GEOGRAPHICAL INFORM~~A~~
SYSTEMS IN ARCHAEOLO~~GY~~

The study of geographical information systems (GIS) has moved from the domain of the computer specialist into the wider archaeological community, providing it with a powerful tool for research and data management. This clearly written but rigorous book provides a comprehensive guide to the archaeological uses of GIS. Topics covered include: the theoretical context and the basics of GIS; data acquisition including database design; creation of elevation models; exploratory data analysis including spatial queries; statistical spatial analysis; map algebra; spatial operations including the calculation of slope and aspect, filtering and erosion modelling; methods for analysing regions, visibility analysis; network analysis including hydrological modelling; the production of high-quality output for paper and electronic publication; and the use and production of metadata. Offering an extensive range of archaeological examples, it is an invaluable source of practical information about GIS for all archaeologists, whether engaged in cultural resource management or academic research. This is an essential handbook for both the novice and the advanced user.

James Conolly is former Lecturer in Archaeology at University College London and now Canada Research Chair in Archaeology at Trent University, Canada. Alongside the archaeological uses of GIS, his research interests include settlement and landscape archaeology, quantitative methods and population history, especially as applied to the origins and spread of agriculture and Aegean prehistory.

Mark Lake is a lecturer at the Institute of Archaeology, University College London, where he coordinates the M.Sc. GIS and Spatial Analysis in Archaeology. His research interests include early prehistory, spatial analysis and evolutionary archaeology. He is a contributor to *Handbook of Archaeological Sciences* and a member of the editorial board of *World Archaeology*.

GEOGRAPHICAL INFORMATION SYSTEMS IN ARCHAEOLOGY

CAMBRIDGE MANUALS IN ARCHAEOLOGY

General editor
Graeme Barker, *University of Cambridge*

Advisory editors
Elizabeth Slater, *University of Liverpool*
Peter Bogucki, *Princeton University*

Books in the series
Pottery in Archaeology, Clive Orton, Paul Tyers and Alan Vince
Vertebrate Taphonomy, R. Lee Lyman
Photography in Archaeology and Conservation, 2nd edn., Peter G. Dorrell
Alluvial Geoarchaeology, A. G. Brown
Shells, Cheryl Claasen
Zooarchaeology, Elizabeth J. Reitz and Elizabeth S. Wing
Sampling in Archaeology, Clive Orton
Excavation, Steve Roskams
Teeth, 2nd edn., Simon Hillson
Lithics, 2nd edn., William Andrefskey Jr.
Geographical Information Systems in Archaeology, James Conolly and Mark Lake

Cambridge Manuals in Archaeology is a series of reference handbooks designed for an international audience of upper-level undergraduate and graduate students, and professional archaeologists and archaeological scientists in universities, museums, research laboratories and field units. Each book includes a survey of current archaeological practice alongside essential reference material on contemporary techniques and methodology.

GEOGRAPHICAL INFORMATION SYSTEMS IN ARCHAEOLOGY

James Conolly

Department of Anthropology, Trent University & Institute of Archaeology,
University College London

Mark Lake

Institute of Archaeology, University College London

CAMBRIDGE UNIVERSITY PRESS

Cambridge, New York, Melbourne, Madrid, Cape Town, Singapore, São Paulo,
Delhi, Dubai, Tokyo

Cambridge University Press
The Edinburgh Building, Cambridge CB2 8RU, UK

Published in the United States of America by Cambridge University Press, New York

www.cambridge.org
Information on this title: www.cambridge.org/9780521797443

First published 2006
Fourth printing 2010

Printed in the United Kingdom at the University Press, Cambridge

A catalogue record for this publication is available from the British Library

ISBN 978-0-521-79330-8 hardback
ISBN 978-0-521-79744-3 paperback

To Lucy and Ella, Paddy and Katy

CONTENTS

FIGURES

TABLES

XVII

BOXES

ACKNOWLEDGEMENTS

Many people facilitated the writing of this book and we would like to take the opportunity to thank: Professors Peter Ucko and Stephen Shennan for their encouragement and advice; Dr Andrew Bevan for many discussions on landscape archaeology and GIS; Dr Cyprian Brookbank for his 'early-adopter' enthusiasm for spatial technologies; Dr Sue College for her keen eye; Drs Andre Costopolous and Andrew Gardner for their opinions on Chapter 1; Professor Yvonne Edwards for her helpful comments on a draft version of the manuscript; Sach Killam for his new user's perspective; Professor Clive Orton for guidance on all matters statistical; Dr Paddy Woodman for sharing her expertise; all of our students from the MSc programme in GIS and Spatial Analysis at the Institute of Archaeology (UCL) whose feedback on drafts of this book has been invaluable; Simon Whitmore at CUP for his patience; and the two anonymous reviewers whose constructive criticism greatly improved the text. Mark Lake's use of GIS has at various times been generously supported by the Natural Environment Research Council and the Leverhulme Trust. James Conolly would like to acknowledge the Department of Anthropology of the University of Auckland for welcoming him as a Visiting Research Fellow and, during the latter phases of writing, the support of the Social Science and Humanities Research Council of Canada (Canada Research Chairs Program).

1

Introduction and theoretical issues
in archaeological GIS

1.1 About this book

The study of geographical information systems (GIS) has now matured to the point where non-specialists can take advantage of relatively user-friendly software to help them solve real archaeological problems. No longer is it the preserve of experts who – in the eyes of cynics – chose their archaeological case studies solely to illustrate solutions to GIS problems. This is, of course, a good thing, because GIS has so much to offer archaeology. Nevertheless, the widespread adoption of GIS brings with it several attendant dangers. The most problematic is that modern GIS packages offer users a variety of powerful tools that are easily applied, without providing much guidance on their appropriateness for the data or questions at hand. For example, many current GIS software packages require just a few mouse clicks to create an elevation model from a set of contour lines, but none that we know of would warn that the application of this method to widely spaced contours is likely to produce highly unsatisfactory results that could lead to a host of interpretative errors further down the line. Conversely, there is a risk that researchers who become over-dependent on the data management abilities of GIS may shy away from tackling more analytical questions simply because it is not immediately obvious which buttons to push. It is our ambition that no archaeologist who keeps this manual near his or her computer will make such mistakes, nor be hesitant about tackling the sorts of questions that can only be answered with some of the more advanced tools that GIS packages offer.

We have adopted an approach that is both practical, because we recognise that many readers will be looking to get a particular job done with a minimum of fuss, and rigorous, because we are equally well aware that poorly described short cuts usually turn out to be the most tortuous routes of all. Practical means that we have focused on the kinds of problems that are routinely faced by archaeological users of GIS, in both cultural resource management and research. It also means that we have tried to give the reader sufficient guidance to achieve all but the most complex tasks without having to consult a raft of supporting literature, apart perhaps from manuals or help files specific to the chosen GIS software. The latter may be required because we simply cannot provide instructions for every GIS software package, although we have provided some package-specific examples to provide concrete illustration of certain operations. Our approach is rigorous in that we always try to explain *why* as well as *how*. In our several years' experience of teaching GIS to archaeology students, this is the best way of ensuring the appropriate application of methods,

Table 1.1 *The main types of question that can be answered using GIS*

Question	Example	Chapter
Location	What artefacts have been found along the proposed route of the new road?	7 & 10
Condition	Where were Roman coins dating to the second century AD found?	7
Trend	How does the density of primary debitage change as one moves away from the prehistoric hearth?	6 & 8
Routing	Does the medieval trackway follow the most energetically efficient route?	11
Pattern	Are the burial cairns distributed uniformly across the landscape, or do they cluster on SE facing slopes?	7 & 9
Modelling	Where would one expect to find more Mesolithic campsites?	8

while also empowering users to develop new applications as the need arises. Indeed, we hope above all else that this manual will inspire a problem-solving attitude to the archaeological use of GIS.

Although we do not envisage many readers methodically working their way through this manual from start to finish, we have tried to maintain a logical progression such that topics are introduced in roughly the order that they might be encountered in the course of developing and using an archaeological GIS. This chapter considers some theoretical issues raised by the use of GIS. Readers who are new to GIS may find it helpful to return after reading Chapter 2, which introduces the basics, and Chapter 3, which illustrates the varied ways in which GIS can benefit archaeological projects. Chapters 4 and 5 are primarily concerned with the construction of a GIS and, in particular, the process of spatial data acquisition. Chapter 6 discusses a common next step in the construction of archaeological GIS, which is the generation of continuous surfaces from point data: for example, an elevation model from spot heights. Chapters 7–11 describe the use of GIS for analysis, that is, answering the types of question listed in Table 1.1. Readers who are using GIS for cultural resource management (CRM) will probably find Chapters 7 and 10 most immediately relevant to their needs, although CRM applications can be found for many of the techniques in the other chapters. Research-orientated readers will probably want to read Chapter 7 and a selection of Chapters 8–11, depending whether their interest is in spatial pattering (Chapter 8), derivatives of continuous surfaces such as slope and aspect (Chapter 9), the analysis of regions (Chapter 10), or the analysis of routes (Chapter 11). Chapter 12 describes methods for presenting the results of analyses for use by others, whether by traditional publication, or delivery via the Internet. Chapter 13 provides advice for the maintenance of spatial data. We suspect that some readers will be tempted to skip this last chapter, but metadata are of vital importance, as the investment in creating a GIS will soon be wasted without them. Finally, we have provided an extensive glossary to aid readers who pick their own path through the book.

1.2 Theoretical issues

As just explained, our primary motivation in writing this manual is to promote the appropriate and creative use of GIS to tackle archaeological problems. In essence, we treat GIS as just one tool – albeit a very powerful one – among the many that may be deployed for archaeological purposes. However, there has been considerable debate about whether GIS is just a tool, or whether it is a 'science' in its own right (Wright *et al.* 1997). It is argued that this matters because if GIS is just a tool then its use may be construed as largely theory-neutral, but if it is a science then its use automatically brings with it a particular theoretical perspective – one that may or may not be welcome. The remainder of this chapter provides an introduction to some of the key issues in this debate.

1.2.1 *The nature of space*

Geographical information systems require two descriptors to describe the real world: *attribute* records what is present while *location* records where it is (Worboys 1995). As will become clear in Chapter 2, the location descriptor is what sets GIS apart from other database systems. More importantly here, it requires a concept of what space is and a means of describing it.

What is space?

Any kind of spatial analysis, whether formal or informal, is ultimately predicated on a concept of space. Western thought has been dominated by two main philosophical ideas about the nature of space, one of which views it as a container and the other as a relation between things.

The **absolute concept** views space as a container of all material objects, which exists independently of any objects that might fill it. The origin of the absolute concept of space may lie with the Greek atomist philosophers (Harvey 1969, p. 195), but in any case it assumed a dominant position in Western thought during the Renaissance, particularly as a result of the success of Newton's laws of motion, which require a fixed frame of reference for the measurement of movement. Kant subsequently developed the absolute concept of space as 'a kind of framework for things and events: something like a system of pigeonholes, or a filing system for observations' (Popper 1963, p. 179). He categorised geography as the study of all phenomena organised according to this 'filing system'; this view remained central to geography until at least the mid 1950s (Harvey 1969, Chapter 14).

In contrast, the **relative concept** views space as a positional quality of the world of material objects or events (Harvey 1969, p. 195), from which it follows that, unlike in the absolute concept, it is impossible to envisage space in the absence of things. Philosophers of science, reacting against Newton's identification of absolute space as God or one of God's attributes, came to favour the relative concept during the nineteenth century. Physicists, however, remained wedded to the absolute concept until the early twentieth century, when the General Theory of Relativity reduced their dependence on Newtonian mechanics. Theoretically inclined geographers followed in the 1950s as they realised that many processes can only be understood if distance is measured in terms of cost, time or social interaction (Watson 1955), none of which can provide the invariant framework required for Kant's 'filing system'.

How can we describe space?

Just as spatial analysis is predicated on a concept of space, so it also requires a 'language' (Harvey 1969, p. 191) with which to describe the spatial distributions of objects and events in that space, and to discuss the processes responsible for such distributions. Formal spatial languages are known as **geometries**, and the two that are most immediately relevant to archaeological users of GIS are *topology* and *Euclidean geometry*. These and other geometries may be distinguished from one another because they are not equally capable of distinguishing the effects of particular transformations, such as stretching, enlarging or rotating.

> **Topology** distinguishes spatial objects that should be considered different on account of the way in which they relate to their neighbours and, for that reason, it has a close affinity with the relative model of space. For example, suppose an excavation plan were drawn on a rubber sheet, then topology is concerned with those aspects of the recorded features that remain invariant when the sheet is stretched or knotted, but not cut or folded. These include stratigraphic relations such as 'contains' and 'abuts', but not the areas covered by different deposits. Indeed, one of the most notable features of topological geometries is that they do not allow one to measure distance or area. Nevertheless, the identification of explicit topological relations is often an important step in the construction of a GIS (Chapter 5), especially if it contains networks such as river or road systems (Chapter 11).
>
> **Euclidean geometry** is the geometry that most of us are taught at school. Devised by Euclid around 300 BC, it is an example of a *metric* geometry, that is, one which includes the concept of distance between points such that the distance from point A to point B is the same as that from B to A. Euclidean geometry has long been associated with the absolute concept of space. Note also that the familiar Cartesian coordinate system (Chapter 2) is not actually an essential feature of Euclidean geometry – it is approximately 2000 years younger – but it is of course a very useful tool for analysing transformations in Euclidean space. Returning to the example of an excavation plan, Euclidean geometry allows one to measure the areas covered by different deposits as well as to state the stratigraphic relations between those deposits.

Since Euclidean geometry allows one to distinguish a larger number of transformations than topology it may be considered more 'specific' (Klein 1939). In GIS terms, a more specific geometry supports a larger number of meaningful questions about the spatial relations in a database.

Space in GIS

As already noted, GIS describe the world in terms of attributes and locations. The two principal data models used in GIS to describe how these should be linked to some extent mirror the two philosophical concepts of space.

The *continuous field* data model proposes a space over which some attribute varies, usually smoothly and continuously (Burrough and McDonnell 1998; Couclelis 1992). A concrete implementation, which provides a discrete approximation of a continuous field, is a raster digital elevation model (DEM). As will be discussed further in Chapter 2, a raster DEM records height above sea level for a set of cells arranged in a regular grid, but the important point to note here is that one can query any cell in the grid and expect to retrieve an elevation value (or a NULL value in the case of missing data), in other words, every location has an attribute value (at least in principle). Since the continuous field model organises information by a set of predetermined locations in space it can be considered to fit quite closely with the philosophical absolute concept of space.

The alternative *entity* data model proposes a set of entities which have a location and which are characterised by spatial and/or non-spatial attributes (Burrough and McDonnell 1998). A typical implementation of this model is a vector map of archaeological survey units, which records the extent of each unit as a closed polygon and associates with each a unique identifier and information such as the weight of potsherds recovered by surface collection (see Chapter 2). In contrast to the previous example, one would not expect to retrieve data about potsherds from locations other than those associated with survey units, in other words, some – possibly many – locations do not have attribute values. The entity model has some affinity to the philosophical relative concept of space, at least to the extent that it organises information by entity rather than by a set of predetermined locations in space. On the other hand, it is worth noting that in practice the locations of entities are given according to a fixed coordinate system that describes a space existing independently of those entities.

We have just suggested a close association between raster maps and the continuous field data model, and between vector maps and the entity data model. This association does indeed mirror standard practice in implementing the two data models. Nevertheless, it is important to be aware that raster and vector maps are themselves data structures rather than data models: it is in fact possible – although usually less convenient – to represent a continuous field as a vector map and a collection of entities as a raster map (e.g. see the discussion of triangulated irregular networks (TINs) in Chapter 6).

1.2.2 *Space in archaeological GIS*
Does it really matter much for archaeological purposes that there are different philosophies of space and that these are at least partially mirrored in the different models of space used in GIS? In our view it does, both for the use of GIS to record archaeological evidence and for its subsequent use to analyse that evidence in the hope of learning about the past. We consider each in turn.

Recording the evidence
Archaeologists routinely, although often implicitly, invoke particular concepts of space and particular geometries to record the spatial organisation of the evidence for past human activity. For instance, the single context recording system used on many deeply stratified urban excavations is essentially predicated on the relative concept of space and emphasises topological relations. Thus there may be few or no

plans of a continuous surface showing the various stratigraphic units revealed at a particular stage in the excavation, since the primary concern is not to record what is present in each quadrat on the site grid, but rather the locations of and relationships between the individual stratigraphic units that provide evidence for past events. This, it may be argued, is better achieved by planning each unit separately and recording the relationships between units on a topological diagram – the Harris matrix (Harris 1979).

In contrast, a programme of field survey by surface collection is more likely to be predicated on the absolute concept of space and to emphasise relationships that require Euclidean geometry. For example, if the purpose is to locate settlements then the results might be recorded on a plan showing the number or weight of artefacts found in each quadrat of a survey grid, since the primary concern is to identify locations with particular attributes, in this case those with many artefacts. Furthermore, if for some reason it was not possible to lay down a regular survey grid then the results might be adjusted to take account of the area covered by each survey unit, something that clearly requires Euclidean geometry.

The requirements of the two different archaeological problems just outlined will best be met using different models of space: the entity model in the first case and the relative model in the second, which in turn suggests the creation of vector and raster maps, respectively (but note the earlier caveat). This illustrates that concepts of space and geometries are important for the very practical business of recording the spatial organisation of archaeological evidence.

Learning about the past

As noted at the outset of this discussion, there has been much debate in geography about whether GIS constitutes a 'tool' or a 'science' (Wright *et al.* 1997) and what theoretical, and indeed ethical, baggage might accompany its use (e.g. Curry 1998; Sui 1994). Archaeologists have engaged in a similar debate (e.g. Wheatley 1993; Gaffney and van Leusen 1995; Gaffney *et al.* 1996; Thomas 1993, 2004; Witcher 1999), albeit with less-explicit concern for ethics and for the feminist critique found in geography (see Kwan 2002). Roughly speaking, those who view GIS as a 'tool' take the view that it is potentially applicable to many kinds of learning, whether that is pursued through the inferential framework characteristic of the natural sciences or through other frameworks provided by, for example, humanist sociology. In contrast, those who view GIS as a 'science' tend to regard it as closely or even inextricably linked to the natural sciences model. Whatever the theoretical arguments about how GIS can and cannot be used, in practice it appears that the history of research-orientated[1] archaeological GIS recapitulates,

---

[1] In this discussion we use the term 'research-orientated' to refer to studies whose purpose is/was to make sense of present/past human spatial organisation. The very earliest archaeological applications of recognisably modern GIS mostly involved the construction of predictive models (e.g. papers in Judge and Sebastian 1988), but the primary purpose of these was often to predict the presence of archaeological evidence without necessarily seeking to explain or understand it (see Chapter 8 in this book).

over a greatly compressed timescale, the parent discipline's experimentation with different modes of learning and its changing emphasis on different facets of human behaviour (see Lake and Woodman 2003 for a more detailed treatment in the context of visibility studies).

'Common-sense' narrative Prior to the advent of the New Geography in the 1960s, most studies of the human use of space proceeded by descriptive synthesis, providing a narrative account of what happens where. The same reliance on description and narrative was broadly true of archaeology up until the late 1960s, especially in its treatment of space. Though both 'traditional' geography and 'traditional' archaeology had developed specific methodologies such as distribution mapping and, in the case of archaeology, seriation, neither were generally very explicit about their theoretical premises, nor about the inferential logic used to justify their claims.

Curiously, the earliest research-orientated archaeological GIS studies generally mirrored the 'common-sense' approach of 'traditional' archaeology (Aldenderfer 1996), even though they were undertaken as recently as the late 1980s/early 1990s. For example, Gaffney and Stančič (1991, 1992) used GIS to establish that Roman towers on the Adriatic island of Hvar are intervisible and then suggested that the location of these towers may have been determined by the need for intervisibility. While it is quite possible that this suggestion is correct, the authors did not attempt to support it by, for example, demonstrating that intervisibility is unlikely to have occurred by chance alone and was not a byproduct of some other favourable attribute.

Scientific explanation During the 1960s the New Geography (Holt-Jensen 1988), and subsequently the New Archaeology (Binford and Binford 1968; Clarke 1968; Binford 1989), adopted a positivist approach to their subject matter. It was hoped that the application of logical thought to observations of actual conditions could produce law-like statements about human behaviour. Even though the initial enthusiasm for Hempel's hypothetico-deductive method (as championed by Fritz and Plog 1970) soon waned as archaeologists struggled to apply it in the context of a historical science, much archaeological research conducted since the 1970s has been conducted in processual vein, that is, broadly predicated on the assumption that the methods of the natural sciences can be used to explain the subject matter of the social sciences. This is manifest in a more rigorous approach to inference and a greater use of quantitative and especially statistical methods.

A parallel development occurred in the early–mid 1990s as the use of GIS for archaeological research rapidly entered what one might term its post-pioneer phase. In 1993 Kvamme urged archaeologists to take an integrated approach to spatial statistics and GIS, having already noted how GIS might be combined with one-sample tests to examine association between site location and environmental parameters (Kvamme 1990c). In the same year van Leusen (1993, p. 120) performed a cluster analysis of the geomorphological properties of Palaeolithic/Mesolithic site viewsheds on the grounds that these would be expected to vary for sites that fulfilled different functions within the subsistence system. From then on there was a clear concern with increasing inferential rigour. Thus Wheatley (1995, 1996) used a one-sample Kolmogorov–Smirnov test to evaluate an explicit hypothesis about the intervisibility of sites. His work was subsequently further refined by Fisher *et al.* (1997), who emphasised that the mere existence of an association between human activity and one or more environmental variables does not in itself provide adequate evidence of a causal relationship. For example, they demonstrated how use of more-restricted control samples can help ascertain whether coastal sites with large viewsheds were deliberately located to have commanding views, or whether this was an unintended consequence of proximity to the sea.

Understanding, experience, symbolism and 'otherness' The antipositivist, or humanist, critique of positivist social science found its way into geography in the 1970s (e.g. Tuan 1974) and was taken up in the development of post-processual archaeology during the 1980s (e.g. Hodder 1982, 1986; Shanks and Tilley 1987a). Since the mid 1990s European archaeological GIS practitioners have been particularly concerned that the use of GIS has, whether intentionally (Wheatley 1993, p. 133) or otherwise (Gaffney *et al.* 1996, p. 132), encouraged the continuation or even re-introduction of a positivist approach that had otherwise been rejected by post-processual archaeology. The following introduction to the use of GIS within a post-processual framework is organised according to three strands of post-processual thought, although we concede that in reality these are not so readily separable.

One strand concerns how we learn about the past. This constitutes a rejection of the notion that the methods of the natural sciences are appropriate for the study of social life, and with it the goal of scientific explanation. Instead, drawing on Idealist thought, post-processual archaeologists often propose that human action can only be understood by taking the perspective of those involved (Hodder 1986). This has been augmented with a phenomenological approach that emphasises the creation of experience through bodily engagement with the physical world (e.g. Tilley 1994; Thomas 1996). Thus Chris Tilley argues in his *A Phenomenology of Landscape: Paths, Places and Monuments* (1994, p. 10) that 'space cannot exist apart from the events and activities within which it is implicated'. From this perspective one of the major problems with traditional GIS analysis has been its association with the absolute model of space and the way in which, as a result, it is claimed to perpetuate Haraway's (1991, p. 189) 'God trick': by making everything visible it not only presents 'a picture of past landscapes which the inhabitant would hardly recognise' but also facilitates 'a kind of intellectual appropriation' (Thomas 1993, p. 25). It is increasingly argued that the way forward is to combine GIS with virtual reality so as to provide some kind of localised experience of past material conditions (see Gillings and Goodrick 1996; Pollard and Gillings 1998; Earl and Wheatley 2002; also Gillings 2005 for a critique). This approach represents a significant break with positivist models of inference, eschewing expert explanation based on the results of statistical tests in favour of multiple understandings, each potentially unique to a particular participant.

A second strand of post-processual thought concerns what aspects of the past we choose to study. The tendency of processual archaeology to focus most attention on the ecological and economic dimensions of human existence has been replaced by an emphasis on meaning and symbolism. Thus, for example, the spread of agriculture across Europe is treated in terms of the replacement of one system of meaning by another rather than the replacement of one mode of subsistence by another (Hodder 1990; Thomas 1991b). Most attempts to move beyond the alleged environmental determinism of earlier GIS applications have treated symbolic landscapes as primarily a product of intervisibility (e.g. Gaffney *et al.* 1996). This, however, risks replacing a determinism based on one suite of environmental variables with a determinism based on another. In response there have been three developments in archaeological GIS. One replaces dependence on the simple presence or absence of a line-of-sight with an attempt to model more complex aspects of visual perception (e.g. Wheatley 1993; Witcher 1999; Wheatley and Gillings 2000). A second development combines Gibsonian psychology with the calculation of many or even all possible views in an attempt to map landscape 'affordances' (Llobera 1996, 2001, 2003). Finally, there have also been a few attempts to model senses other than vision (e.g. Tschan *et al.* 2000; Mlekuz 2004).

The third strand of post-processual thought that we consider here is concerned with the 'otherness' of the past. This involves a recognition that the past might have been very different, in particular that past people might have had very different ways of thinking (Shanks and Tilley 1987b; Thomas 1991a) and, even more profoundly, that the very experience of being an individual might have been quite different from that with which we are familiar (Thomas 1996). So far as the use of GIS is concerned, this perspective has contributed to the objection, already noted above, that GIS representations are built using models of space and spatial languages – such as the absolute model and Euclidean geometry – that are specific to Western thought. More fundamentally, Julian Thomas (2004, p. 201) argues that even if it is 'possible to develop a sensuous, experiential archaeology of place and landscape, which is sensitive to the relationality that renders things meaningful . . . it is questionable how far this process can be facilitated by a microprocessor'. At the root of his doubt is the well-known critique of computational theory of mind (Dreyfus 1972; Searle 1992), which argues that traditional artificial intelligence and computational methods simply do not capture the real nature of thinking and knowledge. Archaeological users of GIS have made suggestions that may go some way to addressing the first of these critiques. For example, Zubrow (1994) 'warped' Euclidean space to investigate the fit between the observed and ideal distributions of Iroquois longhouses. In addition it has been argued (e.g. Wheatley 1993) that cost-surfaces (see Chapter 10) provide another way of representing non-Euclidean experience of distance. It may also be that object-orientated GIS (Tschan 1999) will help us model space as inextricably bound up in events and activities. In contrast, the second critique initially appears less tractable, as it questions the very use of computer methods. However, artificial intelligence researchers, including many specialists in sociological simulation, are actively moving beyond traditional computational theory of mind and tackling issues such as the social construction of emotions (Cañamero and de Velde 2000) and the idea that cognition is not somehow separate from engagement with the world (Maris and te Boekhorst 1996). We suspect that these developments will filter through to GIS, perhaps initially in conjunction with the use of agent-based simulation models (Lake 2004).

1.3 Conclusion

GIS has been described as 'the most powerful technological tool to be applied to archaeology since the invention of radiocarbon dating' (Westcott and Brandon 2000, backcover), but also as a technology without intellectual vigour, overly dependent on simple presuppositions about the importance of spatial patterns in a dehumanised artificial space (cf. Pickles 1999, pp. 50–52). Although there are elements of truth in both these perspectives, we believe that one of the greatest strengths of the use of GIS in archaeology is its diversity. In some cases simply organising our data more efficiently is enough to prompt new ideas about the past. In others, new insights require careful use of spatial statistics. In yet others it is necessary to construct new methods within the framework of conventional GIS. And, finally, we will surely learn even more as a result of the integration of GIS with virtual reality, agent-based simulation and ongoing developments in artificial intelligence. Ultimately, the key to success is to use GIS appropriately, which means remaining cognisant of the theoretical encumbrances inherent within it and having adequate technical command of the powerful and diverse possibilities it offers.

2

First principles

2.1 Introduction

The power of GIS, as with other computer programs, can be deceptive: visually impressive but ultimately meaningless results can appear unassailable because of the sophisticated technologies used to produce them (Eiteljorg 2000). The familiar adage 'garbage in, garbage out' is particularly applicable to GIS, and one of our primary aims throughout this book is to provide guidance on how to use this technology in ways to strengthen and extend our understanding of the human past, rather than to obfuscate it. In this chapter we start by providing an overview of the 'first principles' of GIS: the software and hardware requirements, geodetic and cartographic principles, and GIS data models. These provide the conceptual building blocks that are essential for understanding what GIS is, how it works, and what its strengths and limitations are. Although some of these 'first principles' may be familiar to readers who are experienced in cartography and computer graphics, we nevertheless provide a thorough review of each as they yield the foundation on which we build in later chapters.

2.2 The basics

2.2.1 *GIS functionality*

What does a GIS do? Simply providing a definition of GIS and referring to its abilities to capture and manipulate spatial data doesn't provide much insight into its functionality. More informative is to break some of the basic tasks of a GIS into five groups: data acquisition, spatial data management, database management, data visualisation and spatial analysis. Some of the routine tasks performed under these headings are outlined in Fig. 2.1 and described in Box 2.1.

While each of these tasks are important in themselves, above all GIS should be considered as both an *integrated* and as an *integrating* technology that provides a suite of tools that help people interact and understand spatial information. It is important to stress that although the origins of GIS are strongly rooted in digital cartography, GIS is not just about 'maps' nor is it necessarily only about the digital manipulation of the sorts of information and methods that are usually depicted on maps (cf. Longley *et al.* 1999). The use of GIS has a much broader contribution to make in terms of understanding spatial and even space–time relationships between natural and anthropogenic phenomena (Couclelis 1999). Indeed, it is increasingly common to make the distinction between the software tools used to process geospatial data (GIS), and a geographic information science ('GISc')

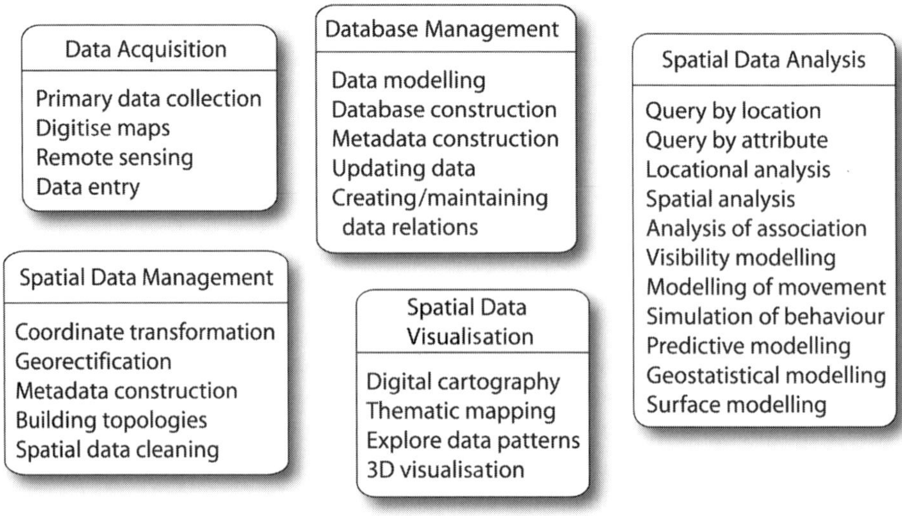

Fig. 2.1 The five main groups of tasks performed by GIS (after Jones 1997, Fig. 1.2).

that is concerned both with the more fundamental conceptual issues of spatial and space–time relationships as well as the impact geospatial technologies are having within the humanities and social sciences (Marble 1990; Curry 1998; Forer and Unwin 1999; Johnston 1999; Longley *et al.* 2005).

2.2.2 *Geographic information*

There is considerable overlap between the aims of the disciplines of archaeology and geography as both share an interest in exploring and interpreting the spatial structure and organisation of human societies at scale from the micro to macro (e.g. Clarke 1977). We thus treat the term 'geographical' as an inclusive one that transcends the discipline of geography (Couclelis 1999). 'Geospatial information' (GI) can therefore be broadly defined as information about natural and anthropogenic phenomena and their relationships with each other. Geospatial information can also describe micro-scale phenomena, such as the patterning of erosion on the facades of historic buildings or the distribution of cut marks on bone (e.g. Marean *et al.* 2001; Abe *et al.* 2002). Most archaeological data – whether artefacts, ecofacts, features, buildings, sites or landscapes – have spatial and aspatial attributes that can be explored using GIS (Fig. 2.2). These attributes include:

- A **spatial location** that tells us where the information is in either a local or global context. A location can be defined by a qualitative term such as 'in Texas' or 'next to the river' or quantitatively using map coordinates. A large component of social-science research uses qualitative positioning data such as counties, cities, census districts or postcodes to form the unit of analysis. Qualitative locations are less commonly used in archaeology

Box 2.1 GIS tasks and descriptions

The acquisition of spatial data GIS is a software platform for the acquisition and integration of spatial datasets. Spatial data include, but are certainly not limited to, topographic maps, site locations and morphology, archaeological plans, artefact distributions, air photography, geophysical data and satellite imagery, all of which can be integrated into a common analytic environment.

Spatial data management GIS uses sophisticated database management systems for the storage and retrieval of spatial data and their attributes. This might involve the transformation of map coordinate systems to enable data collected from different sources to be integrated, the building of vector topologies, the 'cleaning' of newly digitised spatial datasets, and the creation of geospatial metadata.

Database management A major strength of GIS is that it provides an environment for linking and exploring relationships between spatial and non-spatial datasets. For example, given a database on the provenance of a sample of projectile points, and another database that contains information on the morphology of the same points, they can be linked in such a way that it becomes possible to look for spatial patterns in points' morphological variability. Database management, involving conceptual and logical data modelling, is thus an important part of GIS, as is database construction and maintenance to ensure that the spatial and aspatial components of a dataset are properly linked.

Spatial data analysis GIS also provides the ability to undertake locational and spatial analysis of archaeological data, as well as tools for examining visibility (viewsheds) and movement (cost-surfaces) across landscapes. Much work in GIS involves the mathematical combination of spatial datasets in order to produce new data that may provide insight into natural and anthropomorphic phenomena. These range from ecological models that provide predictions of soil suitability for agriculture or erosion potential, or predictive models of potential site location. Tools for geostatistical modelling of spatial data to create, for example, continuous surfaces from a set of discrete observations are also available. GIS can also be a route to the computer simulation of human behaviour and decision making in different types of environments.

Spatial data visualisation GIS has powerful visualisation capabilities used for viewing spatial data in innovative ways (such as thematically or for 'fly-throughs' in three dimensions) that can suggest potential patterns and routes for further analysis. GIS also provide cartographic tools to help produce hard-copy paper maps. Many GIS packages also facilitate the publication of interactive map data on the Internet.

although we may, at times, use locations such as parish, county or survey region. More frequently we use quantitative location data in the form of map coordinates. These include global geographic locational systems, with latitude and longitude being the most common, or national, regional or locally defined Cartesian metric coordinate systems.

- A **morphology** that defines the shape and size of an object, such as 'straight' or '100 m^2'. Qualitative or quantitative descriptors can be recorded as *attribute data* by, for example, recording the size of an archaeological site or the shape of a distribution. Alternatively, it is possible to record spatial morphology directly by mapping the size and shape of a phenomenon, such as an archaeological site on a map. For certain analytical or visual purposes, morphology might be drawn directly on a map, such as the arrangement of a skeleton or the shape of a distribution of artefacts.

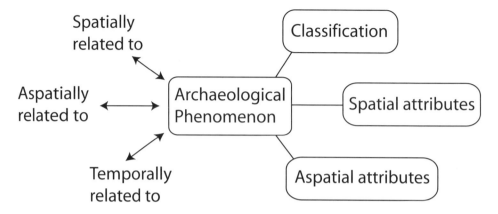

Fig. 2.2 The possible spatial and aspatial characteristics of archaeological data.
A burial, for example, is spatially related to other adjacent burials, aspatially related to
other burials of that gender or age group, temporally related to other burials of that
period, might be classified by the specific position of the body, will have a spatial
location and morphology, and possess any number of aspatial attributes (e.g. lists of
grave goods and qualitative/quantitative characteristics of the skeleton). After Jones
1997, Fig. 2.8.

- Information about **spatial association and interaction** that describes spatial relationships, such as 'path *a* crosses path *b*', 'from settlement *p* one can see settlement *q*' or
  'site *k* is 100 m east of fresh water'. As we discussed in Chapter 1, some types of spatial
  associations are referred to as *topological*, such as when we talk about path or road
  connections. Topological relationships are also described as *orientation-independent*
  because only the connective relationships between objects are important and not their
  orientation or spatial location. *Orientation-dependent* or *directional* relationships are
  those that use relational directions, such as above, below, in front, behind, or the
  cardinal directions east, west, south, north (Jones 1997, p. 25).
- **Temporal relationships** that describe the date and/or associated features in relative
  terms, like 'contemporary with', 'later than', 'earlier than', etc. Temporal relationships
  can be important for ensuring that particular types of analysis, such as settlement
  patterns, are undertaken only on contemporaneous sites.
- One or more **aspatial attributes** that describe the nature of the object. This might
  consist of a biography of a site or object, information about the colour and raw material
  of an object, the time of day that a field was fieldwalked, the shape of the cross-section
  of a feature, or the estimated age of a burial.

The ability to associate aspatial data with spatial objects means that it is possible to explore the spatial characteristics of non-spatial data. For example, given
a database of handaxes that records their spatial provenance and aspatial morphological attributes (e.g. weight, size, shape, raw material, reduction stage, etc.) it is
possible to explore the relationship between their location and their other characteristics. This is an extremely important ability of GIS that has found application
in many areas of archaeological research.

2.2.3 *Components of a GIS*

A GIS is a computer-dependent technology. In addition to the computer itself, there are a number of other important components to a GIS. The most important ones are:

Software In order to qualify as a GIS the software must have: (i) a spatial database that stores and manages spatial objects; (ii) some mechanism of linking attribute data to these spatial objects, either as an internal function of the GIS package, or by providing functions that enable access to external database systems; (iii) a 'geoprocessing engine', which permits the manipulation and analysis of the geospatial information stored in the spatial and attribute databases. None of the many GIS packages currently available perform all tasks equally well. The choice of software consequently needs to be made with respect to several factors, including the tasks it is needed for, what operating system it has to run under (e.g. UNIX or UNIX-like systems such as MacOS X, Linux, Irix, or Solaris; or one of the versions of Microsoft Windows) and the size of the budget for software, hardware and training costs. A large number of packages are available – too many for us to attempt to review – each with their own strengths and weaknesses in terms of ease of use and the range of analytical tools they offer. An afternoon's research on the web will provide a reasonable grounding in the range of software options. If cost is a primary concern, it is worth knowing that one of the more powerful GIS packages, GRASS GIS,[1] is available free of charge under an open-source licence. Excellent comprehensive commercial GIS packages include Idrisi,[2] the ArcGIS suite of programs,[3] and MapInfo,[4] and all may offer discounts for educational users.

Hardware In addition to the computer that runs the software, which could range from a small palmtop computer to a large institutional mainframe, there are several other hardware components that are essential to making a GIS work. These can be divided into two groups. The first consists of input devices, which might be limited to the keyboard and mouse supplied with the computer, but could extend to digitising tablets, flatbed and roll scanners, digital surveying equipment such as global positioning system (GPS) devices and Total Stations, or geophysical sensors. Chapter 5 discusses the various methods for acquiring digital data in some detail. The second group consists of the output devices needed for viewing and sharing information. A computer monitor is the basic piece of display hardware but, with the obvious exception of the WWW, it is not a very convenient device for distributing information to other people. Some type of printer, from standard letter devices to larger colour plotters, is needed for producing the maps, graphs and tables that GIS routinely produces. We review map production and spatial data communication in Chapter 12.

People GIS operators are the most crucial part of the system as they are responsible for the design and analysis of spatial datasets. A GIS is never a fully objective process – data and questions can rarely be simply 'fed' to a GIS and useful results returned – so it is essential that the specialists responsible for digitising, processing and analysing data are closely integrated with both project design and data collection. This is less of an issue when one researcher is conducting both the project design, data collection and analysis, but in large research projects or commercial archaeological units it is

---

[1] http://grass.itc.it.   [2] www.clarklabs.org.
[3] www.esri.com.   [4] www.mapinfo.com.

important to ensure that GIS analysts are included at the earliest stages of the project design to prevent any disjuncture between the envisioned project aims and outcomes. A GIS will rarely contribute in any meaningful way if it is tacked-on as an extra and handed to a 'GIS-person' who has no real understanding of the original goals of the project in question.

2.3 Cartographic principles
2.3.1 *Maps, digital cartography and GIS*
A major element of GIS is the visualisation, management and analysis of spatial data presented in the form of digital maps. It is consequently important to emphasise that all maps, whether paper or digital, simplify the world and present an abstract model of spatial phenomena. Maps can be divided into two basic types:

Topographic maps provide general information about the physical surface of the earth, including natural and human-made features like roads, rivers, settlements and elevation. These exist at a variety of different formats and scales, each suited to particular purposes. Navigational air-charts, for instance, are compiled at a scale which is useful for pilots (1 : 500 000) and emphasise topography, settlements, restricted air-space and airports. In the UK, the Ordnance Survey produce a variety of different topographic maps (in both paper and digital formats) showing elevation, natural and cultural landscape features (including archaeological and historical sites and monuments), roads, towns and villages that are suitable for a range of different applications. The US Geological Survey produce equivalent maps for the USA and most countries have similar organisations (e.g. Canada's Centre for Topographic Information, and Geoscience Australia).

Thematic maps provide specific information about a single feature of the landscape or environment, or display information about a single subject. When the data values vary continuously through space it is common to display them on *isarithmic* maps, which use lines to connect points of constant numeric value, such as elevation (*contours*), temperature (*isotherms*), precipitation (*isohyets*) or even frequencies of hailstorms (*isochalazes*). Other themes are more likely to be displayed on *choropleth* maps, which use shading or symbols to display average values of information in different areas, such as vegetation, geology or numbers of artefacts collected in a survey unit.

To emphasise the differences between traditional paper maps and the dynamical interface that GIS offers it is worth noting some of the constraints of the former (cf. Longley *et al*. 1999, p. 6). Paper maps differ from GIS because they are:

Static The dynamic space-time interactions between objects cannot easily be depicted (e.g. changes in population and settlement patterns, or environmental change). A GIS offers the advantage of enabling exploration of the dynamics of temporal patterning. The University of Sydney Archaeological Computing Lab's TimeMap project[5] is an excellent example of this form of dynamic mapping.

Two-dimensional Multidimensionality cannot be easily depicted on paper. Multivariate spatial data and the three-dimensional representation of topography benefit from multidimensional forms of display available in GIS (e.g. Portugali and Sonis 1991; Couclelis 1999).

---

[5]`www.timemap.net`.

Flat Representing a curved three-dimensional surface, such as the Earth, in two-dimensions often introduces significant distortion in spatial measurements (see below) and GIS provides facilities for improving this.

Precise The traditional methods of cartographic representation do not allow for the depiction of imprecise, 'fuzzy', boundaries (that occur between, for example, vegetational zones, cultural boundaries, etc.). While this remains a problem for some forms of spatial representation in GIS, there are more possibilities for working with less clearly defined boundaries than paper maps traditionally offer.

Difficult to update Once committed to paper, a map is fixed and can only be updated by producing a new map, whereas a digital map may be updated continuously – even in real-time.

Difficult to relate to non-spatial data The attributes of the objects on traditional maps have to be coded and further information can only be found by reference to a gazetteer. A GIS has several advantages over non-digital systems with regards to attribute data: in particular, a GIS offers more comprehensive data retrieval, ease of update and an ability to explore data patterns more quickly compared with its paper counterpart.

A further major advantage of a GIS over traditional mapping is that a GIS permits the organisation of different components of the same map into different thematic map layers (and thus often referred to as *thematic mapping*), which is the basic way that spatial data are organised within a GIS environment. In practice this means that in one GIS digital display many different elements may be combined, each of which can be individually turned on or off, queried, modified, reclassified and edited. Many analytical functions, such as spatial queries, can operate across one or more layers depending on the need of the GIS analyst. Map layers, or subsets of individual layers, can also be combined to produce new maps at will, providing potential insight into relationships between elements on different themes.

2.3.2 *Map projection systems and geodetic datums*

A basic property of a map is that it is has a spatial context – more properly, *geo-referenced* – by implicitly or explicitly referring to positions on the Earth's surface. Obviously with many maps a precise and absolute spatial context is not important; a quick sketch of the route to a friend's house serves a purpose even though it may be inaccurate and relative. However, when precision and absolute spatial context are important, then an explicit system of measurement is required. As the Earth is a complex shape this is not a trivial process and the science of *geodesy* is concerned with the measurement of the morphology of the Earth's surface. The shape of the Earth is best approximated by a flattened sphere, referred to as either an *ellipsoid* or *geoid*, and positions on it can be defined using *polar* or *geographical coordinates* (Fig. 2.3). *Geographical coordinate systems* define degrees, minutes and seconds north or south of the equator as *latitude* and degrees, minutes and seconds east or west from Greenwich Prime Meridian as *longitude*.

This is an elegant and simple solution for locating positions on the planet. It is less suitable for representing the surface of the Earth on a two-dimensional plane, for example, on a paper map or computer screen. The name given to a system used

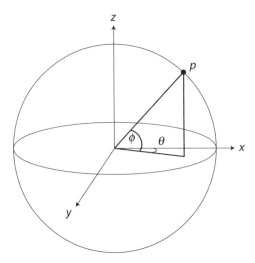

Fig. 2.3 Polar coordinates. The circle of the sphere in the x, y-plane is the equator, and in the x, z-plane it is the meridian. If p is an arbitrary point on the surface of the Earth, then the angle defined by θ is therefore longitude, and the angle defined by ϕ is latitude (after Worboys 1995, p. 143).

to display areas of the Earth's round surface on a flat map is *map projection*, which involves a mathematical *transformation* of the units of longitude and latitude (i.e. *graticules*) to a flat plane. Essentially, a flat map of a large area of the Earth's surface cannot be produced without some form of projection. When mapping areas at the continental or international scale the transformation from three to two dimensions causes profound distortion and spatial error in particular types of measurement. At national and regional scales or larger, the distortion arising from projection to a flat surface causes fewer problems, and national and state mapping agencies have established projections for minimising error within their own boundaries. At very small scales, what we might term subregional or local, the surface of the Earth can be regarded as flat and grid systems can be established and used without reference to geodetic correction. Note here the use of the terms 'large scale' and 'small scale', as this can be a source of confusion. Large scale generally refers to scales of 1 : 50 000 or greater (e.g. 1 : 25 000, 1 : 5000, etc.), and small scale to maps with scales smaller than 1 : 50 000 (e.g. 1 : 100 000, 1 : 1 000 000, etc; Thurston *et al.* 2003, p. 37).

Many forms of map projection have been developed for both global and national mapping purposes and most GIS programs will support many or all of the common ones (GRASS, for example, supports some 123 different projections). Projection systems may be grouped into a *projection family* of which there are three main ones, *conical*, *azimuthal* and *cylindrical*, defined according to how the sphere is projected onto a flat surface (for a mathematical discussion see Iliffe 2000). Each projection family has either a *line of tangency* or two *lines of secancy* that define where the imagined projection surface comes into contact with the Earth, and where there is correspondingly the least distortion (Fig. 2.4). All projections will distort

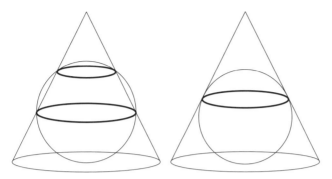

Fig. 2.4 A conical projection with two lines of secancy (left) and one line of tangency (right). The point(s) of contact are also referred to as *standard parallels.*

one or more of the parameters of distance, direction, scale, conformality (shape) and area, although each projection family attempts to minimise distortion in one or two parameters at the expense of increasing it in others.

In addition to the three projection families, there are four projection groups defined on the basis of how this distortion is managed. *Conformal* or *orthomorphic projections* preserve the 90° intersection of lines of latitude and longitude to ensure correct angle measurements between points, but in so doing distort area measurements. *Equal-area projections* preserve area calculations, so that the multiplication of the two edges of rectilinear features represented on a map and globe will be identical (but the properties of shape, angle and scale are then distorted). Projections that maintain distances between one or more pairs of points are described as *equidistant projections*. Any given equidistant projection will only apply to measurements taken in a certain direction: sinusoidal equidistant projections, for example, enforce the measurements parallel to the equator, but distort measurements parallel to the meridian. *True-direction projections* maintain the correct angle from any line measured from the centre of the projection to any other point on the map.

A projection is defined by the combination of a family and then a projection type. For example, a conical projection can be conceptualised as fitting a cone over one of the polar regions as depicted in Fig. 2.4, which is then cut along a meridian as in Fig. 2.5.

The result is a map in which the lines of longitude are straight and convergent, and lines of latitude are concentric arcs. The line of tangency on conic projections is referred to as the *standard parallel* and distortion increases the further one moves away from this line. The amount of distortion can, however, be controlled by altering the spacing of the lines of latitude; if evenly spaced then the projection will be equidistant along the north–south axis (*equidistant conic projection*); if compressed at the northern and southern ends, then the projection becomes equal-area (*Albers equal-area conic projection*).

Azimuthal (or planar) projections represent the Earth's surface on a flat plane using a single point of contact rather than a line of tangency (Fig. 2.6). Azimuthal

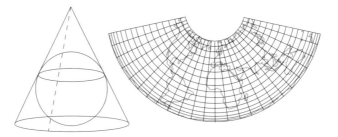

Fig. 2.5 Albers equal-area conical projection with one line of tangency (left) and a meridian (dashed line). The resulting map is to the right, showing the lines of latitude as concentric arcs.

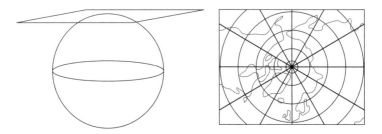

Fig. 2.6 Azimuthal projection with a point of contact at the North Pole. The resulting map has radiating lines of longitude, and concentric lines of latitude. Angle and distance measurements taken along the lines of longitude remain accurate.

(or planar) projections are usually used to map the poles although in theory they can occur anywhere on the Earth's surface. If polar, then the projection is conformal with concentric lines of latitude and radiating lines of longitude. Area distortion occurs as one moves away from the poles, but directions and linear distances from the centre point to any other point on the map are accurate.

Cylindrical projections are conformal and so 90° angles are maintained between the lines of latitude and longitude (Fig. 2.7). Measurements along the line of tangency are equidistant but at further distances from this line area measurements become increasingly distorted.

The most common cylindrical projection is the *Mercator Projection*, which uses the equator as its line of tangency and scales the *y*-dimension (latitude) to reduce the distortion at polar extremes. This projection gives a very misleading view of the world as movement away from the equator causes areas towards the top and bottom of the map to become disproportionately large in area (Snyder and Voxland 1989, p. 10). The *Transverse Mercator Projection* (TM projection), invented by Johann Lambert (1728–1777), rotates the cone 90° so that a meridian becomes the line of tangency. This distorts measurements in the east–west axis but maintains north–south measurements better than the standard Mercator Projection. The TM Projection is one of the standard ways of mapping the globe.

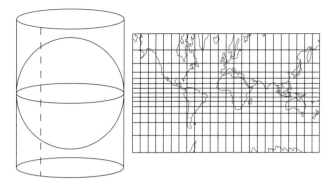

Fig. 2.7 Cylindrical projection with a line of tangency corresponding to the equator and a meridian (dashed line). The resulting map is to the right, showing the lines of latitude as parallel lines.

Finally, the *Universal Transverse Mercator Projection* (UTM) is a twentieth-century modification of the TM Projection that divides the world into 60 vertical zones, each of which are 6° of longitude wide. There is a central meridian in each of these 60 zones that minimises measurement distortion in the east–west to approximately 1 m in every 2500 m (Robinson *et al.* 1995; DeMers 1997, pp. 63–64). Each zone is divided into rows of 8° latitude (12° in the northernmost section) which equates to a 100 000-m wide grid square. The central meridian is given a false easting value of 500 000 m to eliminate the need for negative numbers when specifying east–west coordinates. For the same reason the equator is given a northing value of 0 m for measurements in the northern hemisphere, and 10 000 000 m for measurements in the southern hemisphere. Universal Transverse Mercator coordinates are given by first specifying the zone and then the easting (with 6 digits for 1 m precision) and northing (with 7 digits for 1 m precision). The UTM projection is very popular in GIS and related geospatial technologies like remote sensing because of its global application, minimal distortion and metric coordinate system. Most GPSs are able to record locations in UTM coordinates, making it an ideal system for spatial data collection when a local grid system is not available.

In addition to the projection system used to make the map, it is also important to be aware of which mathematical approximation of the shape of the Earth was used for the construction of a map. The Earth is not an exact ellipsoid, since the surface is not smooth and the poles are not equidistant from the equator. Polar coordinates of latitude and longitude are therefore calculated using a mathematical approximation of the Earth's shape and its centre. Several different approximations have been calculated, often for a specific region of the planet. Clarke's 1866 calculations formed the basis for the 1927 datum of North America (North American Datum 27, or NAD27). NAD27 is being replaced by satellite-derived measurements of an ellipsoid called NAD83 but many organisations still use measurements and locations using the earlier geodetic datum. The Geodetic Reference System

(GRS80), World Geodetic System 84 (WGS84) and European Terrestrial Reference System (ETRS89) are more recent recalculations of the ellipsoid used in Europe. National mapping agencies generally use whichever ellipsoid calculations most closely fit their needs. For example, most national mapping in Great Britain uses the OSGB36 Datum based on the 1830 *Airy* ellipsoid, although the Ordnance Survey have adopted the ETRS89 ellipsoid for more recent mapping derived from GPS receivers.

Coordinate transformation and reprojection

Maps that share a projection system (e.g. UTM) but are based on different ellipsoids (e.g. WGS84 versus NAD27) are not compatible, nor are maps that use different projection systems (e.g. Transverse Mercator versus State Plane) but share the same ellipsoid (e.g. NAD27). For example, the physical distance between two points that have *identical* geographical coordinates, but one based on NAD27 and the other based on NAD83, can be as much as 100 m apart in the USA. For data from multiple map sources to be combined, the maps must share a common projection and geodetic reference system. If this is not the case the projections and/or reference system must be altered through a process called *secondary transformation* or *reprojection*. To compute the transformation, fairly specific information is required about the existing and desired projection systems. Most GIS packages provide tools to transform maps from one geodetic datum to another, and dedicated software tools are also available to help convert between NAD27 and NAD83 (see, for example, the directory of software on the US National Geodetic Survey's website[6] and their online conversion tool[7]). Details about the ellipsoid and projection system used in the construction of a map are typically printed in the corner or are contained in an associated metadata record for digital data (see Chapter 13 for further discussion of metadata elements).

2.3.3 *National and regional grid systems*

Many GIS programs use geographic coordinates of latitude and longitude as the basis for regional maps (most often as *decimal degrees* where minutes and seconds are converted to decimal units so that, for example, 30 minutes 30 seconds is equal to 0.508 of a degree). While decimal degree systems can work well in GIS packages that are able to manage the corrections for spatial measurement, a Cartesian system based on metric units, such as UTM or national (military) grid system, is often a better choice because of the advantages it offers for calculating distances and areas. When a two-dimensional Cartesian grid system is used for mapping, east–west measurements are located on the horizontal x-axis and called *eastings*, and north–south measurements are located on the vertical y-axis and are called *northings* (Fig. 2.8).

At larger scales (e.g. greater than 1 : 1 000 000) most national or regional mapping systems provide metric planar coordinates alongside, or in place of, latitude and longitude. Metric planar coordinates are used in the global UTM projection, the

---

[6]www.ngs.noaa.gov.   [7] www.ngs.noaa.gov/cgi-bin/nadcon.prl.

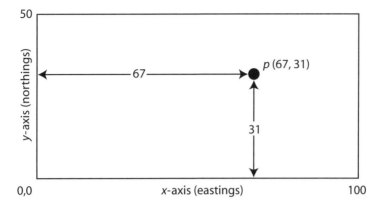

Fig. 2.8 A two-dimensional Cartesian coordinate system. Point *p* is located by reference to its distance from a 0, 0 datum in the *x*- and *y*-planes (respectively referred to as the 'eastings' and 'northings').

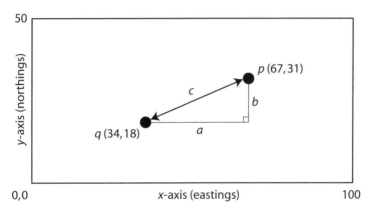

Fig. 2.9 To calculate the linear distance between points *p* and *q* (*c*), Pythagoras' theorem is used: $c = \sqrt{a^2 + b^2}$. As *a* and *b* are known ($a = x_p - x_q = 33$, $b = y_p - y_q = 13$), the calculation is $c = \sqrt{33^2 + 13^2} = 35.5$.

US State Plane system, British National Grid and in most other national grids. National grid systems, such as the US State Plane system, are often better choices for regional mapping projects because the ellipsoid is often selected to maximise spatial accuracy for the specific area covered by that particular system. In parts of the world where national or military grids are unavailable, then UTM is an excellent choice. We must emphasise again our warning from the previous section regarding the inevitable and significant spatial errors that will result from combining data derived from maps with different projections and/or ellipsoids.

Metric planar systems have the important and crucial advantage of allowing the easy calculation of distance and area. For example: linear distance measurements can be calculated using *Pythagoras' theorem* (Fig. 2.9); polygon areas can be calculated using a system that first breaks the shape into smaller *trapezia* and then sums their individual areas to derive the total area; and the geometric centre of a polygon (its *centroid*) can be found by taking the mean of the coordinates of all vertices that define the polygon (for alternatives, see Jones 1997, p. 66; Burrough and McDonnell 1998, p. 63).

2.4 Data models and data structures: the digital representation of spatial phenomena

How does a GIS represent spatial data? The roots of GIS originate with the development of automated mapping in the middle of the last century. In the late 1950s some of the basic computer algorithms for handling geographic information were developed, including the principles for digital cartography, at about the same time that technology had developed to incorporate computer graphics (e.g. Tobler 1959). The *Canada Geographic Information System*, developed in 1963 to manage natural resources, was a natural outcome of these developments and qualifies as the first GIS. It was followed soon after by the development of other systems that were capable of automated mapping (Foresman 1998; Tomlinson 1998). Automated mapping offered considerable time savings over traditional paper methods by providing faster and more accurate facilities for the management and updating of spatial data. These early systems relied on point, line and polygon 'geographic primitives', which still form the building blocks of modern vector-based GIS.

A GIS works by manipulating the digital representations of real world entities. However, a GIS only has a finite set of resources with which to replicate the infinitely complex world and, as a consequence, the digital representations used by GIS are necessarily schematic and generalised. The representation of elements of reality in this way is referred to as a *data model*. In GIS, data models tend to be very simple representations of reality, although as we shall see in later chapters, simple models may become the building blocks for more complex models that are designed to quantify relationships between different entities.

As we saw in Chapter 1, GIS represent spatial data using one or both of the entity and continuous field data models. These are usually implemented as *vector* and *raster* data structures, respectively. Raster and vector data structures store, represent and manipulate spatial information in very different ways. Certain types of entities are more typically represented in one format or the other, although much of the data that archaeologists routinely encounter can ultimately be represented using either structure. Until recently, these two data structures were virtually mutually exclusive: GIS programs tended to rely on either one or the other, forcing users to make a decision as to which they would use. Today most GIS permit the mixing of both raster and vector data as separate thematic map layers, giving users the freedom to decide on the most appropriate structure without necessarily using a different program. The following sections outline the differences between the vector and raster data structures, and provide some examples of ways that different sorts of data are handled by each format.

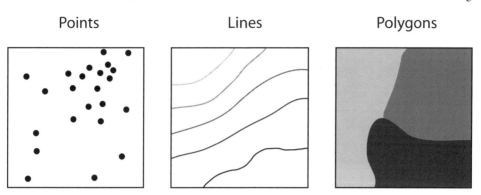

Fig. 2.10 The three vector 'geographic primitives' of points, lines and polygons.

2.4.1 *The vector data structure*

A vector is a mathematical term that refers to one or more coordinates used to define an object in Cartesian space. In the vector structure, real-world entities are represented using one of three geometrical primitives: *points*, *lines* or *polygons*. Each primitive is defined using one or more x, y-coordinate pairs called *vertices*, and are thus described as *discrete* objects because of their precisely defined locations and boundaries (Fig. 2.10). Vertices that are located at the ends of discrete lines, or at their intersections, are called *nodes*.

For example, points are zero-dimensional objects (for they have no length or breadth) defined by a single coordinate pair, and lines and polylines (often also referred to as *arcs* or *edges*) are one-dimensional vectors (having the property of length, but not breadth) defined by two or more coordinate pairs. Polygons, or areas, are two-dimensional objects defined by three or more coordinate pairs. Three-dimensional objects are referred to as *volumes*, but despite the fact that CAD systems routinely use three-dimensional vector objects, the three-dimensional vector structure has not yet been widely implemented in GIS.

The discrete nature of every vector object means that, in addition to possessing its own unique spatial location and morphology, it is a trivial process to provide each vector object with an identification (id) number. On the basis of this unique identifier, each and every object can thus be linked to a set of additional non-spatial attributes that describe additional properties of that object. These properties most often consist of real-world quantitative and/or qualitative variables that give the vector object meaning within the GIS (Fig. 2.11).

Vector topology

An extremely important concept that underlies the vector structure is the geometrical relationships between vector objects, referred to as *topology*. The analysis of topological relationships is explored more fully in Chapter 11, so here it is sufficient to note a few basic concepts. Firstly, topological relationships define

Vector objects   Attribute data

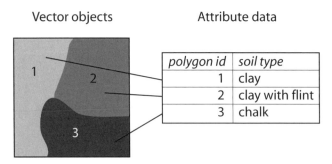

polygon id	soil type
1	clay
2	clay with flint
3	chalk

Fig. 2.11 Vector objects linked to attribute data. In this example, each polygon has a unique id number that links it directly to an attribute table that defines the soil type represented by that polygon.

the connections and relationships between vector objects rather than their spatial location. For example, when two roads cross each other, two different topological relationships can potentially exist between those entities. If the lines simply cross without sharing a node, the lines are not topologically connected. This is equivalent to a road crossing another via an underpass and it is not possible to get from one road to another at the point of intersection. If the roads do share a node, they are topologically linked. In this case, it would be equivalent to the two roads meeting at an intersection. Topological relationships are therefore defined by the presence of shared nodes between vector objects. In practice, many GIS require nodes at both crossing and meeting points, in which case additional methods must be used to provide adequate topological information (see Chapter 11).

Topological relationships also define how polygons relate to each other. For example, two adjacent polygons, perhaps representing separate parcels of land or survey zones, are topologically related if they share one or more nodes or arcs in common (Fig. 2.12). Without common nodes this relationship does not exist, and the polygons then must either overlap and/or have a gap between them. It is entirely possible that they intentionally overlap or have a gap to reflect a real-world spatial relationship; but more usually adjacent polygons have an assumed, if not actual, topological relationship. The calculation of spatial relationships and properties of vector objects is not a trivial process, and is dependent both on the data structure and accuracy of the dataset. During the data collection phase and particularly during the process of digitising vector objects, care should to be taken to ensure that topological relationships are properly maintained and defined. Many vector GIS programs have 'clean-up' routines that can be used to create topologies between objects automatically (Chapter 5).

Some geodatabases, such as ArcGIS, provide a set of topological rules to ensure that vector objects are always related in appropriate ways. For example, polygons that define survey areas might have a 'Must Not Overlap' rule, so that any instances

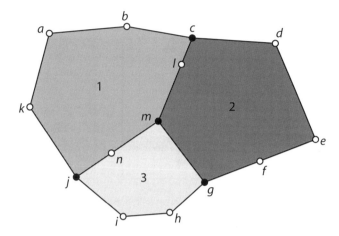

Fig. 2.12 Three topologically related polygons. Polygons 1, 2 and 3 share arcs (edges) defined by nodes *cm*, *mj* and *mg*.

where this occurs are identified and the appropriate action taken (e.g. the overlapping area is subtracted from one polygon, or a new polygon defined by the overlapping area is created).

Topological accuracy also makes for more efficient storage of vector data as vector objects can then share data. Some GIS systems take advantage of this when storing the geometric definitions by only recording an arc (and its vertices) once, and then defining its relationship to polygons. In Fig. 2.12, for example, arcs *cm*, *mj* and *mg* need only be stored once instead of twice for each of the polygon boundaries they define. On large, complex, polygonal maps such as those routinely encountered with soil or geological series, this can result in a significant saving of storage space and computational time, an issue examined in further detail in Chapter 4.

2.4.2 *The raster data structure*
Unlike vector graphics, which use coordinate geometry to define the spatial parameters of objects, raster graphics use a grid matrix of equally sized cells or pixels to represent spatial data (Fig. 2.13). Raster maps are therefore defined only by the number of rows and columns in the grid and the size of each pixel in terms of actual area covered. Each cell also has a value associated with it that represents the attribute status of the object at that location. In a digital elevation model (DEM), for example, each cell has a quantitative value that signifies the mean elevation across the area defined by that pixel, whereas the pixels in a vegetation map may be coded to reflect modal vegetation type. The reliance on pixels and the use of a single attribute per pixel may appear to be very limiting in comparison to the vector structure, but within the simplicity of the raster structure lies its strength. Raster

Point	Line	Polygon

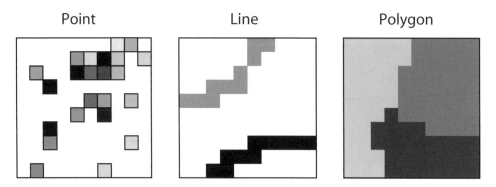

Fig. 2.13 Point, line and polygon primitives as represented on a raster grid.

datasets are easily combined and mathematically manipulated as computers can process and display raster data considerably more quickly than vector data because of the efficiency with which they can store and handle grid data. The simplicity of the structure does not reduce its functionality for, as we shall see in the next chapter, the raster data structure can be used to model some extremely complex spatial phenomena.

A critical variable in the raster structure is the size of the cells, since they define the resolution of a map by providing a minimum unit of representation. Whereas a raster map depicting density of archaeological sites across a large region may consist of a grid of pixels that each represent an area of a square kilometre or more, a raster map showing the density of artefacts across a site may use pixels that define an area of a square metre or less. Although computer processing speed and storage space is continuously increasing, there are nevertheless some practical restrictions on how much information a typical desktop computer can efficiently process. This, of course, varies with the specification of the computer, but loss of performance may be noticed when the total number of pixels is several million or more (e.g. a raster map representing an area of 50 × 50 km with individual pixel sizes of $10 \, m^2$ will require a grid of 5000 columns by 5000 rows and therefore storage of information for 25 000 000 pixels). Decisions relating to resolution need to be made very early on in the model-building process. In the next chapter we show that such decisions can have important consequences for interpretation of the results of analysis and for making sense of spatial patterns.

2.4.3 *Choosing a data structure*
There are many instances where vector systems provide the only sensible means of answering a specific set of questions, or handling the sorts of multiscalar and precisely defined data that one might be interested in exploring. On the other hand, raster data is suitable for powerful spatial modelling, is able to represent continuous datasets more smoothly, and provides image analysis and classification routines suitable for aerial photography and satellite imagery. Many modern GIS systems

are to a large extent 'hybrid' and offer capabilities for manipulating both raster and vector datasets. As a result it is now common to find both data structures being used in a single program environment, thus reducing the choice between the raster versus vector structures to that of appropriateness for the particular needs and questions at hand. From the philosophical perspective adopted in Chapter 1, the vector structure is generally most appropriate when the subject matter has been conceived using the entity model of space. Conversely, the raster structure is usually a better choice if the subject matter has been conceived as a continuous field.

Advantages and disadvantages of the vector structure

Advantages of the vector structure A major advantage of the vector structure is its spatial precision. Real-world entities can be drawn and positioned with an accuracy restricted only by practical limitations such as the precision of the recording equipment. Artefacts, features, sites and other archaeological entities can be integrated in a single environment, each mapped with as much spatial detail as is required for analysis. While centimetre-scale precision would not be required for the analysis of the spatial distribution of sites across a large study region, this level of precision would, however, be essential for the study of the distribution of chert flakes on a knapping floor. Finding the balance between spatial precision and the minimum scale of analysis is crucial: most importantly to prevent spatial errors from influencing pattern recognition. In practice, it is important to recognise that increased resolution also means increased file sizes, with a corresponding burden on storage and processing time. Another significant advantage of the vector structure is that vector objects are maintained as distinct entities and can be easily linked to attribute data records in an internal or external database. For this reason, vector-based GIS programs have traditionally led the way in terms of database integration, as complex attribute queries can be performed with relative ease. A vector map may therefore act as a window into a database, in which each object is described in great detail.

Disadvantages of the vector structure Vector objects are computationally demanding. Every vertex and node of a vector map must be stored in computer memory and drawing vector objects requires a considerable amount of processor time. For this reason, vector data are often much slower to generate on a computer screen than raster data. The manipulation of vector data is correspondingly intensive; spatial queries involving, for example, the calculation of areas of overlap within a large set of polygons needs considerable computer-processing unit (CPU) time. Vector data also impose properties onto real-world objects that do not necessarily correspond with reality. The most important imposition is 'boundedness'. Although many real-world objects do indeed have precise and discrete boundaries, certain types of data are more 'fuzzy' and do not lend themselves to the hard, precise, edges of vector objects. As vector data cannot readily deal with fuzziness or imprecision, this can result in artificial precision in some scenarios. An issue related to fuzzy boundaries is the implied non-varying state of an attribute across a vector object. For example, a polygon used to represent a discrete survey area may possess an attribute value that represents the density of artefacts in that enumeration unit. This implies a continuous distribution of artefacts in that area, which in reality is rarely the case (e.g. Fig. 12.2). An additional attribute could be used to express the variability within a polygon, but there is no simple way spatially to map continuous change with vector objects. Elevation is therefore inherently difficult to represent using discrete vector objects such as points or lines: contour lines, for example, give an indication of topographic variation at set intervals, but it can be difficult to predict elevation values between the lines. There are special vector structures called *triangulated irregular networks* (TINs) that overcome these difficulties (Chapter 6), but the case remains that some types of data are less well suited to the vector structure.

Advantages and disadvantages of the raster structure

Advantages of the raster structure The speed at which raster data can be processed offers advantages for some applications involving very large datasets and there are several other key areas in which the raster structure can offer advantages over vector formats. Firstly, raster data are very good for mapping continuously varying phenomena, such as elevation, as the continuous cell-based structure is akin to a continuously varying surface. The raster structure is also very good at representing real-world entities that have fuzzy boundaries. For example, a distribution of artefacts collected in a ploughed field could be represented more realistically by using raster cells that show the changing density of material rather than a single polygon that arbitrarily defines the site's area with a single density value. When this type of information is crucial, then the raster data structure offers a clear advantage. Secondly, raster datasets can be mathematically manipulated and combined more easily than polygon maps, making it an exceedingly powerful tool for spatial modelling. A simple model of agricultural potential, for example, may be constructed by combining data from several different sources, such as raster maps of elevation, slope, aspect, soil drainage and soil type in a process called *map algebra*. Thirdly, aerial photographs, satellite images and geophysical surveys produce data in raster formats, and the image processing that is often needed to enhance, classify and make sense of these sorts of data can only be performed in a raster environment.

Disadvantages of the raster structure There are three major disadvantages of the raster structure: its fixed resolution, its difficulty in representing discrete entities and its limited ability to handle multiple attribute data. The first problem arises when data collected at different scales need to be integrated. Combining multiscalar datasets could be seen as introducing additional problems regardless of the data model, and might ideally be avoided, but in practice there are many instances when

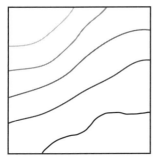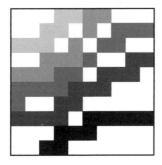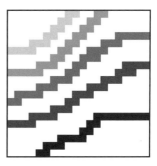

Fig. 2.14 Representing complex curves with raster data can be problematic. The box on the far left shows five vector polylines. The centre box shows the same lines using a 10 × 10 raster grid (i.e. 100 cells). On the far right the resolution has been increasing to a 20 × 20 grid (i.e. 400 cells). This improves the representation, but the raster map still suffers from being blocky and from lost detail.

data collected at different scales must be combined. Field survey data, for example, often mix scales of representation from the larger survey unit (such as a field) to site-based artefact collections where more detail is collected. The representation of multiscalar data is difficult in raster systems and the combination of raster data collected at different scales often results in having to default to the smaller scale and loosing detail. Secondly, problems can arise with representing complex boundaries using raster data because of the inherent limitations of grid data for representing tightly curved objects. Unless the cells are very small in relation to the object being represented and the storage size correspondingly increased, curved lines always will be blocky in appearance (Fig. 2.14).

For this reason complex shapes, such as contour lines, are better modelled using vector objects. Finally, raster data have always been difficult to connect to attribute tables. Although some GIS programs, notably Idrisi and GRASS, provide a facility for linking raster data to a database, in practice this is often more cumbersome than the embedded attribute tables that vector-based GIS programs provide. The raster data structure thus has limitations for the management and querying of multiscalar spatial datasets.

2.5 Conclusion

Geographical information systems (GIS) are a powerful technology that offer a host of analytical possibilities for investigating the spatial organisation of culture and human–environment relationships. These 'first principles' of GIS only define the starting point for exploring the complexity of the human use of space with GIS. In fact, many of these first principles are being constantly challenged by research that is pushing beyond the constraints of two-dimensional mapping to use GIS to model space–time relationships more adequately than the basic vector and raster building blocks presented in this chapter. Nevertheless, GIS is – for the time being at least – still reliant on cartographic principles and a reductionist tendency that restricts its range of possibilities for representing and interpreting the real world. Within these limitations, however, there is still a very broad range of ways that GIS can be used to develop an understanding of human culture in a spatial framework, and the next chapter provides some real-world examples of how GIS can and does work in archaeology.

3

Putting GIS to work in archaeology

This chapter reviews four typical applications of GIS in archaeology: management of archaeological resources, excavation, landscape archaeology and the spatial modelling of past human behaviour. For each application we discuss some general issues concerning the use of GIS in that particular context, followed by a presentation of a case study that illustrates the contribution that GIS has made. Although these examples are in no way exhaustive, they do provide a good overview of the capabilities and potential contributions that GIS can make to archaeological management and research.

3.1 Management of archaeological resources

It is not our intention to discuss the objectives of cultural resource management (CRM), nor the appropriate structure of a spatial database for managing the archaeological record, as these decisions are most appropriately made by government bodies and the archaeologists charged with the tasks of recording and managing the archaeological resource. However, we note that archaeological and historic databases have increasingly been subject to government scrutiny. In the UK, this most recently occurred in a parliamentary review of archaeology that took place in 2003 (APPAG 2003; Gilman 2004). In particular, the UK archaeological databases termed 'Sites and Monuments Records' (SMRs) are under review in light of recent developments in information technology, especially GIS and the Internet (e.g. Newman 2002). This report makes it clear that SMRs should evolve into broader Historic Environment Records (HERs) that include information such as historic buildings, parks and gardens, historic aircraft crash sites, etc. Moreover, the role of HERs as essential vehicles both for the management of the archaeological record and for public education was emphasised.

At the moment, SMRs are still fragmentary due in part to their often ad-hoc nature and the absence of clear guidelines as to what should be recorded. Some guidance and strategies for data collection, standards and maintenance have recently been provided in Fernie and Gilman (2000), ALGAO (2001), ALGAO (2002), but the lack of statutory requirements for their development or maintenance by local authorities is hindering standardisation (APPAG 2003). Several additional recommendations made to the government to improve SMRs include the need to streamline systems and centralise access via the Internet in order to increase their availability to the public (APPAG 2003, p. 19).

The implications of this in terms of the role of GIS are significant. For example, although in 2004 over 90% of SMRs in England reported using GIS for recording and management of data (Bevan and Bell 2004), there is little standardisation of methods and formats of data storage (Newman 2002). There are ongoing studies to introduce national standards specifying how particular sorts of archaeological and historically important information should be recorded within spatial databases, alongside recommendations regarding the role of GIS and the accessibility of spatial data to members of the public. Terminological standards such as the *Monument Inventory Data Standard* (MIDAS) and English Heritage's *National Monuments Record Thesauri*[1] are already in use. While we appear to be some years away from seeing GIS as the primary management system for archaeological and historic data, it is certainly on the horizon. With this in mind, we can make some very general observations and a few brief recommendations for people who might either be considering adopting a GIS for the first time, or considering reviewing and upgrading existing GIS facilities.

Firstly, as should now be clear from the previous chapter, GIS offers many advantages over attribute-only database systems when managing spatial data. Although it is possible to have a perfectly adequate non-GIS database that records site location and other information in a spreadsheet or paper card index, such databases begin to run into significant problems when spatial information becomes a key part of the record. Sites of Special Scientific Interest (SSSI), national parks or large archaeological sites cannot be easily described without reference to their spatial parameters, and recording anything more than the location of a specific point on the landscape becomes very difficult in a standard text-based database. For this reason, spatial databases are far superior as they are able to record morphology and topology in formats that can be queried in ways that attribute-only data cannot. From the perspective of resource management, the advantages of having an integrated system that permits the flexible interrogation of sites within their broader spatial context are enormous. Therefore GIS-based management systems are replacing standard CRM database systems worldwide, although the uptake of GIS in cultural heritage is certainly not uniform, even within Europe (Garcia-Sanjuan and Wheatley 1999).

Vector-based GIS environments are particularly suited to mapping precise boundaries and the linking of attribute data to spatial objects. They have thus traditionally been preferred for resource management. In the UK, nearly all SMRs held by county councils use vector objects to record archaeological spatial data (Bevan and Bell 2004). However, to be truly integrative, an SMR should include several other data layers that may require raster capabilities. Data such as airphotographs, digital elevation models, satellite imagery, historical maps, digital images and resistivity or other forms of survey data will provide a broader range of contextual information. Raster datasets also form the basis of predictive models,

Raster

---

[1]http://thesaurus.english_heritage.org.uk.

which were enthusiastically embraced in the early days of GIS and CRM. There are many reasons to be doubtful of its suitability for *explaining* human–environment relationships (cf. Wheatley 2004), but predictive modelling continues to be an important focus within the sphere of cultural resource management (see Westcott and Brandon 2000 for several examples and Chapter 8 for a discussion of objectives and methods of predictive modelling). An example of using a continuous surface to model 'importance' of known or suspected areas of archaeological significance has also been discussed by Wheatley and Gillings (2002, pp. 219–221).

A GIS will not solve all the data management problems faced by a CRM organisation, and the use of GIS will itself result in a number of issues that have to be addressed – ideally prior to migrating from established systems First, GIS implementation can be expensive. Software and hardware costs, particularly if using a commercial or specially written application, can be enormous. These costs may be relatively minor, however, compared to the costs of acquiring and maintaining spatial data and training personnel to operate the GIS software. Furthermore, while popular off-the-shelf systems such as MapInfo or ArcGIS are powerful and fully capable of dealing with the most demanding CRM and SMR data systems, professional customisation and programming of these systems to meet the specific needs of an SMR or CRM organisation is a worthwhile investment. The customisation of a GIS, while perhaps within the capability of a well-trained GIS operator, is something that is often best undertaken by a professional GIS programmer.

Second, the costs of transferring data from an attribute system to a spatial database can create difficulties because of the increased detail required by the latter. Even the most basic form of spatial data – points – might present difficulties if spatial precision has not been recorded or standardised to an established level. For example, if most site locations are recorded to the nearest 10 m, but a portion of the records only provide locations to the nearest 100 m, then this will immediately call into question the accuracy of any spatial queries that are subsequently undertaken. The only solution is to maintain data about the known or suspected spatial error, or to have spatial locations checked, confirmed or corrected by field personnel (which has cost implications). With more detailed spatial objects – for example, very large sites or historical landscapes – descriptive location records will have to be translated into topologically correct polygons that show their morphology and their spatial relationships to other vector objects such as roads, property boundaries, pipelines and other landscape features.

Third, costs for acquiring digital topographic maps of the area of responsibility also have to be taken into account, as national mapping agencies may not provide free versions of their costly data for commercial purposes. The costs of upgrading data so that it 'works' in a GIS environment cannot be underestimated, indeed, after the investment in training or acquiring GIS personnel, the acquisition of spatial data is perhaps the single most important investment to be made when moving to a GIS.

3.1.1 *Case study I: the Greater London Sites and Monuments Record*

The Greater London SMR is a good working example of a CRM GIS. The software used to manage the SMR is called the Historic Buildings, Sites and Monuments Record (HBSMR)[2] and was specially designed by Exegesis SDM in partnership with English Heritage's National Monuments Record (NMR) and the Association of Local Government Archaeological Officers (ALGAO). Exegesis SDM's HBSMR is built around Microsoft's Access database and is one of the more popular archaeological spatial management systems in use in Britain. Its relational structure – termed the 'Event–Source–Monument' model – permits the use of a sophisticated data model based around separate tables for the attributes of sites or monuments, associated archaeological investigations, and the data that constitutes the archive for that site or monument (Bourn 1999; Dunning 2001). Many SMRs held by county councils in England now use this system to manage their historic and archaeological datasets. The attribute databases link directly to spatial objects and base maps managed in either MapInfo or ArcView GIS, and provide the essential spatial search and query functionality needed to manage the data effectively. The system is based on the 1 : 25 000 Ordnance Survey Meridian series that provides a spatial framework and information on roads, property and administrative boundaries. The archaeological and historical places database consists of spatial objects that define the location and/or boundaries of a broad range of data, from prehistoric sites to larger Roman and medieval structures, and more recent buildings of historical importance. The associated attribute information for each of these locations is defined by English Heritage's *National Monuments Record Thesauri*.[3] A thesaurus is an essential part of any database as it provides a list of preferred terms for describing types of archaeological and historical sites, and establishing relationships between the hierarchical terms used to describe the spatial objects in the SMR. The SMR holds the records of nearly 80 000 archaeological sites, historic places and listed buildings across London's 33 boroughs, and provides the main source of information about the archaeological and historic places in London for archaeologists, researchers, planning consultants and developers. Further information about the Greater London SMR can be obtained from the National Monuments Record section of the English Heritage website.[4]

3.2 GIS and excavation

Archaeology has traditionally possessed a strong conceptual divide between data collection and data analysis, manifested most obviously between excavation and post-excavation activities. For many reasons this division is logical and necessary, not least because there are many tasks that are difficult to perform in the field: cataloguing photographic records; detailed analysis of artefacts, site plans

---

[2] www.esdm.co.uk/HBSMR.asp.
[3] http://thesaurus.english_heritage.org.uk.
[4] www.english-heritage.org.uk/.

and environmental samples; inking-up of drawings; and so on. However, the availability of laptop computers designed for field use means that it is now common for field projects to possess the capabilities for on-site computing. From a GIS perspective, therefore, the most important change in recent years relates to the massive increase in the use of digital recording methods for spatial and attribute data. Many of the routine tasks that were normally assigned to the post-excavation phase of a project can now take place in a field setting and this has eroded the traditional separation between data collection and description, and that of data analysis and interpretation. Beck and Beck (2000) provide a good example of the impact of digital recording on the excavation process, and the implications of eroding the boundary between data collection and interpretation have also been explored by Hodder (1997, pp. 80–104, and 1999). A comprehensive discussion of excavation methodologies and theory, including the impact of information technology (IT) on excavation practices, can also be found in Roskams (2001).

Although it is certainly not a panacea, GIS can play a useful role in an archaeological excavation. As a spatial management tool it is unsurpassed as it allows rapid visualisation of spatial data and can link plans and drawings of archaeological remains directly to database records. On any site with more than a few hundred plans and associated data records GIS can offer major advantages for data management. GIS also enables the visualisation of data patterns at or soon after their collection, which can be invaluable during the course of an excavation, facilitating a 'reflexive' approach to data collection in the way described by Hodder (1999). Data collection therefore becomes a more iterative exercise, allowing ideas about possible patterns and relationships between data to be identified and explored more quickly and efficiently than can occur in traditional paper-based recording systems. A very simple conceptual model of a basic excavation GIS is outlined in Fig. 3.1.

The use of GIS on any excavation requires a considerable amount of forethought and planning. Digital recording technologies bring their own set of disadvantages, particularly the dependence on electricity and the associated costs of buying or renting expensive recording equipment. These costs should be weighed against the potential benefits, such as the time savings in the transfer of information from paper to digital formats, and the interpretative advantages of being able to visualise and explore complex data patterns during the process of excavation. It is increasingly common for excavation projects to record spatial data using a total station or differential GPS, with data transferred directly into a data-logger or computer to reduce the time and the possibility of introducing errors when recording data (Powlesland 1998; Ziebart *et al.* 1998). More recent survey technologies, such as the ArcSurvey package of the ArcGIS family, extend GIS functionality to data collection so that GPS and total station data can be viewed and annotated in real-time on laptop or tablet computers. Alternatively it is possible to record spatial information by photogrammetry – the deriving of spatial data from photographs – which has a long history of archaeological application at both landscape and site levels (e.g. Sterud and Pratt 1975; Anderson 1982; Poulter and Kerslake 1997). Procedures

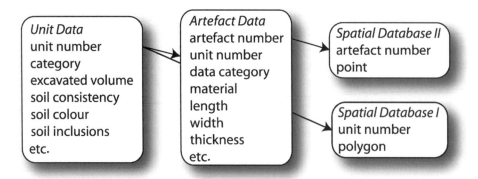

Fig. 3.1 A simple data model for linking excavated unit attribute data and artefact attribute data to a spatial database. The 'polygon' and 'point' fields in the spatial databases contain the *x*, *y*-coordinate data that describes the spatial object, as captured directly in the field or subsequently digitised from paper plans. Such a system allows the visualisation of units as polygons, with an overlay of artefacts as points. Each is directly linked to the attribute databases, allowing context-specific spatial or attribute queries to be preformed (e.g. 'locate all the chert tools within 1 m of hearth features').

for capturing digital data from paper plans is discussed in some detail in Chapter 5, which also considers some of the digital recording technologies that are available to archaeologists.

Three-dimensional stratigraphic modelling

In many situations archaeologists record data in three dimensions that cannot be properly interpreted in the two-dimensional plane offered by most GIS software. While it has been possible for some years to record objects in three dimensions using computer-aided drawing packages such as AutoCAD, and the spatial analysis of three-dimensional data has long been used by prehistorians to understand the patterning of objects (see Spikins *et al.* 2002; Nigro *et al.* 2003, for recent examples), truly analytical three-dimensional GIS remains an elusive target (Hudson-Smith and Evans 2003). Currently, many off-the-shelf GIS packages represent the third dimension by extruding vector objects by a *z* attribute variable to create the impression of a three-dimensional surface or volume, referred to as '2.5D' or 'almost three-dimensional'. While this has some advantages for the three-dimensional visualisation of surfaces or regular three-dimensional phenomena such as buildings, spatial queries like 'retrieve all the objects within a spherical radius of 1 m from this point in three-dimensional space', or the modelling of irregular volumes, are still beyond basic desktop GIS functionality (although three-dimensional 'buffer zones' may be generated in ArcGIS's 'three-dimensional Analyst'). There are, however, programs that have been developed for modelling geological data and these may offer some potential for fully three-dimensional visualisation and analysis of archaeological data. The program 'Vulcan',[5] for example, provides tools for building and visualising volumetric data in three dimensions. A similar set of software produced by C Tech Development Corporation (marketed with the title Environmental Visualisation Systems[6]) offers similar capabilities, as well as three-dimensional geostatistical tools. The ability to build a detailed three-dimensional stratigraphic model of an excavation in order to understand the structure and formation processes of the archaeological record is an exciting possibility that has yet to be fully explored by archaeologists, and we are aware of only the previously cited example of Nigro *et al.* (2003) as an example of its potential.

There have also been a number of projects that have used virtual reality to provide innovative ways of interacting with three-dimensional objects. For example, Gillings and Goodrick (1996) and Exon *et al.* (2000) have explored the possibilities of virtual reality (VR) for the arts and humanities, and provide several examples of potential applications. Purely analytic uses that link GIS with VR remain under development and archaeological examples that combine these two spatial technologies remain to be seen. Interested readers are referred to Fisher and Unwin's (2002) *Virtual Reality in Geography* for examples of the analytic potential of three-dimensional modelling, virtual reality and GIS.

3.2.1 *Case study II: the West Heslerton Project*

West Heslerton is a village in Yorkshire, England, that was the setting for one of the largest English Heritage rescue archaeology projects in recent history. Over 20 hectares of an Anglo-Saxon village and associated cemetery were examined through excavation, survey and remote sensing, providing a comprehensive picture of a crucial period in English history. The project was directed by Dominic Powlesland and is described in a number of publications, both online and in print (see Powlesland 1998, and Haughton and Powlesland 1999, for a full list of references).

Although the project is of major importance for the archaeology of both the Late Roman/Early Anglo-Saxon and the Early/Middle Anglo-Saxon transitions, of particular concern here is its pioneering use of digital recording and presentation of data. All artefacts, features and samples were recorded using a total station, and handheld computers were used in the field as the primary tools for the vector-based recording of over 300 000 archaeological contexts, artefacts, environmental, drawing and photographic records (Powlesland 1998). What marks West Heslerton as different from other projects that were pioneers in the use of digital recording techniques is that it also used GIS to manage, visualise and analyse archaeological spatial data. The software (G-Sys) was written by Powlesland to enable the three-dimensional plotting of point data and the integration of geophysical and remotely sensed data, and digital photographs, with line and polygon vector data.

---

[5]www.vulcan3d.com.
[6]www.ctech.com/products/evs-pro.htm.

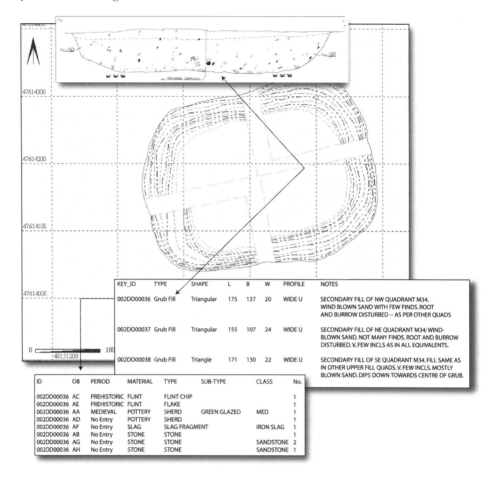

Fig. 3.2 The workings of the West Heslerton WEB-CD, showing the dynamic links between the plans, sections and attribute tables. Arrows depict context-sensitive data records and images obtainable by clicking on the site plan. See Powlesland *et al.* (1998) for details on its construction. Images reproduced with permission.

As well as facilitating the management and analysis of the spatial data, the use of GIS also expedited the publication process. One of the most innovative aspects of the project was its use of digital media to publish the primary record. The scale of data involved, consisting of nearly 30 000 context records and plans, 90 000 object records and close to a million animal bone fragments, alongside the copious photographic, stratigraphic, geophysical and other datasets, meant that traditional paper publication would have been a costly and unwieldy medium to present the full dataset. On what was inexpensively published as the West Heslerton WEB-CD (Powlesland *et al.* 1998), data tables can be searched, and text, plans and section drawings can be interactively linked in ways impossible with traditional publication formats (Fig. 3.2; Powlesland 1997). Although it is now some years since the project finished its fieldwork, West Heslerton remains a milestone in the use of GIS in the field, and for the digital publication of archaeological data.

3.3 Landscape archaeology

Regional survey (or 'field-walking') projects present an obvious environment for using GIS, as the regional and spatial foci are readily aligned to the tools that GIS offers. Whether the survey is organised using systematic testpits or transects, or is more opportunistic and exploratory, using GIS offers enormous benefits over paper-based recording. A number of publications have considered the impact of spatial technologies on archaeological survey and landscape archaeology: for example, papers in Gillings *et al.* (1999) and Bintliff *et al.* (2001) discuss technical and interpretative issues arising from the use of GIS in specific environmental settings, and Lock (2003, pp. 14–77) provides a more general, but very comprehensive, overview. One major challenge facing landscape archaeologists is how to collate data from different projects when data have been collected under different recording systems and methods – for example, papers in Alcock and Cherry (2004) provide a Mediterranean perspective on this problem – and GIS certainly has a major role to play in this endeavour. However, we limit ourselves here to only a more general consideration of the value and role of GIS in landscape archaeology.

The spatial resolution for archaeological landscape data collection varies enormously: it may range from the intensive point plotting of all artefacts across a study region (e.g. Fanning and Holdaway 2001; Ketz 2001), to extensive surveys that seek only to record the location of archaeological sites. In artefact-rich landscapes, such as the Mediterranean, it is often impractical to plot the location of every artefact or even transect, and it is not uncommon for archaeologists to use survey units in the region of 0.5 ha or greater in area, in which counts of artefacts (but not their locations) are tabulated from field walking (Barton *et al.* 1999, 2002; Lock *et al.* 1999; Gillings and Sbonias 1999; Bevan and Conolly 2004). In many cases, projects will use a range of resolutions for different tasks, although this always requires careful documentation to ensure the data recorded at the coarser level are not analysed assuming a higher level of precision. For example, whereas insight into the effects of erosion on artefact visibility could potentially be obtained by investigating the relationship between point-plotted artefact locations and slope values on a 2-m^2 grid, the same investigation with artefact densities collected in units of 50 m^2 would be meaningless unless the slope data were resampled to this level of resolution.

Regardless of the spatial resolution, a common starting point for any landscape-scale project is the digital acquisition (most often as vector data) of the background topographic data, such as extant field systems and boundary walls, buildings, streams, roads, pathways and tracks. This level of detail is dependent on the availability of maps of a sufficiently high resolution, which for all practical purposes is usually a scale of 1 : 25 000 or larger. These background contextual data provide a useful spatial framework for archaeological investigation. For projects working in smaller areas it may be practical to collect these, and also elevation data, as primary data via recording equipment such as a different GPS or a total station (Chapter 5). More often, however, it is more practical to capture elevation data from secondary sources, such as by digitising contours from existing paper maps, then converting these to a continuous elevation model (Chapter 6). In some situations, however, very little high-resolution mapping may be available, in which case it might be necessary to plot data on publicly available lower resolution maps (such as Pennsylvania State University Library's Digital Chart of the World,[7] the US Geological Survey's HYDRO1k series,[8] or commercially available satellite imagery, as described in Chapter 5).

The use of a navigation-grade GPS (i.e. with an accuracy of ± 10 m) will allow the survey units (test squares, transects or tracts) or actual artefacts to be plotted reasonably accurately on base maps of scales of 1 : 25 000 or smaller. With a wide-area-augmentation-station (WAAS)-enabled (see Chapter 5) handheld GPS (± 3 m) such data can be plotted accurately at scales of 1 : 5000 or smaller, and if a differential or survey-grade GPS is used then the spatial accuracy will exceed that of all but the highest resolution base maps (see Chapter 5 for more information on digital recording methods). As outlined in Chapter 2, the use of a metric coordinate system (such as UTM, UK Ordnance Survey, US State Plane, or some form of National Grid) is preferable to latitude and longitude coordinates.

Recording the spatial boundaries of a survey unit within an existing set of map data requires a reasonable degree of map-reading skill and is essential for the accurate placement of archaeological data within the landscape. The use of GPS receivers may improve the accuracy, although since handheld GPS recorders have an error rate of ± 10 m it will be necessary to check and possibly manually adjust spatial locations plotted at scales larger than 1 : 25 000. If survey units are being digitised from paper field maps, then a minimum spatial error should be established by reference to the root-mean-square-error (RMSE) value (see Chapter 5) of the map registration for each session of digitising. If the survey units are tracts (i.e. polygons), then it is also imperative that the topological relationships between the units are properly established: adjacent tracts should share nodes if they truly are adjacent, and must not overlap if they are not. Significant errors can be made, for example, with artefact density estimates because of topological errors in digitised data. Issues related to digitising and polygon topology are discussed in further detail in Chapter 5.

It is worth highlighting here an important point that Thomas (1993, p. 26) has raised concerning an erroneous belief that can potentially arise in GIS-led landscape surveys: that 'data assembled are data understood'. The apparently 'totalising knowledge' that emerges from the assembly of structures, fields, hydrology, soils, elevation and extant archaeological evidence into a GIS does not directly lead to an understanding of the all-important social landscape. Meaningful and

---

[7] www.maproom.psu.edu/dcw/.   [8] http://edcdaac.usgs.gov/gtopo30/hydro/.

substantive interpretations of the complex and often unpredictable relationships humans have with their landscapes cannot be arrived at by assembling data alone, but must be carefully built and explored using a range of sources (e.g. ethnographic, historical, environmental, experiential, archaeological). Each provides insight and interpretative possibilities for developing an understanding of past human behaviour in a landscape context; GIS is but one of several potentially useful tools that can be used to reach this goal and its results should be balanced against other forms of analysis and interpretation.

3.3.1 *Case study III: the Kythera Island Project*

The Kythera Island Project (KIP)[9] serves as a good example of an extensive survey project in an artefact-rich landscape where GIS played an important role in meeting the aims of the project. Kythera, a Greek island that lies between Crete and the Peloponnese, was selected for an intensive study to explore insular dynamics (see Broodbank 1999 for an overview). Here we highlight only the landscape archaeological component of the research, which was built on a detailed study of over one-third of the island's total area of 280 km^2. The geospatial framework used by the project is based on the Greek military grid system established for the island, on which the 1 : 5000 topographic map series is based. These maps were manually digitised prior to the survey and included a range of anthropomorphic features, including roads and tracks, field systems and standing buildings (Fig. 3.3).

A 10-m resolution DEM for the survey area was created from manually digitised contours to aid in the interpretation of land-use, site and artefact taphonomy, and ecological modelling (Bevan and Conolly 2004). The field computing system consisted of three laptops running digital mapping systems, database and GIS. Hardcopies of sections of 1 : 5000 maps defining the day's field-walking objectives were printed out for archaeological surveyors, who then used a combination of local land features such as field boundaries, roads and buildings, together with compasses and GPS receivers, to locate and plot their survey tracts. Individual transects and related artefact counts were also recorded on paper forms, and land-use data was also recorded for each tract. Artefact record sheets were entered into a linked GIS and relational database system by an onsite dedicated data-entry team (Fig. 3.4). Points defining the individual survey tracts were also digitised at the end of each day, which were then linked to the database records. Between 1998 and 2001, nearly 9000 tracts covering an area of 42.5 km^2 were surveyed and digitised and nearly 200 new sites located and documented within the survey area.

The use of GIS during the survey seasons enabled the qualitative assessment of new spatial patterning within a few hours of the data having been collected. Newly discovered archaeological sites, artefact distributions and the conditions influencing the patterning of artefacts were then used to inform ongoing project decisions. The archaeological datum itself could also be immediately revisited,

---

[9]www.ucl.ac.uk/kip.

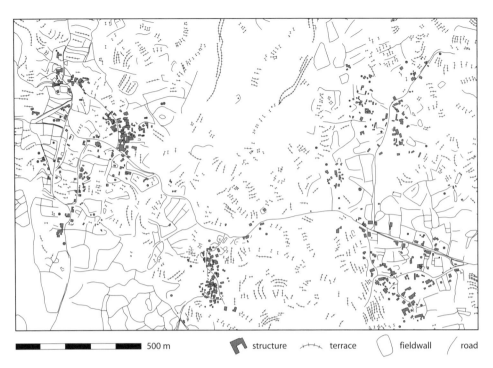

500 m   ◢ structure   ⌒⌒⌒ terrace   ⬭ fieldwall   ╱ road

Fig. 3.3 A small window into the KIP GIS, showing major anthropomorphic features that formed the framework for the archaeological data collection. Source: Kythera Island Project. Used with permission.

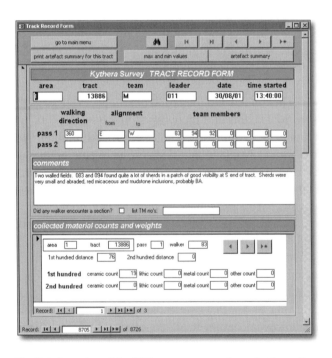

Fig. 3.4 A section of the KIP survey tract attribute database. Source: Kythera Island Project. Used with permission.

Table 3.1 *KIP geospatial datasets*

Data	Extent	Format	Entity	Scale/Resolution
20-m contours	Island	Vector	Arc	1 : 5000
Spot heights	Island	Vector	Point	1 : 5000
2–4-m contours	Survey area	Vector	Arc	1 : 5000
Cultural topography	Island	Vector	Various	1 : 5000
Bedrock geology	Island	Vector	Area	1 : 50 000
Aerial photographs	Island	Raster	Grid	1 : 15 000
Satellite imagery	Island	Raster	Grid	20-m resolution
Digital photos	Local	Raster	n/a	n/a
Elevation	Local	Vector	Point	1 : 2000
Site location	Survey area	Vector	Point	~1 : 15 000
Site scatter	Local/survey area	Vector	Area	~1 : 15 000
Ceramic distribution (i)	Local	Vector	Area	25–400-m^2 units
Ceramic distribution (ii)	Survey area	Vector	Area	<10 000-m^2 units
Geoarchaeology (i)	Subsurvey area	Vector	All	1 : 5000
Geoarchaeology (ii)	Local	Vector	All	1 : 2000

Source: Bevan and Conolly 2004.

checked and confirmed, leading to a very high-quality dataset. Furthermore, the rapid feedback of results to the archaeologists responsible for the data collection had a significant positive effect on team morale. From a management perspective, the KIP GIS also helped with predictions of the time required to complete sections of the survey, and how best to allocate surveyors in the field. These factors were also of enormous value during the field season.

The final KIP GIS dataset consists of a broad range of topographic, geological and archaeological data, collected and processed using a variety of techniques (Table 3.1). These data have formed the basis for an ongoing substantive study of the island's historic landscapes, including the study of past land-use systems, the relationship between ecological features such as watersheds and prehistoric site placement, and Bronze Age demography and settlement patterns (see Bevan 2003; Bevan and Conolly 2004) for recent examples.

3.4 Spatial and simulation modelling

The term 'spatial modelling' refers to the use of geospatial data to simulate a process, understand a complex relationship, predict an outcome or analyse a problem. For example, *regression analysis* can be used to ascertain the relationship between two continuous variables, one of which may be spatial. A well-known example of this type of model is the exploration of the relationship between the proportion of a raw material found in an archaeological assemblage against the distance from the source of the raw material. This is often performed to provide insight into the possible processes governing how that material was transported across the landscape. This

Table 3.2 *The four scales of measurement*

Data type	Description	Example
Nominal	Descriptive categories	Colours: red, blue, black, etc.
Ordinal	Ranked data	Relative sizes: small, medium, large, larger
Interval	Continuous data but arbitrary '0'	Calendar dates: 100 BC, AD 50, etc.
Ratio	Continuous data with fixed '0'	Lengths: 13.4, 16.2, 18.1, etc.

form of modelling was popular in the late 1960s through the 1970s, although the optimism expressed by early advocates concerning the correlation of the regression curves with particular forms of exchange systems (e.g. Renfrew *et al.* 1968; Renfrew and Dixon 1976) was subsequently muted by the simulation studies of Hodder and Orton (1976).

Regression analysis nevertheless still plays an important role in understanding the relationship between quantitative variables (Shennan 1988, pp. 114–134), although in a subsequent chapter we will highlight some of the problems that have been identified with the technique when modelling spatial datasets. More complex forms of archaeological spatial modelling can involve establishing the relationship between known site locations and environmental variables – typically things like elevation, slope, aspect and distance to water – to help predict the occurrence of sites in unsampled areas (i.e. 'predictive modelling', as discussed in detail in Chapter 8). Other types of spatial modelling commonly employed by archaeologists include the use of elevation models to understand visibility (Wheatley 1995; Lake and Woodman 2003; Llobera 2003), elevation and terrain data to understand movement across landscapes (Bell *et al.* 2002), ecological modelling to understand factors related to site visibility and location (Bevan 2003), and quantitative analysis of artefact distributions to model living surfaces (Spikins *et al.* 2002). Spatial modelling can also include the use of simulation studies to understand human decision making in specific environmental situations (Lake 2000a,b). The range and types of data used in spatial modelling are clearly broad in scope, to the extent that it is difficult to provide general guidelines for how best to approach this type of GIS-based analysis.

One common approach to modelling first extracts data from a spatial database in order to explore, clarify and define patterns and relationships (possibly with the aid of separate statistical software). Examples include: the extraction of site locations as x, y-coordinates in order to analyse their relative aggregation at different scales; logistic regression analysis of grid-based environmental variables against site location; or the calculation of statistical indexes such as *Moran's I* to search for spatial dependency (autocorrelation) within a dataset.

In these examples, the data model is not as important as the scale of measurement, that is nominal, ordinal, interval or ratio data (Table 3.2 and see also Chapter 8), which influences the type of quantitative analyses that can be performed. Interval data provide opportunities for a wide range of robust statistical tests but informative modelling can still be performed with lower-order data. Shennan (1988, pp. 65–70), for example, provides a simple case of a non-parametric analysis of site location against a nominal variable (soil type) that provides some insight into the processes structuring site location. Chapter 8 reviews a selection of useful statistical methods for testing the presence and strength of relationships in spatial datasets.

A second approach to spatial modelling involves the mathematical manipulation of one or more datasets to produce new data. A number of different types of modelling, including network, visibility, erosion, movement, cost-surface and some forms of ecological modelling, fall into this category. With the exception of network modelling, which depends on vector topology, raster data are often the preferred data format for building spatial models. Elevation data play a particularly important role as a basic dataset on which visibility, movement and ecological models are built; these can then be used to help understand the human use of space. New geospatial datasets can also be created by combining raster datasets using algebraic expressions. Chapters 9 and 10 examine this form of spatial modelling in further detail and the case studies described below together outline an applied example.

A third approach is *dynamic modelling*, which explores how phenomenon change over time. Certain types of erosion models that use *cellular automata* fall into this category. Archaeologists are also using *agent-based simulation* models within GIS systems to predict and explain certain types of past human behaviour and decision making in an actual landscape setting (e.g. Kohler and Gumerman 2000; Lake 2000a). Agent-based models have also been combined with GIS for predicting visitor movement in national parks (Gimblett 2002) and this technique may well prove useful for CRM (Eve 2004). Integration with simulation modelling is one of the most active, exciting and rapidly developing areas of archaeological GIS. However, building a dynamic simulation in GIS is an advanced topic that falls outside the scope of this book. Interested readers are advised to refer to the two cited volumes above and to review papers in the *Journal of Artificial Societies and Social Simulation*. Gilbert and Troitzsch (1999) provide a more practical introduction to the simulation of social phenomena, although they do not specifically address the use of GIS.

3.4.1 *Case study IV: the modelling of Mesolithic site location and foraging behaviour*

Examples of the application of GIS-based spatial modelling can be found in Lake 2000a,b, Lake and Woodman 2000, and Woodman 2000b. These three linked studies investigate prehistoric hunter–gatherer activity on the island of Islay, Scotland, and, respectively, make predictions about site location, explore the behavioural activities that produce sites, and establish the relationship between site location and the amount of the landscape that can be seen from that position (i.e. a site's 'viewshed').

Table 3.3 *Variables used in Woodman's (2000b) predictive modelling study*

Variable	Description
Elevation	Derived from 10-m contours
Local relief	Maximum elevation range in 500-m radius
Shelter quality	Ordinal-scale measurement of landform shelter based on Kvamme (1985)
Aspect	Derivative of elevation
Exposure	Derivation of aspect to create categories describing exposure
Angle of view	Derivation of slope, to create categories describing horizontal angle of view
Distance to water source	Linear distance to nearest water source
Order of nearest water source	Based on drainage classification using Strahler's method (Strahler 1952)
Distance to modern coast	Linear distance to high-water mark of modern coastline
Distance to Mesolithic coast	Linear distance to reconstructed coastline
Exposure of modern coast	Ordinal-scale measurement (exposed, semi-protected to protected)
Exposure of Mesolithic coast	As above
Topographic location of modern coast	Nominal-scale measurement describing setting of site (e.g. bay, headland, linear coastal or inland)
Topographic location of Mesolithic coast	As above

Woodman's study involved subjecting a selection of 14 environmental variables to a form of statistical modelling called *linear logistic regression analysis* in order to ascertain their relationship to site location. This type of analysis is multistaged, and is dependent on a number of presuppositions that first have to be demonstrated rather than assumed, but ultimately results in an equation of the form $p = a + b_1 x_1 + b_2 x_2 + \cdots + b_k x_k$, where p represents the log odds of site occurrence, $x_1, x_2 \ldots x_k$ are the values of variables such as elevation, distance to water, etc., and a and $b_1, b_2 \cdots b_k$ are derived numeric values established by the statistical analysis (Table 3.3) (Menard 2001). This formula can then be used to construct probability maps of site location. In this particular case, by comparing the predictions for site presence against both random and known settlement locations for inland sites, Woodman was able to show that her model was able to distinguish site locations from random places in the landscape, and thus had value for predicting the likelihood of site occurrence elsewhere on the island.

Lake's (2000a,b) study combined GIS and computer simulation to construct a dynamic model of hunter–gatherer foraging behaviour on Islay. The aim of the exercise was to develop a better understanding of the causal factors underlying the spatial patterning of Mesolithic artefacts located during archaeological fieldwork (Mithen 2000) and to test whether their distribution and composition could be explained in terms of hunter–gatherer decision making that prioritised the

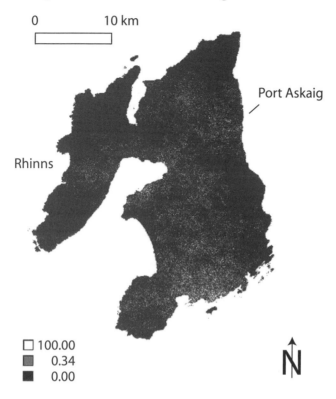

Fig. 3.5 A simulated artefact distribution resulting from one run of an agent-based model. The key shows the number of microliths as a percentage of the maximum number discarded in any map cell. Reproduced from Lake (2000a) with permission; coastline © Crown Copyright, all rights reserved, licence no. 100021184.

acquisition of hazelnuts. The process involved the construction of an agent-based simulation model that provided each agent with a set of goals, decision-making abilities and risk-taking parameters. The agents' environment included a model of hazelnut abundance on the island, which was constructed by combining GIS layers such as measures of land capability with estimated parameters for woodland species' tolerances derived from pollen data and contemporary topological data such as slope and aspect. Agents were then 'set loose' on this digital landscape to search and collect hazelnuts, and share information about the location of hazelnuts. By building in tool-discard behaviour, Lake was able to compare the simulated runs of various scenarios (e.g. varying the location of landing and the willingness to take risks in terms of deciding where to move), and compare the results against the known archaeological record (Fig. 3.5). The model of hazelnut foraging behaviour, as predicted by the simulation, showed a poor correspondence with the archaeological record, suggesting that hazelnut foraging was not a major determinant of hunter–gatherer activity on the island. The lack of fit did not mean that the simulation 'failed' – only that this behaviour does not account for the archaeological evidence and, consequently, that some other explanation must be entertained.

Finally, Lake and Woodman (2000) responded to a well-documented behavioural trait of hunter–gatherers concerning the importance of information acquisition, and hypothesised that Mesolithic sites were situated in positions that provided more extensive views across the landscape than the 'average' view from elsewhere on the landscape. To test this idea, they formally developed a null hypothesis that stated that the amount of landscape visible (the viewshed) from known site locations should be statistically indistinguishable from the quantity of landscape visible from all non-site locations. As the calculation of the viewsheds for all non-site locations would involve deriving information from 90 000 individual locations, they used a technique called *Monte-Carlo simulation* (Chapter 8) to provide estimates of the viewshed parameters for non-site locations. This involved randomly sampling 24 locations from their study area 25 times, and calculating an 'envelope' that provided a statistical range of viewshed characteristics for non-site locations. These values were then compared to the viewshed characteristics of known sites, which were shown to be statistically different. This result was upheld even when sites were compared with non-site locations characterised by similar elevation, slope and aspect values as the sites. The null hypothesis was consequently rejected, allowing them to propose that Mesolithic people on Islay deliberated situated sites in areas that possessed large viewsheds, presumably as part of a strategy for maximising information about their local landscape.

3.5 Conclusion

It should now be clear that the range of tasks and the variety of questions to which GIS can contribute answers are vast. Whether your primary interests are using GIS to facilitate the management of spatial data collected during an excavation, to help predict the probability of site locations in a study area, or to model the movement routes of people across terrain, GIS can play an important role. If you are new to GIS and have been following the chapters sequentially, you should now have a much better idea of how GIS fits into the wider framework of archaeologists' broad interest in the human use of space and landscapes, how GIS works, and how it has been used in the past to help manage and make sense of the archaeological record. The next three chapters look more closely at how one builds a GIS. Firstly, in Chapter 4 we consider data storage and management systems. This is followed by a comprehensive chapter on how datasets can be digitally captured and structured for manipulation and analysis in a GIS environment. Chapter 6 then delves more deeply into the manipulation of spatial datasets, showing how to classify and interpolate data in order to create and structure spatial data for subsequent analysis.

4

The geodatabase

4.1 Introduction

This chapter describes the way that spatial and attribute data are structured and stored for use within a GIS. It provides the necessary information about data models and database design to enable archaeologists unfamiliar with computer databases to make appropriate decisions about how best to construct a system that will work well and efficiently.

A database is a collection of information that is structured and recorded in a consistent manner. A card catalogue that records information about archaeological sites, such as their location and date, is as much a database as a full-fledged web-searchable digital sites and monuments record. Digital databases differ from their paper counterparts mainly in that they are dependent on database software for searching and retrieving records. The complexity of the data structure will also be increased as digital databases are often broken into several different related files. This reduces the amount of duplicated information in a database, improves access speed and also enables the retrieval of small subsets of data rather than complete records. Software that is used to store, manage and manipulate data is referred to as a *Database Management System* (DBMS). The objectives of a DBMS are to store and retrieve data records in the most efficient way possible, from both the perspective of the overall size of the database and also the speed at which that data can be accessed.

The technology of DBMS is a major research focus in computer science. There is consequently a vast and growing literature on database method and theory, but unless one is interested in designing and writing database programs from scratch it is possible to remain largely ignorant of these details. More usefully we can briefly note the four specific functions that a DBMS should provide (cf. Burrough and McDonnell 1998, p. 50), namely: (i) quick access to, and the ability to select subsets of data, potentially by several users at the same time; (ii) a facility for inputting, editing and updating data; (iii) the ability to define and enforce rules to ensure data accuracy and consistency; (iv) the ability to protect data against unintentional or malicious destruction.

A GIS needs to store, manage and retrieve both geographical and attribute data (the combination of which is collectively referred to as a 'geodatabase'). Many GIS programs provide tools for the management of attribute as well as geographical data, although it is also common to use a separate DBMS program, such as Microsoft Access or MySQL, to manage attribute data. The first part of this chapter reviews

Table 4.1 *A flat-file database*

sherd_id	sherd_class	temper	diameter (mm)	site_id	earliest date (BP)	latest date (BP)	area (m²)
1	rim	fine sand	88	1001	1200	1100	8045
2	body	fine sand		1001	1200	1100	8045
3	base	grog		1001	1200	1100	8045
4	body	vegetable		1004	900	700	410
5	rim	vegetable	47	1004	900	700	410
6	body	fine sand		1006	1000	800	8900
7	base	coarse sand		1007	800	400	7980
8	rim	shell	140	1007	800	400	7980
9	rim	grog	134	1009	200	100	1200

the ways that attribute data may be stored and managed in a DBMS, and the second part examines the storage methods for raster and vector datasets.

4.1.1 *Data models: from flat file to relational*

The simplest form of database consists of a single table of data, in which each column contains a field and each row a record. Tables such as these are referred to as *flat-file databases* because there is no depth to the data. All the data are stored in one location and there are no linkages between these records and those in other data tables. Flat-file systems do have some advantages over other logical models as they are very easy to maintain, the data are readily available, and search and find operations are computationally simple. However, they have a major disadvantage which precludes their use for all but the simplest databases, which is that they have no facility for dealing with data that may be redundant. For example, many records in the pottery sherd database shown in Table 4.1 contain duplicated information about the site from which the sherd comes.

This introduces a high level of duplication in the data. Furthermore, some data cells are empty – for example, the field *diameter* is only filled in for rim sherds. The result is both an unnecessarily large and redundant data structure in which a large number of cells either contain repeated data or are null. Flat-file tables are thus only appropriate for the simplest databases, as they soon become unwieldy when information about more than one entity needs to be recorded, as in the above example. An elegant solution to this problem, first defined by E. F. Codd (1970) in what became known as the *Relational Model*, is to break the database into separate tables that each contain a coherent package of information. For example, creating three new tables each containing information on *sites*, *pottery* and *rims* reduces the amount of repeated data and blank entries. The disadvantage is that the system must then manage three tables instead of one, so some mechanism is then needed to extract information from all tables to answer questions such as 'what different types of temper are found on rim sherds from sites with dates before 1000 BP?'.

The advantages of the relational model are its simple tabular structure, uncomplicated relationships, and its associated powerful and versatile query language, called SQL (pronounced 'sequel'). Although the relational model may seem complex to the uninitiated, in practice it is a simple and versatile way of managing large datasets.

The principal component of a *relational database* is a table of data, referred to as a *relation*, which consists of a set of records that contain a number of different fields shared by all records. Each record must be distinct from every other via a unique identifier (such as an id number), referred to as the *primary key*. If no single field contains a unique entry, then two or more fields can be used to define a primary key, in which case it is called a *composite key*. Tables must also meet certain conditions defined by the relational concept of *normalisation* (for examples, see Beynon-Davies 1992, pp. 30–42). This means that records with the same repeating values should be placed into separate tables and be defined by their own primary key. The process of breaking a set of data into separate tables and defining the links between them is referred to as *normalisation*.

For example, in Table 4.1, values for *site_id*, *early date*, *late date* and *area* always occur in groups and should therefore be recorded in a separate table (called 'sites'). The rules of normalisation also require that dependent values in the remaining fields are separated; and so, in our example, *diameter* must also be placed into a different table ('rim measurements') than the *sherd_id*, *sherd_class* and *temper* fields, because it is dependent on a *sherd_class* value of 'rim'. In this case, the rims table needs to inherit the *sherd_id* data so that it is possible to determine which sherd each rim measurement belongs to. The normalised tables and their primary keys are shown in Table 4.2.

Relationships between tables are then created by defining links between a primary key and its equivalent field in another table, referred to as a *foreign key*. In our example, we need therefore to create a new field in the pottery table called *site_ id* that contains the id number of the site where that sherd was found. This field then acts as the foreign key and allows the primary key (*site_id*) in the site table to establish a relation with the pottery table. The variable *sherd_id*, which is present in both the pottery and rim tables, can be used to link those two tables together. The links tables can take the form of either a *one-to-one*, *one-to-many* or *many-to-many* relationship, depending on the number of records referred to by the primary–foreign key link. In this example, the relationship between 'sites' and 'pottery' is one-to-many (as one site may have many sherds) and the relationship between 'pottery' and 'rim measurements' is one-to-one (as no sherd will have more than one rim record – note we are not considering the possibility of conjoining sherds or rims here!). For reasons of storage efficiency and relational coherence, many-to-many relationships need to be turned into one-to-many relationships via the construction of intermediary tables. Normalisation is covered in greater detail in a number of accessible publications, including the University of Texas at Austin's Information Technology Service Data Modelling Pages[1] and Hernandez (2003).

---

[1]`www.utexas.edu/its/windows/database/datamodeling/rm/overview.html`.

Table 4.2 *The three normalised tables: sites (upper), pottery (middle) and rim measurements (lower). Primary keys are defined by a* †*, the foreign key by a* ‡

site_id†	early date (BP)	late date (BP)	area (m^2)
1001	1200	1100	8045
1004	900	700	410
1006	1000	800	8900
1007	800	400	7980
1009	200	100	1200

sherd_id†	sherd_class	temper	site_id‡
1	rim	fine sand	1001
2	body	fine sand	1001
3	base	grog	1001
4	body	vegetable	1004
5	rim	vegetable	1004
6	body	fine sand	1006
7	base	coarse sand	1007
8	rim	shell	1007
9	rim	grog	1009

sherd_id†	diameter (mm)
1	88
5	47
8	140
9	134

The retrieval of data from a relational system using SQL involves defining the relations between entities and the conditions under which certain attributes should be selected. This is discussed in further detail in Chapter 7, where spatial data query methods are also reviewed. Some GIS programs, such as ESRI's ArcInfo and ArcView, have embedded DBMSs that allow basic relationships between tables to be defined and queried. While embedded management systems offer good functionality for data retrieval from databases with simple structures, linking a GIS to a database such as PostgreSQL, MySQL, Oracle or Microsoft's SQL Server, permits the full use of the relational model and SQL for managing and querying attribute data.

Even if the GIS software does provide basic DBMS facilities for managing attribute data there are three good reasons for using an external DBMS instead: (i) an external DBMS will be able to cope with more complex multi-table data relations; (ii) data retrieval will be faster with large volumes of data; (iii) it will permit more complex queries than the basic search and retrieval functions provided in many integrated DBMS found in GIS programs. Nearly all GIS offer facilities for linking spatial data objects to attribute data held in an external relational database, often through SQL and database technologies such as Open DataBase Connectivity (ODBC).[2] SQL is covered in more detail in Chapter 7, although it is worth noting here that many database systems provide graphical query tools so that the user is not required to write raw SQL.

Beyond the relational model: object-orientated systems

Recent post-relational database theory has seen the development of *object-orientated* (or OO) databases. Object-orientated (OO) databases share some of the philosophy behind OO programming languages such as Java. This includes concepts such as packaging data and functionality (behaviour) together into modular units called objects; the *encapsulation* of objects so that they can only change their own state, not the state of others in the system; and *inheritance*, such that new objects may inherit the properties of other existing objects. Object-orientated databases thus differ significantly from relational databases by including information about the behavioural characteristics of entities, which are referred to as its *methods*. The combined table and attributes, including rules defining their behaviour, is referred to as an *object*, and similar objects are grouped together in *object classes*. For example, as applied to GIS, 'burial mounds' and 'causeway enclosures' may be modelled as objects in an OO data model rather than simply entities in a layer. In the OO model, information about the entities are encapsulated within the object, whereas in the relational model, information is obtained via linked records in an attribute table. Embedding the relevant information within the object itself removes the need to search for properties in additional tables, and also provides the possibility of including rules that stipulate the behaviour of the object. The process of retrieving data is similar to the relational model, although in OO databases a derivative of SQL called *Object Query Language* (OQL) is used.

A fully OO GIS that permits a more flexible set of object rules and behaviours is not yet available for the desktop, and has not made a significant impact in archaeology. Commercial OO GIS software systems include Smallworld,[3] which has been designed for organisations with significant asset-management requirements. Note, however, that the geodatabase structure used in ArcGIS is partially OO because vector entities do have defined behaviours and rules to, for example, control the form of topological relationships between vector objects.

4.2 Designing a relational database for attribute data

The users of GIS most often become involved in database theory when they need to design a database to provide storage and access to a set of attribute data. For example, if you have been collecting data from an archaeological survey, you may

---

[2]http://en.wikipedia.org/wiki/ODBC.
[3]www.gepower.com/prod_serv/products/gis_software/en/core_spatial.htm.

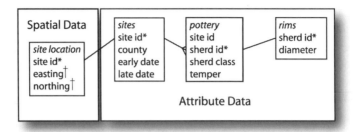

Fig. 4.1 An entity–relationship (E–R) diagram (boxes = entities and attributes, arrows = relationships) for a geodatabase. Asterisks indicate unique values (primary keys). † indicates a spatial attribute used for GIS implementation.

need to create a system to store information about the types of environmental and archaeological data that were collected that can then be linked to a GIS that contains information about the spatial location of, for example, testpits, survey areas, transects and archaeological sites.

The design of a database typically consists of four stages: designing a conceptual model, implementing the model, constructing an external interface (or 'front end'), and deciding on the system for the physical storage of data.

Conceptual model Database design often first begins at the level of the *conceptual model*. This is the most abstract and arguably the most important level of database design, as it concerns the entities (such as sites or artefacts) and their attributes (such as size or type), and their relationships with other entities (such as between artefacts and sites). The term 'entity' in this sense refers to any phenomenon, physical or abstract, that can be described and distinguished from other phenomena (Jones 1997, p. 164). For example, 'artefacts' and 'archaeological sites' are two different types of entities. When designing an attribute database, a useful first step is to make a list of entities and their attributes and the nature of the relationships between them. This can then be modelled using an entity–relationship (E–R) diagram (Chen 1976). The example provided in Fig. 4.1 shows the relationship between the entities discussed previously: 'sites', 'pottery', 'rim measurements'. Note that in this instance a fourth relation has been added that contains the spatial locations of the sites, which would usually be stored in a GIS.

Implementation Following the conceptual design, the next stage is typically to populate the database with a sample of information to ensure that the relations function in the way that is intended, and that it is possible to extract information in the combinations required for subsequent analysis (e.g. using the same example as above, is it possible to extract the locations of sites that possess sand-tempered pottery?).

External interface Assuming the database works, a common next step is to create the external interface, although with smaller single-user systems this may not be necessary. In larger multiuser systems having a 'front-end' is desirable as it provides users with a set of tools to enter and search for data. In addition, as there may be several different categories of user, the external model can be customised to present only the necessary subsets of data to a particular user. For example, the external level of a sites and monuments record database could be designed so that the data seen by archaeologists and municipal planners are organised differently to the data made available to members of the public. It is at this level that an entire database, or sections of it, can be 'locked' so that data cannot be seen or modified by non-administrative users. Facilities for speeding up data entry and reducing input error can also be introduced at the external level, which might include drop-down menus, or 'radio buttons' offering simple yes/no options for data entry. Some database packages provide tools for the design of front-end 'forms', and many provide tools to enable the use of web browsers to view, query and edit data.

Physical storage Some decisions can be made by users regarding where and how information should be stored on hard-disks. GIS and database programmers expend considerable energy on increasing the efficiency of their programs by designing them so that the information they store can be quickly retrieved by the computer. For database end-users, the specifics of the physical model (such as how often a database writes to a disk, how it allocates virtual memory, and how it keeps track of changes to a database) may remain hidden, but the speed of the database and its ability to process requests for information efficiently is ultimately linked to how the database deals with the physical storage of data. A small desktop GIS will probably store data on the same physical device (hard-disk) as the GIS software; but data for large, multiuser, networked systems will likely be spread over many disks and, to prevent data loss in the event of disk failure, duplicated in what is known as a redundant array of inexpensive disks (RAID). If you are designing a database for more than one user, then it is worth investigating network storage and RAID systems in more detail – an afternoon's research on the Internet will provide ample information about available options.

4.3 Spatial data storage and management

As with attribute data, a GIS also requires a database for the storage and manipulation of spatial objects. However, as the data structures for spatial objects are embedded into the GIS program and cannot themselves be manipulated, the spatial object DBMS remains largely 'behind the scenes'. Although it will do its job without complaint or need of user intervention, it is nevertheless worth briefly reviewing the different data structures used to store and manipulate vector and raster datasets in order to reinforce the primary importance of the DBMS in GIS.

4.3.1 *Vector data storage*

In the vector data structure, all objects, whether points, lines or polygons, are represented using one or more *x, y*-coordinate pairs. A set of points, for example, is recorded as a list of coordinate pairs, each of which is given an identification number. Polylines may be stored as a sequence of vertices terminated by nodes and are also given identification numbers. Polygons can be represented in the same manner as polylines and their final node must be the same as their first node in order to close the loop.

This method of data storage is used by CAD and some early GIS programs (e.g. ArcView 3.2), but it is not very efficient because it does not take into account the topological relationships between vector objects. When two polygons share a common boundary, for example, the vertices of the common boundary need to be recorded for each polygon, which results in a very data-hungry system. Furthermore,

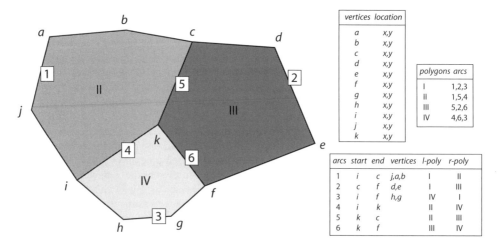

Fig. 4.2 Three topologically related polygons and a simple arc-node storage structure.

there is no way to store relationships – such as adjacency or overlap – between vector objects, so they must be computed at need. A more efficient solution uses a relational model for data organisation and is referred to as *arc-node data structure* (Fig. 4.2). This method structures, stores and references data in a relational DBMS so that points (nodes) construct polylines (arcs) and polylines construct polygons. The directionality of the arcs is recorded in this storage method by a field that defines the beginning and end node plus the vertices in between. Arcs that are used to define polygon boundaries also record which polygons lie on the left and right of the arc. This enables adjacency queries on polygons to be quickly answered with reference to the arc table rather than using a computationally more complex spatial query method.

Any spatial queries performed on these objects can then be answered by reference to these tables. For example, questions such as 'what is the area of polygon III?' can be answered by using the vertices that define arcs 5, 2 and 6 to build triangles, for which areas can be calculated, the sum of which provides the polygon's area. Topological queries, such as 'which polygons are adjacent to polygon IV?' can be answered by finding the arcs that define polygon IV, then using the left and right polygon field for those arcs to define adjacency to other polygons (i.e. polygons II and III).

Although the arc-node structure is arguably more efficient it can limit flexibility, so some recent GIS databases, such as that used in ArcGIS, have moved to a different topological structure managed by what is called a Spatial Database Engine. In this system, the arc-node structure for each object is stored separately in what is termed a Feature Class object. Topological relationships are thus computed at-need rather than stored as an inherent part of a spatial database, although some forms of relationships can be predefined and stored in Feature Datasets, so that, for example, changes in the boundary of one object will automatically result in

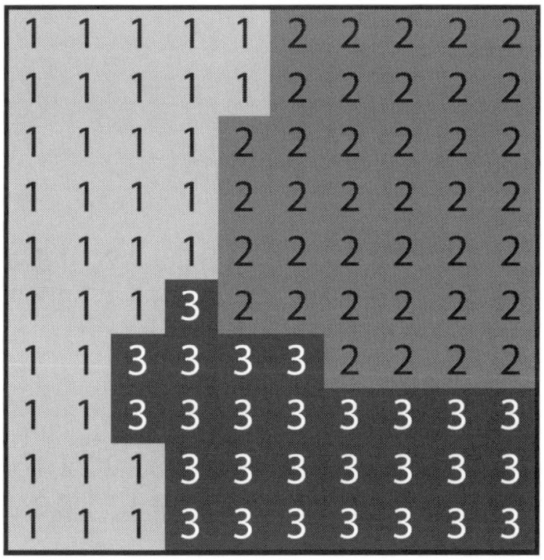

Fig. 4.3 A 10 × 10 raster grid with cell values overlay.

changes to those others that share the same boundary. This permits a high degree of flexibility for defining relationships between spatial entities, but is also computationally more intensive and requires additional memory for recording the structures and relationships between spatial objects.

In Chapter 7 we discuss the mechanics of a broader range of spatial queries that depend on topological relationships.

4.3.2 *Raster data storage*

Consider the raster map in Fig. 4.3. A simple method for storing such a grid of *n* rows by *m* columns is to record the *x*, *y*-coordinate pair of each cell together with its associated attribute value. This, for obvious reasons, is neither very practical nor efficient: there is no mechanism for recording the size of cells and large matrices will have massive memory overheads because every pixel requires three pieces of data (i.e. its *x*, *y*-coordinate and its value). Advances in raster storage systems in the 1980s and early 1990s saw the development of much more efficient methods of storing raster data (Burrough and McDonnell 1998, pp. 51–57). All but the most basic raster storage systems now possess a *header*, which defines the number of rows and columns, the cell size, the geodetic datum, the projection and reference system, and the location of a corner pixel followed by a sequence of cell values (Fig. 4.4).

In some GIS programs, such as Idrisi, the header information is stored as a separate file that shares a name with the file that stores cell values. Using a header results in more efficient data storage because the cell coordinates need not be stored, but large files can still occur with data consisting of long real number strings, as is the case with elevation data (Burrough and McDonnell 1998, p. 51). One method to reduce file size that works well for data that have some degree of positive spatial autocorrelation (Chapter 6) is to record the differences between one cell and the

columns: 10
rows: 10
cell size: 20
minimum *x*: 320
minimum *y*: 153
reference system: metres
1 1 1 1 1 2 2 2 2 2 1 1 1 1 1 2 2 2 2 2 1 1 1 1 2 2 2 2 2 2 1 1 1 1 2 2 2
2 2 2 1 1 1 1 2 2 2 2 2 2 1 1 1 3 2 2 2 2 2 2 1 1 3 3 3 3 2 2 2 2 1 1 3 3
3 3 3 3 3 1 1 1 3 3 3 3 3 3 3 1 1 1 3 3 3 3 3 3 3

Fig. 4.4 A typical raster storage file.

1 1 1 1 1 2 2 2 2 2 1 1 1 1 1 2 2 2 2 2 1 1 1 1 2 2 2 2 2 2 1 1 1 1 2 2 2
2 2 2 1 1 1 1 2 2 2 2 2 2 1 1 1 3 2 2 2 2 2 2 1 1 3 3 3 3 2 2 2 2 1 1 3 3
3 3 3 3 3 1 1 1 3 3 3 3 3 3 3 1 1 1 3 3 3 3 3 3 3

becomes:

1 5 2 5 1 5 2 5 1 4 2 6 1 4 2 6 1 4 2 6 1 3 3 1 2 6 1 2 3 4 2 4 1 2 3 8 1
3 3 7 1 3 3 7

Fig. 4.5 An example of raster file compression using the RLC method.

next. In this way an elevation matrix that contained the sequence {1021.34, 1022.01, 1023.00} could be recorded as {1021.34, 0.67, 0.99} and would thus reduce the number of stored digits in the raster file. Methods that rely on a form of *data compression* may also offer solutions for particular types of data. For example, an array of numbers can be compressed using a system of *run length compression* or RLC. This involves substituting repeating numbers with an integer that defines how many times the number occurs in sequence. RLC would reduce the data array in Fig. 4.4 to the second array shown in Fig. 4.5.

Other forms of compression use regular shapes such as squares, rectangles, triangles or hexagons that *tessellate* in a regular pattern and these are then assigned to data of uniform value, so that only the size and location of the shape and the shared cell value need to be recorded. When square blocks are used the process is often referred to as *quadtree* data encoding. Like the more common RLC method, each may offer some space savings at the expense of computational time.

In practice, a user need not be overly concerned with the specifics of the raster compression system used in any given GIS, as most are able to both import and export non-compressed raster data. The specific format and headers used to read non-compressed data are often particular to an individual GIS, although these details will be included in the software's documentation. Readers interested in additional information on raster data storage and compression are referred to Burrough and McDonnell (1998, pp. 51–57).

5

Spatial data acquisition

5.1 Introduction

This chapter examines the different ways in which spatial datasets are acquired and structured to take advantage of the visualisation and analytical abilities of GIS. It is conventional to distinguish between *primary* and *secondary* data sources because acquisition methods, data formats and structuring processes differ considerably between the two. Primary data consist of measurements or information collected from field observations, survey, excavation and remote sensing. Secondary data refer to information that has already been processed and interpreted, available most often as paper or digital maps. Many users of GIS wish to integrate primary and secondary datasets (for example, to plot the location of primary survey data across an elevation model obtained from a data supplier). Both types of data have advantages and disadvantages, which this chapter examines in some detail. By the end of this chapter you will be familiar with the ways in which both primary and secondary data are obtained, and the issues and procedures for assessing the quality of combined datasets.

5.2 Primary geospatial data

Primary, or 'raw', geospatial data has not been significantly processed or transformed since the information was first captured. Archaeologists generate vast quantities of primary data during excavation and survey, such as the location of settlements, features and artefacts, geoarchaeological and palaeo-environmental data and the location of raw material sources within the landscape. Raw data may also be available from databases of information compiled by other agencies: the location of archaeological sites, for example, can be obtained from Sites and Monuments Records and published site 'gazetteers'. Primary data may also be extracted from remote sensing sources such as aerial photographs, satellite imagery and geophysical survey. This section reviews the two major sources for primary data, namely survey and remote sensing.

5.2.1 *Surveying technologies*

Digital recording is increasingly common on archaeological surveys and excavations and has been greatly simplified in recent years by tablet and handheld computers connected (perhaps wirelessly) to digital recording equipment. This accelerates recording procedures and reduces the probability of errors being introduced in the transfer between paper and digital formats. Key spatial technologies in this regard

Fig. 5.1 A 'total station' consisting of a targetless laser distance measurer and an electronic theodolite.

are *global positioning system* (GPS) receivers and 'self-registering tachometers' or *total stations*. Although both pieces of equipment are expensive, the time savings they offer help to offset their rental or purchase costs.

Total station survey

A total station is a piece of electronic survey equipment that is able to record horizontal and vertical angles and linear distances from itself to a target (using infrared or laser light) and then automatically convert this data into eastings, northings and elevation values via trigonometric formula (Fig. 5.1). Total stations have largely replaced optical *theodolites*, but the latter are still in use in situations where a total station's cost or dependence on electricity causes difficulties. It is possible to establish the position of the total station and all newly measured points with reference to a known coordinate system provided that two or more points with known coordinates (i.e. 'benchmarks') are locally available. Alternatively, a floating local grid independent of any national or global system may be established. The local grid, then, may later be 'tied in' to a national grid, for example by using a GPS to establish the reference.

Coordinate data captured by a total station are either stored on an internal memory card or data-logger, which can then be downloaded to a computer, or the total station may be connected to a computer so that the results of the survey can be immediately visualised and annotated in a program similar to ESRI's Survey Analyst or Leica's GIS DataPRO software packages. If the data are stored on a data-logger it will export a text file that lists the name or code of each object alongside the easting (x), northing (y) and elevation (z) that defines the object's relative or absolute location. This data can then be imported into a GIS program.

Global positioning system survey

The GPS is a satellite navigation system used to provide precise locations to receivers on the Earth's surface. It was initially developed, and is currently maintained, by the US military and first started operation in 1978. The current system consists of 29 satellites launched between 1990 and 2004, each of which circles the Earth twice in a 24-h period at an altitude of approximately 20 100 km. Each satellite continuously broadcasts a time signal from its internal atomic clock. The satellites broadcast two signals, called L1 and L2, the former of which contains a *coarse acquisition code* (C/A code) that is publicly accessible, whereas the latter contains a more accurate *protected* (P) code with access rights controlled by the US Department of Defense. Until May 2000, the C/A code was intentionally degraded, but now this is no longer the case basic GPS accuracy has increased from ~50 m to under 20 m.

A GPS receiver unit, which can range from a small inexpensive handheld unit to an expensive permanent base station, has its own internal clocks from which it is able to ascertain the time it takes for each satellite's signal to travel to the receiver, and thus the distance from the receiver to each satellite. In theory, three satellites are sufficient to provide a three-dimensional location (e.g. latitude, longitude and elevation) on the Earth's surface by establishing the position of the intersection of the distances between the receiver and each satellite. In reality, the internal clocks on consumer GPS receivers are not accurate enough to establish the time differentials to the level of precision required for useful three-dimensional measurements, so an additional (fourth) satellite signal is needed.

In practice, a GPS receiver must often estimate the position of the intersection because of vagaries in its estimate of local time and atmospheric interference with satellite signals lying at low angles in the sky. Correction mechanisms in the GPS receiver and additional data broadcast by the satellite are used to minimise these sources of error. Higher-end receivers are able to reduce error even further by analysing the signal code frequencies to estimate the atmospheric distortion. Important sources of correction are also obtained by additional satellite systems, such as the Wide Area Augmentation System (WAAS) and European Geostationary Navigation Overlay Service (EGNOS). These separately maintained systems consist of networks of ground stations in, respectively, the USA and Europe, that transmit information on the reliability and accuracy of the GPS signals to other satellites that WAAS- or EGNOS-enabled receivers can read.

Inexpensive navigation-grade handheld GPS receivers are suitable for collecting locational information about features on the landscape to within 10–20 m of their true location. It is increasingly common for inexpensive receivers to be WAAS/EGNOS enabled, providing locations ±3 m of their true location in the

USA or Europe. This level of error is acceptable for larger phenomena such as archaeological sites or monuments, but is less suitable for recording local topography or smaller-scale phenomena like artefact locations. For applications that require greater precision and accuracy, a system that provides *differential correction* between the estimated and actual location of the receiver is needed (hence *differential* or DGPS). Mapping-grade receivers that are accurate to between 0.5 and 5 m are suitable for archaeological site survey and larger-scale mapping (e.g. up to 1 : 2500) and receive corrections from other satellites or from radio beacons. More expensive survey-grade systems accurate to the centimetre level consist of a roving unit and a base station (Fig. 5.2). The base station is set up at a location for which the precise coordinates are already known or are first estimated by averaging thousands of readings taken over several hours. Once the base station's actual location is reasonably well established, it begins recording the constantly changing differences between its actual location and its fluctuating real-time location as derived from the satellites. These fluctuating differences are time-stamped. Data collected by the roving unit are similarly time-stamped so that calculated coordinates can be adjusted by the appropriate correction factor determined by the base station either in real time (*real-time kinematic* or *RTK GPS*) or in post-survey processing (*static* DGPS). Positional accuracy is thereby increased to the centimetre level or better, allowing GPS to be used for higher-precision survey work.

Survey coordinates obtained by RTK GPS are stored in the roving unit and then downloaded to a computer as a set of coordinates and feature codes, or downloaded directly to a portable (often a weatherproofed tablet style) computer. As with all GPS technology, however, if the receivers are unable to communicate with the satellites then they are unable to record locations. This reduces their usefulness in situations where there is dense overhead vegetation. Global positioning system survey technology is therefore not suitable for all applications and should be viewed simply as one of several potential methods for spatial data acquisition. The GPS equipment can appear fairly intimidating to the uninitiated, although in reality it is a fairly simple technology to use, and in appropriate conditions is often far faster than using a total station.

5.2.2 *Remote sensing*

The term remote sensing (RS) refers to the collection and interpretation of information about phenomena without physical contact. Our eyes and visual cortex, for example, constitute a type of remote-sensing device that is extremely good at detecting and making sense of differential absorption and reflection in electromagnetic wavelengths between approximately 700 nanometres (nm) and 400 nm (with a corresponding wave frequency between 4 and 7.5×10^{14} Hz), which we perceive as visible light (Fig. 5.3). More customarily, however, RS refers more specifically to the art and science of acquiring and interpreting information about objects and phenomena by measuring their responses to electromagnetic radiation collected using sensors mounted on anything from ground vehicles, to balloons, aircraft and

Fig. 5.2 A differential GPS (DGPS), which typically provides three-dimensional accuracy to ±3 cm or better.

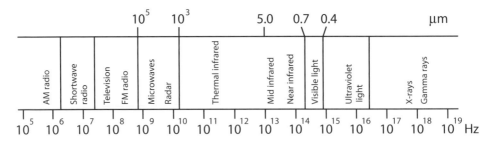

Fig. 5.3 Wave frequencies (in Hz) and lengths (in μm) of the electromagnetic spectrum.

spacecraft. Remote-sensing systems have long been used by archaeologists to collect information about the structure of landscapes, the natural environment, and the location and configuration of archaeological sites and features. The decreasing cost and increasing availability, resolution and versatility of satellite imagery has begun to make a significant impact in archaeology, although the full potential of this rich dataset has not yet been fully explored for expanding our understanding of long-term landscape and environmental history. Although dedicated RS software is needed for sophisticated forms of image correction, enhancement and analysis, many GIS programs provide a good range of tools for the analysis of image data. Moreover, by allowing images to be used as thematic layers with other geospatial information, GIS provides an interpretative framework for both collating, analysing and interpreting RS data about the contemporary and past landscape.

Types of imagery

Remote-sensing image data can be divided into two types, *photographic* and *digital*, depending on whether the information is captured using sensors that record electromagnetic responses as visual or digital data. Digital images can be further subdivided into *panchromatic* or *multispectral* depending on the breadth of electromagnetic radiation they are able to capture.

Aerial photographs are frequently used in archaeological survey and, more recently, high-resolution images from photographic sensors on former spy satellites have been used by the archaeological community. Photographic sensors typically capture high-resolution images of the Earth's surface using colour, panchromatic or infrared film. In general terms, the value of any photograph is primarily a function of the area covered by the photograph and the resolution of the image. This in turn is a function of the altitude of the aircraft (or spacecraft), the focal length of the camera lens, the sensitivity of the lens and the properties of the film (Jones 1997, p. 99).

Digital sensors record the way that natural and anthropogenic phenomena such as water, soil, leafy vegetation, roads and buildings respond to different parts of

(a) Landscape

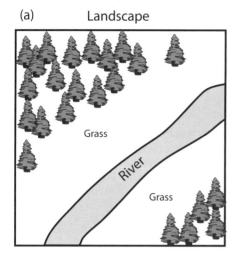

(b) Digital 'image'

190	182	193	190	192	187	78	170	50	48
187	191	190	179	186	190	176	190	59	52
191	193	185	190	176	182	47	65	68	241
198	192	191	173	180	58	68	190	240	251
181	180	182	58	54	67	248	240	248	240
183	179	61	53	61	245	248	240	237	58
188	57	55	51	240	251	235	61	58	54
56	49	60	242	252	235	60	57	140	176
53	67	243	252	235	60	57	165	176	188
54	234	250	240	53	56	57	188	190	193

Fig. 5.4 A hypothetical landscape consisting of three distinct ecological zones (a), the pixel values as recorded by a digital sensor (b). Note that the pixel values express an average for the area they cover, and only one band of several potential bands is shown.

the electromagnetic spectrum, and record this information as a sequence of *bytes*,[1] where each byte corresponds to a pixel value (between 0 and 255; Fig. 5.4). The major advantage of digital sensors is that, unlike optical photographic devices, they record information across a broad range of visible and non-visible wavelengths and are thus referred to as *multispectral* scanners. Typical resolutions for multispectral satellite systems are in the range of 10 to 40 m. This obviously restricts the use of digital imagery to investigating phenomena that exist at much larger scales than can be detected with aerial photographs. However, recent digital imaging systems, such as Space Imaging's IKONOS[2] and DigitalGlobe's Quickbird,[3] can achieve panchromatic resolutions of 1 m or less (Table 5.1), which is equivalent to optical sensors on former spy satellites.

Photographic imagery Aerial photographs are normally classified as *vertical* or *oblique*. Vertical photographs are those taken with the camera axis as vertical as possible. These are often used for *photogrammetry* – the derivation of spatial measurements from photographs – which has long been profitably employed by archaeologists (e.g. Sterud and Pratt 1975; Poulter and Kerslake 1997; Bewley and Raczkowski 2002). When vertical aerial photographs are taken in stereoscopic pairs

---

[1] Satellites transmit data to ground stations in streams of binary data composed of 'bits' which have only two possible values, 0 or 1. As bits cannot individually represent anything more complex than on/off, true/false, 0/1, etc., they are often grouped together in groups of eight, called 'bytes'. Bytes offer considerably more flexibility than bits, having 256 (i.e. 2^8) potential values, and are referred to as 8-bit images.

[2] www.spaceimaging.com.   [3] www.eurimage.com/products/quickbird.html.

Table 5.1 *Major sources of digital satellite imagery*

Source	Type	Resolution (m)
SPOT 5	4-band multispectral and panchromatic	10^a 2.5^b
Landsat-7 ETM+	7-band multispectral and panchromatic	28.5^a 15^b
IKONOS	4-band multispectral and panchromatic	4^a 1^b
Quickbird	4-band multispectral and panchromatic	2.5^a 0.6^b
Radarsat	4-band multispectral	3–100
SIX-C/X-SAR	Radar	Typically 30

[a] Multispectral.
[b] Panchromatic.

and viewed with a stereoscopic reader or displayed using specialised photogrammetric software they can be used to map three-dimensional topography. Vertical photographs are usually obtained using specialised cameras and dedicated aircraft and they are available (often for a fee) from the agencies that acquired them. For GIS and/or mapping purposes, vertical or near-vertical photographs are preferable to oblique photographs as they are subject to less spatial distortion. Oblique aerial photographs can still be used to extract useful information, but they will need to be rectified (see below) and their level of accuracy for mapping and analysis will be less than that obtainable from vertical images. However, as archaeologists are often obliged to use oblique photographs, specialised programs have been developed to help rectify them so they can be used for mapping. The program AirPhoto included with the Bonn Archaeological Statistics Package (BASP)[4] is one example that has been designed specifically for archaeological purposes.

A combination of shadow, vegetation, soil patterns and texture influence the value of aerial photography in detecting or delineating archaeological remains. Visibility can, therefore, change dramatically between the time of day and the season of the year in which the photograph is taken. The ability to detect features can also be influenced by the type of film used. Black-and-white film has an established pedigree in archaeology, but it is being superseded by increasing use of colour aerial photography and colour infrared photography (CIR; e.g. McKee *et al*. 1994).

As aircrafts fly significantly closer to the Earth's surface than satellites, aerial photography will always be available at higher resolutions. However, recently declassified intelligence satellite imagery can approach the spatial resolution of aerial photography and is also suitable for distinguishing landscape features. Former Soviet spy satellites such as the Russian KVR-1000 and US CORONA systems,

---

[4] www.uni-koeln.de/~al001/basp.html.

Table 5.2 *NASA Landsat-7 ETM+ bands*

Band	Wavelength (μm)	Spectral region	Resolution (m)
1	0.45–0.52	Visible blue	30
2	0.53–0.61	Visible green	30
3	0.63–0.69	Visible red	30
4	0.75–0.90	Near infrared	30
5	1.55–1.75	Mid infrared	30
6	10.40–12.50	Thermal infrared	60
7	2.10–2.35	Mid infrared	30
8	0.52–0.90	Panchromatic	15

Source: Jensen (2002).

for example, take panchromatic photographic images with a spatial resolution of between 1.5 and 3 m, which is sufficient to detect archaeologically relevant features (Fowler 1996; Philip *et al.* 2002; Ur 2003).

Digital sensors Digital sensors are conventionally divided into two types, *passive* and *active*, depending on whether the instrumentation is responsible for producing the energy that is reflected off the phenomena being recorded (Table 5.1). Active systems record the reflected response to transmitted electromagnetic radiation, such as microwave and radar imaging systems that transmit microwave energy and receive the reflected energy back from the Earth's surface. The Spaceborne Imaging Radar (SIR-C) and X-Band Synthetic Aperture Radar (X-SAR) project missions (jointly run by NASA, the German Space Agency and the Italian Space Agency) have increased the range of information that can be captured using active microwave and radar imaging systems.[5] Archaeologists have found that in certain conditions these scanners can sometimes detect information through canopy vegetation or buried under shallow soil.[6]

However, many satellite recording systems, like aerial photography, are passive. The first four Landsat satellites launched between 1972 and 1978 by NASA all carried passive multispectral scanners that capture reflected energy from the Earth's surface. These demonstrated the value of satellite imagery for providing data about the terrestrial environment, such as land-use patterns and ecological variability. Landsat-4 and Landsat-5 (launched in 1982 and 1984) carried improved multispectral scanners referred to as the *Thematic Mapper* and included thermal infrared sensors for recording heat energy emitted from the Earth. Landsat-6 (launched in 1993) failed to reach orbit, but Landsat-7 (launched in 1999) uses an *Enhanced Thematic Mapper Plus* (ETM+) to record seven multispectral bands plus an eighth (panchromatic) sharpening band (Table 5.2).

---

[5]http://southport.jpl.nasa.gov/sir-c/getting_data/missions_general.html.
[6]www.jpl.nasa.gov/radar/sircxsar/.

Table 5.3 *Principal applications of Landsat TM spectral bands*

TM band	Spectral region	Principal application
1	Visible blue	Water penetration useful for coastal mapping. Soil/vegetation discrimination, forest type mapping, identification of cultural features
2	Visible green	Vegetation discrimination and vigour assessment. Identification of cultural features
3	Visible red	Chlorophyll absorption for species differentiation. Cultural feature identification
4	Near infrared	Vegetation types, vigour and biomass content. Identifying water bodies and for soil moisture discrimination
5	Mid infrared	Vegetation and soil moisture content. Differentiation of snow from clouds
6	Thermal infrared	Vegetation stress analysis, soil moisture content and thermal mapping applications
7	Mid infrared	Discrimination of mineral and rock types. Vegetation moisture content
8	Panchromatic	Cultural and natural feature mapping

Source: Lillesand and Kiefer (2000: Table 6.3).

The latest SPOT system (SPOT-5, launched in May 2002) collects multispectral data in the green, red and near-infrared bands. DigitalGlobe's Quickbird satellite system, launched in 2001, provides multispectral data in the blue, green, red and near-infrared band at 2.5-m resolution. Multispectral scanners can also be operated from specially equipped aircraft, thereby permitting much higher-resolution – often submetre – data capture.

The different ways that different phenomena reflect the Sun's energy or respond to transmitted energy is described as a *spectral response pattern* (SRP). Analysis of SRPs is used to help identify and distinguish between phenomena that might look similar to the naked eye and thus define a response *signature* for different phenomenon (Eastman 2001, p. 57). In practice, signatures are difficult to define. A major part of satellite imagery interpretation therefore involves the analysis of how different objects and phenomena respond to either reflected solar radiation or radiation transmitted from the recording instrument, under different conditions. At a gross level, different types of vegetation may be distinguishable in the longer red and near to short-wave infrared band (600–900 nm) and differences in soil moisture content may be differentiated by responses in the short infrared bands (i.e. 1400, 1900 and 2700 nm) because wet soil surfaces absorb these electromagnetic wavelengths (Lillesand and Kiefer 2000, pp. 17–20). Table 5.3 provides a generalised example of the how different phenomena respond across different spectral bands. In the same way that archaeological features may be detected in aerial photographs from vegetation patterns, often manifested as 'crop marks', subtle differences in soil moisture content or vegetation may also indicate the presence of past human activity. When attempting to identify features that have an unknown SRP, a 'training' process followed by 'ground truthing' is often needed to help with classification. Chapter 6 describes the processes involved in image classification and enhancement in further detail.

More recent passive systems used by archaeologists include airborne thermal video radiometers (TVR) that measure emitted radiation in the thermal-infrared (TIR) spectral region (3–14 μm). This has been shown to have application for detecting subsurface features: since buried objects cool more slowly than the surrounding soil matrix, differences in emitted thermal energy can be detected by TVR instruments at night (Ben-Dor *et al.* 1999).

Some other RS devices used by archaeologists are ground based, and involve capturing information about subsurface remains, which include ground penetrating radar (GPR), resistivity metres and fluxgate gradiometers (or magnetometers). There is a long and profitable history of geophysical survey in archaeology, the results of which can often be well integrated with other forms of spatial data (Barker 1998, pp. 60–67). Geophysical survey is a specialised archaeological subdiscipline that requires a considerable amount of training and expertise. A good introduction to basic principles can be found in Clark (1996).

Satellite and airborne-derived topographic data It is becoming increasingly common to use satellite or airborne digital data to construct digital elevation models (DEMs) of the Earth's surface. This can offer some advantages over more traditional forms of creating DEMs, such as from manually digitised contour lines (Chapter 6) or through stereoscopic analysis of aerial photographs, because of the faster processing time and larger area coverage that satellite systems offer. Major satellite suppliers offer global or near-global coverage for DEM products. For example, SPOT[7] and Space Imaging[8] can supply elevation on a grid spacing of 30 m or less, derived from analysis of stereo pairs of images. The Advanced Spaceborne Thermal Emission and Reflection Radiometer[9] (ASTER) also provides data on land surface temperature, reflectance and elevation at a 30-m horizontal resolution.

Interferometry is a technique that uses simultaneous signal acquisitions by synthetic-aperture radar (SAR) to collect elevation differences on the Earth's surface, as used by the 2000 Space Shuttle Endeavor's *Shuttle Radar Topography Mission* (SRTM). Here, a radar system installed in the cargo bay and one at the end of a 60-m boom captured elevation data for 80 per cent of the globe at resolutions of up to 30 m, which has recently been made publicly available.[10] These

---

[7]www.spot.com/home/proser/elevat/dem/welcome.htm.
[8]www.spaceimaging.com./products/itm/technical_overview.htm.
[9]http://asterweb.jpl.nasa.gov/.   [10]www.jpl.nasa.gov/srtm/mission.htm.

sources of primary data are useful for regional analyses and may offer time and cost savings over survey or the manual digitising of paper maps to collect elevation data.

Higher-resolution data can be obtained by mounting laser or radar transmitters on specially equipped aircraft, such as Intermap's STAR-3i Interferometric Synthetic Aperture Radar (IFSAR), which is typically mounted on a Learjet.[11] Aircraft-mounted systems such as these can capture elevation data with a horizontal accuracy of under 2 m and a vertical accuracy of 50 cm or better. Even more accurate is aircraft-based laser altimetry, such as Light Distance And Ranging (*LiDAR*), which can record 2000–5000 height measurements per second to produce a DEM with a horizontal resolution of about 1 m and a claimed vertical accuracy of ±15 cm (DeLoach and Leonard 2000; Brock *et al.* 2002). Although this is a very quick way to collect high-resolution elevation data over a large area, the cost of these data products often puts them beyond the budget of most archaeological users.

Archaeological applications

Aerial photographs and satellite images are particularly useful tools for archaeologists as they can provide valuable information about a landscape that may not be available from conventional maps, or would take a considerable amount of time to collect through field survey. Historically, much of the RS performed by archaeologists is based on aerial photography at visible or near-infrared wavelengths, but since the launch of the first satellite digital sensors in the early 1970s and the more recent availability of images from former Cold-War spy satellites, the use of satellite imagery is becoming increasingly common. Aerial photography and satellite imagery have been used to identify and map cultural phenomena such as ancient walls, settlements or other human modifications to the landscape that may only be visible under certain light and vegetation conditions. Some satellite images approach air photographs in the level of detail they show and can also be used to map structures and features.

For example, layers from multispectral systems, typically the red, blue and green (RGB), can be combined to create what is known as a 'colour composite' that mimics information in normal colour image – i.e. green vegetation appears green and water appears blue, etc. It is also possible to produce composite images by combining the infrared, red and green bands to enhance healthy vegetation, which in these composite images will be depicted as bright red. Some systems, such as SPOT and Quickbird, can have their composite images improved through a process of 'pan-sharpening', which uses the higher-resolution panchromatic data to enhance the lower-resolution colour data, providing a good alternative to colour aerial photography.

Geographical information systems have had a major role to play in the archaeological use of photographic and digital imagery. The integrative nature of GIS

---

[11]www.intermap.ca/intermap_STAR-3i_upgrade.htm.

enables imagery to be related to other forms of spatial data, and many programs also include sophisticated image enhancement and analytical tools to help classify and make sense of what can be extremely complex remotely sensed data. The following are three typical examples of the use to which satellite imagery and aerial photographs are typically put within an archaeological GIS.

Prospection One of the values of remotely sensed imagery is its ability to provide a different perspective on what might otherwise be a familiar phenomenon, which can lead to the identification of new or unexpected features that may not have been recognisable from the ground. The history of using cameras in this way can be traced back to photographs taken of Stonehenge from a balloon in 1906 (Capper 1907). During the Second World War many aerial photographs were taken from reconnaissance aircraft and archaeologists were used to help interpret their military significance. After the war, the technique became an established archaeological prospection tool in Western Europe and North America, and there are now copious examples of the use of aerial photographs for the discovery and mapping of previously unknown, or difficult to define, archaeological features. For example, standard black-and-white photographs have been used to identify previously unknown Neolithic encampments in Charente, France (Bouchet and Burnez 1990), to discover and interpret anthropogenic topographic hollows in Mesopotamia (Wilkinson 1993), and to identify new features at the Avebury henge, Wiltshire (Bewley *et al.* 1996). With the opening up of the post-communist skies since the end of the Cold War, the technique has more recently played a major role in the discovery and documentation of archaeological remains in Eastern Europe (Bewley *et al.* 1996, 1998). Specialised photography such as infrared (IR) imaging is sometimes necessary to identify archaeological features that would otherwise be difficult to see with the naked eye. The value of colour IR film, for example, has been demonstrated by its role in identifying prehistoric footpaths in Costa Rica (Sheets and Sever 1991; McKee *et al.* 1994), but interpreting such imagery often requires some form of image manipulation and enhancement.

Declassified intelligence photographs from satellites that carried photographic sensors can be used in ways similar to aerial photographs. For example, Philip *et al.* (2002) and Ur (2003) have successfully used declassified intelligence photographs from the US CORONA satellite series to aid in the discovery and mapping of archaeological settlements in Syria. Russian KVR-1000 imagery has also been used to help identify archaeological remains at the Roman site of Zeugma, Turkey,[12] as well as clarify linear features in the Stonehenge region (Fowler 1996). Spaceborne radar imaging has also been important in some high-profile archaeological discoveries, such as the 1992 finding of the Lost City of Ubar, which has helped popularise radar data.[13]

---

[12]www.ist.lu/ele/html/department/zeugma/remote.html.
[13]www.jpl.nasa.gov/radar/sircxsar/.

Air- and space-borne sensors produce imagery that can be of use for archaeological prospection, but GIS does not necessarily play a significant role unless these images need to be enhanced, classified or used as the basis for constructing maps. Many GIS programs, particularly those with developed raster analysis capabilities such as Idrisi and GRASS, have sophisticated tools for image enhancement and analysis of panchromatic, colour and multispectral data. Other packages, such as Imagine,[14] have been designed specifically for the interpretation of image data. Archaeologists have processed multispectral imagery to help locate archaeological remains on the basis of their particular signatures within the image. Research in the Vale of Pickering, Yorkshire, for example, used air-borne multispectral imagery to identify and map previously unidentified landscape features such as trackways, enclosure systems and barrow cemeteries (Powlesland *et al.* 1997). In the USA, multispectral imagery has been used with equal success in Chaco Canyon to detect and map prehistoric roads, walls, buildings and agricultural systems, some of which could not be identified on standard aerial photography or colour infrared photographs (Sever and Wagner 1991).

Photogrammetry The rise of GIS has led to a resurgence in the use of aerial photography for the purposes of archaeological mapping. The use of aerial photographs to make maps of archaeological sites was pioneered by O. G. S. Crawford in the 1920s and 1930s, and became increasingly common after the Second World War. Although a major archaeological tool, photogrammetry is a discipline in its own right and specialised optical or computer visualisation equipment (as well as a great deal of training) is needed to interpret stereoscopic pairs with the aim of recording three-dimensional data. The limitations of desktop GIS restricts photogrammetry to on-screen digitising of georeferenced aerial photographs to capture two-dimensional data. In the last few years there have been successful attempts to map cultural landscapes using high-definition panchromatic satellite images with resolutions of under 4 m (Fowler 1996). These images come in tiles covering tens or hundreds of square kilometres and have been shown to be a good alternative to aerial photography for regional landscape mapping, such as their use by Ur (2003) for mapping ancient Mesopotamian road systems.

A typical photogrammatic application involves delineating features by tracing their paths with polylines, or defining their boundaries with polygons, but this type of mapping will rarely be as accurate as a field survey. Mapping features from aerial photographs, however, may accelerate map production for extensive features that would be difficult to survey on the ground. An excellent example of this is the mapping undertaken at the Roman town of *Viroconium* at Wroxeter, England. A mixture of vertical and oblique photographs (that had been rectified using points obtained from geophysical survey) were used to aid the mapping of archaeological features (Baker 1992). Aerial photographs have also been used successfully to

----

[14]www.erdas.com.

0   100   200 m   1 dot = 25 sherds

Fig. 5.5 A dot-density overlay on an aerial photograph can provide an excellent visual framework for the qualitative assessment of distribution patterns. © Kythera Island Project. Used with permission.

distinguish and map environmental zones, such as the categorisation of wetlands undertaken for an investigation into the environmental and cultural history of NW England (Cox 1992).

Landscape visualisation Rectifying and georeferencing an aerial photograph or satellite image in order to use it as a background for visualising landscapes can facilitate the interpretation of other spatial data layers. A visual reference to enable contextual detail to be qualitatively assessed can provide profound insight into the spatial relationships between archaeological data and landscape features. Figure 5.5 provides a good example of this by using a georectified aerial photograph as a backdrop to an artefact distribution pattern, which adds a contextual dimension that would be very difficult to replicate in any other way. Aerial photography or satellite imagery can also be used to provide an element of terrain realism to a three-dimensional digital elevation model (DEM). We discuss the construction of DEMs in some detail in the next chapter, so here it is sufficient only to draw attention to the fact that aerial photographs can be used to enhance the three-dimensional visualisation of terrain when *draped* on a DEM. This technique can play an important role in the effective communication of the qualitative aspects of landscape variability in the same way that an aerial photograph can provide an effective backdrop to other data layers.

Acquiring and integrating remotely sensed data

Satellite imagery can either be obtained directly from the government or commercial agencies such as SPOT,[15] NASA,[16] Eurimage[17] or IKONOS,[18] or from academic or other third-party organisations. The US Geological Survey's (USGS) EarthExplorer database maintains archives of Landsat, CORONA and other declassified satellite imagery searchable via an online catalogue[19] and the Canadian Centre for Remote Sensing (CCRS) hosts a similar service.[20] In the UK, the Natural Environment Research Council (NERC)[21] has a range of Landsat, SPOT and air-borne multispectral imagery available for download. MIMAS[22] also provides access to UK coverages of Landsat and SPOT data for the UK higher education community.

Satellite data may be supplied either as photographic prints or negatives, digital images or, as is common for multispectral data, in a file archive. The exact format in which digital imagery is acquired depends on the supplier, so it is important to consult the documentation for the preferred GIS program to establish whether it is able to read the supplied data format. Geographical information system programs that have traditionally been stronger in image processing facilities (such as Idrisi, Imagine and GRASS) can cope with most imagery formats. Other more vector-orientated software, such as ArcView and ArcInfo, may have some limitations. Table 5.4 lists some of the more commonly encountered raster file formats.

The digitisation of features from an image base map is a common way of creating a map. However, the identification and accurate delineation of phenomena of interest is often dependent on image enhancement, analysis and interpretation, which is covered in the next chapter. There are also several preconditions that must be met before image data can be fully integrated with other spatial data. Air photographs and satellite images, unlike maps, lack an inherent reference system for scale and location. It is, however, increasingly common for image data to be supplied rectified and with reference data incorporated into the image. GeoTiff and Spatial Data Transfer Standard (SDTS) formats, for example, are commonly used for distributing referenced raster files. Bear in mind that an embedded reference system may not be the same as the rest of your data. In order to incorporate unreferenced or incompatibly referenced images into a GIS and to relate them to other maps, a new coordinate system must be imposed on the image through a process referred to as *georeferencing*, as described in more detail below. This may necessitate

[15]www.spot.com.   [16]http://landsat.gsfc.nasa.gov.   [17]www.eurimage.com.
[18]www.spaceimaging.com.   [19]http://edcsns17.cr.usgs.gov/EarthExplorer/.
[20]www.ccrs.nrcan.gc.ca.   [21]www.nerc.ac.uk.   [22]www.mimas.ac.uk.

Table 5.4 *Common satellite and image file formats*

Image format	Usual extension
Tagged Image File Format	.TIF or .TIFF
Georeferenced Tagged Image Files Format	.TIF, .TIFF, .GTIF
SPOT GeoSpot Files	.GSP
Windows Bitmap File	.BMP
Hierarchical Data Format	.HDF
National Landsat Archive Production System	.NLAPS
National Imagery Transmission Format Standard	.NITFS
USGS Spatial Data Transfer Standard	.SDTS
USGS ASCII DEM	.DEM
Erdas Imagine files	.LAN or .IMG
ArcGIS Grids	.ADF
Military Elevations (DTED)	.DT0, DT1
Shuttle Radar Topography Mission files	.HGT
Landsat (band-interleaved-by-pixel)	.BIP
SPOT (band-interleaved-by-line)	.BIL
Joint Photographic Experts Group Image File	.JPG

re-projecting or otherwise changing the shape of the image (i.e. 'rectifying', 'warp-ing' or 'rubber sheeting') to make it fit the new reference system more accurately. A related, but more accurate, process of adjustment to correct for relief-based distor-tion is called *orthorectification*. This is necessary to correct the significant terrain displacement in satellite and air-borne imagery in areas of significant vertical relief and requires specialised software and skills to perform accurately.

5.3 Secondary data

The transfer of data from an existing storage medium (e.g. from paper maps) remains a common route of spatial data acquisition. Secondary data, whether digital or ana-logue, have by definition already undergone processing and interpretation and their use therefore should come with an understanding of the potential sources of error in the data. To a greater or lesser extent, all maps are partially subjective, highly transformed and interpreted translations of raw data, and they inevitably contain the biases and intentions of the people or agencies that produced them (Wood 1992; King 1996). Secondary data sources may also contain substantial spatial errors that need to be taken into account when the data are used for spatial analysis or deci-sion making. This includes maps that have been obtained from commercial map suppliers and from national mapping agencies like the UK Ordnance Survey and the US Geological Survey. While these agencies publish information about acqui-sition and processing methods with anticipated error rates, the risk of incorporating erroneous or imprecise data in a spatial model remains very high when using sec-ondary data from these or other sources. Furthermore, if these maps exist only in paper form they will need to be digitised, which can itself be a source of potentially significant error. This is not to say that primary data sources are always preferable; the enormous investment in time and specialised skills required to produce a topographic map from ground survey or aerial photographs means that it is more efficient to use secondary data, albeit with the expectation that some errors will be encountered.

5.3.1 *Integrating secondary map data*

In order to integrate new map data into a GIS project, the following six characteristics need to be considered to ensure compatibility between new and existing spatial information (Burrough and McDonnell 1998, p. 81).

The georeferencing system We have already considered the topic of map coordinate systems in Chapter 2, and here we only need reiterate that maps may have been acquired using a coordinate system incompatible with existing datasets. In order to integrate data collected using a different referencing system it must be re-projected or rectified, which invariably introduces a degree of spatial error. Rectification and the quantification of spatial errors using RMSE values, are discussed in further detail below.

Scale and resolution Combining data collected at different scales can cause interpretative difficulties. In general terms, a map composite constructed from two or more source maps will be no more accurate than the least accurate map, and possibly somewhat worse than this if some maps have been re-projected. In addition, to combine raster datasets that have different resolutions (i.e. pixel sizes) some appropriate conversion of groups of pixels into a single value is necessary before the two layers can be combined.

Data collection techniques If new map data are to be combined with existing data, it is essential that they are compatible, not only in resolution, but also in terms of their collection methods. For example, attempting to combine the results of two separate archaeological surveys of the same area, one of which has been walked using linear transects and one using gridded surface collection, could lead to problems of interpretation when defining counts or densities of artefacts across the site.

Data quality A professionally produced and aesthetically pleasing map gives an impression that the same amount of care was taken with the collection of the primary data used in its construction. Unfortunately, it is not always possible to assess the quality of data merely by examining a map. The data sources, recording instruments, conditions of data collection and, if appropriate, spatial error estimates should be recorded. If this information is not available, the map data should be treated with suspicion.

Data classification methods Integrating secondary data also requires some understanding of the classification system used and whether it is compatible with the objectives of the project. To state the obvious, a map of archaeological sites classified into categories of 'prehistoric', 'Roman' and 'post-Roman', will not be useful for exploring spatial patterning of Iron Age settlements. Less obvious may be the classification of environmental data, such as soil productivity maps, which may be derived from modern agricultural productivity and so not be directly relevant to past agricultural conditions.

Data processing methods When using a map of elevation or some other continuously changing variable, such as temperature, then the method of collection, the density of sample points and the interpolation methods should be considered. For example,

Table 5.5 *Common vector file formats*

Description	Possible file extension
Data eXchange Format	.DXF
Arc/Info Generate files	.E00
ArcView Shape files	.SHP
National Geodetic Survey	.BBK
Digital line graphs	.DLG
UK National Transfer Format	.NTF

if the choice between two DEMs is to be made on grounds of quality, then it will be important to ascertain which methods of interpolation and subsequent filtering (if any) were used in their creation. Digital elevation maps produced from contour data are particularly prone to interpolation errors. Chapter 6 discusses which are the most appropriate interpolation methods for particular circumstances.

Acquiring digital map data

Many maps are available for download from government data suppliers such as the US Geological Survey,[23] the Canadian Centre for Topographic Information,[24] Geoscience Australia,[25] the UK Ordnance Survey[26] and equivalent European and national mapping agencies. Publicly available global datasets at coarser resolutions are available from Land Processes Distributed Active Archive Centre,[27] Pennsylvania State University Library's Digital Chart of the World[28] and are also often provided by GIS companies as part of the software package. The delivery format of the map file may vary considerably. Common vector map file formats are outlined in Table 5.5. The exact process by which data acquired from these or other agencies is imported into a particular GIS program depends on how well that program supports the relevant file format, and is usually explained in the program's documentation. In cases where the preferred software offers no support for the relevant format it is usually possible to find another program that can be used as an intermediary to convert the data to a file format that is supported.

Vector files will be appropriately structured to allow the extraction of only those data layers or spatial objects required for a particular application. Each entity, be it a point, line or polygon, will also have one or more descriptive attributes. For example, map data purchased from the Ordnance Survey of Great Britain contains numerous layers, each defining different types of spatial object. These codes allow the dataset to be separated into different map layers within a GIS environment. Raster files contain less information because of the limitations of the file structure.

[23]http://geography.usgs.gov.   [24]www.cits.rncan.gc.ca.   [25]www.ga.gov.au.
[26]www.ordnancesurvey.gov.uk.   [27]http://edcdaac.usgs.gov/gtopo30/hydro.
[28]www.maproom.psu.edu/dcw.

At the minimum, a raster file will contain a grid of numeric values, but more typically there will be a header file that defines such things as the scale and resolution of the image (Chapter 4). Some GIS programs may require this information to be rewritten in an appropriate format before it can be interpreted by the program.

5.3.2 *Digitising paper maps*

For many parts of the world detailed topographic maps are not available in digital formats. Even when digital maps are available, digital thematic maps, such as geological or soil data, may only exist in paper formats. In some countries it may even be difficult to obtain paper maps for reasons of national security, and regional-based analyses may depend on publicly available maps or remotely sensed data obtained from the resources outlined above. In order to use paper maps in GIS it is necessary to 'digitise' them.

The term 'digitising' refers to the process of transferring analogue information to a digital format, although in this context the term refers more specifically to the delineation and transfer of discrete units of information from paper maps, plans or aerial photographs to a spatial database. Digitising can be performed from within a GIS program if the program supports it (and many packages do) or in a specialised computer-aided drawing (CAD) environment such as AutoCAD. Digitising can be done in one of three ways. Often a specialised piece of hardware called a digitising tablet is used, on which a paper map is placed and individual map features are traced using an electronic 'puck'. Alternatively, the paper map is scanned, georeferenced and displayed on a computer screen so that features may be digitally traced using a mouse in a process called *heads-up* or *on-screen digitising*. More recently it has become common to use programs that automatically find and extract vector data from scanned maps. Programs such as ESRI's 'ArcScan' integrate this process within a GIS environment, but there are also a number of standalone packages as well. Regardless of which method is used, there are four stages to the digitising process: (i) capturing the spatial data; (ii) entering the attribute data; (iii) error checking and 'drawing cleanup', and when appropriate; (iv) linking the spatial data to the attribute data (Fig. 5.6).

Capturing the spatial data

In order that the information being transfered from the paper map is placed in its correct geospatial position, the map needs to be *georeferenced* before any information is captured. When using a digitising tablet, georeferencing involves a mathematical process that transforms the coordinates of the paper map to real-world ones (that is sometimes called 'map calibration'). This requires the identification of a number of *ground control points* (GCPs) on the original map that correspond to locations on the target map. Ideally, more than three GCPs are needed, although more than nine points can soon become redundant. The placement of the points is important to ensure an accurate fit between the paper and digital data. Points should be spread

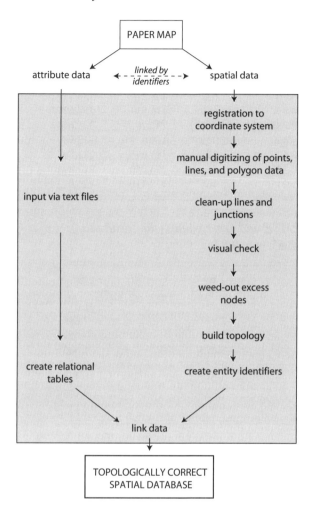

Fig. 5.6 Steps in digitising map data (after Burrough and McDonnell 1998, Fig. 4.8).

evenly around the perimeter of the area to be digitised rather than clustered in the centre or lying along one or two straight lines. The mathematical basis of calibration, and the associated spatial error in the calibration – as expressed using the root-mean-square error (RMSE) – is described in the Box 5.1.

Whether digitising in 'heads-up' mode or via a digitising tablet, capturing information from the map may be undertaken in either 'point' or 'stream' mode. The first refers to a process in which the user manually defines the location of the vertices that define points, lines, polylines or polygons. The last process, stream digitising, is the automatic placing of vertices while the puck or mouse is traced over the map object, with the distance between vertices established by a user-set increment value. The

Table 5.6 *A correspondence table*

GCP	Input x	Input y	Output x	Output y
1	19.682	112.957	115.542	532.924
2	50.304	112.632	408.210	534.677
3	60.892	112.469	476.557	534.677
4	36.785	94.552	294.297	336.644
5	19.520	85.919	119.047	242.009
6	48.675	89.177	383.675	271.802
7	40.531	82.661	296.050	217.474
8	61.217	98.461	478.310	426.022

Table 5.7 *RMSE and error values (the 'residuals').*
RMS: x = 2.55, y = 9.83

GCP	x-error	y-error
1	−0.454	−1.017
2	2.977	7.886
3	−2.139	−9.659
4	−3.273	1.606
5	1.632	−0.555
6	4.252	−19.547
7	−2.627	9.105
8	−0.367	12.179

Box 5.1 Root-mean-square error

When computing the rectification, a GIS program will attempt to use the polynomial function that best fits the points to their new location. However, an exact match is highly unlikely, so it is important to obtain a quantitative measure of the goodness-of-fit between the desired and actual locations of the GCPs. This is usually expressed as a root-mean-square error (RMSE), which can be interpreted as the average spatial error of the rectification. The RMSE may be accompanied by an individual error value for each GCP used for georectification, which gives the linear distance between the desired and actual locations of each GCP after rectification. These are also called the 'residuals'. The residuals for the control points in Table 5.6 are given in Table 5.7, following an affine transformation. The RMSE value is calculated as:

$$\text{RMSE} = \sqrt{\frac{\sum(x_o - x_t)^2}{n}} \tag{5.1}$$

where x_o, and x_t are, respectively, the original and transformed coordinate locations, and n is the number of GCPs. In the example in Table 5.7, the mean of the squares is 6.52 for x and 96.59 for y. The square roots of these two values, 2.55 for x and 9.83 for y, give the RMSE and thus the average spatial error in the rectified map or image. Whether or not this is an acceptable level of error depends on the scale of the maps and the purpose to which they are being put. As a rule of thumb, it is wise to aim for an error of less than 1 : 3000, so if the original image was 1 : 15 000 in scale, then an RMSE of approximately 5 m (15 000/3000 = 5) or less would be acceptable. In the example in Table 5.7 the y-value falls outside this range and the combined RMSE value for both the x- and y-dimensions is 7.18. On this basis, the rectification exceeds the acceptable error limit, so it would be necessary to choose a new set of GCPs and reconfirm that their new coordinates are accurately estimated. It can be helpful when reselecting GCPs to examine the residuals. For example, Table 5.7 shows that GCP 6 has a high error in both the x- and y-dimensions, suggesting that it might be contributing significantly to the overall error. Simply removing this GCP from the next attempt at rectification may therefore reduce the overall RMSE to within acceptable limits.

Combining spatial data from two or more sources will result in a larger RMSE than data from any individual map. This may occur when, for example, a map that contains topographic data is combined with a geology map so that measurements between phenomena on both maps can be taken (e.g. distances from sites to a particular raw material source), or when two raster maps each with cell values that represent two phenomena (e.g. quarterly rainfall amounts) are added together. When data from two maps are added together the combined RMSE can be calculated by:

$$\text{RMSE}_{\text{combined}} = \sqrt{\text{RMSE}^2_{\text{map1}} + \text{RMSE}^2_{\text{map2}}} \qquad (5.2)$$

The combined RMSE can result in a large degree of uncertainty being introduced into spatial data. For example, combining a 1 : 25 000 topographic map with an RMSE of 8 m and a 1 : 100 000 soil map with an RMSE of 32 m means that any point on the combined dataset will only be accurate to ±33 m.

advantage of point digitising is that operator control over the placement of vertices tends to result in a more 'intelligent' selection of vertices that better represent the shape of a polyline or polygon using the fewest points necessary. For some forms of interpolation of elevation data – particularly TINs – the manual capture of 'very important points' (VIPs) at contour vertices produces better results than stream digitising which can result in long strings of redundant vertices. A major disadvantage of point digitising, however, is that it is a very time consuming and tedious process. For that reason, stream digitising is often preferred for capturing complex information such as contour lines. Many GIS programs contain 'drawing cleanup' options, which consist of a set of tools that remove vertices along a polyline

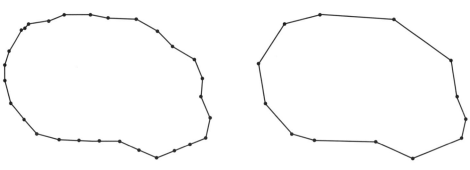

Fig. 5.7 A polygon before (left) and after (right) the removal of redundant vertices. User-specified tolerances are used to determine when vertices are redundant. In this example, 'cleaning up' has resulted in the loss of some detail, but has reduced the space needed to store this polygon by nearly half.

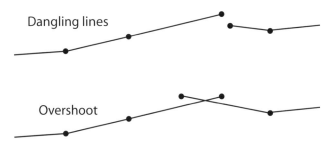

Fig. 5.8 Two common topological errors when digitising line data.

if the resulting locational change falls within a user-specified spatial tolerance (Fig. 5.7). This, in effect, means that a drawing digitised in stream mode can be 'weeded' of redundant information, thus reducing its size close to that of a manually digitised drawing.

Error checking and building topologies

When digitising a drawing, careful attention must be paid to the topology of the vector objects. When digitising a topographic map, for example, it is very important that individual contour lines are connected without overhangs or undershoots (Fig. 5.8) as these topological errors may severely impair subsequent analysis and interpolation. Many digitising programs have functions for helping maintain topologies through a 'snap' feature that automatically finds and connects vertices within a user-defined limit when digitising. Similarly, polygons need to be properly defined, without unintentional 'slivers', 'overhangs' or unconnected vertices (Fig. 5.9). Even when using automated 'snap' functions it is essential to carry out error checking and post-digitising drawing 'cleanup' to ensure a topologically correct spatial database. Some GIS packages have post-digitising automated 'clean and build' functions that first 'weed' redundant vertices and then construct topologies in the manner

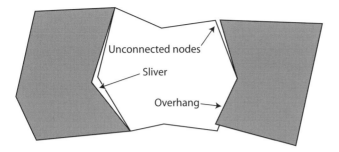

Fig. 5.9 Three common topological errors when digitising polygons.

described in Chapter 2. This ensures a clean, properly structured and efficient spatial database.

Survey projects often record data about many small units across a landscape as polygons (e.g. Bevan and Conolly 2004; Barton *et al.* 2002). The recording of the location and morphology of each unit as polygons, as well as the topological relationships between the polygons, may be captured directly in the field using total stations or GPS equipment, or during post-survey digitising from field maps. In either case it is of utmost importance for the subsequent interpretation of the archaeological data that polygon topology is recorded correctly so that overhangs or slivers are present only when they are true features of the original survey data (Fig. 5.10). Major errors in artefact density calculations can occur with poorly recorded survey units.

Entering attribute data

Digitising does not necessarily involve only the capture of location and morphology. Attribute data, such as contour line values, site codes, etc., are an essential part of a GIS as they provide meaning to the spatial objects. In the case of single attribute data, such as contour line values, it is often easier to enter this information at the time of digitising. Alternatively, and particularly in situations where extensive attribute data need to be entered, it is easier to enter this information in a separate database, spreadsheet or raw text editor. Provided that an identifier is also entered with the attribute data, then this information can be linked to the spatial database once identifiers have been added to each spatial entity.

Linking spatial and attribute data

Once the spatial data have been entered and topological relationships have been built and/or checked, entity identifiers need to be added or confirmed for each spatial object. These identifiers then serve as links to the information stored in the attribute database. The actual mechanics of linking attribute and spatial databases will vary with the GIS software, but typically this involves defining an identifier attribute held in each database and specifying that the two tables should then be linked via

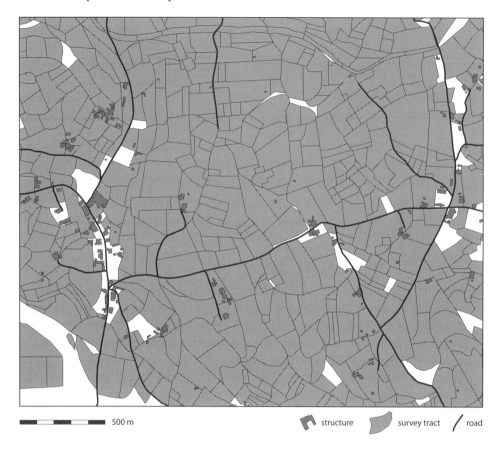

500 m   structure   survey tract   / road

Fig. 5.10 A small section of the KIP GIS, showing survey tract polygon topology. Adjacent polygons often share borders, but do not overlap, and gaps between polygons are intentional and reflect unsurveyed areas. © Kythera Island Project. Used with permission.

this attribute (i.e. as a relational 'one-to-one' or 'one-to-many' join, as described in Chapter 4).

5.4 Map rectification and georeferencing

The integration of paper maps, aerial photographs or satellite images with other map data requires defining spatial coordinates for the new data so that it can be properly positioned and scaled in relation to the exiting map data. This process is called *georeferencing*. In order to accomplish this, a number of locations with known coordinates must be identifiable on the map or image, referred to as ground control points (GCPs). Map data will, typically, have a grid overlay from which coordinates can be obtained, but finding control points may be more difficult on low-resolution images such as satellite data. On images with a 20-m pixel resolution or less it

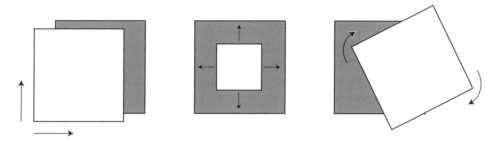

Fig. 5.11 Translation, scaling and rotation.

should be possible to locate road intersections, field boundaries, rock formations, buildings or other features for your control points. If GCPs cannot be defined by comparing the image data with a map, then it may be necessary to obtain GCPs by GPS survey (see Smith and Atkinson 2001).

In its simplest form, georeferencing is a mathematical transformation of one set of coordinates to another. Most of the mathematical calculations required for simple transformations are relatively easy to perform as they consist of a combination of three operations: *translation*, *scaling* and *rotation* (Fig. 5.11). Translation is the simple horizontal or vertical shifting of a set of coordinates. For example, changing the following set of three coordinates {10, 5; 7, 8; 2, 12} to the new coordinates {20, 10; 17, 13; 12, 17} involves a simple translation of +10 units in the x-direction, and +5 units in the y-direction. Scaling is similarly straightforward; changing the new set of coordinates by a scale of 3 would give us {60, 30; 51, 39; 36, 51}. Rotation, while easy to visualise, is a more complicated procedure requiring the trigonometric manipulation of coordinate pairs. In practice, it is often necessary to combine these three operations, so GIS programs use polynomial functions to transform the original coordinate system. The program first defines a function that uses several unknown parameters to link the inputs, which consist of the GCP coordinates on the original image, to the outputs defined by their intended location. It then obtains these parameters by solving the corresponding polynomial equation. Finally, the completed function is applied to all cells or vertices on the original map, thus effecting the transformation.

When translation, scaling and rotation is applied equally across the whole map (i.e. it does not alter the shape of the original image) it is referred to as a first-order polynomial, or *orthogonal* transformation. In many situations a more radical approach may be needed. A second-order polynomial (or *affine* transformation) is able to adjust the shape of the original image by independently scaling the x, y-axis of the original image, then translating, rotating and skewing the image as necessary to make it fit the desired coordinate system. Third- and higher-order polynomials are able to translate, scale and rotate in differing proportions over the entire map, in what is called a *projective* transformation. This is also known as image 'warping' or 'rubber sheeting', which provides a good analogy for what the rectification is attempting to perform. The combined process of correcting distortion and placing in a coordinate system is often called *georectification*.

The manner in which map or image rectification is performed is similar across most GIS packages. Typically, it involves creating a correspondence table or text file that contains a list of GCP locations (as pixel locations defined using x, y-coordinates) on the unrectified map or image alongside their desired new coordinates (as obtained from the base map; Table 5.6). The selection of GCPs will be dictated by the availability of features on the base map and the map or image to be rectified for which coordinates can be identified. These control points should also be widely spaced throughout the image, rather than clustered in a corner or along the edges. The number of control points to use is dependent on how radical the rectification needs to be: simple orthogonal transformation needs only two or three points, but a badly distorted aerial photograph or satellite image requires many control points to compute an accurate warp. Nine well-spaced GCPs are usually sufficient for even a relatively radical rectification, although in some extreme cases 16 or more well-placed points may be needed (Campbell 1996, p. 304).

Some relatively recent GIS packages such as ArcGIS have rectification tools that allow one roughly and manually to position the map or image to be georectified and then select a series of common points to serve as GCPs. These are then used to perform the rectification and calculate an RMSE value in the manner defined above.

5.5 A note on spatial error and map generalisation

An RMSE value provides a measure of how accurately spatial information has been translated to a new coordinate system. The RMSE values will be low when calibrating paper maps that are in good condition and higher when using, for example, photocopies. In some situations, such as when georectifying aerial photographs, RMSE values may be much higher than the guideline values we suggest. In any given situation a judgement will have to made as to whether the spatial error falls within a usable limit. It is essential to record the RMSE for all georectified maps as it may become an important variable when collecting spatial data such as distances. Ideally, the RMSE should be included in the metadata accompanying the dataset (see Chapter 13).

One important point to remember is that maps of different scales will have different resolutions and errors. By its very nature, a 1 : 50 000 map cannot accurately record the morphology of features with a spatial extent much less than 50 m, as at this scale such features would need to be drawn less than 1 mm wide. If this map was digitised, there is nothing to stop it being reproduced at much larger scales and used to collect spatial measurements well beyond the accuracy of the original data. The term 'map generalisation' refers to the errors arising from making spatial inferences from map data that has been reproduced at scales that are incongruous with the limitations set by the original scale of the drawing. This practice can be the source of considerable error and should be avoided. Furthermore, as we have explained, combining maps of two different scales can also result in significant spatial error. When combining maps of different scales it is important therefore to structure questions and condition inferences to the error of the largest scale map used in the analysis. Readers requiring further information on map generalisation and spatial error are referred to João (1998).

6

Building surface models

6.1 Introduction

Surface modelling is an important analytical tool and, particularly in the case of elevation modelling, is often the final stage of GIS project development. Constructing a digital elevation model (DEM) from secondary sources such as digitised contour lines and/or spot heights, or from primary data such as LiDAR or DGPS survey, is a frequent objective of surface modelling (Atkinson 2002). Surface models can also be derived from a wide range of point-based environmental and anthropomorphic data, such as artefact counts or soil chemistry (e.g. Robinson and Zubrow 1999; Lloyd and Atkinson 2004). The derivation of a continuous surface from a set of discrete observations involves a process called *interpolation* and the selection of an appropriate interpolation technique depends on the structure of the sample data plus the desired outcome and characteristics of the surface model. This chapter begins by reviewing some of the more common interpolation methods and is followed by a more detailed review of techniques for building DEMs from contour data.

6.2 Interpolation

Interpolation is a mathematical technique of 'filling in the gaps' between observations. More precisely, interpolation can be defined as predicting data using surrounding observations. It can be contrasted to *extrapolation*, which is the process of predicting values beyond the limits of a distribution of known points. To use a simple example, if n and m are unknown values within the set of numbers $\{2, 4, n, 8, 10, m\}$, then using a simple model of linear change n could be *interpolated* as being equal to 6. Using the same assumption of constant change, m would be *extrapolated* as equal to 12.

It is important to highlight that interpolation may usefully be applied to any quantitative spatial phenomenon that has some degree of structure – in other words, when the values of observations are not random, but have *positive autocorrelation*. This term describes a form of spatial structure in which, over the entire distribution, it is to a greater or lesser extent the case that the closer two observations are together, the more similar their values. This is clearly the case with elevation data (e.g. the closer two places on a landscape are to each other, the more similar their elevations will be) and many other types of natural phenomena. Positive autocorrelation is an important prerequisite for interpolation, as it determines whether attributes can be predicted by looking at neighbouring data points. However, while positive autocorrelation can be assumed for many environmental phenomena such as elevation, rainfall, temperature, etc., it cannot necessarily be assumed for anthropomorphic phenomena, such as the distribution of artefacts across a landscape. The degree to which a set of observations are autocorrelated should therefore be investigated before attempting to model it as a continuous distribution, as only positively correlated distributions will be worth interpolating. In cases where there is weak positive autocorrelation, interpolation methods that use geostatistics to assess the character of spatial variation in a dataset (e.g. *kriging*, as described below) often perform better than simple methods. Both approaches are described in detail in this chapter.

> **Edge effects** The reliability of a prediction of an attribute value at an unsampled location will improve as the number and proximity of surrounding known points increases. It therefore follows that points at areas towards the edge of a distribution will often have less accurate predictions because there are fewer points surrounding it. This 'edge effect' can significantly distort the predicted surface at the edge of the distribution and, as a rough rule of thumb, the outer 10 per cent of an interpolated surface can be considered suspect. For example, in a situation where the distribution of sampled points covers a rectangular area of 100×100 m, then the interpolated surface within the central 80×80 m will have fewer edge effects than the outer 10-m border. When collecting data for an interpolation, such as contour lines to build a DEM, it is wise to include information from the surrounding area to reduce the influence of edge effects. The interpolated surface can then be clipped to the desired extent.
>
> **Types of interpolation** Interpolation algorithms can be characterised in a number of different ways. One characterisation is based on the number of points used: *global operators* use all points collectively to identify a global trend; *local operators* look only to known values in a defined neighbourhood of the unsampled location to ensure that the surface responds to local variability, which typically results in a rougher but locally more responsive surface. Interpolation algorithms can also be distinguished according to whether they are *exact* or *inexact*. The former describes models where the values of the original data points are maintained in the output, whereas inexact methods result in an entirely derived surface, replacing the original data values with those derived from the model. Finally, interpolations can be defined as *constrained* or *unconstrained*, depending on whether upper and lower limits to the model are fixed.

6.3 Global methods

6.3.1 *Trend surface analysis*

Global interpolation methods are extremely valuable for assessing general trends in data but provide poor predictions of local variation. The most commonly used global interpolation method in archaeology is *trend surface analysis*, in which a mathematical surface is fitted to a spatial distribution of quantitative attribute values.

For example, Fig. 6.1(a) shows an artefact distribution, where the size of the artefact has also been recorded. The distribution can be envisaged as a three-dimensional point cloud, where the size of the artefact defines its height above the surface. A trend surface model applied to this distribution is the mathematical equivalent of fitting a sheet of paper through the three-dimensional surface so as to minimise the sum of the distances between each point and the piece of paper (or, more precisely,

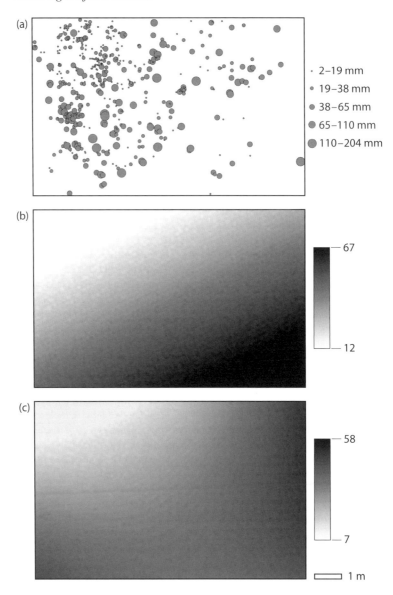

Fig. 6.1 Trend surface analysis of artefact sizes. The upper map (a) is a proportional symbol representation of artefact sizes. Map (b) models size change using a linear trend surface and map (c) a quadratic trend surface. Created using *TREND* in Idrisi.

the sum of the squared distances). A 'first-order' trend surface, as in Fig. 6.1(b), attempts to fit the imaginary sheet of paper without bending it at all, whereas second- (Fig. 6.1c) and higher-order surfaces warp the surface in progressively more complex ways to minimise the average distance between all the points. In effect, the higher-order the surface, the more local the model becomes.

Mathematically, a trend surface is a polynomial model. The term 'polynomial' describes a simple function constructed by the addition of *terms*, typically of the format b_0x, where b_0 represents a number derived from the model, and x is the x-coordinate of the spatial object. The complexity (or *degree*) of a polynomial is defined by the number of its terms. As applied to two-dimensional spatial objects, a first-degree, or linear, polynomial model is given by the equation:

$$z_{x,y} = b_0 + b_1x + b_2y \tag{6.1}$$

where z is the value of the variable to be established; b_0, b_1 and b_2 are coefficients obtained by the regression analysis; and x and y are geographical coordinates (Hodder and Orton 1976, p. 160). Second-degree, or quadratic models, as in Fig. 6.1(c), are given by the equation:

$$z_{x,y} = b_0 + b_1x + b_2y + b_3x^2 + b_4xy + b_5y^2 \tag{6.2}$$

For example, in the linear model in Fig. 6.1(b), the variability in artefact size, z, is modelled as $z = 11.45 + 0.21x + 0.46y$. When applied to artefact sizes in the map in Fig. 6.1(a), both the linear and quadratic models suggest that, in general, artefact size is lowest in the upper left of the distribution, with the linear model showing size increasing towards the lower right. The quadratic model shows sizes increase towards the upper right and lower left of the distribution. As with regression analysis, an R^2 value (often referred to as the 'goodness-of-fit') can be used to assess how well the calculated surface fits the original distribution of values and can be taken as a measure of the proportion of the variation that is explained by the modelled surface (Shennan 1988, pp. 126–131). It is calculated as:

$$R^2 = 1 - \frac{\sum\limits_{i=1}^{n}(z_i - \hat{z}_i)^2}{\sum\limits_{i=1}^{n}(z_i - \bar{z}_i)^2} \tag{6.3}$$

where z_i is the observed value, $\hat{z}_i$ is the value predicted by the model and $\bar{z}_i$ is the mean of all observed values. An R^2 value of 0.095 for the linear model in Fig. 6.1(b) and 0.105 for the quadratic model in Fig. 6.1(c) shows poor correspondence between the modelled surface and the original data points. A higher-order polynomial would probably provide a better fit between the observed and predicted data values, but such models are often overly sensitive to outliers at the edges of distributions which can significantly distort reality (Burrough and McDonnell 1998, p. 109).

Trend surface analysis has value for identifying very general data trends but by itself rarely provides adequate understanding of spatial processes and should be used cautiously. This does not entirely nullify the value of trend surface analysis, but it does suggest that using polynomial surface models to understand archaeological distribution patterns can often result in a gross approximation of more complex patterns. Examples of the use of trend surface analysis to make sense of

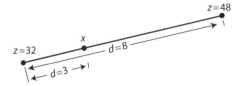

Fig. 6.2 Linear interpolation. Using Eq. 6.4 the z-value at x is predicted as:
$$\frac{(48 - 32) \times 3}{8} + 32 = 38.$$

archaeological data can be found in Hodder and Orton (1976, pp. 155–174), who discuss the technique in considerable detail. Sydoriak (1985) and D'Andrea *et al.* (2002) show its value for assessing intra-site artefact distributions and Bove (1981) and Neiman (1997) have used trend surfaces to help understand the collapse of Classic Mayan civilisation.

6.4 Local methods

Local interpolators are used to model surfaces to provide information about local variability as accurately as possible. They will provide a close or exact fit between the original data observations and the model, depending on whether they are exact or inexact interpolators. Some local interpolation methods take into account trends across the whole study area to establish more precisely the local versus distant influence on attribute values, while others look to only a very small neighbourhood to predict a value. There are many different types of local interpolator but here we review the two most commonly used techniques: inverse distance weighting and splines. Both produce a continuous surface grid from an initial distribution of discrete observations, although exactly how they do this, and their resulting surfaces, vary enormously. In general terms, they are both appropriate for modelling quantitative surfaces of environmental or anthropogenic phenomena including elevation. A further local interpolator that may be used for the interpretation of qualitative data, Thiessen tessellations or polygons, is described in Chapter 10.

6.4.1 *Linear interpolation with inverse distance weighting*

Linear interpolation is conceptually equivalent to drawing a straight line between two points with known attribute values. Any point along this line can then have an attribute value predicted by establishing its relative distance between the points, as given by:

$$z(x) = \frac{(z_u - z_l) \times d_{lx}}{d_{ul}} + z_l \tag{6.4}$$

where z is the interpolated value at point x; z_u and z_l are the upper and lower values; d_{ul} is the linear distance between them; and d_{lx} is the distance between x and the lower value. This is demonstrated in Fig. 6.2.

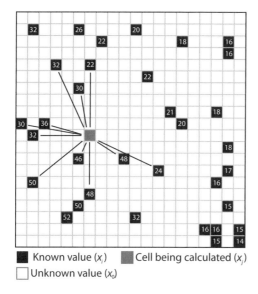

Fig. 6.3 Interpolation is used to calculate values at points within a distribution of points with known values. The distance weighted average of up to 12 nearest neighbours is often used. Distances not lying along the *x*- or *y*-axes are calculated using Pythagoras' theorem (see Fig. 2.9).

However, the use of only two points along a straight line does not always result in accurate predictions of values at unsampled locations. Methods that look to the values and distances from a larger sample of surrounding known points give more reliable results. One common approach is called an *inverse distance weighted* (IDW) predictor, in which the weight given to the sample of surrounding points is inversely proportional to its linear distance raised to a specific power. This is given by:

$$\hat{z}(x_0) = \frac{\sum\limits_{i=0}^{n} z(x_i) d_{ij}^{-r}}{\sum\limits_{i=0}^{n} d_{ij}^{-r}} \tag{6.5}$$

where $\hat{z}(x_0)$ is the unknown value, $z(x_i)$ are known values and d_{ij} is the distance between the unknown and known point. The attribute values of n nearest neighbours are used to establish the unknown value (Fig. 6.3). The exact number of neighbours selected will have an effect on the final surface. Some programs select the nearest 12 by default (hence 'IDW12'), whereas others use a search radius to select between 4 and 8 points.

The distance from each data point to the point being interpolated is then transformed to its reciprocal (i.e. d_{ij}^{-1}), or more often the inverse of the distance raised to a power of two (i.e. d_{ij}^{-2}). The transformed distance is then multiplied by the attribute

Table 6.1 *Attribute, distance values and weighted attributes for Fig. 6.3*

x_j	$z(x_i)$	d_{ij}	d_{ij}^{-1}	d_{ij}^{-2}	$z(x_i)d_{ij}^{-1}$	$z(x_i)d_{ij}^{-2}$
1	46	2.2	0.45	0.21	20.9	9.5
2	48	3.6	0.28	0.08	13.3	3.7
3	36	4.1	0.24	0.06	8.8	2.1
4	30	4.1	0.24	0.06	7.3	1.8
5	48	5.0	0.20	0.04	9.6	1.9
6	32	5.0	0.20	0.04	6.4	1.3
7	22	6.0	0.17	0.03	3.7	0.6
8	30	6.1	0.16	0.03	4.9	0.8
9	50	6.1	0.16	0.03	8.2	1.3
10	50	6.4	0.16	0.02	7.8	1.2
11	24	6.7	0.15	0.02	3.6	0.5
12	32	6.7	0.15	0.02	4.8	0.7
Total			2.56	0.64	99.3	25.4

values of the known point to 'distance weight' the attribute value so that points located further away will contribute less to the prediction. These values are then summed and then divided by the sum of the transformed distances. Inverse distance weighted methods are by necessity exact interpolations, for when d approaches 0, the weight increases to infinity and thus the original data points are maintained in the derived surface.[1] The influence of distance can be modified by changing its weighting: for example, Burrough and McDonnell (1998, pp. 117–118) show how an interpolated surface is significantly altered by modifying the distance function to d_{ij}^{-2}, d_{ij}^{-3} and d_{ij}^{-4}. Table 6.1 provides a worked example and lists the attribute values ($z(x_i)$) and distances (d_{ij}) for the 12 nearest neighbours identified in Fig. 6.3. Both the reciprocal and reciprocal of the square are listed together with the corresponding weighted value. Depending on which of these two weights is chosen, the predicted value for the grey square in Fig. 6.3 would be either $99.3/2.56 = 38.8$, or $25.4/0.64 = 39.7$.

Inverse distance weighting is a good all-purpose interpolation algorithm for well-spaced data points, but determining an optimum set of parameters is difficult; varying the number of neighbours and the distance weighing will significantly alter the surface. Withholding some data points from the model, then comparing these known values with the predicted values at that point is one way of comparing the accuracy of different sets of variables. These differences can be quantified as an RMSE, following Eq. 5.1, and interpolations produced using different weighting values can then be objectively compared. However, short of actually visiting the area

---

[1] For example, if $d = 2$, its reciprocal is $2^{-1} = \frac{1}{2} = 0.5$; if $d = 0.001$, then its reciprocal is $\frac{1}{0.001} = 1000$; if $d = 0$, then its reciprocal is $\frac{1}{0} = \infty$.

being interpolated to check the correspondence between the model and the actual phenomenon, there is no way to ascertain the probability of whether the model is correctly predicting values at unsampled locations. If this level of information is required, then kriging may be a good alternative as it provides a measure of the accuracy of the modelled surface.

6.4.2 *Splines*

'Splines' refer to a good general-purpose interpolation method, best applied to smoothly varying surfaces like elevations. Like the trend surface model, fitting splines produces a polynomial surface, conceptually equivalent to bending a sheet of rubber to pass through the three-dimensional point cloud (and in fact takes its name from the flexible rulers – 'splines' – used by cartographers to draw curved surfaces). More precisely, spline functions are *piece-wise* polynomial functions that are joined together at *break points* to form a *bicubic spline* that passes exactly through the data points (Burrough and McDonnell 1998, p. 119). With all exact interpolators, excessively high or low values can cause unnatural 'pits or peaks' in the modelled surface. *Thin-plate splines* – the usual implementation in GIS packages – solve this by replacing the exact surface with a weighted average to produce a minimum-curvature surface (Franke 1982; Burrough and McDonnell 1998, p. 120). The thin-plate spline interpolation method usually offers the option of setting either a *tensioning* or *regularising* weight. Increasing the weighting of the former adjusts the tension of the total curvature of the surface to produce a rougher surface that improves the fit with the original data, whereas increasing a regularising weight adjusts the third derivative in the curvature minimisation expression to produce a smoother surface.

Like IDW methods, splines are a good all-purpose interpolation method that have the major advantage of retaining small-scale variability in the data. Because of their inherently smooth surface, DEMs generated from splines can produce aesthetically pleasing sloped surfaces. The major disadvantages are that, as with the inverse distance weighting methods, there is no easy way to assess how accurately the model reflects actuality and the smooth surfaces may be inappropriate for some sorts of data.

6.5 Interpolation with geostatistics: kriging

The general interpolators described above perform well on most datasets, but will not necessarily be the best approach for situations where there is weak positive spatial autocorrelation and the density and distribution of points is irregular. In these cases an interpolation method that uses geostatistical methods to estimate better the degree of spatial variation and autocorrelation in a dataset will help ensure that the predictions are optimal and will also provide information on error rates associated with each prediction (Haining 2003, p. 327). Interpolation using geostatistics is known as *kriging* and is a more complex process than the previously discussed techniques. Kriging is conceptually similar to inverse distance weighting in that it uses a variable to weight the contribution of surrounding known values based on their distance from the unsampled location to predict a new value. The major difference is that the weighting value is dependent on the spatial structure and degree of spatial autocorrelation of the sample distribution. The calculation of weighting values first involves the construction of an *experimental variogram* – a mathematical model that predicts what influence distance has on the relationship between known values – and then fitting this to a *theoretical model* defined using an established function.

The use of variograms to derive localised predictions of attributes for unsampled locations is dependent on *regionalised variable theory* (Matheron 1971). This theory states that spatial variation of a variable is a product of a deterministic component and a stochastic (random) component. The deterministic component is a global mean or trend. The stochastic component has two parts: a localised random component correlated with the global pattern and highly localised random noise caused by measurement error or small-scale spatial processes (Burrough and McDonnell 1998, pp. 133–134; Lloyd and Atkinson 2004). This theory can be expressed as the value of a variable z at point x being defined by:

$$z(x) = m(x) + \epsilon'(x) + \epsilon'' \tag{6.6}$$

where $m(x)$ is a function describing the global trend of z at x, $\epsilon'(x)$ is the random but spatially dependent local variation at x and ϵ'' is random noise (DeMers 1997). For example, if z is taken to represent the number of lithic artefacts recovered in a 2×2-m excavation square, then regionalised variable theory might be used to model a situation in which the number of artefacts actually recovered (or predicted to be recovered) is a product of: (a) a general trend of artefacts decreasing in number the closer one is towards the periphery of the distribution; plus (b) a localised trend that has the number of artefacts at the periphery varying from high to low depending on whether the edge of the distribution is slightly upslope or downslope; plus (c) random influence at a highly localised level, such as the presence of a midden at the edge of the distribution which could cause an area to have an unusually high number.

Kriging, by first establishing the relationship between distance and attribute variability, uses regionalised variable theory to establish locally responsive distance weightings. The weighting function is defined as λ_i and the sum of λ_i is equal to 1. When applied to each of the values, $z(x_i)$, from the n neighbours within the search radius, the sum of the modified values will provide the estimated attribute value, $\hat{z}$ at location x_0 (where x_i are the n neighbours):

$$\hat{z}(x_0) = \sum_{i=1}^{n} \lambda_i \times z(x_i) \tag{6.7}$$

In order to derive λ_i, an experimental semi-variogram must be created, which is a plot of the *semi-variance*, denoted by γ, against distance between each pair of

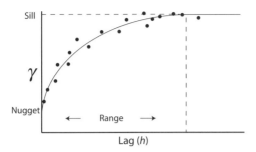

Fig. 6.4 A plot of lag (h) against semi-variance (γ) is a variogram. The observations are shown as data points, to which an exponential theoretical model (solid line) has been fitted.

points in the sample (referred to as the lag, and denoted by h). The semi-variance can be estimated by the formula:

$$\hat{\gamma}(h) = \frac{\sum\limits_{i=1}^{n}[z(x_i) - z(x_i + h)]^2}{2n} \tag{6.8}$$

where n is the number of pairs of points of distance h. The plot of γ against h is the experimental variogram (Fig. 6.4).

The most important stage in kriging is the fitting of a theoretical model to the experimental variogram, of which the most common are spherical, exponential, linear and the Gaussian models (Burrough and McDonnell 1998, p. 136). Close correspondence between the experimental and theoretical semi-variogram is essential for the accurate derivation of λ_i and some measure of the success of the fit is needed to ensure an accurate match. Good kriging software should provide a mechanism for quantifying the fit between the two (e.g. via an R^2 value). Poor fit between the two models may indicate that there are two or more trends in the data that should be modelled separately.

When a good fit is identified, the coefficients of the particular theoretical model fitted to the semi-variogram (based on the variable parameters of the nugget, sill and range, and the type of model used, as shown in Fig. 6.4) are then used to derive the values of λ for each distance between the unknown and known points. As well as an interpolated surface, kriging provides a standard error surface, which can be used to identify areas where the interpolation is less accurate.

There are several different kriging techniques suitable for different forms of data. For samples without high peaks or troughs (i.e. atypically high or low values compared to their neighbours) and without spatial structure (e.g. a trend from high to low values) then *ordinary kriging* can provide a more accurate surface model than methods derived without geostatistics. In instances where there are unusually high or low values *block kriging* can provide a smoother surface by averaging values. *Universal kriging* is a technique that uses trend surface information but still responds to local values. This method works well with data that have a definite trend as it can utilise that data to make more accurate predictions. The technique of *co-kriging* uses information from more than one variable in the distribution (e.g., returning to the example above, perhaps lithic artefacts and slope values). Co-kriging uses the autocorrelation of the variable in question as well as correlation between it and another quantitative variable to make better predictions of the weighting value used in the interpolation.

Despite its complexity, kriging is a valuable alternative to more traditional interpolation algorithms, especially when some measure of the accuracy of the modelled surface is desirable. However, some understanding of the spatial structure of the sample data is essential to ensure that it is being implemented and interpreted correctly. Haining (2003, pp. 325–333) provides a good introduction to models for representing spatial variation. A detailed and informative discussion of kriging with worked examples of calculating kriging weights can be found in Burrough and McDonnell (1998, pp. 132–151) and Lloyd and Atkinson (2004). The latter work is notable as it is one of the few recently published examples of the applicability of kriging to archaeological data. The authors provide two case studies, one of which uses soil phosphate data obtained during the Laconia Survey in Greece (Buck *et al.* 1988) and the other that examines assemblages of Roman pottery from the south of Britain reported by Allen and Fulford (1996). The other notable recent work is Ebert (2002), who uses kriging to predict the quantity of lithic artefacts expected to be recovered during field walking.

Geostatistical tools for the derivation of variograms and the fitting of experimental models are available for many GIS packages, including ArcView (using one of the third-party kriging extensions listed on the ArcSripts page of the ESRI website[2]), ArcInfo, ArcGIS (as a component of the Geostatistical Analyst), GRASS (using Gstat) and Idrisi. There are also a number of freely available non-GIS packages that can be used for geostatistical analysis and kriging, such as R[3] and Variowin[4] (Pannatier 1996). Box 6.1 explains how to produce an interpolated surface using kriging in ArcGIS.

6.6 Creating digital elevation models

The creation of digital elevation models (DEMs) is one of the more common uses of interpolation algorithms in GIS, although with the increasing availability of high-resolution digital elevation data from mapping agencies this need is declining. A DEM is stored, manipulated, viewed and analysed in a GIS either as a raster grid, when it is properly referred to as an *altitude matrix*, or as a triangulated irregular network (TIN). Raster-based DEMs are the most popular method for working with elevation data, although TINs offer advantages in storage overheads and for some

---

[2] http://arcscripts.esri.com/.
[3] www.r-project.org.   [4] www-sst.unil.ch/research/variowin.

Box 6.1 Interpolation using kriging in ArcGIS

Kriging in ArcGIS is performed via the *Geostatistical Analyst* extension. Initiating the Geostatistical Wizard leads to the user being asked to select from a number of different kriging methods, the choice of which depends on the structure of the data as explained above. Once a technique is selected, a range of visualisation tools are provided, including the experimental variogram and directional variogram to assist with the identification of anisotropy. Several different theoretical models can be selected, and it is possible to assess visually how well these each fit the experimental model. Unfortunately there is no way of quantitatively comparing the fit between the experimental and theoretical models. One solution is therefore to use a separate program such as 'Variowin' (Pannatier 1996) to establish the best-fitting theoretical model and then enter the parameters (e.g. model type, nugget, range and sill) into the Geostatistical Wizard. Once this has been entered, the wizard then passes the information to the Spatial Analyst and computes the interpolation, resulting in a modelled surface. The wizard allows for the generation of prediction errors, and also for randomly selecting subsets of data for empirical testing of the accuracy of the modelling distribution.

forms of analysis. Both model formats may be derived from spot heights (points), vector hypsography (contour lines) or a combination of the two.

The quality of a DEM can also be evaluated on the basis of its suitability for particular tasks. Is it, for example, of a suitable resolution for the scale of analysis and/or secondary datasets with which it is to be integrated? Is it a statistically accurate surface? Is it smooth and aesthetically pleasing? Prioritising one or more of these qualities depends very much on the application to which the DEM will be put (Yang and Holder 2000). For example, the aesthetic qualities of a DEM, particularly when viewed isometrically, are important for landscape visualisation and can provide a different perspective on the character of topography and terrain. They can be especially powerful when 'draped' with other information, such as shaded relief, aerial photographs or other datasets (Fig. 6.5). On the other hand, smoothly varying surfaces may not necessarily be the most accurate. In some circumstances it may be more important to ensure that the DEM contains as few errors as possible even if this means sacrificing some other aspect such as resolution or visual impact.

The accuracy of the DEM is essential if it is to be used for spatial analysis. Digital elevation models form the base data for a host of derived surfaces and ecological and environmental models (discussed in further detail in Chapters 9 and 10). The DEM-derived surfaces that are commonly used in archaeological GIS include: the first-order derivatives of slope and aspect (e.g. Kvamme 1985; Woodman 2000b; Barton *et al.* 2002); the second-order derivative of terrain curvature (e.g. Bevan and

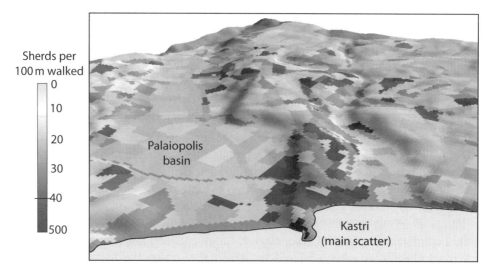

Fig. 6.5 An isometrically viewed DEM, hillshaded and draped with artefact distribution patterns. Source: Kythera Island Project. Used with permission.

Conolly 2004); visibility (e.g. Wheatley and Gillings 2002; Lake and Woodman 2003; Llobera 2003); movement (e.g. Llobera 2000) and cost-surfaces (e.g. Bell and Lock 2000; Bell *et al.* 2002); and hydrological models and watershed extents (Hill 1998; Bevan 2003; Bevan and Conolly 2004; Table 6.2). Digital elevation models are also needed for the construction of taphonomic models, such as soil loss and sediment movement (Burrough and McDonnell 1998, pp. 193–198; Barton *et al.* 2002; see also Chapter 9), although the full potential of quantitative modelling of erosion processes has not yet been fully exploited by archaeological users of GIS.

The quality of DEMs varies enormously depending on the accuracy and structure of the original data and the interpolation methods used. The number and distribution of sample points ('spot heights') is crucial. Generally speaking, the greater their number in areas of highly variable terrain the more accurate the interpolation is likely to be. Whenever possible, therefore, it is better to use primary data collected manually using the techniques described in Chapter 5 so that the distribution of points can be properly controlled. Obviously, this is not a viable option for large-scale regional landscape projects or in situations where survey is impractical or impossible. In many regions, DEMs with grid spacing of 15–30 m are available from satellite sources, but these may not be of sufficiently high resolution for some forms of landscape archaeology. In these situations it is worth investigating the availability of DEMs from government or commercial data suppliers. Note, however, that some commercially available DEMs are actually interpolations of existing contour data and are therefore likely to share the same errors as other interpolated data.

Table 6.2 *Surface models that can be computed from a DEM*

Attribute	Definition	Practical application
Slope/gradient	Maximum rate of change in elevation	Steepness of terrain; difficulty of movement; land capability classification; erosion and artefact movement; predictive modelling
Aspect/exposure	Compass bearing of steepest downhill slope	Solar irradiance; vegetation modelling; movement; site predictive modelling
Profile curvature	Rate of change of slope	Erosion modelling; soil and land evaluation
Shaded relief	Representation of terrain relief via a shadow effect ('hillshade')	Visual assessment of terrain variability
Irradiance	Amount of solar energy falling on a landform	Vegetation modelling; land capability classification; predictive modelling
Viewshed	Location of visible landscape from a given point	Site and settlement location analysis; predictive modelling
Watershed	The region draining to a defined point in the landscape	Settlement location analysis

Source: Adapted from Burrough and McDonnell (1998, pp. 190–192, 204).

6.6.1 *Building a DEM from contour lines*

The creation of a DEM using manually digitised contour lines from paper maps must often be resorted to because of the lack of any alternative sources of information. However, contours do not provide an ideal set of data for creating a DEM. First, it is often difficult to assess how accurately the contour data represents the actual morphology of the landscape in question. If the contours were originally derived from photogrammetric analysis of aerial photographs then they will be more accurate than contours created from interpolated spot heights, but it is often unclear how the contour map was created. Second, as described in Chapter 5, manually digitising contour data will contribute further spatial error to the dataset. Third, as described below, contours are less than ideal datasets for the interpolation routines described in the previous section.

A common but often unsatisfactory approach to interpolating DEMs from contours is to rasterise the contour lines and then use the corresponding grid cells in an IDW, spline or kriging interpolation. Alternatively, the vertices of the polylines may be extracted as points to be used as nodes for one of these routines. In these situations there are good reasons to be cautious about using interpolators such as IDW or splines described previously. Simple interpolators like IDW work best with evenly distributed data, whereas contour lines present a string of points of the same value with potentially very wide spaces between the next string of points. Under these conditions, simple distance weighted algorithms based on nearest neighbour or a fixed radius search are likely to produce significant errors, or 'artefacts' in the

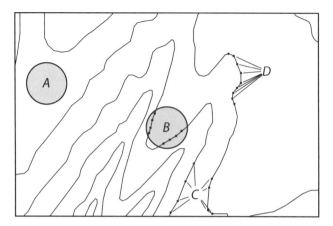

Fig. 6.6 Problems associated with the simple interpolation of contour data. Using a fixed search radius can result in either no points available for interpolation (point *A*) which results in areas with an erroneous predicted value of '0', or a set of points sharing a single value (point *B*), leading to 'plateaus' forming around contour lines. Distance weighted interpolation of nearest neighbours may provide a smoother surface (point *C*), although points located between widely spaced intervals, such as at *D*, will still result in a plateau. Source: Kythera Island Project.

modelled surface (Burrough and McDonnell 1998, Fig. 5.16; Carrara *et al.* 1997, p. 471; Fig. 6.6). Such problems are often clearly visible as alternating plateaus and steep slopes on slope maps derived from the DEM (Fig. 6.7).

Despite the importance of the DEM and the frequent need to use contour lines to create one, there is no established best practice for converting contour data to a continuous surface and the subject remains the focus of considerable debate (see, for example, Carrara *et al.* 1997; Burrough and McDonnell 1998, pp. 121–131; Franklin 2000; Yang and Holder 2000; Merwin *et al.* 2002, for recent technical discussions). One approach is to use interpolation algorithms specially designed to handle contour data, as these are able to manage the irregularity of the point distribution, as demonstrated by examples in Hageman and Bennett (2000). However, a DEM created from contour data cannot be assumed to be accurate and must be checked for errors following interpolation. Some accepted methods for assessing the quality of a DEM include checking that: (i) predicted heights falling on or near the original contour lines have values close or equal to the contour height; (ii) predicted elevations positioned between two contour lines have a value between the two contour lines; (iii) elevations vary linearly between the elevations of the two bounding contour lines; (iv) areas bounded by a single contour interval, for example valley bottoms and hill tops, have a realistic morphology; (v) any artefacts of interpolation (i.e. areas which have unrealistic predictions) are limited to <0.1–0.2 per cent of the modelled surface (Carrara *et al.* 1997, p. 453).

The quality of a DEM can also be assessed by deriving two additional datasets from the modelled surface. Firstly, a contour map with an interval one-half that of

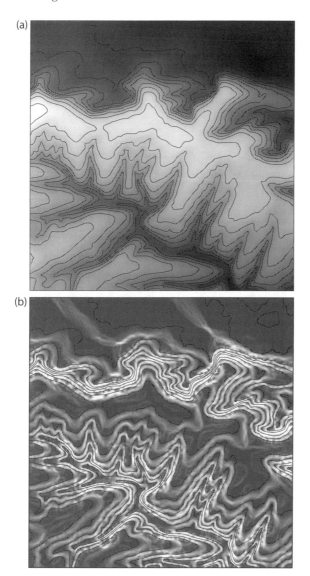

Fig. 6.7 Typical problems of using contour data for interpolation. Although the DEM (a) appears to be an accurate model of surface variability, the derived slope map (b) shows extensive 'tiger-striping' (i.e. alternating light and dark areas that correspond to the location of the original contours). Created by IDW12 interpolation of contour vertices in ArcInfo 7.2. Source: Kythera Island Project.

(a)   (b)

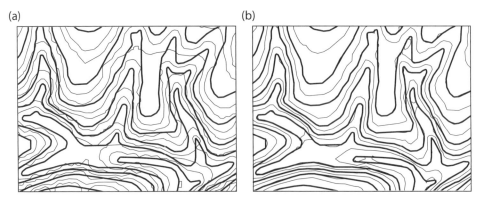

Fig. 6.8 Comparison of original contour lines (thick) with contour lines generated
from surfaces (thin) using (a) IDW interpolation and (b) a TIN. Significantly more
discrepancies between the original and modelled surface are evident in A than B,
because of the problems of using point-based interpolation of contour data. The TIN
was transformed to a grid using *TINLATTICE* and contour lines were generated for
both surface grids using *CONTOUR* at one half of the original interval ratio using
ArcInfo 7.2. Source: Kythera Island Project.

the original contour data can be compared to the predicted contours to identify the
overall accuracy of the interpolation and areas where there may be errors (Fig. 6.8).
Secondly, a slope map derived from a poorly interpolated DEM may show artificially steep slopes interspersed with plateaus in the form of 'tiger stripes' located
along the original contour lines, as in Fig. 6.7. Finally, in critical applications,
the accuracy of a DEM can also be verified by the statistical comparison of the
DEM and original dataset, using methods described in Kvamme (1990b), Wood
(1996, Chapter 3), Carrara *et al.* (1997), Hageman and Bennett (2000) or Yang and
Holder (2000). Common tests include the calculation of RMSE values and examining a frequency histogram of elevation values. The latter method, referred to as
hypsometric analysis, is particularly useful when interpolating from contour data,
as poorly interpolated data often results in 'spikes' corresponding to the original
contour intervals (Wood 1996, Section 3.1.3).

Filtering (smoothing) a DEM (as described in Chapter 9) may help 'iron out'
problems such as those just described. However, as a rule of thumb, if considerable filtering is required to make a DEM visually plausible, it is likely that there
are problems with either the source data, or the method of interpolation, or both.
Because of the problems associated with building DEMs from contours, it is therefore preferable to resample the original data to reduce the effects of contour line
data on the interpolation and/or to select a method that is better able to deal with
this type of data. In this section we consider three common approaches used to
build DEMs from contour data: TINs, linear interpolation based on steepest slope,
and ArcInfo's proprietary *TOPOGRID* algorithm. No one method will be suitable
for all types of terrain and, as accurate DEMs are critical for a wide range of other

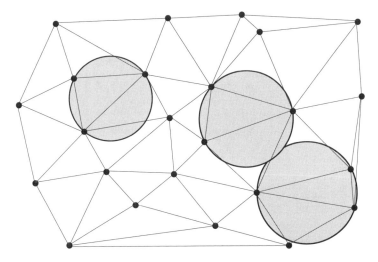

Fig. 6.9 A Delaunay triangulation. No circle that passes through the three vertices of a triangle may contain any other node.

models, it is worth experimenting and comparing different approaches to ensure that the best model is used.

Triangulated irregular networks

Triangulated irregular networks (TINs) are constructed from a set of *mass points* which can be derived from spot heights, the vertices of contours or a combination of both. A TIN is constructed by building a tessellation of triangular polygons from the mass points, configured such that if a circle was passed through the three nodes of each triangle, no other nodes would be included (Fig. 6.9). This is called *Delaunay triangulation*, and it ensures that the closest node from any point in triangle *n* is one of the three nodes used to construct triangle *n*.

However, 'raw' contour data present several problems for TIN building. Firstly, digitised contour lines often contain more data than is needed to represent a surface and sample points along one contour line may lie closer together than points on the adjacent contour. When constructing a TIN, this results in unrealistically flat elevations in parts of the surface model, most often on lobed spurs, or widely spaced contours on hill tops and valley floors (Fig. 6.10a, b). To help avoid redundant points being incorporated in the model, TIN-building programs therefore usually offer the capability of setting a *proximal tolerance* and a *weed tolerance*. The former establishes the minimum distance between points on the horizontal plane, so that if two or more points lie within the tolerance range only one is used as a node in the TIN. More critically, the 'weed tolerance' establishes the minimum distance along a line before a vertex is used in the TIN (ESRI 2002, p. 31).

The accuracy of a TIN will be greatly improved by digitising critical points along contour lines (i.e. capturing only major, rather than all, inflection points) and 'very

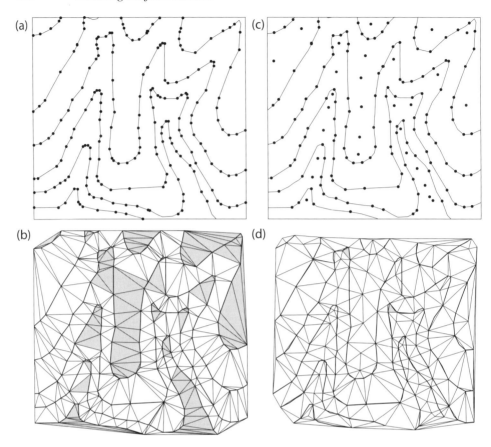

Fig. 6.10 Using all vertices from a contour map (a) results in many flat triangles (shaded grey in b). Resampling the contours and adding spot heights between lobed contours (c) reduces this problem (d). Source: Kythera Island Project.

important points' (VIPs) that define hill tops, pits and saddles. Carrara *et al.* (1997, pp. 470–471) also show that without defining hard breaklines to help guide the construction of triangles, valley bottoms and hill tops are modelled as flat triangles, which results in an unrealistic surface model. One suggested way to do this is to pre-mark these points on the map using a coloured pen so that they can then be manually digitised (with their elevation values) to create the mass points for the TIN (ESRI 2002, p. 57). This will reduce the number of flat triangles and result in a more realistic and accurate surface (Fig. 6.10c, d). To improve the accuracy of the TIN, additional landscape features such as ridges and streams can also be integrated and defined as hard 'break lines'. These lines, which do not necessarily require elevation values, are then maintained as linear features in the TIN and interrupt surface smoothness, which is particularly important for the accurate modelling of hydrological processes.

The resulting TIN is a very versatile model and can be used 'as is' to derive attributes defining elevations, slope, aspect, shaded relief and viewsheds without requiring additional layers. Spikins *et al.* (2002) demonstrate an innovative use of TINs to reconstruct buried land surfaces using the three-dimensional coordinates of artefacts. Triangulated irregular networks also offer advantages over raster grids with regards to storage and processing time for smaller study areas, because the density of triangles can be adjusted to the complexity of the terrain and the needs of the model, with extra triangles used for areas of highly variable relief. However, with large study areas, this advantage disappears because of the computationally demanding task of generating vector polygons. The major disadvantage of TINs is that the elevation surface often retains a triangular imprint, imparting an unrealistic, although not necessarily inaccurate, feel to a surface model.

Finally, in order to integrate TIN elevation data with other grid datasets, or for other modelling purposes, it may be necessary to convert the TIN into a raster grid. This is a straightforward process that involves laying a grid of desired resolution over the TIN with individual cell values being calculated by linear interpolation or a bicubic average to the nearest vertex. However, slope maps derived from this grid are also susceptible to the retention of the original triangular surface.

Linear interpolation between contours
One of the most basic algorithms that can be used on contour data is a linear interpolation along a line drawn between two contours. These methods first involve rasterising the digitised contour at the resolution of the final grid. The rasterising must be done at a sufficiently fine resolution to ensure that no pixel has two contour lines passing through it, as this can cause significant errors. Linear interpolators then look to these contour lines to derive values for pixels that lie between them. For example, Idrisi's *INTERCON* linear interpolator works by projecting four straight lines (top–bottom, left–right, and two intersecting diagonals) through the pixel to be interpolated until each line intersects with a contour line. The slopes of each of the four lines are established by calculating the change in attribute value divided by the length of the line. The line with the maximum slope is chosen and the interpolated value estimated by its position on this line, as defined by Eq. 6.4. Without going into detail, this interpolator can produce some significant errors or 'artefacts' in the surface model depending on the configuration of the original contour lines. Filtering the DEM will smooth it, but will not completely remove the errors (Eastman 2001, pp. 120–121). For this reason, *simple* linear interpolation of contour data is not advisable; in most circumstances the alternatives discussed next will produce better results.

A generally reliable linear interpolator is the 'flood-fill' method, as included in the GRASS GIS package 'r.surf.contour'. In this method, for each cell in the input map that is not a contour line cell, a 'flood fill' – an even outward expansion in all directions – is generated from that spot until the fill comes to two unique values. The flood fill is not allowed to cross over the rasterised contour lines, thus ensuring

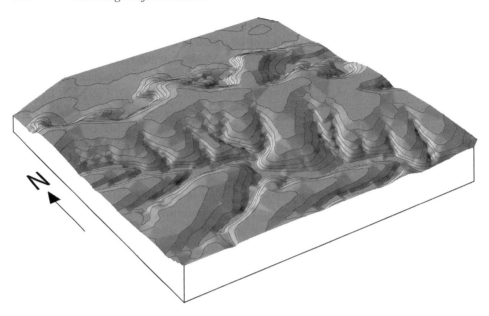

Fig. 6.11 Isometric view of a hillshaded DEM generated using *TOPOGRID* in ArcInfo 7.2. Hillshade generated with *HILLSHADE* using an azimuth of 315° and an altitude of 60°. Tiger striping is still present on south-facing slopes, although less pronounced than in DEM produced using IDW in Fig. 6.7. Original contours have been overlaid for reference. Source: Kythera Island Project.

that an uphill and downhill contour value will be the two values chosen. Unlike *INTERCON*, which uses a simple linear interpolation, r.surf.contour uses the linear inverse distance weighted average to derive the new attribute:

$$z = \frac{\left(d_u^{-1} \times z_u\right) + \left(d_d^{-1} \times z_d\right)}{\left(d_u^{-1} + d_d^{-1}\right)} \tag{6.9}$$

where z is the interpolated value, d_u is the distance to nearest upslope contour, d_d is the downslope distance to the nearest contour, and z_u and z_d are the two bounding contour values (Wood 1996, Section 3.2.1). This results in a more accurate surface and r.surf.contour is a justifiably popular approach to building altitude matrices from contour data.

Topogrid

A well-established and robust method of creating DEMs from contour data is ArcInfo's *TOPOGRID* algorithm, which was designed to produce hydrologically correct elevation surfaces (Hutchinson 1989; Hutchinson and Dowling 1991). It will build a surface from contour data alone but to work optimally it requires additional datasets like spot heights, the locations of rivers, lake polygons, stream channels and ridge lines. Elevation data are initially used to construct a stream network that is then used to ensure the hydrogeomorphic properties of the DEM. As it is a propriety algorithm, the interpolation algorithm is not fully documented, although it uses a form of thin-plate splines, with a roughness weighting to allow for abrupt changes in topography (ESRI 1999). Using it with contour data alone significantly reduces the accuracy of the model for hydrological applications, but usually produces a DEM that is nevertheless acceptable for other purposes. The derived slope map does exhibit some plateaus (Fig. 6.11), although it is often smoother than simple point-based interpolation (e.g. Fig. 6.7).

6.7 Conclusion

Surface models are an important analytical tool, although the process of transforming a set of discrete observations to a continuous distribution is rarely straightforward. Some of the methods reviewed in this chapter, such as trend surface analysis, may provide a useful picture of general patterning, but rarely provide a complete picture of spatial processes and need to be carefully interpreted. Although IDW and splines are good all-purpose interpolators for evenly spread data points, the results need careful examination to establish that they accurately represent the phenomenon in question. Other interpolators, such as kriging, require proper consideration of geostatistics before creating the model. Digital elevation models, in particular, form a crucial dataset for a variety of spatial models and analyses, so it is essential that the interpolation is as appropriate and error free as possible. When attempting to create a DEM from contours, special attention is needed to deal with some of the problems inherent in this form of representation. Many GIS packages offer several types of interpolation, including kriging, with push-button simplicity. However, verifying the accuracy of the original data, selecting a method appropriate for that data and the desired output, and then assessing the interpolated surface is time wisely spent.

7

Exploratory data analysis

7.1 Introduction

Selecting and classifying geospatial data on the basis of their location and attributes starts the process of data exploration, pattern recognition and the interpretation of spatial data. The first part of this chapter examines queries as part of the analytical process in GIS. A query is a formal request for a subset of data based on one or more selection criteria and forms a core function of GIS. The second part of this chapter then considers the subject of classification, which refers to the grouping or placing of data into categories on the basis of shared qualitative or quantitative characteristics. This chapter also discusses methods for the classification of multispectral satellite image data, which is an important process in the interpretation of remotely sensed imagery.

7.2 The query

There are three types of query performed in GIS: (i) *phenomenal* or attribute queries, which question the related non-spatial data tables of spatial objects (e.g. 'select all sites that have obsidian artefacts'); (ii) *topological* queries, which question the geometric configuration of an object or relationship between objects (e.g. 'select all sites within Smith County'); (iii) *distance* queries, which ask something about the spatial location of objects (e.g. 'select all sites within 100 km of an obsidian source').

In Chapter 4 the concept of the relational model was introduced for managing both attribute and spatial datasets. This is the most commonly encountered data structure in GIS. Its associated retrieval language, SQL, can be used as the 'engine' to find subsets of data on the basis of defined selection criteria. As powerful as SQL is, however, it was not designed to handle spatial datasets. Consequently, most GIS programs separate the querying of spatial (i.e. map) data from the querying of attribute data. SQL is more frequently used for the latter, which is termed a phenomenal query. Spatial queries are often evoked using special tools and query engines provided by the GIS software. This is not exclusively the case, however, and a version of SQL called *Spatial SQL* has been defined to enable map data to be queried using a procedure similar to that used for attribute data (Egenhofer 1991, 1994; Open GIS Consortium 1999). Database developers such as Oracle and PostgreSQL have also added basic spatial query extensions to their relational systems (respectively called Oracle Spatial and PostGIS).

7.2.1 *SQL*

SQL is a basic tool for querying relational databases. Every major commercial DBM that uses the relational model understands and accepts SQL statements, although many desktop products (such as Microsoft Access) also use graphical interfaces for query construction. Most GIS systems such as Idrisi, GRASS and ArcGIS are able to process SQL statements (or pass them to an external relational database), and many also offer a graphical interface (e.g. ArcGIS's Query Builder) to help construct attribute queries. The SQL language is relatively easy to understand and the basics are straightforward to learn. It is, however, a large and complex topic and we are only able to provide examples of the more common types of query.

Clauses and operators
The 'select' clause SQL uses a simple structure for selecting a set of records from one or more tables of data. The most powerful SQL component is the *select* clause, which retrieves one or more fields (variables) from a table of data specified using a *from* clause. For example, the SQL statement to retrieve a list of 'site_id' numbers from the sites table defined in Table 4.2 is:

```
SELECT sites.site-id FROM sites;
```

Note that in this and the following examples, SQL commands are always given in capital letters and the clauses in lower case. Clauses must be followed by the name of the table and, if specified, columns are separated from the table name by a full stop.

The 'where' clause Introducing conditions to specify what data we are interested in requires use of a *where* clause to restrict the selection set to records that meet the specified criteria. A *where* clause needs to invoke a *conditional operator* to define the conditions for selection in a query statement. The four mathematical operators, GREATER THAN ($>$), LESS THAN ($<$), EQUAL TO ($=$) and NOT EQUAL TO ($<>$), are designed for queries of quantitative attribute data. For example, the SQL statement for selecting all sites less than a hectare in size is given by:

```
SELECT sites.site-id FROM sites WHERE sites.area < 10000;
```

This statement would return a list of 'site_id' numbers only for those sites that were smaller than 10 000 m^2. It is also possible to use the equality and inequality operators to extract qualitative data, for example, 'date EQUAL TO ($=$) Bronze Age'. The LESS THAN and GREATER THAN functions do not apply to qualitative data and their use in these cases will return an error.

Both quantitative and qualitative data may also be selected using *logical operators* that also follow a *where* clause (Table 7.1). For example, the following statement could be used to retrieve all sites between 1 and 2 hectares (inclusive):

```
SELECT sites.site-id FROM sites WHERE sites.area
BETWEEN 9999 AND 20001;
```

Table 7.1 *SQL logical operators*

Logical operator	Description
BETWEEN *n* AND *m*	Finds all values between values *n* and *m*
IN *n*	Find the matching values of *n*
LIKE {%, _}	Find value using wildcard '%' (multiple characters) or '_' (single characters)
EXISTS	Searches a table for a row that meets a specified criterion
UNIQUE	Searches rows to find duplicate values
ALL	Compares a value against all values in another set
ANY	Compares a value against any value in another set
IS NULL	Finds missing values (not '0')

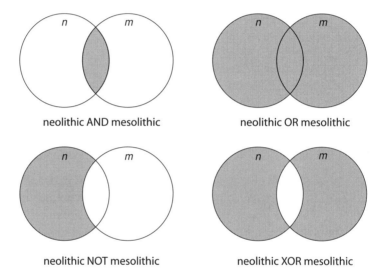

Fig. 7.1 The Boolean operators. The shaded component represents the selection set.

The LIKE operator may also have a '%' added to act as a multicharacter 'wild card' (i.e. LIKE '%lithic' would return 'palaeolithic', 'neolithic' and 'mesolithic').

Boolean operators Another class of operators use *Boolean logic* to define a selection set through the actions of *union, intersection, difference* and *exclusion*. Queries use *Boolean algebra*, which consists of four logical operators: AND (intersection), OR (union), NOT (difference) and XOR (exclusion) to define sets of data. The function of the operators can be explained by reference to a sample dataset of archaeological sites, some of which are Mesolithic, some of which are Neolithic, and some of which contain both periods. It is possible to define new sets of data on the basis of attribute states defined by the Boolean operators. Figure 7.1 shows the results of the

Table 7.2 *Example of the results of a grouping and aggregate SQL statement*

site_id	Number of rim sherds
1001	3
1002	4
1004	2
1006	1
1007	2
1009	1

four algebraic expressions where the shaded components of the circles represents the selection set. Boolean logic can also be used in spatial queries in a similar fashion: 'sites <1 km from a river OR <500 m from a lake'.

Relational queries
The greatest advantage of the relational model is that sets of data can be retrieved from across two or more tables (relations) by specifying the primary and foreign keys. We can, for example, query the relations in Table 4.2 to obtain a list of site_id numbers that contain rim sherds (as recorded in the pottery table) by using what is called an *inner-join* expression to define the link between the relations 'sites' and 'pottery'. Inner joins follow a *where* clause and are specified with an equals sign, as in the following example:

```
SELECT sites.site-id FROM sites, pottery
WHERE sites.site-id = pottery.site-id
AND pottery.type = rim;
```

This would list all the site ids for the selection-specific criteria in the order they occur in the tables, so that a site that contained six rim sherds would be listed six times. This isn't the most practical way of viewing the results of the query, so SQL has two grouping clauses (*orderby*, *groupby*) and five aggregate functions (*count*, *sum*, *average*, *min* and *max*) for summarising data. We could improve the former query by using the optional clauses of *groupby* and *count* to provide output with a new field giving us the number of times that site occurs (which is effectively giving us the number of rims discovered at each site).

```
SELECT sites.site-id
COUNT pottery.site-id AS 'number of rim sherds'
FROM sites, surveyors WHERE sites.site-id = pottery.site-id
AND pottery.sherd`class = rim
GROUPBY sites.site-id;
```

The output from this query is shown in Table 7.2.

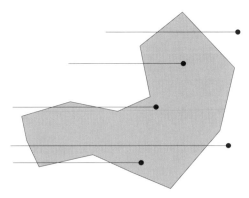

Fig. 7.2 The point-in-polygon problem. A spatial query asking whether any point is inside or outside a polygon is solved by extending a line in a single direction from the point.

7.2.2 *Spatial queries*
Spatial queries are queries that require examination of the spatial properties of the objects to provide the selection set. They can be divided into two types: topological and distance (buffering) queries.

Topological queries
Topological queries pose questions about the geometrical relationship between two or more objects. Imagine, for example, two map layers where points represent 'archaeological sites' and 'states' are represented by polygons. The question 'select all archaeological sites in Maine' is thus a topological query as it depends on establishing whether a point lies within the boundaries of a polygon. The process of retrieving this data is what is called a *point-in-polygon* operation (Haines 1994; Worboys 1995, pp. 215–218). Other related types of topological questions are termed *line-in-polygon* operations and *polygon-overlay* queries. It is worth examining these in more detail, as they provide considerable insight into both the abilities and mechanics of spatial queries.

Point-in-polygon The *point-in-polygon* test is the most straightforward of the topological queries and is sometimes referred to as a *containment query*. The most common strategy to determine whether a point is inside a polygon uses an algorithm that counts the number of times a hypothetical line, extended infinitely in a single direction, intersects the polygon boundary (Haines 1994). If it intersects an odd number of times, the point is inside the polygon, if an even number of times, then the point is outside the polygon (Fig. 7.2). Manber (1989) provides a point-in-polygon algorithm based on this theorem. To minimise the time needed to conduct point-in-polygon searches, a bounding rectangle is usually initially defined to reduce the set of points that need to be tested (Jones 1997, pp. 189–190).

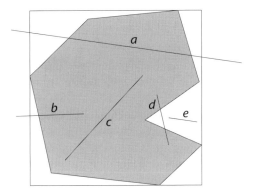

Fig. 7.3 The line-in-polygon problem.

Containment queries on raster datasets are more trivial. Assuming that polygon features are represented by a pixel value unique to that polygon, any pixel sharing that value lies within the polygon (Foley *et al.* 1990).

Point-in-polygon operations are used to answer queries similar to:

- What proportion of the Bronze Age barrows in Wiltshire is located on chalkland?
- Select all artefacts that come from building N in settlement S.
- How many sites were found in the last survey zone?
- Are there any Late Iroquoian villages in Simcoe County?

Line-in-polygon A more computationally demanding test is needed to determine the relationship between a line and a polygon. The first stage of a *line-in-polygon* test is to define the minimum rectangular boundary of the polygon and then determine whether this intersects or contains the line in question (Fig. 7.3). Lines that potentially intersect the polygon will be partially contained by the polygon, as with lines a, b and d. This does not, however, take into account those lines that are entirely contained by the polygon, such as c. This possibility is accounted for by performing a point-in-polygon test for the end nodes of the line. It is possible, however, for both nodes to be outside the polygon, yet the line still passes through it, as with a. Furthermore, in the case of the concave sides of polygons, both nodes may be within the polygon but the line can still have an external segment, as with line d.

Various solutions have been devised to solve this problem, some of which are outlined in Foley *et al.* (1990). In a topologically aware GIS environment, nodes placed at the intersections of lines and polygons enable calculation of exactly how much of each line falls within the polygon. Questions that require a line-in-polygon test will be similar to:

- Which counties does Offa's Dyke pass through?
- How many kilometres of Roman road are found in Surrey?
- How many public footpaths are there in the Avebury World Heritage Site area?

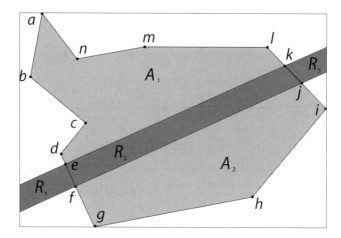

Fig. 7.4 Polygon overlay.

Polygon overlay A similarly complex problem occurs when the spatial properties of two overlapping polygons are investigated. Imagine, for example, that it is necessary to determine the area of overlap of polygon *A*, which defines an archaeologically sensitive area, by polygon *R*, which represents a proposed highway extension (Fig. 7.4).

The computational process is similar to the line-in-polygon problem in that it involves using nodes at each point of intersection (nodes e, f, k, j in Fig. 7.4). There are several ways that this can be managed by the GIS software, but typically it depends on examining topological relationships. For example, the area of the polygon, R_2, defined by the vertices e, f, k, j can be established by standard geometric principles, as defined in Chapter 2. More sophisticated algorithms are needed when polygons have internal 'islands', or have two or more areas of overlap because of a convexity in the underlying polygon. For that reason topological databases are not solely limited to arc–node structures but also record relationships such as 'contains' or 'borders left', to facilitate all possible configurations and morphologies of polygons. Polygon overlays are used to answer queries similar to:

- What proportion of the survey area is under cultivation and has been field walked?
- How many hectares of the proposed new urban zoning falls in archaeologically sensitive areas?
- What is the amount of arable land that lies within a 5-km radius of the site?

Worboys (1995, pp. 218–222) provides further information on the implementation of topological operations in a GIS.

Distance (buffering) queries
The second type of spatial query, a buffering query, involves the selection of a subset of a dataset based on its distance to a defined point, line or polygon feature. For example, the result of a buffer zone of distance n around a point will be a circle of

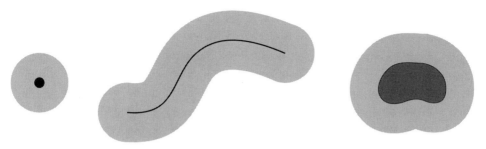

Fig. 7.5 The effects of buffering a point, line and polygon feature by the equivalent number of units.

radius *n*. If a line feature is buffered, the result will be a linear polygon with rounded ends. A buffered polygon will produce an enlarged version of itself (Fig. 7.5).

Determining whether any given point, line or polygon falls within the buffer zone is then a matter of determining its topological relationship with the polygon defined by the buffer, as in the manner described for topological queries. Buffering operations are necessary to answer questions like:

- What proportion of sites fall within 1 km of the coast?
- What is the change in density of sherds moving away from the centre of site *k* in 100-m intervals?
- What is the difference in the average amount of high-grade arable land falling within 5 km of sites of type A versus sites of type B?
- What proportion of all scrapers are found within 2 m of hearth features?

7.2.3 *Using attribute and spatial queries: an example from Shetland*
Now that we have introduced basic query logic and the sorts of attribute and spatial queries that can be answered by a GIS, we provide some examples that demonstrate their application to archaeological questions. In doing so, we will demonstrate how the combination of attribute and spatial queries often constitute the first steps of exploratory data analysis (EDA). We will use a simple dataset from Neolithic west Shetland in Scotland that consists of the locations of archaeological sites (coded as either chambered cairns or stone houses), elevation and land capability (Fig. 7.6). These data were obtained from Müller (1988).

Attribute queries
We can begin to investigate the relationship between the types of site size and their distribution patterns by using SQL with a combination of mathematical and logical operators. We could, for example, begin by dividing the data into different sets by defining a query to find sites defined as 'chambered cairns'. The SQL statement for this is:

```
SELECT site.site-type FROM sites
WHERE site-type = 'chambered cairn';
```

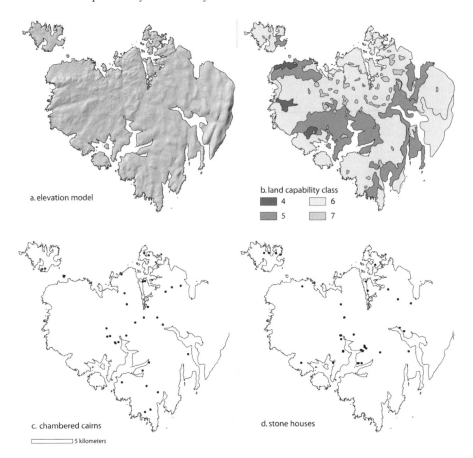

Fig. 7.6 West Shetland study area elevation (as shaded relief), land-use capability and the distribution of Neolithic chambered burial cairns and stone houses (Müller 1988). Land capability represents major divisions only (4 = limited value for crop production; 5 = grassland, grazing, possible crop production; 6 = land suitable only for rough grazing; 7 = unsuited to agriculture; Bibby *et al.* 1991). Total size of study area is 2587.5 hectares. Elevation and coastline © Crown Copyright, all rights reserved, licence no. 100021184. Land capability maps © The Macaulay Land Use Research Institute 2004, all rights reserved.

This simple query begins the process of data exploration and allows us to find structure in the data. In this particular example, we can start to see evidence of spatial clustering and different distribution patterns for chambered cairns and stone houses (Fig. 7.6c, d). Using this information we can begin to unpack the locational differences between the two monument classes and explore the factors that may have conditioned their placement in the landscape.

Spatial queries
The limited set of data that we are using in the previous and following example is not sufficient to build a comprehensive understanding of the reasons underlying

Table 7.3 *Observed number of cairns and houses in each land-use category*

Land class	Cairns		Houses	
	n	(%)	n	(%)
4	0	0.0	0	0.0
5	13	38.2	28	58.3
6	21	61.8	20	41.7
7	0	0.0	0	0.0
Total	34	100.0	48	100.0

Table 7.4 *Contribution of each land class to the study area*

Land-class code	Hectares	%
4	459.6	1.8
5	6 766.2	26.1
6	17 741.9	68.6
7	914.5	3.5
Total	25 882.2	100

the placement of these monuments in west Shetland. However, simply to illustrate further the initial stages of an exploratory analysis, a useful next step is to define the spatial relationships of the different classes of site with the land-use map. This is a containment query requiring a point-in-polygon operation that will establish which points lie within each polygon class. The precise mechanics of how this is performed depends on the GIS program (in ArcGIS it is carried out using the 'select by' query function), but the outcome of the query is shown in Table 7.3. This shows us that most of the burial cairns are situated in land capability class 6 (rough grazing), whereas most of the stone houses are land capability class 5 (grassland with some agricultural potential). However, there is a danger in inferring that each type of site is preferentially located in a particular zone. This can only be established by determining what proportion each land class contributes to the total study area and testing to see whether the distribution is significantly different from that expected by chance alone.

Determining the specific proportion each of the four land-use categories contributes to the study area is another spatial query. In this instance, all the polygons of a particular class are selected and the total area of the selection set is calculated (Table 7.4). Tables 7.3 and 7.4 provide us with all the information we need to determine whether burial cairns and stone houses are differentially distributed according to different classes of land in west Shetland. The next section describes how to substantiate these observations using a χ^2-test.

Table 7.5 *Summary statistics of elevation values (m) for cairns and houses*

Statistic	Cairns[a]	Houses[b]
average elevation	48.3	21.4
standard deviation	24.3	12.6
median elevation	45	20
minimum elevation	5	2
maximum elevation	106	49

[a] $n = 33$.
[b] $n = 48$.

As a further example of a spatial query, we have compared the elevation of the two classes of archaeological sites. The precise way this is performed in a GIS again depends on the software, but the algorithm will be relatively trivial: as elevation data are stored in a raster grid and the sites are stored as points, so finding the elevation for each site is simply a matter of correlating a site's x, y-location with its corresponding pixel on the raster map and extracting the pixel's value. Table 7.5 shows the summary statistics for the elevation values of burial cairns and stone houses in our study area.

The results suggest that cairns are generally situated at higher elevations than houses. However, a further statistical test – for example, a Kolmogorov–Smirnov test (see below) – would need to be undertaken to substantiate this observation.

7.3 Statistical methods

Statistics play an important role in GIS-led research because they are used to explore, clarify and ascertain the significance of relationships in spatial and attribute datasets. There is a large variety of statistical techniques and five of the most common are described below. The first three (the chi-squared, Wilcoxon and Kolmogorov–Smirnov tests) are referred to as *non-parametric* tests because they do not rely on an estimate of parameters of the distribution of the variable of interest in the population. They are therefore appropriate tests for small samples, especially when little is known about the parameters of the parent population, or when the parent population cannot be safely assumed to be normally distributed (i.e. as in Fig. 7.9, see p. 131). As the name suggests, *parametric* statistics require an understanding of the shape of the population. The most common parametric test, the Student's t-test, depends on the sample being normally distributed.

Statistical testing is dependent upon a number of concepts and terms, the most basic of which are defined in Table 7.6. Shennan (1988) and Baxter (1994) are good starting points for readers requiring more details than we are able to provide here.

Table 7.6 *Basic statistical terms and concepts*

Term	Definition
Population	In statistical terms, a population is any set of phenomena with one or more shared attributes. 'Iroquoian longhouses', 'palaeolithic handaxes' and 'Folsom sites' are all populations
Sample	A sample is a subset of a population. 'Seneca longhouses', 'British palaeolithic handaxes' and 'Folsom sites in New Mexico' are all samples of the populations defined above
Null hypothesis	The null hypothesis usually defines a state of non-significance – in other words, that there is no difference between the two samples being tested and that they are therefore most probably drawn from the same population
Alternate hypothesis	The alternate hypothesis usually states that the samples are most probably drawn from different populations
Significance level	The level of probability, or 'critical value', at which the null hypothesis should be rejected. Convention is that the probability (p) is set to 0.05 or less, meaning that there is only a 5% chance of making a Type I error
Type 1 and 2 errors	A Type 1 error occurs when a null hypothesis has been incorrectly rejected. A Type 2 error occurs when a null hypothesis has been incorrectly accepted
Scale of measurement	Data can be measured at nominal, ordinal, ratio or interval scales of measurement. These categories are defined in Table 3.2

7.3.1 *Non-parametric tests of significance*

The chi-squared test

The chi-squared test is an excellent starting point for situations when it is necessary to test the significance of observations made at nominal scales of measurement. It is an extremely versatile test that has a wide range of applications both in GIS and more broadly in archaeology and the social sciences. Examples of situations where a chi-squared test might be appropriate would be when comparing the number of sites found on different types of soil or geology, testing the correlation between different types of artefact found in different areas of an archaeological site, or assessing the relationship between number of surface artefacts collected in different types of settings.

The chi-squared test begins with the construction of a *contingency table*, where the count (not percentages) of observations against data categories are recorded. For example, earlier in this chapter we established the number of different types of Neolithic site found on different types of land in west Shetland, reproduced in Table 7.7. These constitute our *observed* values. Our initial hypothesis is simply that there is a significant difference between the numbers of the two different types of monument found in the different land classes. The null hypothesis can therefore be stated as 'there is no difference between the observed numbers of the different

Table 7.7 *Observed number of cairns and houses on each land class*

Land class	Cairns	Houses	Total
4	0	0	0
5	13	28	41
6	21	20	41
7	0	0	0
Total	34	48	82

Table 7.8 *Expected number of cairns and houses on each land class*

Land class	Cairns	Houses	Total
4	0	0	0
5	17	24	41
6	17	24	41
7	0	0	0
Total	34	48	82

monument types on the different land classes'. The level of significance at which we will reject the null hypothesis is set at 0.05.

In order to determine whether there is any relationship between the numbers of different sites found on the two different land categories, a table of *expected* values for each category is needed against which the observed values can be compared. For a two-sample test such as this, expected values are usually calculated by multiplying the row total by the column total and dividing by the total number of observations, as in Table 7.8.

The chi-squared formula is given by:

$$\chi^2 = \sum_{i=1}^{k} \frac{(O_i - E_i)^2}{E_i} \tag{7.1}$$

where χ^2 is the chi-squared value, k is the number of categories and O_i and E_i are the observed and expected number of cases in each category. For every category, the expected value is then subtracted from the observed value and this number is multiplied by itself and then divided by the expected value. Once this has been done for all categories, the sum of these values is the χ^2. Using the data from Tables 7.7 and 7.8, we therefore have the following (Table 7.9).

It is now left to establish whether the χ^2-value of 3.22 is large enough for us to reject the null hypothesis of no correlation. However, as large tables will naturally have larger χ^2-values, a measure called the *degrees of freedom* (v) is used to 'weight'

Table 7.9 $\frac{(O_i - E_i)^2}{E_i}$ *values*

Land class	Cairns	Houses	Total
4	0	0	0
5	0.94	0.67	1.61
6	0.94	0.67	1.61
7	0	0	0
Total	1.88	1.34	3.22

the significance of the χ^2 based on the size of the table. For a two-sample test it is given by:

$$v = (r - 1)(c - 1) \tag{7.2}$$

where v defines the degrees of freedom, r is the number of rows and c is the number of columns. In our example $v = 3$. We can now compare the calculated χ^2-value with the expected value of χ^2 given 1 degree of freedom, at the predetermined significance level of 0.05. More formally, if for v degrees of freedom $\chi^2_{calc} \geqslant \chi^2_{\alpha}$ we will reject the null hypothesis, but if $\chi^2_{calc} < \chi^2_{\alpha}$, then we accept the null hypothesis. In this scenario, $v = 1$ and $\alpha = 0.05$. A statistical table must be consulted that gives the percentage points of the χ^2-distribution, which is provided in Table 7.10. In this case, it can be seen that for 3 degrees of freedom $\chi^2_{0.05} = 7.81$. As $3.22 < 7.81$, we therefore cannot reject the null hypothesis, which means that we must conclude that in this sample there is no significant difference between the observed numbers of cairns and houses in relation to land capability class.

This result may at first seem counter-intuitive, for the data in Table 7.7 appear to show that there are more houses found in land class 5 and more cairns found in land class 6. What the chi-squared test has told us is that, while our observations suggest a relationship, the difference in patterning between houses and cairns is not sufficiently pronounced given the sample size to allow us to make a claim that a difference exists. What constitutes 'reasonably confident', however, is a matter of some debate. As a rule of thumb $p < 0.05$ – a 95 per cent confidence level – is acceptable for most situations, although a more conservative or relaxed level of significance may sometimes be appropriate. Decreasing the significance level to $p < 0.1$ (i.e. 90 per cent confident) would correspondingly increase the chance of incorrectly rejecting the null hypothesis, referred to as a *Type 1 error*.

We could further investigate the relationship between land capability and monument type by comparing our observed distribution with an expected distribution based on the percentage of each land class in the study area. For example, as land class 7 constitutes 3.5 per cent of our study area, we should expect to find 3.5 per cent of all cairns and 3.5 per cent of all houses located in that region (Table 7.11).

Table 7.10 *Critical values of* χ^2 *for v degrees of freedom and critical values* (α) *of 0.10 to 0.0001. Calculated using built-in functions of the statistical program 'R'*

				α		
v	0.10	0.05	0.025	0.01	0.005	0.001
1	2.71	3.84	5.02	6.63	7.88	10.83
2	4.61	5.99	7.38	9.21	10.6	13.82
3	6.25	7.81	9.35	11.34	12.84	16.27
4	7.78	9.49	11.14	13.28	14.86	18.47
5	9.24	11.07	12.83	15.09	16.75	20.51
6	10.64	12.59	14.45	16.81	18.55	22.46
7	9.04	14.07	16.01	18.48	20.28	24.32
8	13.36	15.51	17.53	20.09	21.95	26.12
9	14.68	16.92	19.02	21.67	23.59	27.88
10	15.99	18.31	20.48	23.21	25.19	29.59
11	17.28	19.68	21.92	24.73	26.76	31.26
12	18.55	21.03	23.34	26.22	28.30	32.91
13	19.81	22.36	24.74	27.69	29.82	34.53
14	21.06	23.68	26.12	29.14	31.32	36.12
15	22.31	25.00	27.49	30.58	32.80	37.70
16	23.54	26.30	28.85	32.00	34.27	39.25
17	24.77	27.59	30.19	33.41	35.72	40.79
18	25.99	28.87	31.53	34.81	37.16	42.31
19	27.20	30.14	32.85	36.19	38.58	43.82
20	28.41	31.41	34.17	37.57	40.00	45.31
21	29.62	32.67	35.48	38.93	41.40	46.80
22	30.81	33.92	36.78	40.29	42.80	48.27
23	32.01	35.17	38.08	41.64	44.18	49.73
24	33.20	36.42	39.36	42.98	45.56	51.18
25	34.38	37.65	40.65	44.31	46.93	52.62
26	35.56	38.89	41.92	45.64	48.29	54.05
27	36.74	40.11	43.19	46.96	49.65	55.48
28	37.92	41.34	44.46	48.28	50.99	56.89
29	39.09	42.56	45.72	49.59	52.34	58.30
30	40.27	43.77	46.98	50.89	53.67	59.70

This, however, is investigating a subtly different hypothesis than that suggested previously: not that there is a difference in the observed numbers of cairns or houses in relation to how the other monument type is distributed across the four different land classes, but that there is a difference in the numbers of cairns and houses given the sizes of the different land classes. In this case, a chi-squared test returns a value of 30.7 for 3 degrees of freedom, which is well within the limits for a 99.9 per cent level of confidence. This allows us to state that there is a statistically significant relationship between land capability class and monument distribution. Examination

Table 7.11 *Expected numbers of monuments based on land-class areas. See Table 7.7 for observed values*

Land class[a]	Cairns	Houses	Total
4 (1.8)	0.6	0.9	1.5
5 (26.1)	8.9	12.5	21.4
6 (68.5)	23.3	32.9	56.2
7 (3.5)	1.2	1.7	2.9
Total	34.0	48.0	82.0

[a] Values in parentheses are percentages of the total land-class area.

Table 7.12 $\frac{(O_i - E_i)^2}{E_i}$ *values adjusted for area*

Land class	Cairns	Houses	Total
4	0.6	0.9	1.5
5	1.9	19.1	21.0
6	0.2	5.1	5.3
7	1.2	1.7	2.9
Total	3.9	26.8	30.7

of the contributions to the chi-squared statistic shows that this is mainly caused by the many more houses observed on land class 5 than expected (Table 7.12).

The Wilcoxon (Mann–Whitney) test

The Wilcoxon or Mann–Whitney test is another good and relatively straightforward non-parametric statistical test. Unlike the χ^2, however, it can be used to test for differences between two samples of ordinal or continuous data. The only prerequisites for this test are that the two samples are randomly and independently drawn, that the variable is potentially continuous (i.e. decimal places to the nth place are possible, if not necessarily logical), and that the measures within the two samples have the properties of at least an ordinal scale of measurement, so that it is meaningful to speak of 'greater than', 'less than' and 'equal to' (Lowry 2003, Chapter 11a).

Examples where the Mann–Whitney test may be appropriate include situations where it is necessary to compare the sizes of sites from two study areas, sizes of artefacts from two excavation trenches, or numbers of artefacts recovered in field-walked transects taken across two different sites.

For the purposes of illustration, we use a hypothetical example of artefacts recovered from ten transects walked across two sites, referred to as site *A* and site *B*. The

Table 7.13 *Artefacts recovered from ten transects over sites A and B*

Site A	Site B
23	44
22	32
18	20
15	12
9	10
4	10
2	4
1	2
1	1
1	1
Total 96	136
Mean 9.6	13.6

data are given in Table 7.13, with the transect results ranked from highest to lowest for each site.

The question we wish to answer is whether the data support an argument that the densities of material recovered from sites *A* and *B* are equivalent, assuming that the transects are equal length for both sites and that they are a random sample drawn from the total population of transects that could have been made across each site. The data in Table 7.13 show that on average more artefacts were recovered from the transects in site *B*, and a boxplot of these numbers shows that the range in the number of artefacts collected in the transects from site *B* is also greater than site *A* (Fig. 7.7).

To claim that observed differences are sufficiently pronounced and that the transects are thus samples from two different populations (and therefore that sites *A* and *B* do have different surface densities of artefacts), requires a statistical test.

The null hypothesis is that the samples are drawn from the same population and consequently that there is no significant difference in artefact density between these two sites. As with all statistical tests, a level of significance for rejecting the null hypothesis must be established. Here, we will use 0.05, so that if $p < 0.05$, we will reject the null hypothesis and conclude that the samples are drawn from different populations.

The test begins by re-sorting the sample values into a single ranked group of size $N = n_a + n_b$, where n_a and n_b are the number of observations for sites *A* and *B* (Table 7.14). Each value is then ranked, according to where it sits in the total list. When there is more than one instance of a value (as in this case with values 1, 2, 4 and 10), then each receives the mean of the rankings for that value. For example, value 1 is ranked 1, 2, 3, 4 and 5, so all instances of value 1 receive the ranking of $15/5 = 3$. These ranked values are then returned to each of the samples, as in Table 7.15 (note that the order is reversed).

Table 7.14 *Ranked transect values for sites A and B*

Value	Rank	Site
1	3	A
1	3	A
1	3	A
1	3	B
1	3	B
2	6.5	A
2	6.5	B
4	8.5	A
4	8.5	B
9	10	A
10	11.5	B
10	11.5	B
12	13	B
15	14	A
18	15	A
20	16	B
22	17	A
23	18	A
32	19	B
44	20	B
Total	210.0	
Mean	10.5	

Table 7.15 *Ranked measures for sites A and B*

Site *A*	Site *B*
3	3
3	3
3	6.5
6.5	8.5
8.5	11.5
10	11.5
14	13
15	16
17	19
18	20
Total 98.0	112.0
Mean 9.8	11.2

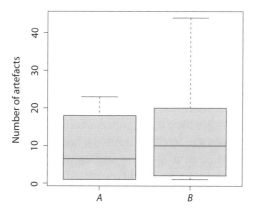

Fig. 7.7 Boxplot of artefacts recovered from transects taken across sites *A* and *B*. The box is bounded by the first and third quartiles and so contains 50 per cent of the observations. The transverse line within the box marks the median value, while the transverse lines at the ends of the 'whiskers' mark the minimum and maximum values.

The Mann–Whitney test calculates a measure U for each sample, which is given by:

$$U_a = n_a n_b + \frac{n_a(n_a + 1)}{2} - W_a \tag{7.3}$$

and

$$U_b = n_a n_b + \frac{n_b(n_b + 1)}{2} - W_b \tag{7.4}$$

where n_a and n_b refer to the number of observations (transects) for site A and B, and W_a and W_b denote the sum of the ranks for sites A and B (as given in Table 7.15). By substituting the values in Eqs. (7.3) and (7.4), then $U_a = 10 \times 10 + (10(10 + 1)/2) - 98 = 57$ and $U_b = 10 \times 10 + (10(10 + 1)/2) - 112 = 43$. If the null hypothesis is true (that site B does not show a different concentration of artefacts than site A), we can expect $U_a \leqslant U_b$. This is in fact not the case, but we need to consult a statistical table that provides values of U for critical values of p to determine whether or not the difference is significant.[1] In this example, n_a and n_b are both equal to 10, and at $p < 0.05$ the upper and lower limits of U are 27 and 73 for a one-tailed test and 23 and 77 for a two-tailed test. As our alternate hypothesis proposes that sites A and B are different we use a two-tailed test (a one-tailed test should be used if a hypothesis of difference in one direction is proposed). Our lower and upper estimates of U, namely 43 and 57, fall within the wider boundaries of the two-tailed test and we therefore cannot reject null hypothesis: there is no statistical difference in artefact density between the two sites.

The Kolmogorov–Smirnov test

Another useful non-parametric method is the Kolmogorov–Smirnov test (or K–S test). Like the Mann–Whitney test, it can be used on two independent observations measured at the ordinal scale or above and it is not dependent on the observations being normally distributed. It is useful for a broad range of problems, particularly when the restrictive conditions of a parametric test cannot be met. To provide an example, we refer to Campbell's (2000) study of archaeological landscapes on the Pacific island of Rarotonga, where he has recorded the size of agricultural terraces (termed *repotaro*). Terraces are used by members of corporate groups called *matakeinanga*, each of which resides in a territory termed a *tapere* (Campbell 2000, pp. 63–64). To demonstrate the value of a K–S test, differences in *repotaro* sizes between the two corporate group territories are investigated. The data are taken from Campbell 2000, Appendix 1.

A graphical comparison of *repotaro* sizes (in square metres) for two *tapere*, Takuvaine and Tupapa, is given in Fig. 7.8 and shows that the 14 *repotaro* from

---

[1] An online calculator for critical values of U can be accessed at
http://faculty.vassar.edu/lowry/ch11a.html. See Lowry (2003) for details.

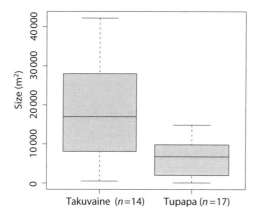

Fig. 7.8 Boxplot of *repotaro* sizes for the Takuvaine and Tupapa Tapere.

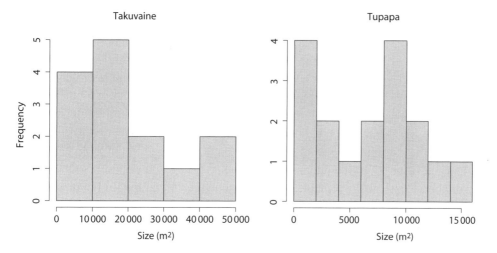

Fig. 7.9 Frequency distributions of *repotaro* sizes for the Takuvaine and Tupapa Tapere.

Takuvaine are, on average, larger than the 17 recorded for Tupapa. Visual assessment of the shape of the distribution of the samples (Fig. 7.9) shows that they are not normally distributed, so a non-parametric method is an appropriate way to investigate differences. The null hypothesis is that the two samples of terraces are drawn from the same population and that there is no significant difference in size between the two groups.

In order to calculate the K–S statistic, the data need to be converted to a cumulative distribution. The K–S test measures the maximum difference in the cumulative distributions of the two categories (referred to as D) and compares this difference against the difference predicted if the samples were drawn from the

Table 7.16 *Critical values of D, Kolmogorov–Smirnov test for two populations (Arsham 2003), where n_1 and n_2 are the two sample sizes*

α^a	Critical value
0.10	$1.22 \times \sqrt{(n_1 + n_2)/(n_1 n_2)}$
0.05	$1.36 \times \sqrt{(n_1 + n_2)/(n_1 n_2)}$
0.025	$1.48 \times \sqrt{(n_1 + n_2)/(n_1 n_2)}$
0.01	$1.63 \times \sqrt{(n_1 + n_2)/(n_1 n_2)}$

[a] α is the significance level.

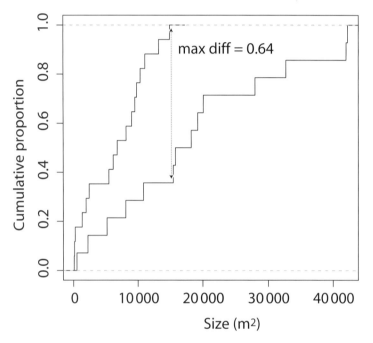

Fig. 7.10 Cumulative proportion distribution of *repotaro* sizes for Takuvaine and Tupapa Tapere. Location of maximum difference marked by dashed line.

same distribution:

$$D = \max|S_1(x) - S_2(x)| \tag{7.5}$$

where D is the K–S statistic, and $S_1(x)$ and $S_2(x)$ are the two cumulative distributions. In this example, a plot of the cumulative distribution curves shows a maximum distance of 0.64, at $\sim$10 500 m^2 (Fig. 7.10). To ascertain whether a value of $D = 0.64$ is significant or not, a table of critical values must be consulted. Consultation of Table 7.16 for $n_1 = 14$ and $n_2 = 17$ for $p < 0.05$ provides a minimum value

Table 7.17 *Mesolithic artefact densities (artefacts per hectare) from coastal and inland survey areas on Islay*

Coastal	2.66 3.75 1.78 0.65 0.43 5.15 0.20 2.07 0.40 0.70 7.26 0.41 0.72 0.53 0.92 3.92 3.26 0.20 0.09 0.53 0.60 0.30 0.04 0.20 0.16 0.23 0.03 0.06 0.03 6.36 0.45 0.44 0.06 0.46 4.44 0.57
Inland	2.09 0.53 1.06 4.60 0.35 1.09 0.53 1.37 14.89 1.17 0.43 0.18 8.64 0.02 0.13 0.20 0.48 0.27 0.31 0.17 0.43 0.25 0.16 0.52 0.08 0.91 0.14 0.10 0.09 0.58 6.38 1.56 0.55 1.42 1.26 1.27 0.61

Source: Woodman (2000b, p. 457).

of 0.36. Our *D* value of 0.64 exceeds this, so we therefore can reject the null hypothesis and conclude that the *repotaro* sizes are not drawn from the same population. In other words, Takuvaine *repotaro* are significantly bigger than those in Tupapa Tapere.

Although this test is easy to perform by hand and critical values of *D* are provided in statistical tables (e.g. Lindley and Scott 1984), many statistical packages also include K–S testing and will calculate *D* and return a number for a given critical value of *p*.

7.3.2 *Parametric tests of significance: Student's t*

Parametric tests depend on knowledge of the characteristics of the distribution of data. The *t*-test is the most common parametric method used to assess the probability that two samples have been drawn from two different populations. In theory, the size of the samples can be as few as ten observations, but an essential prerequisite for performing a *t*-test is that the sample data are normally distributed since the results are meaningless if this condition is not met. Larger samples (e.g. 30+) are more likely to meet the condition of normality (if their parent is also normal) and this can be verified either by visual assessment of a histogram or boxplot or, more robustly, by using a statistical test such as a Kolmogorov–Smirnov test for normality, the Shapiro–Wilks' *W* test or the Lilliefors test. In addition, it is necessary to ascertain whether the variances in the sample scores are roughly equivalent, as there are two forms of the *t*-test depending on whether or not this is the case. Equivalence of variance can be established by an *F*-test. Tests for normality, the *F*-test and the *t*-test itself, are included in major statistical packages, including R.

We have used data from Woodman's study of Mesolithic site location on Islay for a worked example (Woodman 2000b, p. 457). The dataset consists of 36 coastal and 37 inland survey areas, each of which has a value that describes the density of Mesolithic artefacts. These samples can be used to test the hypothesis that there is a difference in artefact density between coastal and inland survey areas as part of a wider study into Mesolithic site location (Table 7.17).

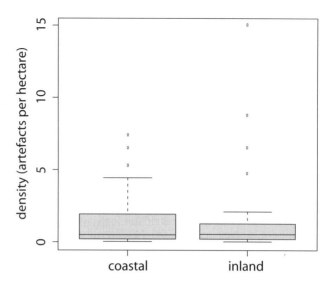

Fig. 7.11 Boxplot of artefact densities for coastal and inland survey areas.

The mean artefact density is 1.39 artefacts per hectare for coastal areas and 1.48 for inland areas, suggesting that the latter zone on average possesses a higher density of artefacts than the former. Boxplots of the two samples, however, show that there is considerable overlap in the sample distributions (Fig. 7.11).

A skewed sample distribution is a common occurrence with archaeological datasets and contravenes the requirements of the Student's t-test. However, rather than use one of the non-parametric tests it is often possible to transform samples and 'normalise' the shape of their distributions, and in so doing, make them suitable for a parametric test. In this example, by taking the natural log of each of the density values, the distribution begins to resemble more closely a normal distribution (Fig. 7.12).

The Shapiro–Wilks test is commonly used to establish that each sample is not statistically different from a normal distribution (in this case returning $p = 0.18$ and $p = 0.74$ for the logged values from the coastal and inland samples, showing that they are not statistically different from a normally distributed sample). An F-test may then be used to establish that the two samples have equivalent variances. In this case the result, $p = 0.55$, indicates that the t-test can be taken assuming this condition.

The t-test itself returns a p-value of 0.91, much higher than the critical value of 0.05 (or less) needed for rejecting the null hypothesis. This indicates that the two samples are not statistically different. Thus, although the coastal sample has a higher mean density than the inland survey sample, the difference is not sufficiently

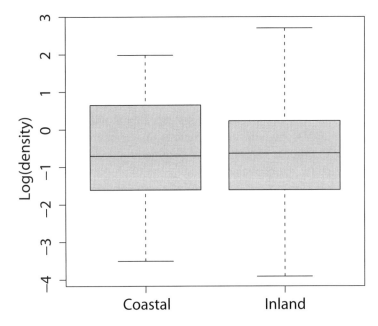

Fig. 7.12 Boxplot of logged artefact densities for coastal and inland survey areas.

large enough to conclude that the density of Mesolithic artefacts for all coastal areas is different from all inland areas of Islay.

Comprehensive statistical packages such as S-Plus, SPSS and R are able to perform the non-parametric and parametric tests described in this section (as well as a range of other more specialised techniques described in the next chapter). At the time of writing, these statistical procedures were also available online from *VassarStats: Web Site for Statistical Computation*[2] (Lowry 2003). Boxes 7.1 and 7.2 provide guidance on the use of R, which is an OpenSource package that integrates with GRASS GIS.

7.4 Data classification

This final section introduces a number of statistical methods of classification useful for visualising patterns within attribute data. As defined in the introduction to this chapter, classification involves the grouping or placement of data into groups. Members of each category should be more similar to each other than they are to non-members on the basis of qualitative or quantitative characteristics. The reasons for classifying spatial data are to simplify an otherwise complex matrix, to discover structure and patterns and to facilitate comparative analysis. There are a wide variety of *classification systems* that, for our purposes, are usefully divided into *qualitative*

---

[2]http://faculty.vassar.edu/lowry/VassarStats.html.

Box 7.1 Using R

R is a versatile and powerful object-orientated statistical programming language that can be used for everything from simple univariate statistical tests to more complex statistical and geostatistical modelling. It can be linked to GRASS GIS so that data and spatial parameters can be read directly into R without the need for separate data entry (see sections on using R within GRASS in Neteler and Mitasova 2002). As with GRASS, R is provided free of charge under the GNU General Public Licence. It can be obtained for a variety of platforms from `http://cran.r-project.org`.

As R is an object-orientated language actions are performed on objects referred to as *named data structures*, which might be a number vector, array, list or matrix. One of the simplest and most useful objects is a list (or *numeric vector*) of data in the form of $x_1, x_2, x_3 \cdots x_n$. To set up a vector called **site-1** consisting of 10 numbers the following R command would be used:

```
> site-1 <- c(64, 23, 42, 2, 23, 9, 42, 2, 11, 6)
```

Alternatively, if the data were in a delineated ASCII file called **site1.txt** the command

```
> site-1 <- read.table("site1.txt")
```

performs a similar function. Mathematical operations can then easily be performed on this object. For example, it is possible to calculate the natural logarithm of the variables in **site-1** and store them in a new vector called **site-1log** using the command

```
> site-1log <- log(site-1)
```

Several operations can be performed on numeric vectors, including operations for basic descriptive statistics and graphical display of the distribution pattern. For example, these three separate commands:

```
> summary(site-1)
> box.plot(site-1)
> hist(site-1)
```

respectively return basic descriptive statistics (i.e. the minimum, first quartile, median, mean, third quartile, maximum of the distribution) and a boxplot of the distribution and histogram of the distribution.

Box 7.2 Univariate statistics in R

Given two lists of numbers, say **site-1** and **site-2**, the statistical tests described in the first part of this chapter are quickly and easily performed. For example, the Wilcoxon test is performed by the command

```
> wilcox.test(site-1, site-2)
```

which in this example returns a result in a format similar to the following, showing that the two samples are most likely drawn from the same population:

```
data: site-1 and site-2
W = 51, p-value = 0.9697
alternative hypothesis: true mu is not equal to 0
```

Other tests are equally easily performed. The Kolmogorov–Smirnov test is called with the command

```
> ks.test(site-1, site-2)
```

and a *t*-test assuming equal variances is called by

```
> t.test(site-1, site-2, var.equal=TRUE)
```

The prerequisites for a *t*-test, namely that both samples are normally distributed, can be determined with the Shapiro–Wilks test:

```
> shapiro.test(site-1)
```

and equivalence of variance can be established using the *F*-test with the following command:

```
> var.test(site-1, site-2, var.equal=TRUE)
```

In all these cases the output takes a form similar to that shown above for the Wilcoxon test, namely some summary information followed by a *p*-value that indicates the degree of confidence that the samples are drawn from two populations.

For more information about R, see Venables and Smith (2003).

---

and *numerical*. Qualitative classifications are those that use a descriptive attribute as the basis for dividing objects into different categories. For example, an artefact typology based on the shape of the pot (e.g. 'open mouth' vs. 'closed mouth'), or type of tool (e.g. 'scraper' vs. 'burin' vs. 'projectile point') are qualitative. Spatial data can also be classified using descriptive terms: archaeological sites might be divided into different periods, or landscape data classified on the basis of environmental and formation processes (e.g. 'loess terrace' vs. 'Holocene alluvial plain' vs. 'palaeochannel' vs. 'gravel island' etc.).

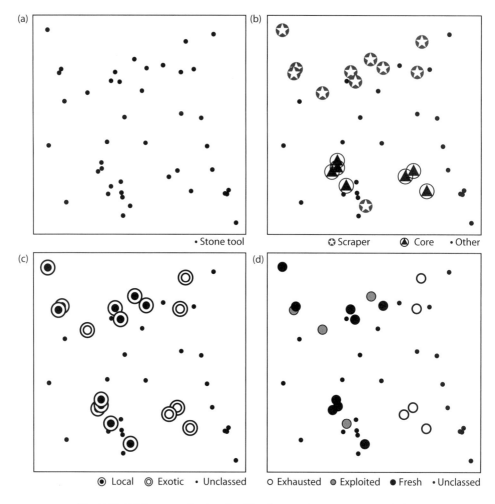

Fig. 7.13 Different qualitative classifications on the same stone-tool dataset: (a) unclassified distribution, (b) scraper vs. core locations, (c) raw material distribution and (d) reduction sequence classification. Some patterning in location of cores and scrapers is evident in (b), but the spatial and attribute patterns would require statistical validation using techniques described in Chapter 8.

7.4.1 *Qualitative classifications*

One consequence of an object possessing several attributes is that several different maps may derive from the same base data depending on which attribute is used to construct the groupings.

Figure 7.13 shows a hypothetical distribution of stone tools across a living surface, where each artefact is represented by a point and is associated with an attribute table that describes what sort of tool it is (e.g. 'scraper', 'core', etc.), its stage in the reduction sequence (e.g. 'early', 'exhausted') and the raw material on which it has been made (e.g. 'local chert', 'exotic chert', etc.). By differentially classifying objects according to these different qualitative variables, it is possible to generate several different maps that permit the visual assessment of spatial organisation of the artefacts. For example, Dibble *et al.* (1997) uses this method to highlight spatial patterning of stone tools to assess behavioural versus post-depositional effects at the French Acheulian site of Cagny-l'Epinette.

Qualitative classes may also form the basis for qualitative modelling following their *reclassification* into rank-order categories (e.g. Fig. 7.14). Burrough and McDonnell (1998, pp. 171–172) describe a simple example where land quality, LQ, for small-holder crop production may be modelled as a function of nutrient supply, oxygen supply, water supply and erosion susceptibility. In this example, rank-order classifications are derived from polygon maps of soil depth (shallow, moderate, deep), soil series (five classes) and slope (flat, moderate, steep). Erosion susceptibility is constructed by combining soil and slope data (e.g. 'if soil series is S_2 and slope class is flat, then erosion susceptibility $= 1$'). Assuming that high values mean less suitable, then the overall suitability of land for crop production can be determined by the highest value in the manner suggested by Burrough and McDonnell (1998, p. 172):

$$\text{Suitability} = \max(\text{LQ}_{\text{water}}, \text{LQ}_{\text{oxygen}}, \text{LQ}_{\text{nutrients}}, \text{LQ}_{\text{erosion}})$$

This is obviously a great simplification of the potential factors involved in the relative suitability of land for crop production, but it does nevertheless serve as a useful illustration of how qualitative data classes may be converted into rank-order numeric variables and subsequently combined in order to produce new data from the constituent elements of several original datasets.

7.4.2 *Numerical classifications*
The subject of numerical classification has received considerable attention in archaeology, particularly in terms of artefact analysis (e.g. Baxter 1994; Shennan 1988). Our concern here is more specifically with the application of numerical classification as applied to spatial datasets, although numerical classifications can be divided into two types: *univariate* and *multivariate*. Univariate methods are those that deal with only a single variable – for example, the classification of slope values – into discrete categories, whereas multivariate methods deal with the classification of two or more variables – as, for example, commonly encountered with multispectral satellite imagery – into clusters or categories that reflect real structure in the data.

Univariate classifications and statistical generalisation
Univariate classifications may be applied to geospatial data in order to simplify or generalise a dataset, as is the case with choropleth mapping (see Chapter 12). For instance, a sample of several hundred testpits, each of which have a number of artefacts ranging from 0 to 36, might be grouped into four new categories called 'no evidence', 'low intensity', 'medium intensity', 'high intensity'. The strategy

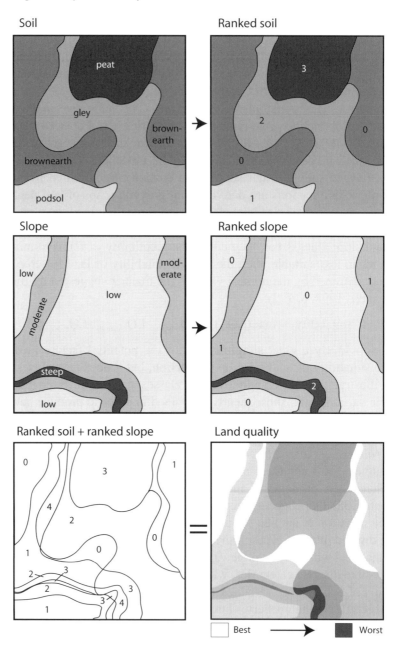

Fig. 7.14 Hypothetical reclassification of qualitative variables to rank-order variables, for the purpose of qualitative prediction of land quality for horticulture. Soil and slope maps have been ranked into numerical categories (0 = most suitable, to 3 = least suitable). These ranked attributes are combined using polygon overlay (if vectors), or with map algebra (if rasters). The result is a new map with five land categories showing modelled land-quality variability. See FAO (1974, 1976) and Rossiter (1996) for guidelines on qualitative predictions of this kind, and Wilson (1999) and Hoobler *et al.* (2003) for applied examples.

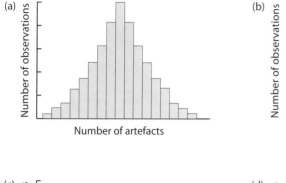
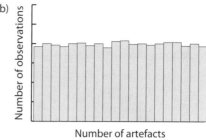
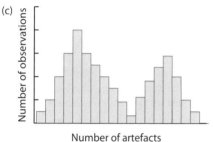
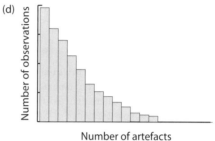

Fig. 7.15 Four idealised distributions: (a) normal, (b) rectangular, (c) bimodal, (d) skewed (to the right).

for both defining the groups and for deciding which testpits should be placed in which group can be done arbitrarily (e.g. perhaps 0 artefacts = 'no evidence', 1–5 = 'low', 6–18 = 'medium', 18–36 = 'high'), but there may then be little correspondence between the data and the categories; if there is only one testpit that contains between 6 and 18 artefacts, for example, the classification would not be representing 'natural' breaks in the datasets. It is therefore essential to have some understanding of the shape of data distribution in order to classify it appropriately. Figure 7.15 shows four idealised examples of distributions, each of which is best classified using one of the following classification methods.

- **Standard deviation and quantile** In situations where the data distribution can be shown to be normal, or close to normal (i.e. similar to the histogram in Fig. 7.15a), then classifications using *standard deviations* or *quantiles* to define data categories will be most useful. Standard deviation methods use the statistical deviation from the mean number of objects per observation, typically in steps of ±0.5 or ±1.0, to construct classes (Fig. 7.16). When applied to choropleth mapping, the effect often serves to illustrate highs and lows, with different colours used for the upper and lower end of the data range (e.g. blues for standard deviations to the left of the mean and reds for standard deviations to the right). Quantile classifications divide the number of observations into equally sized groups, such as *quartiles*, which each contain 25 per cent of the number of observations, or *quintiles* which each contain 20 per cent of the number of observations.

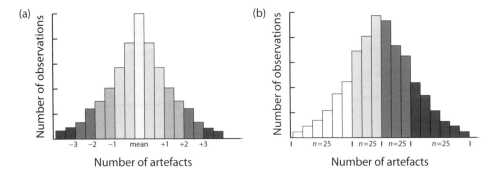

Fig. 7.16 Classification of normally distributed data: (a) by standard deviation, (b) by quartiles (n = number of observations).

- **Equal interval or equal step** Rectangular, or near rectangular, distributions (i.e. where objects have the same number of observations) are rare in archaeology. In cases where such a pattern does exist, categories can be defined with *equal intervals*, such that each category contains the same range of values (e.g. 1–8, 9–16, 16–24, 24–36). This is the simplest form of classification, although it is not a good way to depict data variability if the distribution is not linear. For example, if there are more instances of lower-valued data (e.g. 75 per cent of trenches contained fewer than 8 artefacts), then in the resulting map 75 per cent of the data will reside in a single class and any spatial patterning in the 1–8 artefact range will be masked.
- **Natural break** This is perhaps the most common form of general classification for quantitative data. The classification method attempts to find the most suitable class ranges ('breaks') by testing them against the distribution of the entire dataset so that the resulting class ranges reflect the structure of the distribution. The statistical method most often used for this is called *Jenks Optimal Method*, which attempts to find natural clusters in the data so as to create classes that are internally coherent but distinctive from other classes (Jenks and Caspall 1971; Slocum 1998). The process involves an iterative comparison of class means against a measure of the mean values for the entire dataset in order to maximise what is referred to as a *goodness of variance fit* (GVF). The optimal partition for each subset is the one with the smallest total error (the sum of absolute deviations about the class median or, alternatively, the sum of squared deviations about the class mean). The calculation is straightforward (see Dent 1999, p. 148) and can be carried out by hand. However, as it is an iterative process that involves starting with an arbitrary classification, then redefining classes and re-calculating the GVF in order to find the most 'natural' classification, it is best carried out on a computer. In an idealised situation, such as in Fig. 7.15(c), if the maximum number of artefacts was 36 then the natural-break method would create two classes of 1–21 and 22–36. In other cases, such as with the skewed distribution in Fig. 7.15(d), natural-break methods will often provide suitable categories, although a classification based on an arithmetic or geometric progression may be better (see below). The three major disadvantages of natural-break methods are that they are difficult to replicate, as small changes in data values can change the classification scheme, the bin ranges are difficult to read as they do not lie on intuitive breaks, and outliers can receive undue visual importance as they are given their own category.
- **Equal area** Instead of using the data values as the basis for determining the individual class range, divisions in the data are established so that each class shares an equal

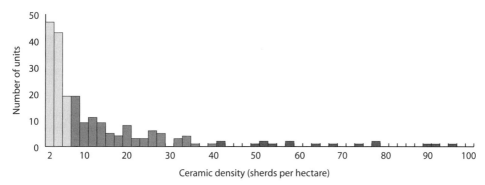

Fig. 7.17 Distribution of sherd density. Nearly 90 per cent of the 456 units have fewer than 100 sherds per hectare. As the maximum value is nearly 10 000 sherds per hectare, only the far left of the distribution curve is shown. Colour coding shows geometric progression classes used for Fig. 7.18(f).

proportion of the map area. In certain applications this may provide a useful alternative to classifications that are based on the data distribution curve itself, because equal-area class breaks can be used to examine how the data are distributed in terms of their spatial area. The major disadvantage is that large polygons may end up in a class by themselves.

• **Geometric intervals** In cases where distributions are skewed, as in Fig. 7.15(d), it may be difficult to obtain a representative classification using the pevious techniques. One alternative is to use a geometric progression to define intervals. The method is suitable for classifying distributions that show very pronounced rates of change, as class ranges increase exponentially in the manner of X^1, X^2, X^3, etc. The formula

$$X^n = \frac{H}{L} \qquad (7.6)$$

can be used to determine the multiplier X, where n is the number of desired classes, H is the highest value and L is the lowest value (Dent 1999, p. 406). Class upper limits are defined as

$$L \times X^1, L \times X^2, L \times X^3, \ldots, L \times X^n \qquad (7.7)$$

For example, Fig. 7.17 shows the skewed distribution curve produced from a dataset of ceramic densities from 256 survey units, where the lowest recorded value is 1 and the highest is 9902. Five classes defined using geometric progression can therefore be constructed by substituting the appropriate values in (7.6):

$$X^5 = \frac{9902}{1}$$

$$X = \sqrt[5]{9902} = 6.3$$

From (7.7), class upper limits are therefore established as: $1 \times 6.3^1, 1 \times 6.3^2, 1 \times 6.3^3, 1 \times 6.3^4, 1 \times 6.3^5 = 6.3, 39.7, 250.0, 1575.3, 9924.4$.

In the same way that reclassifying and regrouping data using qualitative attributes can result in significantly different maps, different numerical methods applied to the same dataset can produce very different impressions of the data. Figure 7.18

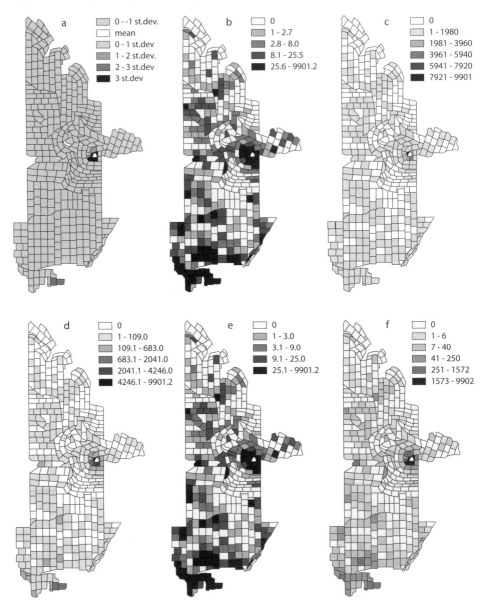

Fig. 7.18 Six possible numerical classifications of the same dataset; (a) standard deviation, (b) quintile, (c) equal interval, (d) natural break, (e) equal area, (f) geometric progression. Source: Kythera Island Project. Used with permission.

shows how the six different methods described create six very different maps, even though the base data are identical. As the data show significant skew (Fig. 7.17), classifications based on standard deviation (a) and equal interval (c) obscure spatial patterning. Quintile (b) and equal-area (e) classification methods produce similar results and both lack detail in the upper ranges because of the large class range of 25–9901; this is a common problem with skewed distributions, as the fewer large numbers get lumped together in a single class. The natural-break classification (d) is an improvement, but while the category 1–109 is 'natural', reference to Fig. 7.17 shows that about 90 per cent of the data fall within this group and therefore spatial patterning within this range might be masked. The geometric-interval classification (f), based on Eqs. (7.6) and (7.7), corrects this by mimicking the actual distribution curve; the lower values are subdivided, which permits a better understanding of the spatial properties of the lower (majority) data values.

Multivariate classifications

Classifications that aim to discover and define grouping in a set of data using two or more variables are referred to as multivariate. These methods are best known in archaeology as applied to artefact analysis and several textbooks explain the various techniques that can be used to both discover, describe and test patterning statistically within multivariate datasets (e.g. Shennan 1988; Baxter 1994; see also Aldenderfer 1998 for a recent review of quantitative approaches in archaeology). Multivariate classification is an important component of spatial data analysis in at least two instances: for finding clusters within a set of spatial objects using two or more of their attributes and for the determination of classes in multispectral image data. The former can be useful when attempting to discover grouping in objects on the basis of attributes derived from GIS analysis. For example, several quantitative variables (e.g. similar to those described in Table 3.3; elevation, slope, aspect, distance to water, visibility, etc.) may have been collected for a distribution of archaeological sites across a study region. An exploratory multivariate analysis could then determine whether sites are clustered in groups defined by their measured characteristics. Multivariate analyses such as *factor analysis* or *principal components analysis* will permit the visual assessment of clustering, which can then be confirmed and refined by using a *k-means* or *discriminant function analysis*. For datasets that consist of both quantitative and qualitative data, a coefficient matrix, such as a *Jaccard coefficient*, may be used as the basis for techniques such as *principal components analysis* or *hierarchical cluster analysis*. Analysis of this sort might, for example, reveal two distinct groups of sites, one of which is situated on higher elevations with south-facing slopes and good visibility, while a second group is found at lower elevations on low slopes and closer to water sources. Readers are referred to the previously cited texts for descriptions on how these statistical techniques are used.

Methods related to *predictive modelling*, a technique that seeks to predict the probability of encountering a phenomenon in unsampled areas based on knowledge gained from sampled areas, may provide insight into a suspected pattern. While data patterns might be apparent from visual inspection of a spatial dataset, statistical analysis is useful for confirming patterning and determining the relative contribution of each of the variables. Chapter 8 introduces several statistical techniques, including predictive modelling, for investigating patterns and relationships in spatial datasets.

7.4.3 *Classification of remotely sensed imagery*

In Chapter 5 we reviewed how image data can be used in archaeology. In many cases an image may be useful 'as is' and needs no further modification or analysis before it can be used as a visual reference, or for collection of spatial data. In other cases, particularly with multivariate imagery from satellite sensors, the data require processing and analysis to extract meaningful information. This often involves two separate processes: image enhancement followed by image classification. The manipulation, classification and interpretation of remotely sensed imagery is a discipline in its own right and we cannot possibly do it justice in the context of this book. The following only outlines the basic philosophy underlying remote sensing; readers requiring more comprehensive information are referred to Lillesand and Kiefer (2000), Campbell (2002) or Lillesand *et al.* (2003), for excellent introductions to these techniques.

As we have previously described, a digital image usually consists of one or more separate bands (i.e. raster grids) of data where every pixel within each band is assigned a value of between 0 and 255. Raster-based GIS packages such as Idrisi and GRASS include a range of tools designed specifically for enhancing and classifying image data. Image enhancement involves the manipulation of pixel values to make the dataset easier to classify and interpret. Idrisi, for example, contains a range of analytical modules specifically designed to enhance image data, such as the tool 'STRETCH'. This performs a *contrast stretch* on an image, which is useful if the image's pixel values are clustered in a narrow band within the 0–255 range. It re-scales the range of values to provide a broader range of data categories for cluster analysis, using techniques such as *histogram equalisation* to help improve the contrast between high and low data values. Other forms of image enhancement include the construction of *colour composites* to produce an image similar in appearance to a colour photograph, or *false colour composites* to make certain features, such as leafy vegetation, stand out. For example, by combining the bands 3 (visible red), 2 (visible green) and 1 (visible blue) from a Landsat ETM image, a colour composite is created. A false colour composite designed to emphasise near-infrared (NIR) elements of an image would use bands 4 (NIR), 3 and 2. Vegetative indexes, such as the *Normalised Difference Vegetative Index* (NDVI), which is a ratio of reflectivities measured in the red and near-infrared portions of the electromagnetic spectrum, can be used to provide a measure of the relative amounts of green vegetation within an image. Eastman (2001, pp. 27–34) provides a good overview of these and other digital image processing techniques and describes their implementation using Idrisi.

Landscape   Digital image   Classified map

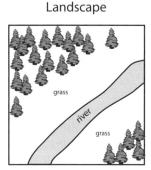

190	182	193	190	192	187	78	170	50	48
187	191	190	179	186	190	176	190	59	52
191	193	185	190	176	182	47	65	68	241
198	192	191	173	180	58	68	190	240	251
181	180	182	58	54	67	248	240	248	240
183	179	61	53	61	245	248	240	237	58
188	57	55	51	240	251	235	61	58	54
56	49	60	242	252	235	60	57	140	176
53	67	243	252	235	60	57	165	176	188
54	234	250	240	53	56	57	188	190	193

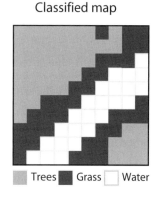

░ Trees ■ Grass ☐ Water

Fig. 7.19 A hypothetical landscape consisting of three distinct ecological zones (left), the pixel values as recorded by a digital sensor (centre) and a possible classification (right). Note that the pixel values express an average for the area they cover and that the classification has focused on distinguishing between the three ecological zones. Alternative classifications might, for example, attempt to find classes within the forest zone reflecting the predominance of different tree types or species.

Following any enhancements and corrections for atmospheric distortion, image classification can then be undertaken in order to discover and define the relationship between pixel values (i.e. recorded electromagnetic radiation) and features on the Earth's surface (Fig. 7.19). Image classification can proceed using either unsupervised or supervised methods.

Unsupervised classification

This involves grouping pixels of similar spectral value into classes without prior knowledge of either class composition or what the classes may represent. This process is also known as *spectral clustering*. In single band images, clusters can be identified by the analysis of a histogram of pixel values. If two bands are being used, their pixel values can be plotted on x, y-axes and clusters defined on the resulting graph. For multispectral images, the process of identifying clustering patterns involves multivariate statistics, such as principal components analysis, as described in the previous section. Most image analysis programs have facilities in which it is possible to specify the number of desired clusters. In other cases the program may automatically define and then group pixels to maximise the variation in the image with little subsequent user input. Alternatively, groups can be manually defined, and pixels allocated using a statistical function. Most simply, each pixel is assigned to its nearest cluster (e.g. Idrisi's 'MINDIST' function). Pixels may also be assigned to classes on the basis of some other statistical relationship with the cluster groups (e.g. whether it falls within a set distance). Assessing whether the classified image makes sense in terms of the landcover it represents involves comparing the resulting classification map with known ground features (Eastman

2001, pp. 30–32). Classes that either do not make sense, or are not useful from an interpretative perspective, can become the focus of additional data collection to create a training sample for a supervised classification. This exercise is referred to as *ground truthing* and is an essential part of unsupervised classification.

Supervised classification

This method often produces better results than unsupervised classification, but it requires some background understanding of the landscape being studied. The process begins with the user defining groups of pixels to act as *training areas*, each of which consists of a sample of pixels that define a known phenomenon. By defining known groups of pixels in this way it is possible to derive the central tendency and dispersion (such as mean and standard deviation) for each cluster defined by the training areas. A *classification algorithm* is then used to classify pixels outside of the training areas into one of these clusters. These range from simple techniques that involve placing a pixel into the class that has the nearest mean pixel value to its own value (e.g. '*maximum likelihood classification*'), to more complex Bayesian methods that depend on specifying the likely proportion each class makes to the image, which can help assign 'difficult' pixels. Some desktop GIS programs support quite complex classification facilities, notably Idrisi and GRASS. However, image classification and interpretation can be a complex process and it is advisable to consult an introductory book on remote sensing and image interpretation for further details on the philosophy underlying this technique. The Idrisi manual (Eastman 2001) offers a very good overview of remote-sensing principles and how they can be implemented in Idrisi. The GRASS online tutorial[3] also discusses image processing and classification procedures in further detail.

7.5 Conclusion

The three types of exploratory data analysis described in this chapter – queries, parametric and non-parametric statistical tests, and data classification – are by themselves informative and useful devices for finding, verifying and visualising data patterns. Spatial patterns, however, require a separate set of statistical tools in order to ascertain their structure and significance. The next chapter discusses this in further detail and introduces a range of methods for identifying spatial relationships in archaeological datasets.

---

[3]http://mpa.itc.it/markus/osg05/neteler_grass6_nutshell2005.pdf.

8

Spatial analysis

8.1 Introduction

Spatial analysis lies at the core of GIS and builds on a long history of quantitative methods in archaeology. Many of the foundations of spatial analysis were established by quantitative geographers in the 1950s and 1960s, and adopted and modified by archaeologists in the 1970s and 1980s. For a variety of reasons, spatial analysis fell out of fashion both in archaeology and in the other social sciences. In part this was because of the perceived overgeneralisation of certain types of mathematical models, but also because of a shift towards more contextually orientated and relativist studies of human behaviour. Recently, however, there has been a renewed interest in the techniques of spatial analysis for understanding the spatial organisation of human behaviour that takes on board these criticisms. In the last decade there have been several advances within the social sciences, particularly geography and economics, in their ability to reveal and interpret complex patterns of human behaviour at a variety of scales, from the local to the general, using spatial statistics. Archaeology has participated somewhat less in these recent developments, although there is a growing literature that demonstrates a renewed interest in the application of these techniques to the study of past human behaviour. In this chapter we review some historically important methods (e.g. linear regression, spatial autocorrelation, cluster analysis) and also highlight more recent advances in the application of spatial analysis to archaeology (e.g. Ripley's K, kernel density estimates, linear logistic regression). Readers requiring more in-depth discussion of methods of spatial analysis are advised to consult the sources that we have made use of for this review, particularly Bailey and Gatrell (1995); Fotheringham *et al.* (2000b); Rogerson (2001) and Haining (2003).

8.2 Linear regression

Linear regression has long been a staple of quantitative analysis. It is used to model the relationship between two continuous variables, and is one of the more important methods in spatial statistics. Consequently we have described the technique, and some associated potential pitfalls, in some detail.

Linear relationships between two quantitative variables may be expressed in terms of the degree of *correlation*, of which there are three basic possibilities: positive correlation, zero correlation or negative correlation. Two variables are said to be positively correlated when there is a simultaneous increase in value between two numerical variables (Fig. 8.1a) and negatively correlated when one variable

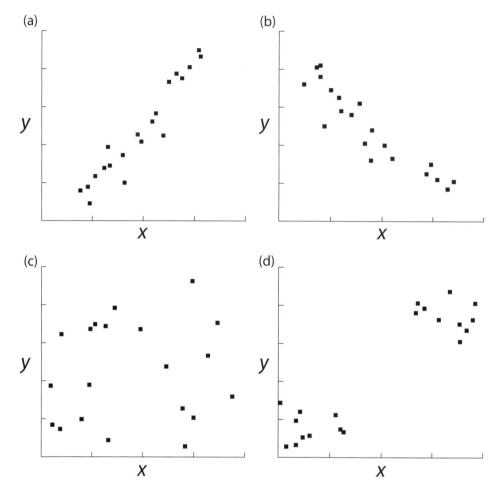

Fig. 8.1 Idealised correlation patterns: (a) positive, (b) negative, (c) zero, (d) spurious positive correlation in an uneven, clustered, dataset.

increases while the other decreases (Fig. 8.1b). Zero correlation occurs when there is no relationship between the two variables (Fig. 8.1c). Figure 8.1(d) shows a more complex relationship between two variables where there is a degree of positive correlation, although there is also a strong clustering pattern and *heteroscedasticity* (unevenness) in the data distribution that reduces the predictive value of the model. We will examine the first two examples initially, then return to cases of zero or spurious correlation later.

When examining the type and strength of correlation between two variables, one variable is considered to be *dependent* and the other *independent*. When plotted on an x, y-graph, the independent variable is plotted on the x-axis and the dependent variable is plotted on the y-axis. The difference between the dependent and independent variables is important and can be thought of as close to that of cause and effect.

To use a well-known archaeological example, the proportion of a particular type of raw material can often be shown to decline with the distance from the source of the raw material – i.e. distance and proportion are negatively correlated, as predicted by Renfrew's 'law' of monotonic decrement (Renfrew and Dixon 1976). In this case, it is the proportion of material that acts as the dependent variable, as its value is determined by its distance from the source. In situations where the suspected causal relationship is more ambiguous, for example between the number of artefacts and the size of an archaeological site, it is possible to speak of *interdependence*. In these cases, which variable is x and which is y is only significant in terms of what the regression analysis is specifically attempting to model.

While it is acceptable simply to describe the relationship between two quantitative variables as either positively or negatively correlated, it is often more useful to express this in terms of the strength of the relationship. The standard measure of the linear correlation between two variables is the *Pearson correlation coefficient*, symbolised by r and given by

$$r = \frac{\sum (x_i - \bar{x}) \times (y_i - \bar{y})}{\sqrt{\sum (x_i - \bar{x})^2 \times \sum (y_i - \bar{y})^2}} \qquad (8.1)$$

where $\bar{x}$ and $\bar{y}$ are the mean values of the independent and dependent variables. Values of r range from $+1.0$ for a perfect positive correlation to -1.0 for a perfect negative correlation. The midpoint, $r = 0.0$, denotes a complete absence of correlation between two variables. For example, the two variables listed in columns one and two in Table 8.1 possess a correlation coefficient of $+0.96$, meaning that they are highly positively correlated – as the x-value increases, so too does y in a highly predictable manner.

The correlation coefficient is usefully visualised as a 'line of regression' placed to minimise the sum of the vertical distances (actually the sum of the squared distances) from each point (the 'residuals') as illustrated in Fig. 8.2. In contrast to r, which simply describes the strength of the correlation and whether it is positive or negative, the r^2-value gives a better indication of the predictive power of the independent variable and can be interpreted as a proportion of the variation in the values of y that are determined by x. To convert this to a more tangible example, imagine that x and y are taken to refer, respectively, to site size and artefact count (so that artefact count is acting as the dependent variable). A correlation coefficient of 0.96 converts to a coefficient of determination, r^2, of 0.88. This indicates that 88 per cent of the variation in artefact count can be explained simply by site size. Note that it would be acceptable to turn this around and recompute the correlation coefficient using site size as the dependent variable (i.e. as y), if the purpose of the analysis was to predict site size on the basis of artefact count.

Two quantities of the line of regression, its slope (a), which defines the rate of change and the point at which the line crosses the y-axis (b, called the *intercept*),

Table 8.1 *Sample x- and y-values and the calculations for deriving r in Eq. 8.1 and Fig. 8.2*

x_i	y_i	$x_i - \bar{x}$	$y_i - \bar{y}$	$(x_i - \bar{x}) \times$ $(y_i - \bar{y})$	$(x_i - \bar{x})^2$	$(y_i - \bar{y})^2$
0.17	365	−0.32	−563.15	180.21	0.102	317 137.92
0.21	401	−0.28	−527.15	147.60	0.078	277 887.12
0.22	243	−0.27	−685.15	184.99	0.073	469 430.52
0.25	502	−0.24	−426.15	102.28	0.058	181 603.82
0.30	580	−0.19	−348.15	66.15	0.036	121 208.42
0.32	780	−0.17	−148.15	25.19	0.029	21 948.42
0.33	602	−0.16	−326.15	52.18	0.026	106 373.82
0.40	702	−0.09	−226.15	20.35	0.008	51 143.82
0.41	440	−0.08	−488.15	39.05	0.006	238 290.42
0.48	900	−0.01	−28.15	0.28	0.000	792.42
0.50	832	0.01	−96.15	−0.96	0.000	9 244.82
0.56	1 023	0.07	94.85	6.64	0.005	8 996.52
0.58	1 100	0.09	171.85	15.47	0.008	29 532.42
0.62	890	0.13	−38.15	−4.96	0.017	1 455.42
0.65	1 400	0.16	471.85	75.50	0.026	222 642.42
0.69	1 480	0.20	551.85	110.37	0.040	304 538.42
0.72	1 435	0.23	506.85	116.58	0.053	256 896.92
0.76	1 542	0.27	613.85	165.74	0.073	376 811.82
0.81	1 703	0.32	774.85	247.95	0.103	600 392.52
0.82	1 643	0.33	714.85	235.90	0.109	511 010.52
Mean 0.49	928.15					
Sum 9.8	18 563			1 786.51	0.849	4 107 338.50

are collectively referred to as the *regression constants* and are given by:

$$b = \frac{\sum\limits_{i=1}^{n}(x_i - \bar{x})(y_i - \bar{y})}{\sum\limits_{i=1}^{n}(x_i - \bar{x})^2} \tag{8.2}$$

and:

$$a = \frac{\sum\limits_{i=1}^{n} y_i - b \sum\limits_{i=1}^{n} x_i}{n} \tag{8.3}$$

The slope and intercept values allow for predictions to be made for y for any given value of x, as given by:

$$y = a + b \times x \tag{8.4}$$

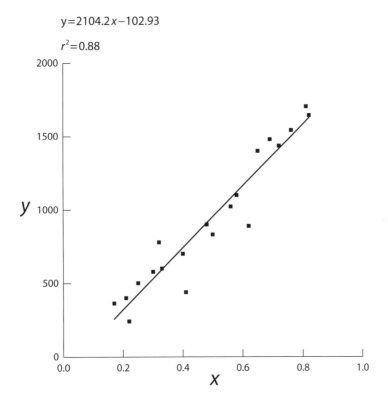

$y=2104.2x-102.93$

$r^2=0.88$

Fig. 8.2 A line of regression fitted to the *x*- and *y*-values in Table 8.1, shown with the coefficient of determination (r^2) and the regression equation.

For example, if Fig. 8.2 showed the correlation between the size of a site in hectares (x) and the number of artefacts recovered from surface collection (y) and $a = -102.93$ and $b = 2104.2$, then it would be possible to predict the number of artefacts from a site of 0.9 ha by substituting these values into Eq. 8.4: $y = (-102.93) + 2104.2 \times 0.9 = 1790.9$.

Predictions also have an associated standard error, calculated as

$$s_{y-\hat{y}} = \sqrt{\frac{\sum_{i=1}^{n}(y_i - \hat{y}_i)^2}{n-2}} \tag{8.5}$$

where $\hat{y}$ is the predicted value of the dependent variable. Using the data from Table 8.2, the standard error of the prediction is the square root of 348 999.1 divided by 18, which equals 139.2. One standard error is roughly equivalent to 68 per cent of observations if the residuals are normally distributed. In this example, assuming that this is the case, then the prediction for the number of artefacts on a site 0.9 ha in size is 1790.9 ± 139.2, which has a 68 per cent probability of being correct. If

Table 8.2 *Data for the calculation of standard error for the regression analysis of the variables given in Table 8.1*

y_i	$\hat{y}_i$	$y_i - \hat{y}_i$	$(y_i - \hat{y}_i)^2$
365	254.8	110.2	12 147.6
401	339.0	62.0	3 850.0
243	360.0	−117.0	13 687.6
502	423.1	78.9	6 222.1
580	528.3	51.7	2 669.8
780	570.4	209.6	43 926.3
602	591.5	10.5	111.2
702	738.8	−36.8	1 350.6
440	759.8	−319.8	102 266.9
900	907.1	−7.1	50.2
832	949.2	−117.2	13 728.8
1 023	1 075.4	−52.4	2 748.1
1 100	1 117.5	−17.5	306.5
890	1 201.7	−311.7	9 7140.7
1 400	1 264.8	135.2	18 279.0
1 480	1 349.0	131.0	17 169.4
1 435	1 412.1	22.9	524.7
1 542	1 496.3	45.7	2 092.0
1 703	1 601.5	101.5	10 307.9
1 643	1 622.5	20.5	419.7
Sum			348 999.1

greater accuracy is needed, then doubling the standard error to ±278.4 provides a 95 per cent probability of being correct.

The Pearson correlation coefficient (r) and the coefficient of determination (r^2) are included in nearly all computer statistical packages, including Microsoft Excel, SPSS, S-Plus and R. However, the use of Pearson's r for describing relationships can be problematic and it is worth reviewing the major pitfalls into which unexperienced users often stumble. Firstly, *it is unwise to assume a causal relationship solely on the basis of an observed correlation.* For example, while it may be generally observed that there is a strong positive correlation between the size of an archaeological site and the age of the director of the excavation, there is no causal relationship in either direction between these two variables. In cases where a causal relationship is suspected, it is always worth investigating the possibility that there are intermediary variables (e.g. in the sequence of: age → seniority → size of funding grant → size of archaeological site).

Regression analysis also depends on a number of assumptions that must be shown to be true before any measured correlation can be shown to be meaningful (cf. Shennan 1988, pp. 139–142). For example, the predictive value of the statistic is dependent on the variation around the line of regression being *homoscedastic* or evenly distributed. If this is not the case the variation is described as *heteroscedastic*.

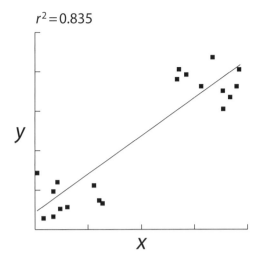

r²=0.835

Fig. 8.3 A line of regression fitted to a heteroscedastic point distribution. There is a strong positive correlation ($r = 0.91$), but the coefficient of determination ($r^2 = 0.84$) is meaningless.

Although a heteroscedastic distribution can be subject to regression and a formula obtained, the results are largely meaningless. Figure 8.3, for example, shows two random clusters of points that individually have an r^2 of 0 but collectively have an r^2 of 0.835. The heteroscedastic nature of the distribution, however, means that x has very little predictive value for y. Similarly meaningless results can occur when one or two outliers from a random distribution result in a line of regression with a strong positive or negative value. In these cases, visual inspection of the scatterplot is essential to ensure that the distribution of points is evenly spread along the x- and y-values. If this is not the case and clustering or outliers are evident, then the latter should be removed (and separately accounted for) and clusters investigated separately. Even if obvious outliers are not present, analysis of residuals in the ways described by Shennan (1988, pp. 139–144) can provide considerable insight into the structure of a linear relationship.

Thirdly, linear regression attempts to model linear relationships between variables, but a non-linear trend might be apparent in the data, as in Fig. 8.4. When visual inspection of an x, y-plot suggests a non-linear pattern, it is appropriate to transform one or both variables prior to performing a linear regression, especially as this will not reduce the predictive nature of the model. Common transformations include the square, the square root, the natural log or $\log_{10}$ of one or both variables. Experimentation with different transformations is often needed to obtain the optimum correlation coefficient with data that exhibit curvilinear tendencies. Shennan (1988, pp. 135–165) provides a comprehensive discussion of transformations of variables to improve linear regression.

Fourthly, one assumption of regression analysis as applied to spatial data is that each of the two observations on the x- and y-variables should be independent and

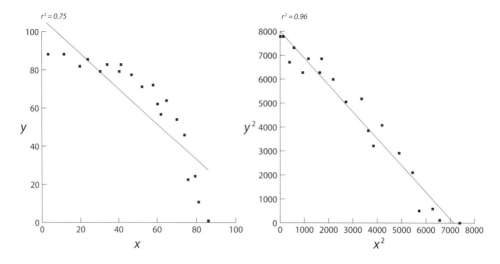

Fig. 8.4 Transforming a variable to improve the correlation coefficient. The scatterplot on the left has a slight curvilinear trend, which can be transformed to a linear trend by squaring the x- and y-variables, as shown on the right. The regression equation for the transformed data therefore becomes $y^2 = a + b \times x^2$, or $y = \sqrt{a + b \times x^2}$.

not spatially autocorrelated (see Section 8.3), nor should the residuals be spatially autocorrelated (Rogerson 2001, p. 154). If both x and y have high spatial autocorrelation then the variance and standard error of r, which is a function of the number of observations as defined in Eq. (8.5), will be underestimated because Pearson's r assumes that each pair of observations are independent of each other (Haining 2003, p. 279). The correlation coefficient will as a consequence be overestimated. Although an assessment of autocorrelation using methods such as Moran's I can be made on each of the two variables prior to the regression, spatial dependence can also be assessed by mapping the residuals from a regression analysis and visually searching for evidence of spatial autocorrelation (Fotheringham *et al.* 2000b, pp. 162–165).

For example, imagine that the relationship between the amount of prehistoric and medieval pottery from a sample of surface collection areas was being investigated (Table 8.3). There is a null hypothesis of no correlation (i.e. higher or lower amounts of prehistoric pottery have no bearing on how much medieval pottery is recovered, and vice versa). A Pearson's r analysis (8.1) returns a value of 0.4 with medieval pottery as the dependent variable, suggesting a slight but definite positive correlation between the two pottery types, perhaps indicating that the prehistoric and medieval sites overlap to a certain degree.

A plot of the residuals of y, however, shows considerable positive spatial autocorrelation (Fig. 8.5). High positive deviations between predicted and observed medieval pottery cluster in the centre and upper right, and high negative deviations only appear in the upper left and the bottom of the survey area. This indicates that the observations are not independent. This in turn warns that the results of the

Table 8.3 *Counts of prehistoric and medieval pottery
recovered from ten surface collection areas*

Area	Prehistoric	Medieval	Predicted	Residual
1	30	2	21.1	−19.1
2	6	3	8.4	−5.4
3	56	56	34.9	21.1
4	42	23	27.5	−4.5
5	21	45	16.4	28.6
6	59	12	36.6	−24.6
7	56	65	34.9	30.1
8	21	30	16.4	13.6
9	43	9	28.1	−19.1
10	33	2	22.7	−20.7
Sum	367	247	247.0	0.0

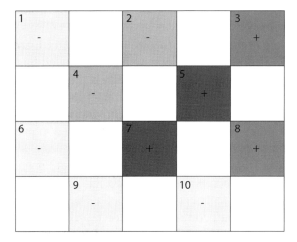

Fig. 8.5 A plot of the residuals of predicted versus actual medieval pottery. Numbers in
upper left of squares refer to individual surface collection areas as defined in Table 8.3.

correlation analysis are not necessarily valid and that r will be overestimated; thus
any judgement of the significance of the correlation becomes problematic.

When a plot of the residuals exhibits positive spatial autocorrelation then the
regression analysis may be improved either by investigating additional explanatory
variables by producing *added-variable plots* (Haining 1990), by using the technique
of *spatial regression* (Rogerson 2001, pp. 187–188), modelling the residuals as a
function of the surrounding residuals (Bailey and Gatrell 1995), or by employing
a geographically weighted regression (GWR) technique as developed by Fotheringham and colleagues (Fotheringham *et al.* 1998). Extensive discussion and many
worked examples of GWR are provided in Fotheringham *et al.* (2002a).

Alternatively, it is possible to control for the influence of autocorrelated variables on the sample by first establishing the number of spatially independent pairs of observations (n') from all observations n and using only the former to establish the significance of the correlation (Clifford and Richardson 1985; Haining 2003, pp. 278–279). These and other common problems with regression analysis are summarised in Table 8.4.

8.3 Spatial autocorrelation

The term 'spatial autocorrelation' refers to the degree of correlation between pairs of observed values and the distance between those observations in spatial distributions (Cliff and Ord 1981). Positive spatial autocorrelation describes a state where attribute values exhibit a tendency to be more similar the closer they are together (e.g. such as elevation, where the closer two sample points are together, the more likely they are to share a similar elevation). If there is no apparent relationship between spatial proximity and attribute value, then the distribution exhibits zero spatial autocorrelation. Negative spatial autocorrelation occurs when similar attribute values are located away from each other (Worboys 1995, pp. 157–158).

Having an understanding of the spatial autocorrelation of a data distribution provides important supporting information for certain types of modelling procedures. In particular, the linear regression of autocorrelated data is problematic for reasons described in the previous section. On the other hand, interpolation is only a valid exercise for data with some degree of positive autocorrelation. While this can be assumed for many environmental phenomena, such as elevation, rainfall, temperature, etc., it cannot be assumed for anthropogenic data. Creating a continuous surface of artefact densities from, for example, a sample of testpits is only useful if the sample data show some degree of positive autocorrelation (which is assessed within the technique of kriging as described in Chapter 6). Thus interpolation methods that incorporate measures of autocorrelation into their procedures – such as the technique of kriging described in Chapter 6 – typically produce continuous surfaces that are more accurate than other methods.

More generally, there has been some optimism that measures of spatial autocorrelation may have wider application in archaeology (Williams 1993), but thus far the most successful applications have been constrained to the analysis of Mayan terminal monument dates (Premo 2004).

The most common method of measuring autocorrelation is using *Moran's I* statistic (Moran 1950):

$$I = \left(\frac{n}{\sum\limits_{i}^{n}\sum\limits_{j}^{n} w_{ij}} \right) \left[\frac{\sum\limits_{i}^{n}\sum\limits_{j}^{n} w_{ij}(x_i - \bar{x})(x_j - \bar{x})}{\sum\limits_{i}^{n}(x_i - \bar{x})^2} \right] \tag{8.6}$$

Table 8.4 *Some common problems, consequences and solutions with regression analysis*

Problem	Consequences	Diagnostic	Corrective action
Residuals non-normal	Inferential test is likely to be invalid	Shapiro–Wilks test (Chapter 7)	Transform *y*-values
Heteroscedastic	Biased estimation of error variance and invalid inference	Plot of residuals against *y*	Transform *y*-values
Non-independent variables	Underestimation of variance and invalid inference	Moran's *I*	GWR, added-variable plots, spatial regression
Non-linear relationship	Poor fit and non-independent residuals	Scatter plot	Transform *y*- and/or *x*-variable
Outliers	Can severely affect model estimates and fit	Scatter plot	Delete outliers
Non-interval or ratio data	Linear regression not valid		Logistic regression

Source: Adapted from Haining (1990, pp. 332–333); Rogerson (2001, p. 146).

where subscripts i and j refer to the spatial objects of which there are n, $\bar{x}$ is the mean of all attributes and w_{ij} is a weighting function to reduce the impact of distant points. If the variable of interest x is first transformed to a z-score $\{z = (x - \bar{x})/s\}$ then formula can be simplified to (Rogerson 2001, p. 167):

$$I = \frac{\sum_i \sum_j w_{ij} z_i z_j}{(n-1) \sum_i \sum_j w_{ij}} \tag{8.7}$$

The weighting function w_{ij} is most often an inverse distance measure ($\frac{1}{d_{ij}}$). For area data a measure of *binary connectivity*, where $w_{ij} = 1$ if i and j are adjacent and $w_{ij} = 0$ if not, is frequently used instead (Rogerson 2001, p. 167).

The expected value of Moran's I, if there is no spatial autocorrelation, is defined by $E(I)$:

$$E(I) = -\frac{1}{n-1} \tag{8.8}$$

Values of I larger than $E(I)$ indicate positive autocorrelation and values lower indicate negative autocorrelation (Fotheringham *et al.* 2000a). The statistical significance of any departure from this expected value can be tested using an assumption of normality (i.e. that the values of x_i are drawn from a normal population). In cases where n is 'large' the standardised statistic

$$Z = \frac{I - E(I)}{\sqrt{\text{var}(I)}} \tag{8.9}$$

can be used where the variance of I under an assumption of normality is

$$\text{var}(I) = \frac{n^2(n-1)S_1 - n(n-1)S_2 + 2(n-2)S_0^2}{(n+1)(n-1)^2 S_0} \tag{8.10}$$

where

$$S_0 = \sum_i^n \sum_{j \neq i}^n w_{ij} \tag{8.11}$$

$$S_1 = \frac{\sum_i^n \sum_{j \neq i}^n (w_{ij} + w_{ji})^2}{2} \tag{8.12}$$

$$S_2 = \sum_k^n \left(\sum_j^n w_{ij} + \sum_j^n w_{ji} \right)^2 \tag{8.13}$$

Less restrictively, an assumption of randomisation can be used (i.e. where observed I is compared to an expected I if x_i was randomly distributed) (Hodder and Orton 1976, p. 178). In this case, the variance of I is given by

$$\text{var}(I) = \frac{nS_4 - S_3 S_5}{(n-1)(n-2)(n-3) \left(\sum_i^n \sum_j^n w_{ij} \right)^2} \tag{8.14}$$

where

$$S_3 = \frac{n^{-1} \sum_i^n (x_i - \bar{x})^4}{\left(n^{-1} \sum_i^n (x_i - \bar{x})^2 \right)^2} \tag{8.15}$$

$$S_4 = (n^2 - 3n + 3)S_1 - nS_2 + 3 \left(\sum_i^n \sum_j^n w_{ij} \right)^2 \tag{8.16}$$

$$S_5 = S_1 - 2ns_1 + 6 \left(\sum_i^n \sum_j^n w_{ij} \right)^2 \tag{8.17}$$

The variance can then be used in (8.9) to calculate a Z-value, which can then be compared to a normal distribution for significance (Fotheringham *et al.* 2000b, p. 204). In cases where n is 'small' then it may be necessary to simulate the parameters of I using Monte-Carlo methods (see Box 8.1) for which Fotheringham *et al.* (2000b, pp. 204–209) provide a worked example.

Box 8.1 Monte-Carlo simulation

Monte-Carlo simulation predates the rise of computing, but it only really became an important form of statistical sampling in the second half of the the last century, particularly in physics (Robert and Casella 2004). More recently it has emerged as an increasingly important method of statistical sampling in the social sciences, as it provides a way of estimating the parameters of complex populations. Monte-Carlo simulation thus has an important role to play in GIS.

The basis of the technique is common to that of statistical sampling: that a random sample of individuals from a population will show some correspondence to the population parameters, and thus the latter can be estimated from the sample. In many cases where populations are large and potentially diverse it is unclear how a random sample should be generated, how many samples should be taken or whether any given random sample is at all representative of the population. Monte-Carlo simulation reduces this uncertainty by taking repeated random samples (often 1000 or more). It is then possible to examine the distribution of values of some statistic (usually the mean) across the samples.

For example, a common archaeological GIS problem is whether the average viewshed size of a sample of archaeological sites is different from the average viewshed size of the background landscape. Viewshed calculations are computationally intensive, and thus even for a modestly sized study area it is unrealistic to attempt to establish the viewshed size for every cell. Taking a random sample of points in the landscape and comparing this with the archaeological sample is the only realistic option, but then it may not be clear whether the random sample is representative of the background population. A Monte-Carlo simulation approach to this problem will take several random samples and so provide a better estimate of the population parameters.

A common starting point for Monte-Carlo simulation is to take 1000 simple random samples each consisting of 1000 individuals and then to average the results. Note that this is computationally equivalent to taking 1 000 000 samples, which may exceed the population size! In cases like this it is acceptable to reduce the size and number of the samples; for example, Lake and Woodman (2000) used 100 random samples of 30 locations to estimate the parameters of the viewshed characteristics of their study area (see Chapter 3). A result is significant if the statistic for the sites falls on the edge of or outside the range of values of the statistics for the non-site samples.

Obviously this is not a task that can be performed manually – ideally it requires a simple program that selects the random samples, calculates their viewshed size and stores the results in a log file. Repetitive tasks like these are relatively easy to program in, for example, Visual Basic for ArcGIS. Alternatively, sets of random x, y-locations can be generated in a spreadsheet or statistical package such as R, saved as text files, and then imported into the GIS to be used as the basis for the calculations.

In other applications, such as spatial analysis, Monte-Carlo techniques are used to establish what a random distribution actually looks like. This is important in Ripley's *K* (this chapter) where a known distribution of points must be compared to a random distribution to establish whether or not it is distinctive (i.e. is clustered, or regular). Although still computationally intensive, 1000 samples of 1000 points is a good starting point as it increases the confidence that the characteristics of a random sample are accurately estimated.

Robert and Casella (2004) provide a good introduction to Monte-Carlo methods.

Although Moran's *I* can be calculated by hand, it soon becomes unwieldy when there are more than ten or so objects. It is much easier to use a statistical computer package, particularly when computing the significance of the statistic (as the previous formulae might suggest!). Modules for calculating Moran's *I* are readily available for many popular GIS packages (e.g. Spatial Statistics for ArcView (Monk 2001), r.moran for GRASS and AUTOCORR for Idrisi) and are included in dedicated geostatistical packages such as G+.[1] It is also included in the freely available CrimeStat[2] spatial statistics program (Levine 2002).

The degree of positive spatial autocorrelation in a spatial dataset may assist with the interpretation of certain anthropogenic phenomena. For example, the spatial structure of 'event horizons' such as the spread of agriculture (Sokal *et al*. 1989; Gkiasta *et al*. 2003) or the collapse of the Classical Mayan state (Kvamme 1990d; Williams 1993; Neiman 1997), depend to a large extent on establishing positive autocorrelation between the dates and locations at which the event is first observed. A recent use of measures of spatial autocorrelation in archaeology can be found in (Premo 2004), who applies autocorrelation statistics to contextual terminal dates of Mayan sites within local neighbourhoods to provide further insight into Mayan 'collapse'. While examples such as these do depend on adequately sampled data, there are certainly many more potential archaeological applications of the analysis of autocorrelation than have yet been realised.

8.4 Cluster analysis

Archaeologists frequently use points to represent the location of artefacts, features and sites. The analysis of point distribution patterns is therefore an important tool for describing, interpreting and explaining the spatial characteristics of these phenomena. Point distribution patterns are often described in terms of their configuration vis-a-vis three idealised states – namely random, clustered or regular (Fig. 8.6a–c). In reality, spatial arrangements, whether artefactual or settlement, can rarely be so simply described. Analysis of distribution patterns needs to be sensitive to the fact

---

[1] www.gammadesign.com/.
[2] www.icpsr.umich.edu/NACJD/crimestat.html.

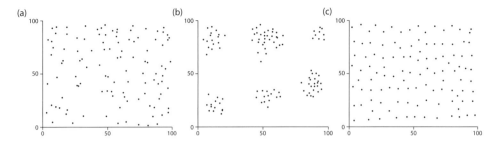

Fig. 8.6 Idealised point distributions: (a) nearly random, (b) nearly clustered, (c) nearly regular.

that several different smaller-scale patterns may exist within a study area and that different types of patterning often exist at different spatiotemporal scales.

In the case of settlement pattern analysis, regular spacing of sites has been taken to reflect either a form of competition between settlements, the existence of site catchments, or a combination of both as a result of demographic growth from an initial random distribution (Hodder and Orton 1976, pp. 54–85; Perlès 2001, pp. 132–147). Clustering of sites may result from a number of factors, but localised distribution of resources and the emergence of polities or regional centres have often been highlighted (Roberts 1996, pp. 15–37; Ladefoged and Pearson 2000). In contrast, random distributions have usually been treated as the statistical null hypothesis, though several commentators provide good examples of how apparently random distributions can be conditioned by less-obvious environmental, biological and social variables (Maschner and Stein 1995; Woodman 2000b; Daniel 2001). In general terms, the interpretation of archaeological settlement distributions is in need of new theory building coupled with renewed empirical and experimental investigation. Recent work by Premo (2004) on Mayan site distribution provides a good example of such an approach.

One major issue in the analysis of point distributions is the effect that the size of the study area has on the detection and characterisation of patterning. Figure 8.7 shows how adjusting the scale of analysis has a major influence on both the homogeneity, intensity and clustering tendencies of point distributions. In the entire study area, $A1$, the pattern is homogenous with a clustered structure (i.e. clustering occurs relatively evenly) such that a frequency distribution of the distances to each point's nearest neighbour would be normally distributed. At smaller scales, for example in area $A2$, the pattern is heterogeneous with a strong left to right gradient. A neighbourhood density function would be positively skewed with a bimodal tendency. Area $A3$ is similarly heterogeneous, although its density value is significantly lower than $A2$. Area $A4$ has a high intensity and homogenous distribution, although here it is far more regular than seen elsewhere.

The dichotomy of dispersion vs. nucleation created by many point-based analyses provides only a coarse characterisation of human settlement patterns. In particular,

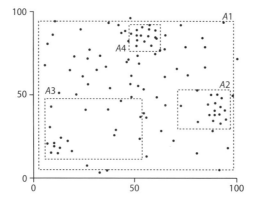

Fig. 8.7 Several smaller-scale point patterns are apparent in the near-random distribution of points in area *A*1. For example, areas *A*2 and *A*3 can be described as containing clustered distributions, while *A*4 is better described as regular.

analyses that are sensitive at only one scale (like nearest neighbour analysis) may overlook more complex, multiscalar, spatial patterns.

8.4.1 *Nearest neighbour analysis*

A favourite, if now old-fashioned, technique used by archaeologists to analyse point distributions is nearest neighbour analysis. Clark and Evans (1954) first explored the utility of nearest neighbour analysis in ecology (Box 8.2), and the New Geographers were soon applying it to human settlement patterns (Dacey 1960; Haggett 1965). Its use for archaeological settlement pattern analysis followed some time later in the early 1970s (Hodder and Hassell 1971a; Clarke 1972; Hodder 1972; Whallon 1974; Washburn 1974; Hodder and Orton 1976) and continued through the 1980s and 1990s. The technique retains its prominence in archaeology both in general textbooks (e.g. Wheatley and Gillings 2002) and in culturally specific studies (e.g. Perlès 1999; Ladefoged and Pearson 2000). Its popularity is a product of two factors: it is straightforward to calculate (see Box 8.2) and it provides an easily interpreted coefficient.

There are, however, several significant limitations to nearest neighbour analysis. It was initially designed to detect spatial patterning between 1st nearest neighbours and thus is not suited to identifying multiscalar effects.

For example, Fig. 8.8 shows a hypothetical distribution of a number of sites represented by points. A single-order nearest neighbour analysis applied to the point distribution in the left panel would detect the presence of clusters, and a *K-means* statistic (described below) could be employed to show that the optimum number of clusters was probably eight. However, neither of these analysis would be able to identify the fact that there is also a higher-order scale producing three clusters. Furthermore, if we include the finer artefact-scale resolution represented on the right panel (rather than just an approximation of the centre of the artefact distribution), then clustering can be shown to exist at three different spatial scales:

Box 8.2 Clark and Evans' nearest neighbour statistic

This useful but problematic statistic is calculated by dividing the mean of the observed distance between each point and its nearest neighbour (denoted by $\bar{R}_o$) by an expected value of R if the distribution was random ($\bar{R}_e$). This latter is estimated using the equation:

$$\bar{R}_e = \frac{1}{2\sqrt{\lambda}} \qquad (8.18)$$

where λ is the density of points in the study area (i.e. the mean intensity of points), as given by Eq. (8.22).

The ratio of $\bar{R}_o$ to $\bar{R}_e$ (denoted by R) provides the statistic:

$$R = \frac{\bar{R}_o}{\bar{R}_e} \qquad (8.19)$$

If $\bar{R}_o$ and $\bar{R}_e$ are equal – in other words, the observed mean nearest neighbour distance is equivalent to that predicted if the distribution were random – then their ratio (R) will be equal to 1. In a clustered distribution, the mean distance between points will be less than when they are randomly distributed. Thus an R-value less than 1 indicates a clustered distribution. If R is greater than 1 (up to its theoretical maximum of 2.15), this indicates that the points are more regularly spaced.

The significance of R is dependent on the sample size and density of the point distribution. It is known that the variance of mean distances between neighbours in a random distribution is

$$V[R_e] = \frac{4 - \pi}{4 \times \pi \times \lambda \times n} \qquad (8.20)$$

where n is the number of points and λ is the mean intensity of points (Rogerson 2001, p. 162). As we can estimate the variance, a z-test can therefore be used to test the null hypothesis of random distribution:

$$z = \frac{(R_o - R_e)}{\sqrt{V[R_e]}} \qquad (8.21)$$

Tables of the standard normal distribution can be used to assess significance: z-values of 1.96 or greater indicating significant uniformity and values of -1.96 or lower indicating a significant tendency towards clustering.

(i) artefacts forming sites (clusters i–x); (ii) sites forming primary clusters (clusters 1–8), and (iii) primary clusters forming secondary clusters (clusters A–C).

Increasing the nearest neighbour measurement to the second, third, ... , nth neighbour may detect clustering at different scales, but the statistical validation of patterning then becomes difficult (Hodder and Orton 1976, p. 41). Nearest neighbour analysis is also significantly influenced by the size of the area to be analysed,

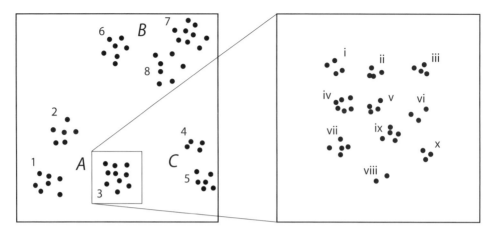

Fig. 8.8 Multiscalar patterning: three large clusters (*A*, *B*, *C*) are each composed of smaller clusters (1–8), which themselves consist of smaller clusters (e.g. i–x for cluster 3).

with regular, random or clustered distributions partially dependent on the shape of the study area. The size of surrounding area included in the analysis also can significantly influence the identification of clustering; the greater the amount of empty space surrounding a central distribution of random points, the more likely it is that the pattern will be identified as clustered. There are 'workarounds' for these problems but the technique nevertheless remains a somewhat blunt instrument with which to describe point distribution patterns.

8.4.2 *Ripley's K*

As GIS-led approaches to the collection and management of archaeological survey data are able to store data at several different scales within the same environment (e.g. artefacts, sites and regions), more sophisticated and spatially sensitive techniques are required to identify and characterise distribution patterns. One technique that addresses some of the inherent problems of nearest neighbour analysis is *Ripley's K-function* (Ripley 1976, 1981). The technique was designed to identify the relative aggregation and segregation of point data at different spatial scales and the shape of the study area has little effect on the assessment of patterning. The statistic is defined for a process of point intensity λ, where $\lambda K(r)$ defines the expected number of neighbours in a circle of radius r at an arbitrary point in the distribution (Pélissier and Goreaud 2001, p. 101). The K-distribution is a cumulative frequency distribution of average point intensity at set intervals of r. Significance intervals are generated by Monte-Carlo simulation of random distributions of the points and a 95 per cent confidence interval can usually be obtained within 1000–5000 iterations (Manly 1991). These estimates can be compared with the observed values of K to provide a statistically robust measure of cluster size and cluster distance in the dataset. For clarity of presentation the cumulative

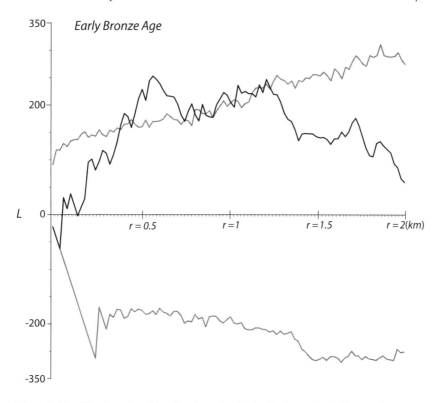

Fig. 8.9 Identification of multiscalar clustering in the Kytheran Early Bronze Age using Ripley's K. The presence of clusters of settlements between 500 and ~700 m is attested by the peak at that position on the x-axis, with significant but less obvious clustering occurring between ~700 and 1250 m (for details see Bevan and Conolly in press).

K-distribution is usually transformed to $L(r) = \sqrt{K(r)/\pi} - r$, where the expectation under randomness ($L(r) = 0$) is a horizontal line (Fig. 8.9). $L(r) < 0$ means that there are fewer than expected neighbours at distance r, suggesting a regular pattern, and $L(r) > 0$, means that there are more neighbours than expected at distance r, indicating a clustered pattern (Pélissier and Goreaud 2001, p. 102).

Ripley's K is available within comprehensive statistical packages such as R, as a module in the freely available spatial statistics package ADE-4[3] (Thioulouse *et al.* 1997) and within the third-party extension for ArcView Spatial Statistics[4] (Monk 2001). Although it is more complex than the Clark and Evans nearest neighbour statistic, and it may take longer to calculate because of the necessity of simulating the parameters of a random distribution, Ripley's K offers a much better route to investigating the spatial structure of point patterns. Bevan and Conolly (in press), for example, have used the technique to investigate the changing nature of settlement

---

[3]http://pbil.univ-lyon1.fr/ADE-4/.
[4]http://arcscripts.esri.com/.

patterns on the island of Kythera. They were able to show not only the presence of clustering during different phases of settlement on the island, but also how both the structure of the distribution and the size of clusters of settlements changed over time, reflecting different settlement strategies.

8.5 Identifying cluster membership

If clustering is identified in a distribution of point data, the second phase of analysis usually consists of defining the number and location of those clusters. There are a number of techniques that may be used to achieve this objective, which can be divided into three groups depending on whether they use *hierarchical* (Sokal and Sneath 1963; Sneath and Sokal 1973), *partitioning* (Ball and Hall 1970) or *density* methods for cluster definition (Silverman 1986). Hierarchical methods start with individual objects and progressively group them into fewer higher-order clusters so that eventually all objects assume membership of one group. Partitioning methods begin with the complete distribution, and break it into a number of smaller units, while density approaches identify dense concentrations of objects. In this section we describe three approaches: hierarchical cluster analysis, *k*-means partitioning and density analysis.

8.5.1 *Hierarchical cluster analysis*

This approach to clustering has a very long history of application in archaeology. It works by creating a 'distance matrix' between objects based on their attribute states, and as applied to spatial data the linear distances between all points in the dataset form the basis of the matrix. For example, the relationships between the points in Fig. 8.10 can be converted to a distance matrix (Table 8.5), which can be used to construct a *dendrogram* defining the hierarchical grouping of individual points (Fig. 8.11).

The construction of the dendrogram begins in an agglutinative manner by defining each separate point as a group unto itself, then locating the pair that possess the smallest distance. In this example, this occurs between points 1 and 5, which are 0.7 units apart. The pair of points with the second smallest distance (7 and 9) are then grouped together. Individual points and grouped pairs may link to existing groups on the basis of a specified rule, which defines the cluster method and ultimately the shape of the resulting dendrogram. For example, one of the simplest methods is called *Single-Link Cluster Analysis* (SLCA) which joins points to groups or groups to groups on the basis of a shared level of similarity between any member of the two groups. In this scenario, point 10 therefore would link to the pair (7, 9), and point 4 would link to the pair (1, 5). Additional points are then progressively joined leading to the dendrogram depicted in Fig. 8.11.

Examination of Fig. 8.11 provides some indication of the spatial structure of the point distribution in Fig. 8.10. Two major clusters can be distinguished, one consisting of points 8, 10, 7 and 9, and a second consisting of 6, 3, 2, 4, 1 and 5, with 6 sitting as an outlier in that group. Within the first group, point 8 stands out from the main distribution. With such a small distribution the additional insight

Table 8.5 *A distance matrix for hierarchical cluster analysis*

	1	2	3	4	5	6	7	8	9
2	7.8								
3	7.3	4.3							
4	4.1	3.7	4.5						
5	0.7	7.0	6.7	3.4					
6	7.3	12.1	13.7	9.3	7.5				
7	13.6	19.7	20.7	16.6	14.0	7.7			
8	12.7	19.8	20.0	16.3	13.3	8.8	3.8		
9	14.4	20.7	21.6	17.5	14.9	8.7	1.0	3.7	
10	16.6	22.8	23.8	19.7	17.1	10.8	3.1	5.2	2.2

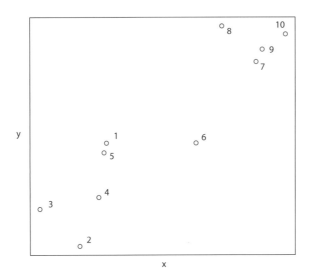

Fig. 8.10 A simple point distribution.

that this brings over visual assessment of the distribution is marginal, although hierarchical analysis applied to larger datasets may help make sense of more complex arrangements. However, a major problem with SLCA is that links between groups are created very easily, so large chains of small clusters often result and outliers are connected to other clusters based on a connection with only one member. Better methods, such as *Average-Link Cluster Analysis*, use average similarity scores of groups to define the level at which additional members cluster. Even more sophisticated approaches to group definition offer further advantages, such as *Ward's Method* which seeks to maximise the homogeneity of clusters by defining clusters so that the *error sum of squares* (ESS) – the sum of the squared distances of all points from the means of the clusters to which they belong – is minimised.

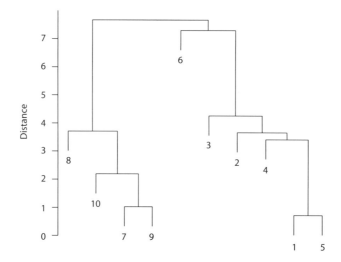

Fig. 8.11 A single-link cluster analysis of the point distribution in Fig. 8.10.

Clusters created using Ward's Method are typically easier to interpret than single-
or average-link methods because long chains of small groups occur less frequently,
resulting in more homogeneous clusters and a more easily interpreted dendrogram.
For example, Ward's (1990) method was used to construct the dendrogram in Fig.
8.12. The results are arguably better than the results from SLCA, in that 3, 2 and 4
form a cluster distinct from 1 and 5, with 6 as an outlier from the latter pair.

   Shennan (1988, pp. 212–232) provides a comprehensive review of several hierarchical clustering methods. In general terms, the advantage of hierarchical methods
is that it is possible to view clustering at a range of different scales, beginning with
small groups of two or more objects and building eventually into larger clusters that
include many smaller groups. This advantage, however, can then present difficulties
when deciding exactly how many clusters may exist in a dataset, as the number
of clusters is defined by an arbitrary level of similarity (or error sum of squares in
the case of Ward's method) chosen by the analyst. For this reason it is often wise
to avoid dependency on a hierarchical method and instead to use complementary
statistics, such as k-means analysis, to help ascertain the optimum number of clusters in a dataset. Most popular statistical packages, such as SPSS, S+ and R, offer
a range of hierarchical clustering methods.

8.5.2 *k-Means analysis*
When the number of objects is large (e.g. >100), the dendrogram produced from
a hierarchical cluster analysis is not easily interpreted and it becomes difficult to
ascertain the level of similarity at which cluster groups should be defined. Better are
methods that allow the desired number of clusters to be specified beforehand so that
a range of solutions can be compared and an optimal solution chosen. k-Means analysis is one such method. The major difference between k-means and hierarchical

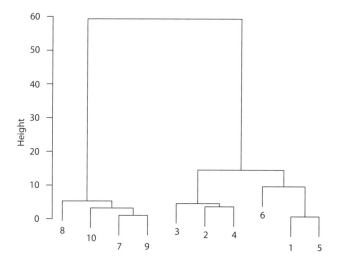

Fig. 8.12 A cluster analysis of the distribution shown in Fig. 8.10 using Ward's method.

clustering is that k-means is a *partitioning* clustering technique, because instead of grouping similar objects together, it divides up a group of objects into a specified number of clusters. Cluster centres are initially defined by the selection of random points from the distribution which act as 'seeds', and the remaining objects are then added to the cluster which they are nearest. As new objects are added to a cluster, the centre of the cluster is recalculated, and if a previously assigned object now lies closer to another cluster centre it is reassigned. This *iterative reallocation* is a major strength of the k-means technique, although because the seeds that define the clusters are random, different optimum solutions may result and solutions may not be replicable. Once all objects have been allocated, each cluster's sum of squared Euclidean distances (i.e. the squared distance between each object and the centre of its cluster) is calculated to provide an assessment of the clustering solution.

One way to determine the optimum number of clusters is to examine the rate of decrease in the total sum of squared distances over the increasing number of cluster solutions. As the number of cluster solutions increases towards the number of points in the distribution, the sum of squares reduces towards 0. The rate of decline, although generally exponential, reduces at points where increasing the number of clusters does not drastically alter the total sum of squares. The way that this is usually measured is to plot the natural log of the percentage of the total sum of squares for an increasing number of clusters (k). In situations where the distributions are reasonably highly clustered, this can be a useful technique for identifying the optimum number and membership of groups. One good example of this is the k-means analysis of distribution of medieval castles on Okinawa Island by Ladefoged and Pearson (2000), which suggested that the optimum clustering solution was three (Fig. 8.13).

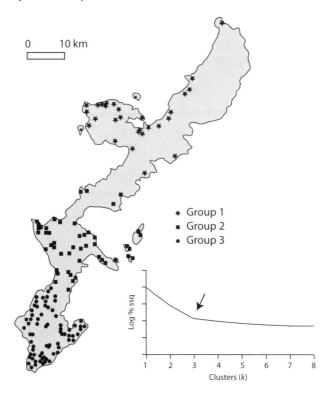

Fig. 8.13 A *k*-means cluster analysis of medieval castles on Okinawa Island, Japan, with the 'elbow' at solution 3 in the associated graph of the decreasing per cent sum of squares (redrawn from Ladefoged and Pearson 2000, Figs. 2–4).

More complex distributions prove difficult to cluster in such a straightforward manner. For example, the distribution of 1795 points in Fig. 8.14 represent the spatial arrangement of stone artefacts from Trench 4b from the Lower Palaeolithic site of Boxgrove, England (Roberts and Parfitt 1999, Fig. 279). The Clark and Evans *R*-statistic is 0.69, with a *z*-value of 24.8, which allows a null hypothesis of randomness to be safely rejected. The question remains as to the number and location of cluster groups in this distribution, which presents significant challenges because of the diffuse nature of the distribution pattern and the lack of clear lines of division between higher and lower density areas.

The only clear 'elbow' is at the two-cluster solution, as shown in Fig. 8.15. The result is a distribution divided in two with the dividing line roughly corresponding to an area of reduced density running through the middle (Fig. 8.16). There are, however, difficulties with this solution that highlight some of the problems with *k*-means analysis. In particular, the dividing line between the left and right clusters appears to be less than optimally positioned. This has arisen because of the relatively simple manner in which *k*-means calculates centroids as the mean of the *x*- and *y*-coordinates.

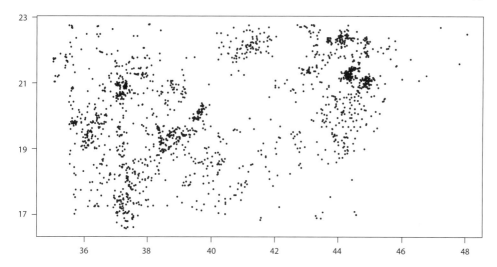

Fig. 8.14 Distribution of stone artefacts from horse-butchery trench 4b at the Lower Palaeolithic site of Boxgrove, England (Roberts and Parfitt 1999, Fig. 279). Source: The Boxgrove Project. Used with permission.

In some solutions this can result in points that lie towards the peripheries of cluster groups being placed into different clusters even though they form a coherent group. These difficulties are to a large extent created because of the nature of this point distribution, which is characterised by a number of small high-density clusters interspersed with a lower density 'carpet' that forms diffuse clusters that bleed into each other. Identifying the optimum number of clusters, and their membership, can be very difficult in these situations, although subdividing the distribution and applying *k*-means to each subunit may help. In general, however, complex spatial distributions such as this example are difficult to cluster using *k*-means, and may not usefully contribute to the interpretation and understanding of the behaviour that created the dataset.

More sophisticated partitioning algorithms like *Partitioning Around Medoids* (PAM; Kaufman and Rousseeuw 1990; van de Laan *et al*. 2002), may provide additional insight. Alternatively, examining cluster patterning through the generation of density measurements can be informative.

8.6 Density analysis

There are many distributions where clustering is evident, but the definition of membership is very difficult to define because of the quantity of points, or because of the 'fuzzy' boundaries of concentrations. In these situations, the problem of how best to define cluster location and size may benefit from approaches that describe the changing density (or, more properly, the *intensity*) of material. These approaches fall under a category of spatial modelling called *intensity analysis* and allow archaeologists to describe and visualise the changing frequency of observations that occur

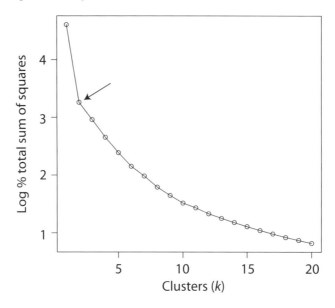

Fig. 8.15 Rate of change of sum of squares (expressed as log percentage of total sum of squares) for 1–20 cluster solutions. The deviation ('elbow') in the rate of change at $k = 2$ (arrow) suggests two clusters is an optimum solution.

within a given area, often to compare different phenomena within the same area or against the same phenomenon in different areas.

If $N(a)$ denotes the number of observations of a phenomenon occurring in A, then the *mean intensity* of the phenomenon, M_1 is given by:

$$M_1 = \frac{N(a)}{A} \tag{8.22}$$

For example, the mean surface intensity for a distribution of 1795 artefacts in a study area of 62 m^2 is calculated as $1795/62 = 28.95$ artefacts per square meter. The same principle could be applied to subregions of the study area, for example, individual 1-m squares, and the first-order intensity function calculated for each square. In this case, the intensity is given by $\lambda(x)$ as we are calculating it for a subset of a.

More usefully, however, the size of the observation area can be reduced to a 'moving window' to derive measures of local density, $\lambda_n(x_i)$, on a regular lattice across the study area. This can be formally expressed by the equation:

$$\lambda_n(x_i) = \frac{N[C(x_i, r)]}{\pi \times r_i^2} \tag{8.23}$$

where x_i is the location at which the intensity is being calculated, and N is the number of artefacts in $C(x_i, r)$, which is a circle of radius r around point x_i. This calculation is referred to as the *naive estimator* (Fotheringham *et al.* 2000a, p. 147).

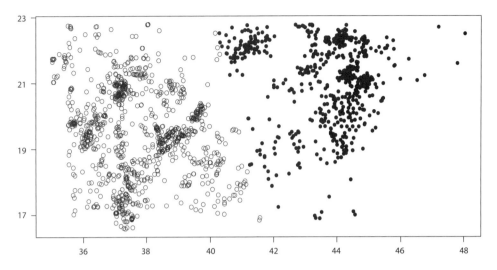

Fig. 8.16 The two-cluster solution of a k-means cluster analysis.

Obviously the area of observation (r) and the grid cell size will have a pronounced influence on the resulting density surface. Some insight might be gained by comparing localised surfaces (i.e. smaller search radii) against generalised surfaces (i.e. larger search radii) to investigate small-scale versus large-scale influences on distribution patterns (Fig. 8.17).

Note that as the search area decreases, local densities will increase for smaller clusters – e.g. 5 artefacts falling within a search radius of 0.25 m will result in a local density of $5/(\pi \times 0.25^2) = 25.5$, whereas 5 artefacts falling in a search radius of 1 m would produce a local density of $5/(\pi \times 1^2) = 1.2$.

8.6.1 Kernel density estimates

A more sophisticated density measure called *kernel density estimation* (KDE) produces smoother and more readily interpreted results than simple density techniques (Silverman 1986).

Kernel density estimation is a non-parametric technique in which a two-dimensional probability density function (the 'kernel') is placed across the observed data points to create a smooth approximation of its distribution from the centre of the point outwards. The two parameters that can be manipulated are the shape of the kernel placed over each data point (although in many GIS packages this is set to a quadratic function and cannot be changed) and the variance (or radius) of the kernel, referred to as the bandwidth and denoted by h. The density value for each cell is then established by adding together values of the density distributions (each of which will be a fraction of 1, unless the data points represent populations) that overlie that grid cell. Experimentation with different values of h is advised, and more detailed guidelines can be found in Wand and Jones (1995); archaeological

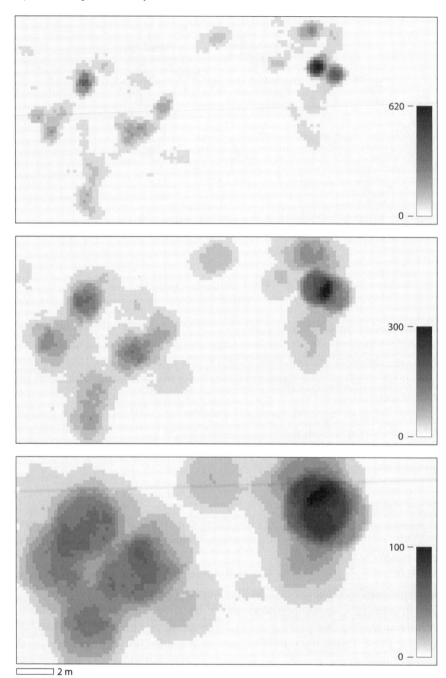

Fig. 8.17 Three intensity surfaces of the artefact distribution in Fig. 8.14: 0.25-m radius (top), 0.5-m radius (middle), 1-m radius (bottom). All calculated on a 10-cm grid. Intensity values are expressed in artefacts per square meter.

applications are described in Beardah and Baxter (1996) and Beardah (1999). In general, using too wide a radius will result in an overly smoothed distribution, whereas too narrow a radius will produce peaks around data clusters that may not reflect the actual distribution. Figure 8.18 shows the result of KDE using the same point data as for the simple density calculations shown in Fig. 8.17. The result is a smoother and more easily interpreted continuous surface for cluster identification.

8.7 Local functions

Finally, simple density measures can be replaced by other neighbourhood functions to produce continuous surfaces that show the changing nature of an attribute. For example, if the count of artefacts is replaced with an attribute variable, y, then a local estimate of y at point x is given by:

$$\hat{y}(x_i) = \frac{\sum y(r_i)}{n(r_i)} \tag{8.24}$$

This returns a continuous surface showing the mean of the variable. This interpolation is local because values are estimated using the values surrounding each cell and it can be contrasted to the global trend surface of artefact sizes in Fig. 6.1. However, in common with the other density functions, this method is highly influenced by edge effects and should be interpreted with caution.

In certain situations it might be important to identify whether a local region deviates from the global trend. This might occur, for example, with survey data if one was interested in exploring whether some enumeration unit (e.g. fields) had neighbours with higher artefact densities than the global pattern and could be defined as a 'hot spot'. An appropriate method to answer this question is Getis's G_j^* statistic (Ord and Getis 1995):

$$G_i^* = \frac{\sum\limits_j w_{ij}(d)x_j - W_i^*\bar{x}}{s[(nS_{1i}^* - W_i^{*2})/(n-1)]^{1/2}} \tag{8.25}$$

where s is the sample standard deviation of the observation values x, and $w_{ij}(d) = 1$ if region j is within a distance d from region i (Rogerson 2001, p. 174). Finally:

$$W_i^* = \sum_j w_{ij}(d) \tag{8.26}$$

and

$$S_{1i}^* = \sum_j w_{ij}^2 \tag{8.27}$$

For example, consider the distribution of artefacts recovered from the five fields in Fig. 8.19. The question is whether the high values around field 5 represent a

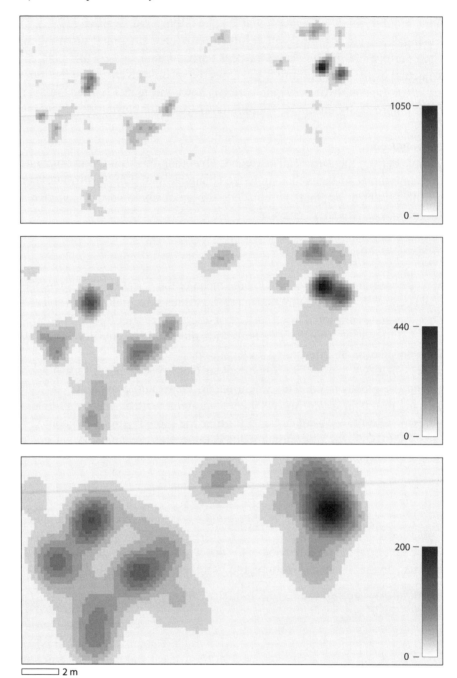

2 m

Fig. 8.18 Kernel density estimates of the artefact distribution in Fig. 8.14 using a diameter of 0.25-m radius (top), 0.5-m radius (middle), 1-m radius (bottom). Densities expressed as artefacts per square meter. Compare to Fig. 8.17.

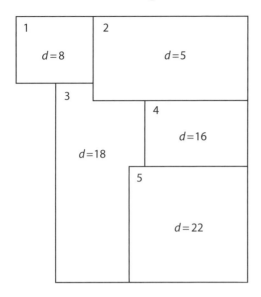

Fig. 8.19 Distribution of artefact densities (*d*) in five fields. Does field 5 and its two neighbours represent a local 'hot spot'?

statistically significant local cluster distinct from the global pattern. From these observations the values in Table 8.6 can be established to complete Eq. 8.25 so that:

$$G_i^* = \frac{56 - 3 \times 13.8}{7.1\sqrt{(5 \times 3 - 9)/4}} = \frac{14.6}{8.7} = 1.67$$

The statistic G_i^* can be taken as a standard normal random variable with a mean of 0 and a variance of 1 (Rogerson 2001, p. 174). We can therefore use the normal (*z*) distribution to establish whether the calculated value of G_i^* is sufficiently large that it falls within the critical region for a specified significance level, thus allowing the null hypothesis to be rejected. For a one-sided test, if $p < 0.05$ then $z = 1.645$, which is less than our calculated G_i^*. We can therefore reject the null hypothesis and conclude that field 5 is located in an area of locally high values.

8.8 Predictive modelling

The term 'predictive modelling' refers to the method of predicting the value (or probability of occurrence) of a dependent variable in an unsampled location using one or more independent variables. As applied to archaeology, it is most closely associated with attempts to predict the probability of archaeological settlements occurring in unsampled landscapes on the basis of quantitative assessment of the locational characteristics of settlements in a surveyed area (Kvamme 1983; Judge and Sebastian 1988; Kvamme 1990a; Westcott and Brandon 2000). In this narrow sense, predictive modelling is subject to the charge of environmental determinism

Table 8.6 *A distance matrix for Getis's G_i^* statistic*

ij	$w_{ij}(d)$	x_j	$w_{ij}(d)x_j$
5, 5	1	22	22
5, 4	1	16	16
5, 3	1	18	18
5, 2	0	5	0
5, 1	0	8	0
Sum	3	69.0	56
Mean		13.8	
St. dev.		7.1	

for its reliance on a limited range of environmental variables (Gaffney and van Leusen 1995). While it is certainly true that environmental variables influence the choice of settlement location, it is also true that these are not the only factors that people consider when choosing where and how to settle a landscape. Several writers have shown how cultural factors ranging from the influence of 'supernatural' phenomena to the location of pre-existing settlements can play an important role in influencing the human use of space (Ingold 1993; Tilley 1994, 1996; Bradley 1998, 2000; Barrett 1999; Tilley and Bennet 2001). The integration of experiential variables in GIS to improve understanding of the multiple factors that influence human settlement location remains a major challenge. To date most work in this vein has concerned visibility, although as we discuss in Chapter 10, concern with visibility does not automatically overcome the charge of environmental determinism. In the meantime, active research in developing predictive models remains focused on environmental and ecological variables, no doubt in part because of the ease with which these can be measured.

Despite the above critique, we suggest that predictive modelling can be genuinely informative in two situations. The first is cultural resource management (CRM), where it is often necessary to predict the presence of archaeological material in order to prevent or mitigate damage from construction or agricultural practices. From a CRM perspective what normally matters is whether the prediction is correct, not whether it contributes to an explanation of site location. Suffice it to say that numerous examples of predictive modelling have shown that environmental variables such as relief, soil type, drainage and permeability, slope, aspect, distance to water, etc., do – at times only moderately but occasionally significantly – improve archaeologists' ability to predict the occurrence of settlements (Kvamme 1983, 1985, 1990a; Duncan and Beckman 2000; Warren and Asch 2000; Woodman 2000b). The second situation where predictive modelling is useful is in understanding the extent to which site location may have been influenced by a complex interplay of environmental factors (cf. Wheatley 2004). In this case the goal is ultimately explanation, but providing one remains alert to the fact that correlation does not necessarily imply a causal relationship, predictive modelling provides a valuable tool for identifying multivariate patterning.

The construction of a predictive model is usually undertaken in four stages: data collection, statistical analysis, application of the model and finally model validation (cf. Duncan and Beckman 2000, p. 36; Warren and Asch 2000, p. 13). Note that validation may lead to further refinement. We consider each stage in turn.

8.8.1 *Data collection*

Predictive modelling works on the assumption that it is possible to differentiate between areas of the landscape that have evidence of past occupation (i.e. 'sites') and areas of the landscape that do not ('non-sites') on the basis of one or more landscape attributes. It follows that the construction of a predictive model requires information about the location of sites and about the distribution of the relevant landscape attribute values.

Ideally, site and non-site locations are established by a programme of random or possibly cluster sampling of the landscape, as is common practice in north America (e.g. Kohler and Parker 1986; Kvamme 1992a). This approach has the virtue of allowing estimation of the actual frequency of sites, which in turn allows one to make absolute predictions about the presence or absence of sites. The alternative approach, known as case control, typically makes use of existing data about the presence or absence of sites, and is more common in Europe, where extensive sampling of the landscape is often not practical (Woodman 2000b). Case-control data only support relative rather than absolute predictions of site presence, that is, statements of the form that it is 2.5 times more likely that there is a site at location A than there is a site at location B. Note that it is best to avoid the practice of identifying sites and then randomly picking other locations to serve as non-sites, since if the latter have not been examined they may in fact contain sites, which will then inevitably undermine the ability of the model to identify landscape attribute values that discriminate between site and non-site locations. However the site and non-site locations are identified, it is common practice to split them into a *training sample* used to build the model and a *testing sample* withheld for the purpose of testing its accuracy. This procedure is known as *split sampling* and it is usual to place 50 per cent of locations in the training sample and 50 per cent in the testing sample. When the locations have been obtained by cluster sampling then they should be split by cluster rather than by individual location (Kvamme 1988, p. 395).

A wide variety of landscape attributes have been used for predictive modelling. The primary datasets often consist of a combination of elevation, soil, hydrology, geology and vegetation maps. Once input into the GIS these can then be used to derive further secondary datasets such as relief for a set of different catchment sizes (i.e. the range of elevation values in a circumscribed area), slope and aspect, distances to annual and permanent streams, soil productivity, erodibility, permeability

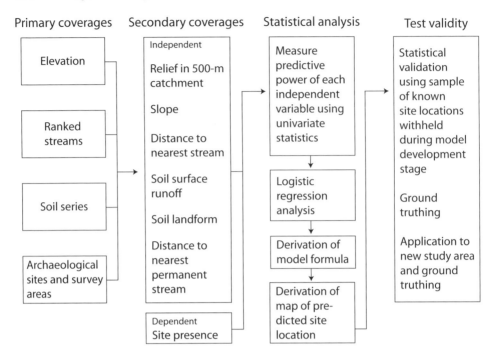

Fig. 8.20 Generalised flowchart of stages in the generation of a predictive model. Adapted from Warren and Asch's flowchart for their predictive model of site location in Montgomery County, Illinois (2000, Fig. 2.4). The six independent variables shown here are only a sample of a much wider range of potentially useful variables. See Warren and Asch (2000) and Woodman (2000b) for examples.

and drainage, vegetation type, exposure, shelter quality, viewshed size, etc. (see Fig. 8.20). Of course, not all the data collected will necessarily turn out to have predictive power.

8.8.2 *Statistical analysis*

Once the data have been assembled, the first task is to identify the landscape attributes that significantly discriminate between the site and non-site locations. This is normally achieved by univariate analysis of each attribute in turn. Depending on the type of data (e.g. nominal in the case of soil types or ratio in the case of distances, elevation and slope) the most appropriate statistical test will probably be one of those described in Chapter 7, such as the chi-squared test, the Kolmogorov–Smirnov test or, if normally distributed, Student's *t*-test. The potentially useful discriminators are those attributes for which it is possible to reject the null hypothesis that their values at site and non-site locations are drawn from the same population. Before these attributes are finally selected for inclusion in the predictive model it is wise to investigate whether any of them either confound, or interact, with others. Confounding occurs when one attribute can substitute for another in predicting the presence or absence of a site (Woodman 2000b, p. 452), from which it follows that the confounder need not be included in the model. Interaction occurs when one attribute modifies the relationship between another and the presence or absence of a site (Woodman 2000b). For example, in her predictive model of Mesolithic settlement on Islay (see Chapter 3), Woodman found that there is a low chance of finding sites at locations where water sources are small and elevation is high, but a much greater chance of finding them at locations where water sources are small and elevation is low. When attributes interact in this way they should be replaced by hybrid variables that specifically represent the nature of the interaction. Woodman (2000b, pp. 452–453) describes methods that may be used to identify confounding and interaction.

Once the appropriate attributes have been identified, the next step is to build the predictive model itself, for which the preferred technique is *logistic regression analysis* (Stopher and Meyburg 1979; Hosmer and Lemeshow 1989; Menard 2001). Logistic regression differs from linear regression in two ways that make it particularly well suited to predictive modelling. The first is that logistic regression is able to use a combination of variables of different scales (i.e. a mix of nominal, ordinal, interval and/or ratio data). The second is that logistic regression seeks to fit an 'S'-shaped probability curve (hence 'logistic'). The 'S'-shaped curve allows the predicted probabilities of site presence to switch fairly rapidly from low to high, thus avoiding the long sequence of intermediate values (representing uncertainty) that would be produced by a normal linear function. In the case of archaeological predictive modelling, the probability curve is fitted along an axis of discrimination determined by differentially weighting the contribution of the chosen attributes in such a way as to maximise the difference between site and non-site locations (Warren and Asch 2000, pp. 6–9). A number of statistical packages offer the ability to perform this task, including SPSS, R and S+. What all of them output is an intercept a, and a series of regression coefficients $b_1, b_2, \ldots, b_n$ that determine the weighting applied to each of the n attributes $x_1, x_2, \ldots, x_n$. The predictive model is an equation that takes the form

$$V = a + x_1 b_1 + x_2 b_2 + \cdots + x_n b_n \tag{8.28}$$

where V (often referred to as a 'score') is the log odds of site presence.

8.8.3 *Application*
Once logistic regression has been used to build the model it must be applied on a cell-by-cell basis to the study area. The first task is to calculate the score, V, for every map cell by implementing Eq. 8.28 in map algebra (see Chapter 9). In cases where the variables are ratio scale (e.g. elevation) then the coefficients are applied directly to the variable (e.g. if x_1 refers to elevation and the regression coefficient b_1 is 0.345, then the raster map containing elevation data would be multiplied by 0.345). In cases where nominal scale data are used, then the results of the analysis will define a set of numeric *design variables* for each nominal category that can

be inserted into the map algebraic formula (see Warren and Asch 2000, p. 19, for a concrete example). Once the score, V, has been calculated for each map cell, i, it must then be converted to a probability of site presence, p_i. This is achieved by implementing the following equation (Haining 2003, p. 262) in map algebra:

$$p_i = \frac{V_i}{1 + \exp(V_i)} \tag{8.29}$$

Depending how the training sample was collected, the resulting raster map will provide either an absolute or relative probability of a site existing in each map cell.

8.8.4 *Validation*

The fact that it has been possible to construct a predictive model does not in itself guarantee the accuracy of its predictions. This can be assessed using the testing sample that was withheld from the model-building process. The basic idea is to establish how many of the observed sites from the testing sample fall within the area where sites are predicted to be found. For example, if 16 out of 25 observed sites fall in the area where sites are predicted, then the model could be expressed as correctly predicting site location 64 per cent of the time. In reality, however, matters are not quite so simple, for two main reasons:

Prediction is probabilistic Very few, if any, models predict site occurrence with absolute certainty of presence or absence. Consequently it usually only makes sense to talk about the model correctly predicting site presence at some specified probability, p, between 0.0 and 1.0. Models tend to be more accurate at low probabilities and less accurate at high probabilities.

Non-sites matter Often it is possible to specify a probability for the occurrence of sites that is so low that all observed sites do actually fall within the area where sites are predicted, in other words, so that the model is 100 per cent accurate. However, the corollary is usually that a large number of non-sites also fall in the area where sites are predicted, so the model is very inaccurate at predicting the lack of archaeological sites. This would clearly be very undesirable if the purpose of the model was, for example, to identify a route for a new road that minimised the damage to archaeological sites.

Clearly then, it is important to consider the accuracy of a model with reference to the problem at hand. One method that facilitates this is the production of cumulative per-cent-correct prediction curves for both sites and non-sites (Kvamme 1988). Figure 8.21 shows just such a graph, in which the number of sites falling in areas where they are predicted decreases as the probability of site occurrence increases, while the number of correct non-sites increases as the probability of site occurrence increases. In this case, if it was important to avoid damaging sites then one might choose to avoid areas with even a relatively low probability of site occurrence. However, a further complication which arises at this point is that the relevant area is likely to be so large (since these are cumulative probabilities the area in question includes all locations with a low probability or greater) as to render the prediction virtually worthless. There are at least two solutions to this dilemma. One is to pay

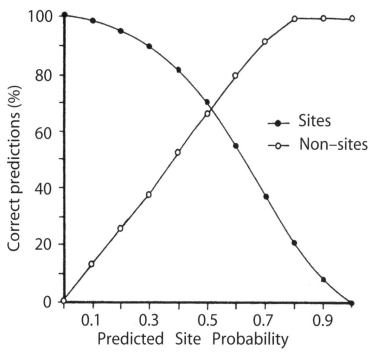

Fig. 8.21 Cumulative per cent correct predictions for model sites and non-sites for all probabilities of occurrence. Reproduced with permission from Kvamme 1988, Fig. 8.11B

attention to the trade-off between correctly predicting site and non-site locations, while another is to examine the predictive *gain* offered by the model. Kvamme (1988, p. 329) defines the gain, G, as:

$$G = 1 - \frac{\text{\% of total area where sites are predicted}}{\text{\% of observed sites within area where they are predicted}}$$

$$(8.30)$$

G, which is calculated for a specified probability of site occurrence, ranges from 1 (high predictive utility) through 0 (no predictive utility) to -1 (the model predicts the reverse of what it is supposed to). The most important property of this measure is that it can distinguish a correct but relatively worthless model from an ostensibly less correct but more useful one. For example, a model that correctly predicts 80 per cent of sites and predicts site occurrence over 70 per cent of the landscape is probably not very useful, which is reflected in the low gain of 0.13. On the other hand, a model that correctly predicts 70 per cent of sites and predicts site occurrence over a mere 5 per cent of the landscape would provide a better basis for many decisions, which is reflected in the gain of 0.93. Further suggestions for testing predictive models can be found in Kvamme (1988).

8.9 Conclusion

This chapter has introduced some techniques useful for investigating the patterns and relationships in spatial datasets. It is impossible to do full justice to the very large literature on techniques of spatial analysis, so we have chosen to highlight approaches that are within the grasp of the majority of archaeologists, whether numerically inclined or not. Although this chapter has reviewed a number of 'traditional' techniques – nearest neighbour, hierarchical and k-means cluster analysis, for example – we have also highlighted recent approaches to the explication of spatial processes, such as Ripley's K. We encourage further investigation of modern spatial analytical techniques as described by Haining (2003) and Fotheringham *et al.* (2000a).

9

Map algebra, surface derivatives and spatial processes

9.1 Introduction: point and spatial operations

In this chapter we introduce a number of point and spatial operations that can be performed on continuous field data. We begin with the use of map algebra, before moving on to the calculation of derivatives (e.g. slope and aspect) and spatial filtering (e.g. smoothing and edge detection), all of which are widely used by archaeologists. In the final section we introduce more specialised techniques that have archaeological potential.

Map algebra is a point operation, whereas the other techniques discussed in this chapter are spatial operations. Point operations compute the new attribute value of a location with coordinates (x, y) from the attribute values in other maps at the same location (x, y), (Fig. 9.1b). In contrast, spatial operations compute the new attribute value of a location from the attribute values in the same map, but at other locations – those in the neighbourhood (Fig. 9.1a). The neighbourhood used in a spatial operation may or may not be spatially contiguous. For example, slope is usually calculated using the elevation values in a neighbourhood comprising the four or eight map cells immediately adjacent to the location in question (see below), but we saw in Chapter 6 how inverse distance weighting interpolates elevation values from some number of nearest spot heights, irrespective of how far away those spot heights actually are. The use of point and spatial operations requires an appropriate data structure as well as careful consideration of whether the results are actually meaningful:

1. **Data structure** Point operations require that attribute values in different maps can be accessed using the same spatial index, which is most easily achieved by 'stacking' raster maps of the same resolution, as depicted in Fig. 9.1(b). Spatial operations can, in principle, be applied to a variety of data structures. For instance, slope can be calculated using elevation data stored as a raster elevation model or as a TIN (Chapter 6). In practice, however, many spatial operations are most commonly, or even only, performed on raster data because the regular array of values greatly simplifies the necessary algorithms.

2. **Interpretation** So far as the process of computation is concerned, most point and spatial operations can be applied to any information that can be stored using the requisite data structure. Whether the results will be meaningful is an entirely different matter! For example, the map 'calculators' included in many GIS packages will allow the user to multiply a nominal soil map by elevation, even though '134 m × clay' will rarely be meaningful. This does not necessarily mean, however, that operations should only ever be used for the purposes for which they were originally envisaged. For instance, many

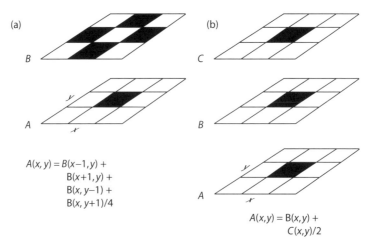

$$A(x,y) = B(x{-}1,y) + \\ B(x{+}1,y) + \\ B(x,y{-}1) + \\ B(x,y{+}1)/4$$

$$A(x,y) = B(x,y) + \\ C(x,y)/2$$

Fig. 9.1 Calculation of a mean value as a spatial operation (a) and as a point operation (b).

spatial operations were developed for application to models of terrain, where they have a 'natural' or common-sense interpretation. Thus few users will have much difficulty attaching a meaning to the rate of change of elevation, which is of course slope; and, similarly, pathways traced along routes which maximise the rate of change of elevation in a downhill direction are easily interpreted as the expected flow-lines for water runoff. Archaeologists have, however, found good reasons to calculate both the rate of change of values and 'flow lines' for non-elevation data. For example, Llobera (2003, p. 40) calculated the 'slope' of a cumulative viewshed map (see Chapter 10) since this allowed him to investigate how the extent of visibility changes as a result of movement through the landscape. As so often with GIS, it is ultimately up to the user to work out which methods will produce meaningful results in a given context.

9.2 Map algebra

The term 'map algebra' refers to the mathematical manipulation and combination of raster grids on a cell-by-cell basis (Tomlin 1990). This is an important capability of GIS and is essential for many forms of modelling and analysis. Conceptually it is straightforward: imagine two raster grids, A and B, covering the same location at the same resolution. Each cell in grid A contains the value 2, and each cell in grid B contains 3. The result of adding grid A to grid B will be a new map where each cell contains the value 5. Similarly, multiplying grid A by grid B will result in a new map where each cell contains the value 6. Obviously, when cells within a raster map have different values that reflect some form of spatial variability (e.g. vegetation, elevation, etc.), then the results of combination with other raster maps will be a new set of continuously varying data. This will occur, for example, when combining data in ways similar to the example shown in Fig. 7.14.

More complex algebraic combinations are, of course, possible. For example, the well-known Normalised Difference Vegetation Index (NDVI) shows variation in green vegetation across a land surface, with 'greener' areas having higher numbers than non-green areas. It is calculated from the near-infrared (NIR) and visible-red (VIS) image bands from a remote sensing satellite such as the SPOT or Landsat systems:

$$\text{NDVI} = \frac{(\text{NIR} - \text{VIS})}{(\text{NIR} + \text{VIS})}$$

Similarly, creating a map that shows the probability of site location as derived from a logistic regression formula (Chapter 8) also requires some long, but not necessarily complex, map algebra. This often takes the form of a polynomial:

$$\text{predictive\_map} = (0.345 * \text{elevation\_map})$$
$$+(0.2194 * \text{slope\_map})$$
$$+(1.34 * \text{distance\_to\_water\_map}) \dots$$

Note that it is necessary for grids to be the same resolution in order to be combined via map algebra. If this is not the case, one or more grids will have to be resampled to the desired resolution.

Map algebra is also used to transform a single raster map into a new map via a mathematical expression. For example, some remote-sensing and predictive modelling applications require that cell values be replaced with their logarithms in order to interpret the results.

In many GIS packages map algebra is handled via a calculator-like interface similar to the one in Fig. 9.2, which provide push-button capabilities for combining raster maps. Some packages, such as GRASS, also provide a command-line interface, which is often more convenient for repeating calculations. GRASS is also interesting for another reason: it is unique in allowing the new value of a cell with coordinates (x, y) to be computed from the values of cells with different coordinates, say $(x + 1, y + 1)$. This is a very useful facility since it allows complex spatial operations (as defined above) to be implemented in map algebra (see Box 11.1 for an example).

9.3 Derivatives: terrain form

The vast majority of archaeological GIS include a model of terrain. Often this is simply used to provide a visual backdrop for the display of, for example, site locations. In other cases, however, the model of terrain is intended to support some kind of analysis, perhaps because terrain is thought to have influenced some aspect of past human activity, or alternatively the recovery of evidence of past activities. Take, for example, the traditional settlement pattern of the western Yorkshire Dales in England: farmsteads are typically located neither in the valley bottoms nor on

Fig. 9.2 ESRI's ArcGIS 'raster calculator'. Source: ESRI. ArcGIS software and graphical user interface are the intellectual property of ESRI and used herein with permission. Copyright © ESRI. All rights reserved.

the hill tops, but instead at elevations between 190 m and 260 m. This is probably for a variety of reasons including proximity to springs, ease of passage between dwellings when the valleys were more wooded and/or marshy, and not least the fact that animal manure need only be moved downhill to fertilise the hay meadows. The simplest possible GIS model of the location of such farmsteads would be a reclassified elevation map delineating the areas located between 190 and 260 m above sea level. Of course, a model as crude as this would have little to say about the specific locations of individual farmsteads. For that we might need to include additional information such as the distribution of springs and watercourses, but also the other aspects of terrain, such as the availability of flat(ish) land for building, and shelter from prevailing winds. The point here is that there is more to terrain than simply elevation. In this section we discuss measures of terrain form that are themselves continuous fields: slope, aspect, plan convexity and profile convexity. Later, in Chapter 10, we discuss the use of GIS to identify discontinuous regions of terrain.

9.3.1 *First-order derivatives: slope and aspect*
Definitions
The *slope* calculated by GIS packages is the maximum rate of change of the elevation at a given location and the *aspect* is the azimuth (compass direction) of this rate

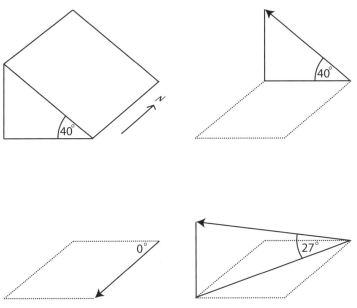

Fig. 9.3 The slope experienced while traversing terrain depends on the direction of travel. Moving due west over an east-facing 40° slope means a rate of ascent of 40°, whereas north or south movement is at 0°. Moving at a NW or SW heading to a 40° slope changes the ascent angle to 27°. Hence our propensity to 'zig-zag' up steep slopes to minimise the angle of ascent.

of change in the downhill direction. The notion of a maximum rate of change is important, since as Fig. 9.3 illustrates, the actual slope experienced when moving over terrain may vary according to the direction of travel, a point which we consider further when discussing cost-surface analysis in Chapter 10. Technically, slope and aspect are first-order derivatives of the surface in just the same way that acceleration is a first-order derivative of velocity – the only difference is that slope is a rate of change across space whereas acceleration is a rate of change in time.

Calculating slope and aspect

Almost all GIS software packages provide push-button functionality for calculating slope and aspect from elevation data. Nevertheless, the results may vary from package to package because several different algorithms have been devised to calculate derivatives of continuous field data. Fortunately it appears that the well-known packages mostly use the two algorithms that have been found to perform best in tests: Zevenbergen and Thorne's method and Horn's method (Burrough and McDonnell 1998, p. 192). Box 9.1 presents a method for calculating slope and aspect in the absence of push-button functionality.

The units of measurement used for slope and aspect are not dependent on the algorithm used to calculate them; some GIS packages offer the user a choice:

Box 9.1 How to calculate slope and aspect from first principles

---

Horn's method This generally produces good results, but is not practicable unless the GIS package in question provides spatial map algebra (e.g. GRASS) or allows the construction of quite elaborate spatial filters. According to this method, the tangent of the maximum rate of change (steepest slope), S, is given by

$$\tan S = \sqrt{(\delta z/\delta x)^2 + (\delta z/\delta y)^2}$$

and the tangent of the aspect, A, by

$$\tan A = -(\delta z/\delta y)/(\delta z/\delta x)$$

where the partial derivatives $\delta z/\delta x$ and $\delta z/\delta y$ give the slope in the east–west and south–north directions respectively. They can be calculated as follows:

$$\delta z/\delta x = (z_{x+1,y+1} + 2z_{x+1,y} + z_{x+1,y-1}$$
$$- z_{x-1,y+1} - 2z_{x-1,y} - z_{x-1,y-1})/8\Delta x$$
$$\delta z/\delta y = (z_{x+1,y+1} + 2z_{x,y+1} + z_{x-1,y+1}$$
$$- z_{x+1,y-1} - 2z_{x,y-1} - z_{x-1,y-1})/8\Delta y$$

Note that $z_{y,x}$ is the elevation value at row y, column z and Δx and Δy are the east–west and south–north map resolutions (i.e. the grid spacing).

Slope may be expressed as degrees of inclination from the horizontal, or as a percentage such that $0° = 0\%$ and $90° = 100\%$. The relationship between these units is simply:

$$\text{slope}_{\text{per cent}} = 100 \times \tan(\text{slope}_{\text{degrees}}) \tag{9.1}$$

$$\text{slope}_{\text{degrees}} = \arctan(\text{slope}_{\text{per cent}}/100) \tag{9.2}$$

Aspect is usually expressed as degrees of rotation from some origin, with a separate value for flat areas where aspect is undefined. It is important to establish exactly what scheme is used by a GIS package as the meaning of the values may not be self-evident. For example, GRASS returns 0 for flat areas and then numerical values which increase counter-clockwise from an azimuth infinitesimally north of east, so that north is $90°$, west is $180°$, south is $270°$ and east is $360°$. It is common practice to reclassify aspect values to the compass directions N, NE, E, ..., W and NW. In the case of GRASS, this could be achieved with the rules shown in Fig. 9.4.

Using slope and aspect

Slope and aspect are commonly included in archaeological predicative models of site location (see Chapter 8). They do, however, have properties which demand that they be treated with caution.

0			= 0 Flat
0.0001	thru	22.4999	= 3 E
22.5	thru	67.4999	= 2 NE
67.5	thru	112.4999	= 1 N
112.5	thru	157.4999	= 8 NW
157.5	thru	202.4999	= 7 W
202.5	thru	247.4999	= 6 SW
247.5	thru	292.4999	= 5 S
292.5	thru	337.4999	= 4 SE
337.5	thru	360	= 3 E

Fig. 9.4 A GRASS GIS rule file to reclassify aspect values to the compass directions N, NE, E, ..., W and NW.

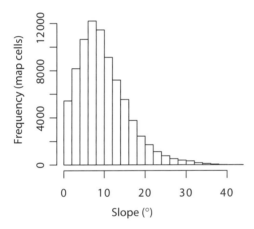

Fig. 9.5 A histogram of slope values in Dentdale and Garsdale, UK, calculated from Ordnance Survey elevation data. Despite being an area of highly variable relief, the distribution of slope values is strongly skewed such that, although the maximum slope is 43.1°, 75 per cent of cells have slopes <13° and 50 per cent have slopes <8.7°.

Slope Values calculated from elevation maps are seldom uniformly or normally distributed (Fig. 9.5). Rather, it is often the case that relatively slight slopes are most frequent, with steeper slopes less frequent and slopes >15° comparatively rare. The non-normal distribution of slope values rules out the use of parametric statistical tests for investigating whether archaeologically significant locations are associated with particular magnitudes of slope. As described in Chapter 7, one solution is to use a non-parametric test, such as the Kolmogorov–Smirnov test, to compare the slope values at archaeologically significant locations with those at a number of randomly chosen locations. The parameters of the distribution of slope values should be established

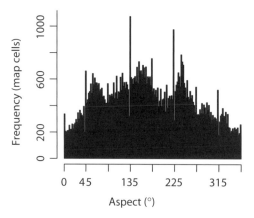

Fig. 9.6 A histogram of aspect values in Dentdale and Garsdale, UK, calculated from Ordnance Survey elevation data.

empirically as they are likely to differ from one study region to another. Note that the same is also true of many other products of elevation data, including aspect and viewshed size.

Aspect Values calculated from elevation maps are usually more uniformly distributed than slope values, as can be seen from the histogram in Fig. 9.6. However, it is not uncommon for the distribution of aspect values calculated in a raster system to contain artefacts of the method of calculation. For example, Fig. 9.6 shows a series of low but wide peaks at 90° intervals and high but narrow peaks at 45° intervals. Mystics will be disappointed to learn that the hills of northern England do not resemble a series of octangular pyramids orientated exactly on the cardinal directions! Rather, these peaks of higher frequency are the result of calculating aspect using the eight cells in the immediate neighbourhood of each location. As we have stressed elsewhere, GIS maps are models, and not always very good ones.

Those who wish to use slope and aspect for statistical analysis should note that they are not wholly independent variables, because slopes of 0° are necessarily correlated with undefined aspect. That said, it is generally the case that elevation, slope and aspect are not closely correlated in areas of varying elevation (Kvamme 1992b), although it may be worth checking this on a case-by-case basis (e.g. Lake and Woodman 2000).

Displaying slope and aspect

When displaying a slope map it may be necessary to increase the number of colours allocated to low slope values in order to reveal variation in all areas of the map. This is a direct result of the skewed distribution of values mentioned above. Figure 9.7(a) shows a map of slope values drawn with shades of grey allocated to equal-size classes of slope. Figure 9.7(b) shows the same information, but displayed with shades of grey allocated to variable-size classes of slope chosen to equalise the area they represent: note how it provides better differentiation of the low slope

(a)   (b)

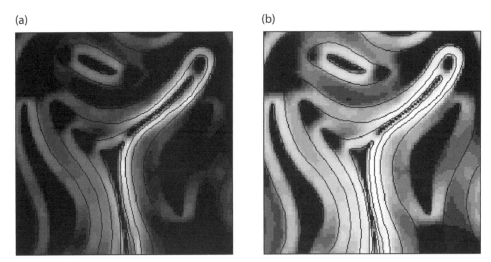

Fig. 9.7 Slope classes in (a) are shaded using an *equal-interval* method, obscuring variability at the low end (darker colours) of the range. This in corrected in (b) by defining classes using an *equal-area* classification.

values. Burrough and McDonnell (1998, p. 193) and Mitasova *et al.* (1995) provide alternative suggestions for suitable class sizes.

One of the most common applications of slope and aspect is the production of shaded relief maps. Shading makes it possible to display elevation data with a three-dimensional appearance, as if illuminated by low sunlight. The effect is particularly useful with high-resolution topographic survey data to help visualise, for example, partially ploughed-out earthworks. It is also mercilessly revealing of algorithm artefacts, particularly of the 'terraces' sometimes produced during interpolation from contour data (Chapter 6). Once the slope and aspect have been calculated from elevation data, shading can then be applied to other data, such as land-cover classes or even aerial photographs, giving an impression of relief (Fig. 9.8).

Most GIS packages provide push-button functionality to produce shaded relief maps. The simplest implementations shade the surface so that cells whose aspect faces away from a hypothetical light source (conventionally placed at 45° above the horizon in the NW) are shaded more darkly than those facing the light source. More sophisticated implementations not only allow the user to vary the position of the light source, but also estimate the amount of light reflected from each cell as a function of aspect, slope and the reflectance of the land cover. Horn (1981) provides a detailed review of the various methods that are used.

The principles used to calculate shaded relief are taken to their logical conclusion in the calculation of solar gain, also known as irradiance. Solar gain is not a presentational device, but a genuinely analytical model of the amount of solar energy falling on each location in a landscape. The calculation of solar gain is

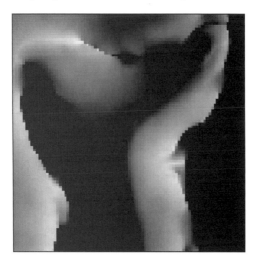

Fig. 9.8 A hillshade model integrated with a DEM to create a shaded relief model.

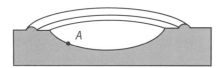

Fig. 9.9 Point *A* on the pond barrow has the same slope and aspect as point *B* on the bell barrow, but they differ in plan and profile convexity, as described in the text.

relatively complicated – see Burrough and McDonnell (1998, pp. 202–203) for a brief introduction – but it has been usefully incorporated into predictive models of site location (Duncan and Beckman 2000).

9.3.2 *Second-order derivatives: profile and plan convexity*
While the first-order derivatives of elevation, slope and aspect, provide useful and easily interpreted information about terrain, they do not directly tell us about its shape. For that it is necessary to calculate the second-order derivatives, profile and plan convexity, which measure change in the first-order derivatives.

By way of illustration, suppose a colleague had conducted a high-resolution topographic survey of a Bronze Age barrow cemetery and provided you with the slope and aspect values for an unspecified location near the centre of a perfectly formed round barrow of unspecified type (Fig. 9.9). With just this information it would be impossible to distinguish between a bell barrow and a pond barrow. If, however, your colleague had instead provided you with the profile and plan convexity, then the type of barrow would have been immediately apparent: any location near the centre of a bell barrow would be located on a slope that is convex in both profile and plan, giving it positive values, whereas any location near the centre of a pond barrow would be located on a slope that is concave in both profile and plan, giving it negative values.

In practice, the main applications of profile and plan convexity are in geomorphology, since quantitative measures of terrain form can provide useful information about the formation processes that gave rise to particular landscapes (Clowes and Comfort 1982). Such information may in turn be of value to archaeologists, especially those studying earlier prehistory. There are, however, a variety of ways in which profile and plan convexity could be of direct use to archaeologists (we do not seriously anticipate their use to classify round barrows!). Returning to the example of the placement of Yorkshire Dales' farmsteads, both profile and plan convexity might provide proxies for shelter, such that locations with negative values are more sheltered than those with positive values. Alternatively – and in a less processual vein – the ability to map qualitative aspects of terrain such as 'roundedness' opens up the possibility of enhanced dialogue with those who espouse a phenomenological approach to landscape. Indeed, we suspect that such dialogue might fare rather better if GIS-using archaeologists showed a greater willingness to experiment with the more abstract higher-order derivatives of continuous field data. Those interested in such an endeavour should consult the work of Marcos Llobera (2001) on, for example, prominence, as well as that by Lake and Woodman (2003) on the settings of stone circles.

9.4 Continuity and discontinuity

It is possible to emphasise change in continuous field data, often in the hope of identifying boundaries that may mark the edges of archaeological features such as walls, buildings or even entire settlements, depending on the scale of analysis. Conversely, it is also possible to de-emphasise change to, for example, smooth an otherwise 'problematic' DEM. Both are most commonly achieved using spatial filtering applied to raster maps.

9.4.1 *Spatial filtering*

Spatial filtering is in some respects similar to the inverse distance weighting method of interpolation discussed in Section 6.4.1. Like that method, it computes the value of a given cell as a function of the values of cells in a neighbourhood and the result is often, although not necessarily, some kind of weighted average. Unlike interpolation, however, the aim is not to estimate the value of unsampled cells, but to modify existing data in such a way as to increase or decrease the spatial autocorrelation between neighbouring cells. As we saw in Chapter 8, an increase in correlation means that the values of neighbouring cells will become more similar, while a decrease means that they will become less similar.

The neighbourhood used in spatial filtering is usually a square window, often called the *kernel*. The new (filtered) value of the central cell in the window is computed as a function of the cell values covered by the window. The window is moved over the entire map, ensuring that all cells eventually receive a new filtered value. The process is said to be *sequential* if the new value of a cell is used in calculating the value of a neighbouring cell, or *parallel* if all calculations use the original (unfiltered) cell values. Most archaeological applications require parallel filtering.

Spatial filtering is described mathematically by the equation:

$$C_{ij} = f \left(\sum_{i-m}^{i+m} \sum_{j-m}^{j+m} c_{ij} \times \lambda_{ij} \right) \tag{9.3}$$

What this says is that the central cell (C_{ij}) is some function (f) of each of the surrounding cells (c_{ij}) in a window of radius m, where the value of each cell c_{ij} is multiplied by a weight λ_{ij} and these values are then summed to determine the value at the centre of the kernel value. Note that each cell may be multiplied by a different weight depending on the type of function and the distance of the cell. For example, a type of spatial filter called *Laplacian*, described in further detail below, weights the values of pixels in such a way that locations where rapid changes in values occur are highlighted. To achieve this effect the weights may be negative in value depending on the size of kernel, as in the following example for a 7×7 kernel:

```
 0   0  -1  -1  -1   0   0
 0  -1  -3  -3  -3  -1   0
-1  -3   0   7   0  -3  -1
-1  -3   7  24   7  -3  -1
-1  -3   0   7   0  -3  -1
 0  -1  -3  -3  -3  -1   0
 0   0  -1  -1  -1   0   0
```

GIS packages that offer spatial filtering may require the user to specify the weights and probably also the radius of the window. The more analytically orientated packages also provide a choice of functions, for example the Idrisi 'FILTER' module provides nine predefined filters as well as the option for user-defined functions (Eastman 2001, p. 87).

9.4.2 *Low-pass filters: smoothing*
Low-pass filters decrease the correlation between neighbouring cells: they have the effect of smoothing away local variability (often referred to as *noise*). Figure 9.10 shows the application of a low-pass filter to a 5×5 matrix.

Using low-pass filters
Low-pass filters have been used to smooth (or 'blur') data in an archaeological GIS for a variety of reasons, some more appropriate than others:

(a)

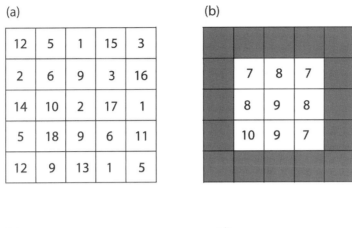

(b)

(c)

(d)

Fig. 9.10 A simple low-pass filter. In this example the 25 cells values in (a) have been replaced by the mean of themselves plus their 8 nearest neighbours. This new value is stored in a separate map (b). The process transforms a 'rough' surface (c) to a 'smooth' surface (d). Note that new values are not calculated for the cells at the edge of the map as erroneous values would be calculated for these owing to them having fewer than 8 neighbours.

Presentation Smoothed surfaces often look more visually attractive than the raw data. For example, it may be preferable to overlay labels and other graphics on the continuous tone representing smoothed quadrat counts of, say, microliths, rather than overlay them on the the 'blocky' representation of the raw counts. However, we suggest that it is generally better to avoid such uses of smoothing unless: (a) the original measurements are also made available; and (b) the smoothed surface is not being used to support an argument that is untenable given the variability in the original data.

Enhancement of terrain models As we saw in Chapter 6, terrain models often contain interpolation artefacts, in which case there may be a temptation to smooth them away. Smoothing for purely aesthetic reasons has the disadvantage that it misleads others about the quality of the terrain model. One common analytical reason for smoothing is the removal of 'pits' that would otherwise disrupt the simulated flow of water in hydrological modelling (see Chapter 11). Another is to remove interpolation 'terraces' that would otherwise erroneously disrupt the line-of-sight in viewshed analysis, although this has the significant disadvantage of lowering peaks and ridges which are often important determinants of viewshed extent.

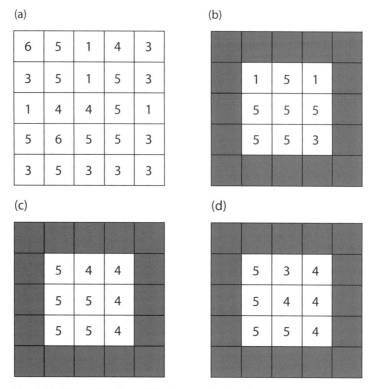

Fig. 9.11 The application of filtering to calculate the (b) mode, (c) range and (d) diversity of map (a).

Identification of trend By reducing local variability it may be easier to identify trends in data. The use of smoothing for this purpose can be appropriate when the process is of an informal exploratory nature, but for more analytical purposes it is better to model a trend surface (Chapter 6) as this provides a measure of the fit.

Computing low-pass filters

Low-pass filters typically compute the central cell as some kind of average of the cells in the window (the kernel):

- The **mean** is used on ratio and interval data (Fig. 9.10), for example elevation or pottery counts. The mean can be calculated quite simply by applying equal fractional weights and then summing the results. For example, if the window is of radius $m = 1$ then all nine weights $\lambda_{i-1,j-1} \ldots \lambda_{i+1,j+1}$ should be set to 1/9 since summing one-ninth of nine cells gives their average value.
- The **mode** (most common value) provides a more appropriate average of nominal and ordinal data such as, for example, a map showing the most frequent artefact type in each cell (Fig. 9.11b).

An alternative use of low-pass filtering is not to smooth existing data, but to create a new map that provides a measure of its local variability. The following functions measure (but do not increase) local variability:

- The **range** is used on ratio and interval data to describe the maximum difference between cell values in the window (Fig. 9.11c).
- The **diversity** (the number of different values in the window) provides a more appropriate measure of variability in nominal and ordinal data (Fig. 9.11d).

9.4.3 *High-pass filters: emphasising change*
High-pass filters have the opposite effect of low-pass filters: they enhance (or 'sharpen') local variability (*noise*).

Using high-pass filters
The most common archaeological application of high-pass filtering is edge detection. For example, given a high-precision topographic survey it may be possible to identify the walls of a buried building by locating areas of rapid rate of change of elevation (Fig. 9.12). The same technique can also be applied to crop marks in aerial photographs, where the change is not in elevation but the tones recorded in the (digitised) image.

In such cases the purpose of edge detection might be:

> **Detection** of features barely discernible to the human eye;
> **Extraction** of features for automated mapping (by thinning and vectorising the results);
> **Quantification** of the fragility of the traces of features, perhaps for conservation purposes.

Edge detection can also be used visually to examine terrain models for interpolation artefacts, although a slope map is often just as effective for this purpose.

Computing high-pass filters
High-pass filters are defined in map algebraic terms as:

$$\text{High\_pass\_map} = \text{Original\_map} - \text{Low\_pass\_map}$$

High-pass filters can be created by implementing the above formula in map algebra. Figure 9.12(b) shows a high-pass filter calculated in this way using a kernel radius of 1. It is more common, however, to use specially designed sets of kernel weights. For example, the previously described Laplacian edge filter is calculated by summing the products of each pixel value multiplied by its kernel values. In a 3×3 kernel the appropriate individual pixel weights are:

```
-1   -1   -1
-1   +8   -1
-1   -1   -1
```

This result emphasises the edges of polygonal areas with higher or lower values than the surrounding area. The above Laplacian filter applied to the elevation data in Fig. 9.12(a) produces the image in Fig. 9.12(c).

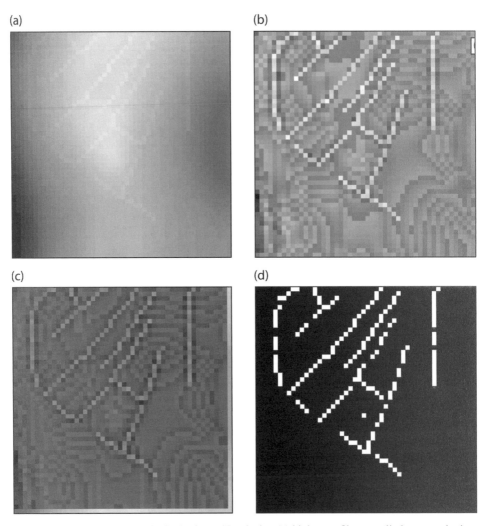

Fig. 9.12 Map algebraic (b) and Laplacian (c) high-pass filters applied to a synthetic DEM containing traces of a field system (a). Extraction of values >1 from the map algebraic result produces a map of the field system (d).

The more raster-orientated GIS packages such as GRASS and Idrisi also offer other specialised edge-detection filters such as the zero-crossing and Sobel edge-detector filters.

9.5 Surface processes: erosion
This section discusses soil erosion modelling as an example of a spatial operation that models a real-world process operating continuously across space. We have chosen soil erosion modelling for two reasons: first, it has several archaeological

Table 9.1 *The universal soil loss equation:* $A = R \times K \times L \times S \times C \times P$

Variable	Description
A	Annual soil loss (ton h^{-1})
R	Erosivity of the rainfall, where $R = 0.11abc + 66$ and a is average annual precipitation (cm), b is the maximum one-day precipitation occurring once in 2 years (cm), and c is the maximum total precipitation of a shower occurring once in 2 years (cm)
K	Erodibility of the soil
L	Slope length factor: $L = (l/22.1)^{0.5}$, where l is slope length (m)
S	Slope factor: $S = 0.0062 \times s^2 + 0.065$, where s is the slope (%)
C	Cultivation parameter
P	Production parameter

Source: Burrough and McDonnell 1998, Box 7.2.

applications and, second, it provides a good illustration of the kinds of issues that are likely to confront those using the more specialised GIS functions.

Archaeologists may gain insight from the modelling of soil erosion in a variety of applications, including:

> **Conservation:** as archaeological sites may benefit from the identification of those at risk from natural erosion, especially in upland areas;
>
> **Prediction** of site location: as this may be enhanced by the identification of areas where soil has been deposited in sufficient quantity to ensure the preservation of archaeological features;
>
> **Landscape history:** which may require an appreciation of the effects of human land-use practices on soil erosion and thus, ultimately, landform.

9.5.1 *Computing soil erosion*

Prior to the widespread availability of GIS, quantitative soil erosion modelling essentially involved constructing an empirical predicative model of the likely soil loss at a given location. This approach, epitomised by the well-known universal soil loss equation (USLE), links observed rates of soil loss with the erosivity of the rainfall and attributes for the eastern USA (Wischmeier and Smith 1978). The latter usually include the erodibility of the soil, the slope, the slope length, the type of cultivation and any measures taken to impede erosion (Table 9.1).

A number of organisations provide data to simplify the calculation of the USLE for agricultural and soil management purposes. For example, the US National Soil Erosion Laboratory (NSERL)[1] and the Ontario Ministry of Agriculture and Food[2] publish tables of data giving values of R, K, C and P for local areas and conditions. The USLE can be implemented in a GIS by applying map algebra to raster maps

---

[1] http://topsoil.nserl.purdue.edu/usle/.
[2] www.gov.on.ca/OMAFRA/index.html.

of the various attributes. Note, however, that it is not a model per se but a set of empirically derived relationships between environmental variables and land use for the eastern USA. Its applicability outside this region is questionable, and in areas such as the Mediterranean the USLE has been shown to have little predictive value for estimating rates of soil erosion (Grove and Rackham 2003, p. 255).

The USLE provides a basic generalised model of erosion but it fails to harness the ability of GIS to implement operations that are truly spatial. More recent GIS-based approaches attempt to predict soil loss by modelling the actual process of erosion (Nearing *et al.* 1994), namely, the transport of sediment over a land surface. Examples of this approach include the AGricultural Non-Point Source Model (AGNPS) (Young *et al.* 1989) and the Areal Non-point Source Watershed Environmental Response Simulation model (ANSWERS; Beasley and Huggins 1991).

Process-orientated erosion models typically work by allowing sediment to 'flow' downhill from each map cell to its lowest neighbour. Since cells may also receive sediment from their uphill neighbours the end result at any particular location can be either erosion – a net loss of sediment – or deposition – a net gain of sediment. Depending upon how the model is implemented the results may be viewed as one or more of: a revised elevation model; a map of revised sediment thickness; or a map of the changes in elevation or sediment thickness (see figures in Mitas *et al.* 1996 for examples). Theoretically, the amount of sediment that moves between any given two cells is dependent upon factors that affect three processes: the detachment of soil particles from the parent material; the transport of those particles by some agent, such as water or wind; and the deposition of transported particles. The factors most commonly included in process-orientated GIS erosion models are those that measure the contribution of landform, soil type, land cover and rainfall intensity to detachment, transport and deposition (Box 9.2).

9.5.2 *Issues in erosion modelling*
Three issues stand out as particularly relevant to archaeologists and we discuss them in some detail as they also apply to many kinds of advanced modelling in GIS.

Choosing a model
The simplest way of choosing a model is to find one that has been implemented in the GIS package with which you are most familiar and/or which the relevant project uses. However, since considerably more time is likely to be spent gathering input data than learning which buttons to press, it may be quicker in the long run – and more scientifically defensible – to choose according to properties of the model rather than the software. Most models draw on the same basic understanding of the physical processes that cause erosion, but all differ in how exactly they model those processes. This is true in terms of both the spatial resolution and the specific parameters used to characterise the processes. For example, while AGNPS assumes that rainfall is constant over the entire region, ANSWERS allows several 'rain gauges' to be specified, each recording temporal variation in rainfall in a given subregion. Similarly, AGNPS requires that soil properties be specified in terms of

Box 9.2 Parameters required for the ANSWERS[a] erosion model

Soil

- Total porosity (per cent pore space volume of soil)
- Field capacity (per cent saturation)
- Steady-state infiltration rate (mm h^{-1})
- Difference between steady-state and maximum infiltration rate (mm h^{-1})
- Infiltration exponent accounts for the rate of decrease in infiltration capacity against increasing moisture content
- Antecedent soil moisture (per cent saturation)
- Soil erodability (K in the USLE)

Land use

- Potential rainfall interception by land cover (mm)
- Surface covered by specified land use (%)
- Roughness coefficient of the surface (a shape factor)
- Maximum roughness height of the surface profile (m)
- Manning's *n* (a measure of flow retardance of the surface)
- Relative erosiveness (function of time and USLE *C* and *P*)

Watershed

- Tile drain coefficient
- Groundwater release fraction (contribution of groundwater flow to runoff)

Rainfall

- Intensity at specified times during event (mm h^{-1})

Channels

- Width
- Roughness
- Slope (if not same as overland slope)

Management practices

- One of a choice of four best management practices (BMPs)

———
[a] http://soils.ecn.pardue.edu/~aggrass/models/answers/.

percentages of sand, silt and clay, while ANSWERS requires information about the porosity, saturation point and infiltration rate. Consequently, there are at least three criteria that could be used to choose a model:

> **Spatial resolution:** the match between the spatial resolution and the study region;
> **Parameters:** the match between the parameters required and those that are available or can be most easily obtained;
> **Theoretical preference:** which is likely to require expert advice.

Assembling input data

As Table 9.1 and Box 9.2 show, erosion models require large numbers of parameters. Some of these, such as elevation and the distribution of soil types, may be available from published sources in digital form (and almost certainly for a fee). It is important to check that the resolution is adequate for the problem at hand. The distribution of land cover can also be derived from satellite remote-sensing data, although this may require fieldwork for ground truthing (see Chapter 7). The properties of soil types and the effect of land-cover types on, for example, flow rates, may require extensive investigation in the field and laboratory. The key point here is that with erosion modelling in particular, and advanced modelling in general, the use of GIS is often the easiest and cheapest part of the whole endeavour. High-quality input data are more likely to have greater influence on the usefulness of the results than expenditure on more sophisticated software.

Palaeoenvironmental reconstruction

By running an erosion model on the palaeoenvironment it may be possible to predict where sites are buried or to enhance understanding of landscape history. A key issue, of course, is the quality of the available palaeoenvironmental reconstruction. All archaeologists will be familiar with issues of temporal resolution and other sources of uncertainty, such as the differential preservation of pollen from different tree species. The additional problem facing those undertaking GIS-based process-driven modelling of erosion is that the requirement for spatially continuous input is not immediately met by the palaeoenvironmental evidence, which almost always constitutes point data, such as that from boreholes. This problem, which is common to most GIS-based modelling of past landscapes, including viewshed analysis (Chapter 10), must be overcome by some form of interpolation. One response to the additional uncertainty introduced by the need for interpolation is simply an outright rejection of GIS-based modelling of past landscapes, but this seems to us overly pessimistic. Instead, we suggest two criteria that can be used in determining whether to proceed:

1. If the effect of uncertainty in the input data can be measured in such a way that the results can be qualified with a probability or a confidence interval. This might be achieved by running the model with a range of different input values reflecting the possible states of the palaeoenvironment.
2. If the uncertainty is commensurable with the inferential logic of the project. For example, a project that seeks to infer unknown human land-use practices from their contribution to the evolution of the modern environment requires reasonable certainty about the palaeoenvironment because its logic is to infer an unknown process from a known start and end point. In contrast, a project where the land-use practices are known and the aim is instead to reconstruct the palaeoenvironment requires less certainty because the logic is that the end point and process will be used to infer the unknown start point by a process of 'reverse engineering'.

9.6 Conclusion

In this chapter we have discussed the application of spatial operations to continuous field data, such as elevation. The calculation of slope and aspect is almost routine in research-orientated archaeological GIS, although as we explained, there are various pitfalls to be avoided. The calculation of plan and profile convexity is less common, but has its uses for both geomorphological and possibly also more phenomeno-logically orientated research. Low-pass filters have various applications – some more desirable than others – while high-pass filters can be used to assist in the interpretation of aerial and satellite imagery and even, in some cases, automated mapping. The final part of this chapter discussed soil erosion modelling as an example of a spatial operation which attempts to model a real-world process of interest to archaeologists. In the next chapter we extend our discussion of modelling and introduce the derivation and analysis of regions.

10

Regions: territories, catchments and viewsheds

10.1 Introduction: thinking about regions

A GIS can be used to create, represent and analyse many kinds of region. Some regions have an objective reality, at least to the extent that they are widely recognised and have a readily detectable influence on aspects of human behaviour. The most obvious examples of this kind are sociopolitical regions such as the territories of modern nation states. Other regions have an objective reality in another sense: that they are defined by some natural process. A good example of a natural region is the watershed; that is, the area within which all rainfall drains to some specified point in a drainage network. A third kind of region is essentially just analytical in the sense that it is created for a specific short-lived purpose and may never be recognised by anyone other than the analyst. For example, an archaeologist might determine the region containing all land within 100 m of a proposed high-speed railway line in order to identify at-risk archaeological sites, but it is the list of sites and their locations, not the region, that is fed back into the planning process.

Regions are readily represented as polygons in a vector map, or less efficiently as cells coded in such a way as to distinguish between inside and outside a region in a raster map. Where the extent of regions are known in advance of GIS-based analysis, as is often the case with sociopolitical regions, their generation and manipulation within a GIS is mostly an issue of data capture and map query.[1] Consequently, the reader whose primary concern is to map and manipulate known regions should consult Chapters 5 and 7, where we discussed these operations in detail. Our principal concern in this chapter is with the use of GIS to build models of regions whose extents are not known in advance of GIS-based analysis.

The use of GIS to model regions resonates so closely with certain theoretical developments in archaeology and geography that it is important to be aware of them, since they often provide the implicit, if not explicit, justification for many GIS-based analyses. As noted in Chapter 1, there is a long history of intellectual traffic between geography and archaeology (Goudie 1987), stretching from the local antiquaries and travelled dilettantes of the sixteenth–nineteenth centuries, who engaged in various combinations of survey, map making, exploration and antiquarianism, to the influence of humanistic geographers such as Ted Relph (1976) and Yi-Fu Tuan (1974,

---

[1]The exact reality of supposedly objective regions is sometimes contested, in which case a more sophisticated approach may be required, such as representation using a raster map with cells coded according to some measure of the degree to which there is consensus about whether or not they fall in the region.

1978) on the development of phenomenological approachs to landscape archaeology. Along the way, the New Archaeology was strongly influenced – particularly in its European guise – by the New Geography, whose classic texts *Locational Analysis in Human Geography* (Haggett 1965) and *Models in Geography* (Chorley and Haggett 1967) provided the stimulus for *Analytical Archaeology* (Clarke 1968) and *Models in Archaeology* (Clarke 1972). Like the New Archaeology which it partially inspired, the New Geography was to a considerable extent born of a growing interest in (and availability of) techniques of measurement and comparison, and a dissatisfaction with the tradition of descriptive synthesis and narrative (Wagstaff 1987). Of particular significance for the treatment of regions, however, was the move to replace chorology – the study of the character and interrelations between places and regions, which formed the backbone of traditional geography – with spatial analysis – the study of geometric arrangement and patterns of phenomena (see e.g. Bunge 1966). In other words, according to the New Geography, place and region should be treated as the result of processes of interaction, not objective entities awaiting study. This view inspired a distinctive spatial archaeology as defined by the contributions to *Spatial Archaeology* (Clarke 1977) and *Spatial Analysis in Archaeology* (Hodder and Orton 1976), and the development of site catchment analysis (Roper 1979).

The notion that regions should be treated as the outcomes of processes both inspired and continues to provide theoretical justification for many of the common GIS techniques for modelling and creating regions. For example, the creation of regions using Thiessen polygons (Section 10.2.2) betrays certain assumptions about processes of spatial differentiation, while the use of cost-surfaces (Section 10.3.1) typically acknowledges factors such as the cost of transport. Consequently, the uptake of GIS in archaeology has led to a tension between the availability of techniques ideally suited to the agenda of the 1970s spatial archaeology and the fact that much of this agenda has been discarded by post-processualists more concerned with a situated contextual meaning than the identification of general processes. We will not attempt to adjudicate on this matter, but instead simply lay out the assumptions behind the various techniques and encourage users to think creatively about their application.

10.2 Geometrical regions

Geometrical regions are defined in abstract spatial terms and do not take account of the content of space. As a result they are mostly analytical, since very few real-world spatial processes are unaffected by what is 'on the ground'. Geometrical regions are most commonly produced by buffering (also called proximity analysis) and tessellation.

10.2.1 *Buffering*

The simplest kind of buffer is a region containing all locations within a certain proximity to particular geographically referenced entity (the origin). The proximity is usually specified in terms of a maximum distance, or both a minimum and

Fig. 10.1 Multiple buffer zones around a point.

maximum distance. In Fig. 7.5 we illustrated the result of a distance or buffer query performed on point, linear and areal entities. A single buffer generated from a linear entity such as a river or road is often referred to as a corridor. It is also possible to create multiple buffers, in which case minimum and maximum values are usually chosen so as to produce a set of contiguous buffers (zones) of ever increasing distance from the origin (Fig. 10.1).

The presence or absence of a specified location within a particular zone provides categorical information about the distance from that location to the origin. If the zones are made suitably narrow with reference to the map resolution, then the effect is analogous to the process of creating a continuous proximity surface by spreading (see Section 10.3.1). In this case, the presence of a specified location in a particular zone does essentially record the actual distance from that location to the origin. Single and multiple buffers can also be generated from multiple origins, in which case the buffers are computed according to the distance from the nearest origin (Fig. 10.2).

Since buffers are discrete entities they are most efficiently represented as polygons in a vector map. Consequently, almost all vector-based GIS software provides push-button functionality for the computation of single and multiple buffers from one or more origins. A particular virtue of the vector representation of buffers is that they may then be included in spatial queries implemented using polygon overlay (Chapter 7). In this way it would be easy, for example, to identify all archaeological sites that fall within the jurisdiction of a particular local authority and which are also located within 50 m of a proposed new road. It is, however, also possible to represent buffers in raster databases. While single buffers can be represented by Boolean maps, with cells coded 1 if they are inside the buffer and 0 if they are outside, multiple buffers must be represented by coding cells according to the category value of the buffer in which they fall. Traditionally, raster buffers are created by

Fig. 10.2 Multiple merged buffers. Each merged zone reports the distance to the nearest point without indicating which point.

reclassifying a continuous proximity surface, but many raster-based GIS packages now offer push-button functionality for this task.

We have included buffers as examples of geometrical regions because they are almost always calculated solely on the basis of Euclidean distance. However, Euclidean distance is not necessarily the most appropriate measure of proximity: other measures that have potential application in archaeology include travel time, the concentration of chemicals diffusing from a source, intervisibility and measures of the possibility of flooding. Map algebra and reclassification can be used to create buffers representing distance conceived in terms of categorical attributes, such as intervisibility and location on the floodplain. Buffers representing distance conceived in terms of continuous attributes, such as travel time, must usually be derived from the results of spreading (see Section 10.3.1 below).

10.2.2 *Tessellation*
Tessellation is simply the process of dividing an area into a set of smaller tiles such that there are no gaps between the tiles. Raster maps are one example of a tessellation, but in this case the tiles (i.e. map cells) are not normally interpreted as meaningful regions. Here we are more interested in tessellations constructed for analytical purposes. By far the most common of these is a method referred to variously as Dirichlet tessellations, Voronoi diagrams or, more frequently, Thiessen polygons. Given an initial distribution of points, the tessellation divides an area so that each point is enclosed by exactly one polygon which also contains all the space that is closer to that point than any other. The polygon may then inherit an attribute of its defining point so that it becomes in fact a simple form of interpolation. This method can be used for interpolation of categorical point observations, such as to create continuous soil maps from borehole data (Fig. 10.3).

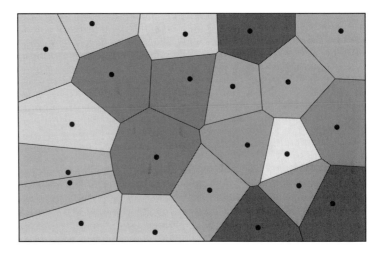

Fig. 10.3 Thiessen polygons. Differential shading represents attribute state.

The New Geography pioneered the use of Thiessen polygons to define the spheres of influence of urban centres, an idea which found its way into Clarke's (1968) manifesto for the New Archaeology. Thiessen polygons were subsequently used to define 'territories' for archaeological site types, including Neolithic long barrows (Renfrew 1976), hillforts (Cunliffe 1971) and Romano-British settlements (Hodder and Hassell 1971b). In these cases they implemented a clear rationale for allocation of territories: that control should be ascribed to the nearest site. To the extent that this rationale is made explicit, the use of Thiessen polygons represented an improvement on ad hoc methods such as the 'squeezing' of circular buffers (Dennell and Webley 1975; see Steinberg 1996; Perlès 2001, pp. 139–143 for more recent uses). However, few archaeologists would today accept the underlying assumptions that influence is independent of the cost of transport, the size of the centre and a myriad of other social and cultural factors (see, for example, Milner's 1996 review of Peregrine's 1995 application).

There are no 'textbook' methods for adjusting tessellations to reflect how the content of individual tiles influences their extent through factors such as the cost of transport. This is not surprising, since geometrical methods for constructing regions ignore the content of space; spreading provides a more appropriate method when the latter is important. It is, however, possible to adjust the extent of individual tiles according to the relative importance of each of the points from which the tessellation was generated. In this case the 'importance' may be a measure of anything from population size to the presence or absence of a religious centre.

The basic premise of gravity modelling is that the intensity of interaction between locations is directly proportional to some quantity at those locations and inversely proportional to the intervening distance (Hodder and Orton 1976, pp. 187–195). For example – and very crudely – it predicts more interaction between large settlements

Box 10.1 Weighting Thiessen polygons

One possible equation to weight Thiessen polygons, and thus to model the boundary between two settlements, i and j is:

$$D_{xj} = \frac{D_{ij}}{1 + \sqrt{P_i/P_j}}$$

where P_i and P_j are the two population sizes, D_{ij} is the distance between them and D_{xj} is the distance from settlement j at which the boundary may be drawn (Hodder and Orton 1976, p. 188).

Constructing weighted Thiessen polygons based on this gravity model in a GIS involves first establishing the smallest convex hull around each point using its neighbouring points as vertices. Weighted polygons may then be constructed by first connecting a series of point locations with line segments and erecting perpendiculars to those line segments at the point defined by D_{xj}, and then extending those perpendiculars until they intersect. An alternative is provided by Aurenhammer and Edelsbrunner (1984). Weighting Thiessen polygons is not provided as a built-in function of desktop GIS, so implementing this algorithm in mainstream commercial GIS packages will likely require the writing of a script. Alternatively, freely available standalone programs such as Gambini (Tiefelsdorf and Boots n.d.) or VPPlants (Gavrilova n.d.) perform this function, and the latter permits the export of the results so they can be placed back into a GIS.

than between small settlements, and that the amount of interaction is less if the settlements were far apart rather than nearby. For example, Jochim (1976, pp. 55–62) has used gravity modelling to investigate the 'differential "pulls" of various resources on [site location]' in Mesolithic Germany. One very simple method for adjusting the size of Thiessen polygons – by weighting them according to the relative size or importance of the individual points – is described in Box 10.1. An alternative approach that employs weighted boundaries to allow for dominance of one territory over another was devised by Renfrew and Level (1979) and is called the XTENT model. There are, however, very few applications beyond their trial formulation, largely because of the acknowledged subjectivity in determining the value of the constant that determines whether territories are likely to be more or less autonomous.

10.3 Topographical regions
It is often appropriate to define regions according to the outcome of processes. Unlike the geometric regions discussed above, regions defined by processes must necessarily take account of the content of space, since the outcome of the relevant

processes will be at least partly determined by what is 'on the ground'. We have chosen to label such regions 'topographic' for the simple reason that the processes most frequently chosen to define regions, whether natural or anthropogenic, happen to be those significantly affected by elevation and its products. For example, watersheds are defined by the flow of rainfall over a land surface (see Chapter 11), which is in large part a function of slope. Similarly, regions defined by the maximum distance that can be travelled without exceeding a certain cost are also likely to be strongly influenced by the steepness of slopes. We must stress, however, that the techniques described in this section are not limited in their application to topography. Indeed, there is scope for applying them to the cultural content of space, for example, to model movement through sacred landscapes in which particular places are vested with meanings that make them attractive or perhaps forbidden destinations. This is an area where archaeologists could perhaps show greater creativity in co-opting GIS functionality to their own ends (but see Wheatley 1993; Llobera 2000).

10.3.1 *Accessible regions*

The explanation of human land-use patterns often, if not always, requires understanding of the potential for – and constraints on – movement through the landscape. In other words, it requires that an attempt be made to establish the relative accessibility of different locations. The classic example of explicit interest in accessibility is site catchment analysis, which is an investigation of the resources available within a region (catchment) accessible from a site (Finzi and Higgs 1972; Higgs and Finzi 1972). Such analyses have variously modelled accessibility as a function of distance (Higgs *et al.* 1967), time (Higgs *et al.* 1967), energetic expenditure (Foley 1977) or territorial packing (Cassels 1972; Dennell and Webley 1975), all of which can – at least in principle – be modelled using GIS. The influence of distance and territorial packing can be modelled as geometrical regions using techniques described above, such as buffering and the fitting of Thiessen polygons respectively. The influence of time and energetic expenditure can be modelled using topographic regions derived from cost-surfaces, which is our concern here.

A cost-surface, or more properly, *accumulated cost-surface*, models the cost of moving from a specified origin to one or more destinations. The cost of moving to each destination is accumulated by a *spreading function* that 'spreads' out over a *cost-of-passage map*. Accumulated cost-surfaces and cost-of-passage maps are usually created as raster maps, since this greatly simplifies the necessary algorithms. Most GIS software requires a minimum of three input maps to create an accumulated cost-surface: a map specifying the origin, a map specifying a destination at which the calculation may cease and a cost-of-passage map. The first two requirements are trivial, but the amount of work that may be required to generate an appropriate cost-of-passage map should not be underestimated.

Before discussing how to create a cost-of-passage map in more detail, it is important to note that the costs used to determine accessibility need not necessarily be measured using a functional currency such as energetic expenditure or elapsed time. In principle, it is possible to employ costs that represent cultural influences such as attraction to or repulsion from burial mounds, or other significant places. Indeed, Llobera (2000) has described in detail how the cultural influence of monuments can be combined with the energetic cost of traversing terrain. Although advanced GIS skills are needed to tackle such a model, it nevertheless suggests that the obstacles to progress in this area lie as much with the difficulty of calibrating models of cultural influence as with the limitations of GIS technology.

Cost-of-passage maps

The cost-of-passage map models the cost of traversing each individual map cell. The cost is often referred to as a *friction* and the cost-of-passage map as a *friction map*. The cost of moving over a cell depends on the mode of transport as well as the attributes of the cell. For example, a map cell that falls in a river may be costly to traverse on foot, but cheap to traverse by boat. The combination of mode of transport and cell attributes determines whether the cost is isotropic, partially anisotropic or fully anisotropic (Collischonn and Pilar 2000).

> **Isotropic** costs are independent of the direction of travel. For example, the cost due to land cover is usually the same irrespective of the direction in which one is travelling: scrub offers the same resistance whether one is travelling north or south, as does a metalled (i.e. gravel or pebble) surface.
>
> **Partially anisotropic** costs are dependent on the direction of travel, but the direction of maximum cost is the same for all cells in the map. For example, a kayaker incurs a greater energetic cost paddling into a head wind than with a tail wind, but the wind direction itself may be constant across the map.
>
> **Anisotropic** costs are dependent on both the direction of travel and the attributes of individual map cells. For example, the maximum cost of walking across a cell is likely to be incurred when walking uphill in the direction of steepest slope, but this direction is potentially different for every cell in the map.

In most published archaeological cost-surface analyses the relevant mode of transport is walking (e.g. Bell and Lock 2000; Bell *et al.* 2002; van Leusen 2002), which incurs both isotropic and anisotropic costs.

Isotropic cost-of-passage The most important determinants of isotropic cost when walking are surface roughness and landcover. So-called 'terrain coefficients' have been developed to model the effect of surface roughness on energetic expenditure (Soule and Goldman 1969), although the additional costs seldom exceed 10 per cent of the cost on a smooth surface (Passmore and Durnin 1955). The energetic expenditure incurred in moving through different types of land cover has not been studied so systematically, partly because there are so many possibilities, ranging from paved surfaces, through various kinds of farmed and natural vegetation, to rock and water. Fieldcraft manuals (e.g. Langmuir 1997) provide a starting point

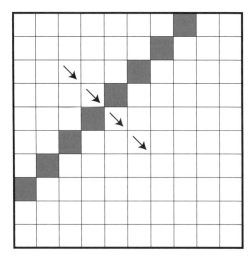

Fig. 10.4 Linear barrier breached by diagonal moves.

for ascertaining the relative costs of some land-cover types, but ultimately it may be necessary to undertake field trials. Van Leusen's (2002, Chapter 16) attempt to model Iron Age and Roman trade networks provides a useful example of the kinds of decisions that must be made when considering the effect of land cover on the cost of movement.

Thus far we have assumed that all map cells can be traversed, albeit with varying costs, but sometimes it is more appropriate to mark some cells as absolute barriers to movement. For example, one may wish to model the impact of defensive earthworks, territorial limits, sacred areas or dangerously fast-flowing rivers. Some GIS software packages provide for the inclusion of barriers by allowing one to place special (often negative) values in the cost-of-passage map. Where this is not the case, a similar effect can be obtained by the simple expedient of inserting exceptionally high values in the cost-of-passage map: the values chosen should be orders of magnitude greater than the maximum value ascribed to the traversable cells. In both cases, a potential problem may arise if the map resolution is such that a linear barrier is represented by a string of single map cells. As van Leusen (2002, Chapter 16) points out, if the chosen spreading algorithm allows movement along the diagonals as well as the cardinal directions, then in some circumstances (Fig. 10.4) the barrier can be breached. One solution to this problem is to add additional cells to the barrier, which can normally be done using a function that 'grows' regions.

The converse of modelling barriers is modelling features that can be expected to canalise movement. In many cases these will be real physical phenomena, such as roads or rivers, in which case the relevant land-cover type should be coded with a suitably low value in the cost-of-passage map. In other cases it may be that movement is canalised by habit rather than any specific land-cover type. Where

(a) (b)

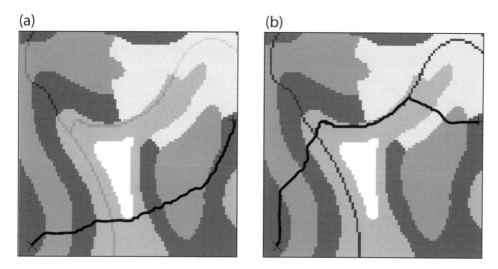

Fig. 10.5 Least-cost paths (black lines) derived from isotropic cost-of-passage maps in which roads (grey lines) are assigned (a) a relative cost and (b) a fixed cost.

this is known to have been the case, it can be modelled by reducing the relevant cell values in the cost-of-passage map. Although modifying the cost-of-passage map will negate the value of any attempt to calculated cumulated energy costs (if, in fact, that is desired), this effectively encourages movement along routes that are known or are suspected to have been preferred. A large reduction to a fixed value will accord greater influence to habitual movement than a smaller reduction made relative to the costs in the surrounding cells (Fig. 10.5).

Anisotropic cost-of-passage Walking is a good example of a mode of transport that incurs anisotropic costs, in this case due to the increased energetic requirements of traversing slopes. There are two aspects to modelling the cost of walking on slopes. The first is to determine the magnitude of the slope that is actually experienced, the *effective slope*, and the second is to ascribe a cost to traversing a slope of that magnitude.

> **Effective slope** differs from the slope recorded in a slope map in two ways. First, slope maps record the maximum rate of change of elevation across a map cell, but one may not necessarily be travelling in the direction of the maximum rate of change. Since aspect maps typically record the azimuth of the downward direction of the maximum rate of change, it follows that the slope that is experienced when traversing a map cell varies from zero to the slope, according to whether the direction of travel is perpendicular to, or parallel with, the aspect, respectively. Second, a given slope may be either downhill, or uphill, depending on whether travel is in the same or opposite direction to the aspect. Taking these two considerations together, it is possible to calculate the effective slope ε using Eq. 10.3 below, where α is the difference between

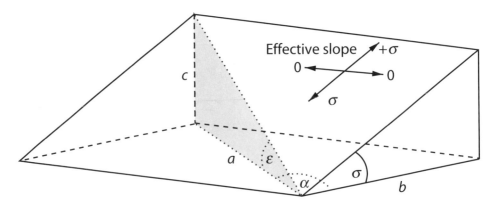

Fig. 10.6 Calculation of effective slope.

the aspect and the direction of travel, σ is the slope, and a and b are as defined in Fig. 10.6. Assuming $a = 1$, then (10.3) may be derived thus:

$$\cos \alpha = b/a$$
$$\cos \alpha = b \tag{10.1}$$

and since:

$$\tan \sigma = c/b$$
$$c = b \tan \sigma \tag{10.2}$$

it follows from (10.1) and (10.2) that:

$$\tan \varepsilon = c/a$$
$$= b \tan \sigma$$
$$= \cos \alpha \tan \sigma$$
$$\varepsilon = \arctan(\cos \alpha \tan \sigma) \tag{10.3}$$

It is important to note that the effective slope calculated using (10.3) is correct only if the difference angle was calculated using a *reversed* aspect map, i.e. an aspect map that records the azimuth of the *upward* direction of the maximum rate of change. Providing this is the case, then the cosine term ensures that the effective slope varies from the slope $(+\sigma)$ uphill to minus the slope $(-\sigma)$ downhill, as shown in Fig. 10.7.

Once the effective slope values have been calculated they must be ascribed appropriate costs. Laboratory experiments have demonstrated that the energy expended during walking is least on a slight downhill slope of 4–6° , increases slightly on the flat and then increases rather more rapidly and non-linearly on steeper uphill slopes (Minetti *et al.* 1993; Rose *et al.* 1994, p. 62). The energy expended also increases on steeper downhill slopes, but at a slower rate than on the equivalent uphill slopes. Llobera (2000, p. 71) has put together data from a number of sources to suggest the relationship depicted in Fig. 10.8.

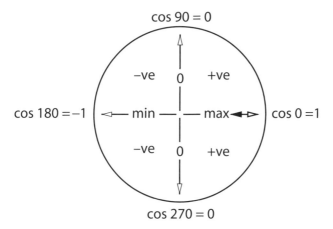

Fig. 10.7 The sign of the effective slope indicates whether movement is up-slope or down-slope.

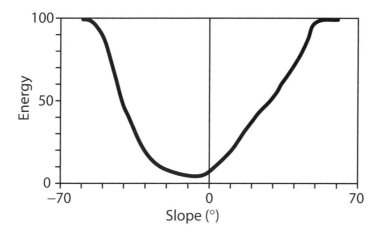

Fig. 10.8 Energetic cost of traversing different slopes according to Llobera. Redrawn from Llobera (2000, Fig. 2).

Van Leusen (1999, pp. 216–217) describes some of the functions that have been used in archaeological studies to model the cost of walking on slopes of differing magnitudes. These have included treating cost in terms of speed, and relative and absolute energetic expenditures.

Speed Gorenflo and Gale (1990) recommend use of the following equation to model the effect of slope on the speed of walking:

$$v = 6e^{-3.5|s+0.05|} \tag{10.4}$$

where v is the walking speed in $km\,h^{-1}$ and s is the slope in degrees (note that $|s+0.05|$ is the absolute value of $s + 0.05$, i.e. it is guaranteed to be positive). Verhagen *et al.*

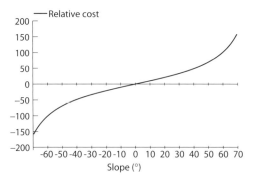

Fig. 10.9 The energetic cost of traversing different slopes according to Bell and Lock (2000).

(1999) used this equation for calculating the accessibility of settlements, but note that since they appear to use slope rather than effective slope their analysis is not fully anisotropic.

Relative energetic expenditure Bell and Lock (2000) propose a function that is based on changes in potential energy rather than laboratory-derived estimates of actual metabolic energy expenditure. They demonstrate that the relative cost of ascending slopes can be modelled as the ratio of the tangents of the slope angles, s. Consequently, a map of relative cost, C, can be obtained using the equation:

$$C = \tan s / \tan 1 \tag{10.5}$$

where a slope of $1°$ is used as the reference point. This equation has the virtue of simplicity while nevertheless producing a non-linear relationship between slope and cost (Fig. 10.9). On the other hand, it has the disadvantage that the relationship is symmetrical[2] about a slope of $0°$. As Bell and Lock themselves acknowledge, this is not compatible with the results of laboratory studies of actual metabolic energy expenditure during walking.

Absolute energetic expenditure Van Leusen (2002, Chapter 6) proposes the following equation to calculate the metabolic energy expenditure (in watts) of walking:

$$M = 1.5W + 2.0\,(W + L)\left(\frac{L}{W}\right)^2$$
$$+ N\,(W + L)\left(1.5V^2 + 0.35V\,|G + 6|\right) \tag{10.6}$$

where M is watts expended, W is the weight of the walker's body (kg), L the weight of any load (kg), V the speed of walking (km h^{-1}), N is a 'terrain factor' and G the slope (%). The terrain factor makes it possible to incorporate the effect of land cover on the ease of movement and assumes a paved surface as the reference, such that $N = 1$ for a road, $N = 1.5$ for a surface that is one and a half times as costly to traverse as a road and so on. Note that the term $|G + 6|$ ensures that the minimum cost is associated with downhill slopes of 6 per cent rather than flat land (Fig. 10.10). Van Leusen has used this equation (albeit without the adjustment to minimum cost) to model Iron Age and Roman trade networks in the hinterland of Wroxeter Roman city (van Leusen 2002, Chapter 16).

---

[2] Albeit positive in the uphill direction and negative in the downhill direction.

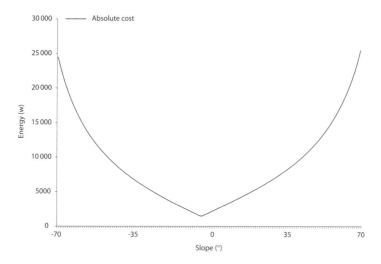

Fig. 10.10 The energetic cost of traversing different slopes according to van Leusen (2002).

It is important to recognise that none of the above methods for calculating the cost of traversing a slope of a given magnitude are anisotropic unless they are applied to the effective slope. The difference angle and thus effective slope are easily calculated using map algebra, provided that the direction of travel is known in advance. This may be true when modelling the cost of travelling along known pathways (see, for example, Krist and Brown's 1994 study of historic native American trails in Michigan), but more often the purpose of cost-surface analysis is to predict an unknown direction of travel. Under these circumstances the difference angle and thus effective slope can only be calculated by the spreading function during the process of calculating the accumulated cost-of-passage surface, because it is only then that the direction of travel is resolved (see below). Consequently, when undertaking anisotropic cost-surface analysis it is vitally important to choose GIS software that not only calculates the effective slope, but also allows the user to specify how that information is transformed into a cost. At present the only widely used software with this functionality is Idrisi (Eastman 1997, Chapter 15).

The accumulated cost-surface

An accumulated cost-surface is calculated by applying a spreading function to a cost-of-passage map. The spreading functions used for this purpose are designed to minimise the accumulated cost at the destination(s), from which it follows that an accumulated cost-of-passage map models the *minimum* cost of moving from a specified starting point to the specified destinations (often all cells in the map). One of the best-known algorithms is that devised by Tomlin (1990) and shown in simplified form in Fig. 10.11. Figure 10.11(a) shows an origin, O, and destination, D, on an isotropic cost-of-passage surface. Inspection of the cost-of-passage surface

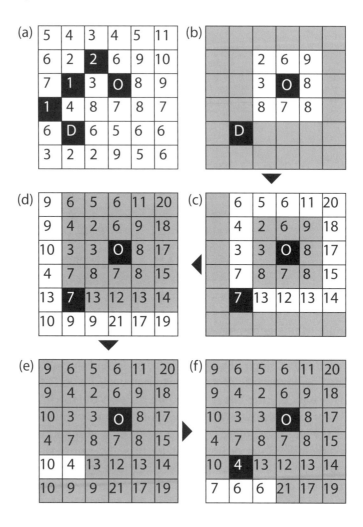

Fig. 10.11 Stages in the iteration of a basic spreading function.

suggests that the black map cells constitute the least costly route from the origin to the destination. Figures 10.11(b–f) show how this would be calculated. Note that the cells depicted in grey are those whose values remained unchanged in that step. At the start, all cells are initialised with an accumulated cost of zero. Then, at each step, a window comprising the eight immediate neighbours is moved over each cell that has at least one non-zero neighbour, starting with the origin. The accumulated cost is calculated as the cost of traversing the cell at the centre of the window, plus the lowest accumulated cost among its neighbours. Calculation of a complete accumulated cost-surface for the map in Fig. 10.11(a) takes five steps.

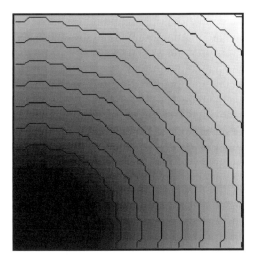

Fig. 10.12 An accumulated cost-surface showing algorithm artefacts.

1. (Fig. 10.11b) The first step considers only the cells in the eight-cell neighbourhood of the origin.
2. (Fig. 10.11c) The eight cells considered in step one are reconsidered and their accumulated costs found not to change, but the accumulated costs for the cells neighbouring them can now be calculated.
3. (Fig. 10.11d) The 24 cells considered in step two are reconsidered and their accumulated costs found not to change, but the accumulated costs for the cells neighbouring them can now be calculated.
4. (Fig. 10.11e) The 36 cells considered in step three are reconsidered and two cells are now found to have lower accumulated costs. As it happens, one of those is the destination.
5. (Fig. 10.11f) The 36 cells considered in step four are reconsidered yet again and a further three cells are found to have lower accumulated costs. No additional changes are possible, so this is the final result.

Production versions of Tomlin's algorithm usually include modifications to take account of the increased journey length when travelling diagonally across a cell rather than in the cardinal directions. They may also include modifications to improve efficiency, such as Eastman's (1989) *push-broom procedure*, which has been implemented in Idrisi.

The spreading functions found in GIS software are often poor. Douglas (1999) has pointed out that a uniform isotropic cost-of-passage map – i.e. one in which the cost of passage is the same for all cells in all directions – should yield an accumulated cost-surface on which the accumulated cost increases as a series of concentric circular rings of increasing radius. As it turns out, most GIS software packages actually produce a series of concentric polygons, as can be seen in Fig. 10.12. This is simply wrong and will undermine the validity of any further analyses based on the accumulated cost-surface. The reason is often nothing more complicated than the use of an eight-cell neighbourhood, which only allows costs to be accumulated in the directions N, NE, E, SE, S, SW, W and NW. Douglas has proposed a solution for this problem based on an analogy with the processes of refraction and diffraction in the transmission of light, but unfortunately it has yet to be implemented in any widely available software.

Using cost-surfaces

Accumulated cost-surfaces are usually calculated as the precursor to further analysis, often the derivation of least-cost paths, which we consider in Chapter 11. Here we are more concerned with their use to delimit discrete regions such as territories or site catchments. Indeed, the availability of GIS has fuelled renewed interest in site-catchment analysis (Gaffney and Stančič 1991; Hunt 1992; Saile 1997; Stancic *et al.* 1997), which had fallen from favour in the late 1970s. In this context it is important to recognise that technical advances do not necessarily overcome fundamental shortcomings in particular forms of analysis. Consequently, anyone contemplating undertaking a GIS-based site-catchment analysis would do well to acquaint themselves with Roper's (1979) review of a large number of earlier studies. In many cases the problems she identifies are not insurmountable, but nor will they be automatically overcome by the use of GIS.

Delimiting site catchments The initial creation of an appropriate cost-of-passage map is the first step in using a cost-surface to delimit a site catchment. This must reflect the relevant factors, such as terrain, land cover, etc., that are believed to have influenced the size of the area which could be exploited from the site in question. The influence of those factors must be measured in a suitable currency, such as travel time or energetic expenditure. Once the accumulated cost-surface has been calculated, the boundary of the catchment can be extracted as follows:

1. Decide on the maximum value of the chosen currency beyond which resources could not have been exploited, for example: the maximum travel time that would allow travel to, extraction of, and return travel from a resource within a day. This decision will, of course, require numerous assumptions about the organisation of resource acquisition. Indeed, it could be argued that it is precisely when there is uncertainty that the application of GIS becomes most useful, since it readily facilitates the comparison of catchments derived using different assumptions.
2. Differentially code each map cell according to whether or not its accumulated cost exceeds the chosen maximum. In many cases this is easily achieved using map algebra similar to the following:

    catchment = (accumulated_cost_surface <= maximum)

    which would produce a map with cells coded 1 if they fall within the catchment and 0 otherwise.
3. If desired (see below), convert the raster representation of the catchment to a polygon in a vector map.

Analysing site catchments Most studies of site catchment proceed by analysing the composition of resource types (or other landscape attributes) present within the catchment(s). The ultimate aim may be to:

- Determine whether a community of a given size was likely to have been self-sufficient;
- Estimate the maximum population at a site;
- Determine the mode of subsistence practised by the site's inhabitants, e.g. farming versus foraging;
- Determine whether the specific range of resources available was likely to have been a factor influencing site location, perhaps by comparing the catchments of sites with those of randomly chosen locations (e.g. Zarky 1976).

Whatever the motivation, it is a simple matter to analyse the composition of a site catchment using GIS, providing the relevant resources have been mapped. This is, of course, a significant caveat, since such mapping is likely to require a substantial effort in palaeoenvironmental reconstruction. While the difficulties that may be encountered in producing an adequate palaeoenvironmental reconstruction have little to do with GIS per se, it can nevertheless be argued that the use of GIS does tend to highlight the disjuncture between the desire for a spatially continuous reconstruction and the point nature of most palaeoenvironmental data. This is largely because GIS software does not readily lend itself to the 'eyeballing' of, say, vegetation extents, but rather to the construction of *explicit* models from which such extents may be deduced, which is in turn often more revealing of the sparseness of data.

Assuming that the relevant resource maps are available, then the composition of a site catchment may be analysed using one or both of two methods:

Polygon overlay is appropriate for use with vector maps of discontinuous resources. As described in Chapter 7, it can be used to answer queries such as establishing the proportion of a site catchment that is cultivable land.

Cross-tabulation allows similar queries to be made of raster maps. In this case, the result of cross-tabulation would be a table showing how the values in the raster map are distributed between those cells within the site catchment and those outside it (Fig. 10.13). Cross-tabulation can be applied to raster maps representing continuously varying resources as well as those representing discontinuous (e.g. types of) resources. Since the former produces a table containing one row (or column) for every unique resource value, many of which will represent very few map cells, it is usually more helpful to reclassify such a map into a set of classes. For example, one might reclassify a map of solar gain into the classes low, medium and high.

10.3.2 *Visible regions*

The calculation of viewsheds (regions of intervisibility) has become a very popular use of GIS in academic research. Much of this work has concerned the placement of monuments in the landscape, for example: Wheatley's (1995) study of the intervisibility of earthern burial mounds (long barrows) in central southern England; Woodman's (2000a) study of the reciprocity of view between stone burial chambers (chambered cairns) in the Orkney Islands of Scotland; Fisher *et al.*'s (1997) investigation of whether stone cairns on the Scottish island of Mull were deliberately placed so as to overlook the sea; and Llobera's studies of the prominence of monuments (Llobera 2001) and the manner in which they become visible as one approaches them.

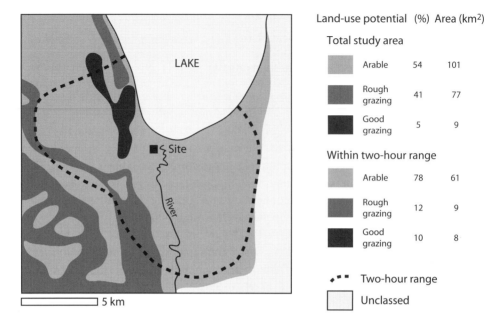

Fig. 10.13 Cross-tabulation of land-use potential within a two-hour territorial limit of a site (after Vita-Finzi 1978, Fig. 87).

The calculation of viewsheds also has applications in cultural resource management and planning more generally. For example, Batchelor (1999) calculated the area visible from Stonehenge in order to investigate which of several proposals for re-routing roads near the World Heritage Site would have least visual impact.

Definitions

Intervisibility Visibility analysis in GIS is founded on the automatic determination of whether any given pair of points are intervisible. This process is normally carried out on a raster digital elevation model (DEM) and works by projecting a straight line-of-sight from the viewpoint to the target. If the elevations of all intervening map cells fall below the line-of-sight, then the two points are held to be intervisible. If, on the other hand, the elevation of one or more intervening cells falls above the line-of-sight, then the line-of-sight is interrupted and so the two points are held not to be intervisible.

Viewshed The viewshed of a viewpoint is the set of target cells that can be seen *from* the viewpoint (see reciprocity, below).

> **Single viewshed** The simplest result from a viewshed analysis is a binary map marking target cells as visible or not visible from a specified viewpoint. Some software packages provide additional information. For example, GRASS creates a map in which each target cell is marked with the declination (angle in the vertical plane) at which it

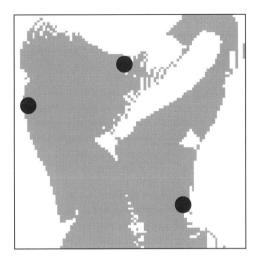

Fig. 10.14 A multiple viewshed created by the merging of the viewsheds of each of the three locations.

Fig. 10.15 A cumulative viewshed created by the addition (overlay) of the viewsheds of each of the three locations.

is visible from the specified viewpoint. Other useful information, such as the azimuth (angle in the horizontal plane) can be obtained by post-processing, as described by Wheatley and Gillings (2000, p. 22).

A **multiple viewshed** map is the logical union of two or more viewshed maps (Fig. 10.14). The values in a multiple viewshed map are either 1 (visible from one or more viewpoints) or 0 (not visible from any viewpoint). Each map cell in a multiple viewshed map records whether it is visible from at least one viewpoint.

Cumulative viewshed is the term introduced by Wheatley (1995, p. 173) for the map algebraic sum of two or more binary single viewshed maps (Fig. 10.15). The cell values in a cumulative viewshed are integers ranging from zero to a theoretical maximum of the number of viewpoints, although this will only occur if at least one cell is visible from all viewpoints. Each map cell in a cumulative viewshed map records the number of viewpoints from which it is visible.

A total viewshed map (Llobera 2003) is usually created using one of two methods. The first is to calculate the viewshed from every single map cell in turn and then sum all these viewsheds. Such a map is effectively the cumulative viewshed of every possible viewpoint, from which it follows that each map cell records the number of other map cells *from which it is visible*. The second method is to use a dedicated program (such as the r.cva module available for GRASS) which calculates the viewshed from every single map cell, counts the number of cells in the viewshed and then records this at the viewpoint. Unlike the first method, this produces a map in which each cell records the number of other map cells *which are visible from it*. It is possible to obtain the second type of map using the first method by careful choice of observer and target offsets (see reciprocity, below). The cell values in a total viewshed are integers ranging from zero (or one if the line-of-sight algorithm being used treats a viewpoint as visible from itself) to a theoretical maximum of the number of cells in the map, although this maximum is unlikely to be obtained with models of natural terrain.

Isovist field is the the term used in planning and architecture to refer to a total viewshed. An isovist is 'the set of all points visible from a given vantage point in space' (Benedikt 1979, p. 47) and an isovist field is created by summing isovists for every possible vantage point in an environment (Batty 2001). An isovist field is thus directly equivalent to a total viewshed created using the first method described above.

Issues in visibility analysis

The potential pitfalls in GIS-based visibility analysis have been well rehearsed in the archaeological literature (Wheatley and Gillings 2000). Here we distinguish between *computational*, *experimental*, *substantive* and *theoretical* concerns.

Computational issues These stem from the way in which visibility analysis is programmed in individual GIS software packages. In the case of commercial software the end user generally has no control over this, beyond the initial choice of software, and even then informed choice is often hampered by lack of adequate documentation. In the case of open-source software the end user can change the way in which visibility analysis is programmed, but only if they or a collaborator have the necessary programming skills.

The two most important computational issues have to do with the ability of the GIS software to calculate *theoretical* intervisibility accurately, given perfect data:

Algorithm Different GIS software packages use different algorithms for calculating intervisibility. In particular, they vary in how they calculate the elevation of a map cell on the line-of-sight, whether they treat the viewpoint and targets as points or cells, and how they compare the elevation of a map cell with the elevation of the line-of-site (Fisher 1993). Consequently, different GIS software packages produce different results, even from the same data (Fisher 1993; Izraelevitz 2003).

Curvature of the Earth Since the surface of the Earth is not flat, but curved, there is a maximum distance beyond which a target of a given height cannot be seen, even at sea with perfect visibility. The effect of the curvature of the Earth's surface is to

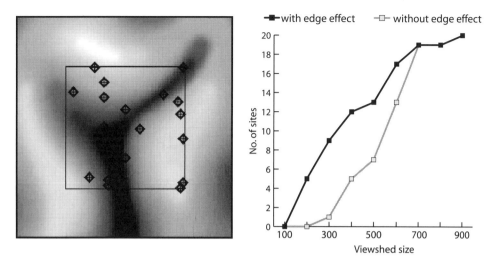

Fig. 10.16 The edge effect in visibility analysis.

reduce the elevation of a target by approximately 7.86 m for every 10 km from the viewpoint, which is potentially significant for many archaeological visibility analyses. Unfortunately, many GIS software packages do not take account of the curvature of the Earth when calculating intervisibility. Where necessary, this problem can be overcome by modifying the digital elevation model to curve it gently downwards away from the viewpoint, as described by Ruggles and Medyckyj-Scott (1996, p. 133). Note, however, that when calculating multiple, cumulative or total viewsheds, this modification must be made individually for each viewpoint in turn.

Experimental issues These arise as a result of the way in which a visibility analysis is conducted once all substantive decisions (parameters, data, purpose) have been made. They are under the control of the end user, although there may be constraints such as the speed of the available computer(s). The most important experimental issues include the following:

The edge effect is particularly influential if the aim of a visibility analysis is to compare the size or shape of two or more viewsheds. Since intervisibility decays with distance (see substantive issues), it is usually only calculated for target cells that fall within some specified radius of the viewpoint (the maximum viewing distance). When the distance between a given viewpoint and the edge of the map region is less than that radius it follows that the viewshed may be artificially truncated, thus invalidating comparison with the viewsheds of other viewpoints that were further from the edge of the map (Fig. 10.16). The simplest solution is to perform the visibility analysis on a map region which is surrounded by a buffer zone of the same width as the maximum viewing distance; this is then discarded during subsequent analysis. For an example see the study by Lake *et al.* (1998), which clearly demonstrates the edge effect.

Reciprocity If, as is usually the case, one takes account of the heights of the observer and target above ground level (the observer and target 'offsets') then it is possible for the target to be visible to the observer while the observer remains invisible from

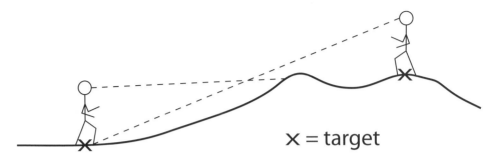

Fig. 10.17 Differing observer and target offsets prevent exact reciprocity of intervisibility.

the target (Fig. 10.17). The greater the disparity between the observer and target offsets, the greater the probability that intervisibility will not be reciprocal. Lack of reciprocity may be interesting, as has been demonstrated for the placement of Orcadian chambered tombs (Woodman 2000a) and Hellenistic city defences (Loots 1997). It only becomes a problem in cases of poor experimental design, for example, when one attempts to produce a total viewshed in which each cell records the number of other map cells *which are visible from it* by summing the viewsheds of every possible viewpoint; in this case it would be important to reverse the observer and target offsets to achieve the desired result.

DEM quality Accurate determination of the theoretical intervisibility between two points crucially depends on the digital elevation model providing an accurate representation of reality. Given that the calculation of intervisibility is particularly sensitive to the elevation of peaks and crests, it is best to create the DEM using an exact interpolation method in conjunction with a comprehensive network of spot heights on local elevation maxima and (less importantly) minima. When there are real doubts about the accuracy of the DEM it may be advisable to create a probabilistic viewshed as described by Fisher (1991).

Sensitivity When intervisibility must be calculated over large distances there is an increased likelihood that very small changes in observer height will result in large differences in viewshed size or shape. This is further compounded by any inaccuracy in the DEM, as well as other factors such as uncertainty about the height of intervening vegetation (see below). For this reason it is good practice to repeat visibility analyses for a range of parameter values in order to understand whether the results are – hopefully – robust, or instead, highly sensitive to small changes (see Lock and Harris 1996 for a discussion).

Substantive issues These determine the choice of parameter values and data for visibility analysis. They include:

Palaeoenvironment Most, if not all, published visibility analyses use a modern DEM. This may provide an adequate model of the later prehistoric topography in a rural area; it is much less likely to be adequate for earlier prehistory or in a built-up area.

Palaeovegetation The so-called 'tree factor' (Wheatley and Gillings 2000, p. 5; cf. Chapman and Gearey 2000) is invariably raised at every conference presentation of a visibility analysis. It is obvious that the presence of tall vegetation can have a significant effect on intervisibility; it is not quite so obvious what to do about it.

Fig. 10.18 A probabilistic viewshed.

The simplest solution (where it cannot be demonstrated that the palaeovegetation was low) is to add the average height of vegetation to the relevant map cells in the DEM. In practice it is usually difficult to obtain palaeoenvironmental reconstructions of sufficient spatial resolution. In any case, the blocking effect of vegetation depends on both the time of year (whether it is in leaf) and its density within a given map cell. For this reason a more promising solution might be to provide a probabilistic measure of blocking analogous to that described by Fisher (1991) for modelling DEM quality, although this is likely to require the development of new algorithms.

Contrast A target that contrasts with its background may, for practical purposes, be visible over greater distances than one that blends in with its background. Contrast is a function of the innate properties of the target, atmospheric conditions and lighting (Felleman 1986). For example, a newly built chalk burial mound gleaming white in oblique sunlight may be visible from further afield than a grassed-over burial mound viewed through light rain on a generally overcast day. The visibility tools available in current GIS software packages do not model the effect of contrast on intervisibility. The simplest solution is to set the maximum viewing distance on the basis of real-world experiments viewing an analogous target in analogous conditions. However, such use of a single maximum viewing distance fails to account for any gradual reduction in the probability of intervisibility with increasing distance, just as it also fails to account for daily and seasonal variations in atmospheric conditions and lighting. Consequently, a more nuanced approach adds a probabilistic element. In the case of effects related to distance (for example the size of the target) it is possible to produce a map in which the probability of actual intervisibility declines with distance. This can be achieved by post-processing the calculated viewshed using a combination of buffering and map algebra, as described by Wheatley and Gillings (2000). A similar solution could be developed for effects related to the horizontal angle of viewing. In the case of effects related to specific conditions, such as weather, it is possible to produce a map in which the probability of actual intervisibility reflects the extent to which a given map cell is always visible, or only visible under a limited set of circumstances (Fig. 10.18). One way of producing such a map is as follows.

1. Calculate a binary viewshed map for each condition using the appropriate maximum viewing distance.
2. Use map algebra to multiply each binary viewshed by the number of units of time (e.g. hours or days) for which the relevant condition holds.
3. Sum the binary viewsheds.
4. Use map algebra to divide the sum of all the viewsheds by the total number of units of time (e.g. 24 hours, 365 days).

More sophisticated methods for modelling the factors that contribute to contrast have been developed to assess the visual impact of proposed wind turbines: the work of Bishop (2002), in particular, is potentially of great relevance to archaeologists conducting visibility analysis.

Height of observer The choice of observer height is not straightforward – even when there is good skeletal evidence for the population in question – because GIS software only accepts one height value when the target may have been of interest to many people of different heights. This is not a trivial issue: Lock and Harris (1996) have demonstrated in their analysis of visibility from Danebury Iron Age hillfort that observer height can significantly alter the calculated viewshed. One solution is to calculate the viewsheds for a range of heights. Depending on the research question, it may then be appropriate to create a probabilistic map showing the likelihood of a person of unknown height being able to see each map cell.

Acuity of vision GIS software does not take account of acuity of vision, since to do so it would need information about the observer's eyesight as well as the contrast and size of the target (and even that presupposes one observer and a fixed target). A rather crude solution treats the maximum viewing distance as a proxy for acuity and then repeats the analysis for several different distances representing a range of acuity.

Theoretical issues These determine the frame of reference and purpose of GIS-based visibility analysis. Lake and Woodman (2003) have argued that developments in GIS-based visibility studies have tended to recapitulate those in archaeological theory more generally. Important theoretical issues include:

Inferential strategy One of the most popular reasons for using GIS to calculate intervisibility is to compare the viewsheds of archaeological sites, for example, burial mounds, with those of other places that lack evidence for human activity. Given an appropriate experimental design (see Chapter 8) it may then be possible to attribute some level of statistical significance to the results, which may in turn provide a means of testing a hypothesis about the reasons for site location (see Fisher *et al.* 1997; Lake *et al.* 1998; Wheatley 1995 for examples). Such analysis can be performed manually in the field (for example Bradley *et al.* 1993), but the use of GIS generally allows a much larger number of non-site locations to be sampled and often also provides the only realistic means of mitigating the impact of modern building.

Perception There has been significant interest – albeit mostly among European archaeologists – in using GIS visibility tools to investigate perception of landscape, often in an attempt to demonstrate that GIS can be applied in a broadly post-processual framework. Frequently, however, such studies (e.g. Gaffney *et al.* 1996) have failed to move beyond establishing whether certain points, for example stone circles or rock art, are intervisible. It can be argued that demonstrating the existence of a line-of-sight between points of interest has little to do with perception, which is more properly construed as the process of moving from sensory input to cognitive representation. A small group of researchers are cognisant of this and, most notably, Marcos Llobera (1996, 2001, 2003) has been developing methods which have as their theoretical foundation Gibson's (1986) ecological approach to visual perception. Wheatley and Gillings (2000) also find inspiration in Gibson's work, although for practical purposes they draw more on Higuchi's (1983) eight visual indices of the visual and spatial structure of landscape. As it stands, these more sophisticated approaches to perception largely constitute the development of methodology: the challenge now is to make substantive contributions to specific archaeological problems.

Visualism A frequent criticism of GIS-based visibility analysis is that it privileges vision over sound, smell and touch, which does more to perpetuate Renaissance ideals than reflect the relative importance of vision in the more distant past (Witcher 1999; Wheatley and Gillings 2000). Tschan *et al.* (2000, Fig. 10) illustrate a hypothetical 'perception shed', which records the combination of senses that may be used to perceive each cell in a raster map. They suggest that hearing and smelling, as senses 'subject to distance as a process' (Tschan *et al.* 2000, p. 45), could be modelled by adapting existing visibility analysis tools, although they do not provide a worked example.

Another critique related to that of visualism is that the plan shape of a viewshed depicted in a GIS map bears little resemblance to the experience of people on the ground and is therefore of limited interpretative value (Thomas 1993). Those working in a theoretical framework for which this is a problem will wish to consider whether virtual reality provides a means of overcoming the 'specular' (Thomas 1993) means of representation afforded by two-dimensional GIS mapping. The potential benefits of virtual reality have been discussed by Gillings and Goodrick (1996), while Exon *et al.* (2000) provide a substantial case study that combines 'traditional' GIS and virtual reality in an investigation of the visual relationship between Stonehenge and its surroundings.

10.4 Conclusion

The extents of archaeologically significant regions are often known prior to GIS-based analysis, in which case their content can usually be analysed using methods discussed in Chapter 7, such as polygon overlay. In contrast, this chapter focused on the use of GIS to help define regions whose extents are not already known. In the first part we introduced methods that can be used to create geometric regions, such as buffers and Thiessen polygons. These techniques do not take account of the content of space. In the second part of the chapter we turned our attention to what – for convenience – we have labelled 'topographic' regions. The methods used to create these kinds of regions do take account of the content of space. Cost-surfaces allow one to define regions on the basis of accessibility, which may be physical and/or cultural. Visibility analysis provides a means of defining regions as sets of locations that are intervisible, although we have suggested that it will often be most appropriate to think of such regions in probabilistic terms. One important kind of topographic region that does not appear in this chapter, however, is the watershed, or rainfall catchment. We discuss this region in Chapter 11 where we are better able to explore its derivation from a hydrological network.

11

Routes: networks, cost paths and hydrology

11.1 Introduction

It is often appropriate to model the spatial organisation of human activity in terms of point locations and the relationships between them; for example the movement of goods between settlements or the intervisibility between forts. This chapter discusses the various network analysis tools that can be used to study such relationships. It also discusses techniques for predicting the likely path of an unknown route between point locations, as well as the flow of water and watersheds.

Given that the bulk of archaeological data is ultimately point based it is surprising that network analysis has not featured more prominently in the archaeological application of GIS. Of course, what is a point at one scale of analysis may be a region at another, and it is thus important to recognise that the applicability of network analysis is determined by the way in which the problem is framed rather than the geographical extent of a particular study. A few published archaeological network analyses have investigated subjects ranging in scale from the colonisation of new territory (Allen 1990; Zubrow 1990) and the location of 'centres' (Bell and Church 1985; Mackie 2001) to the connectivity of rooms in individual buildings (Foster 1989). There is no reason why this range could not be extended to even smaller extents: to, for example, investigate patterns of refitting among lithic artefacts in a single stratigraphic unit.

11.2 Representing networks

We are all familiar with networks such as road and rail networks, and also the idea of social networking – that a friend or business associate knows somebody who knows somebody else who can provide ... These examples demonstrate that networks can be conceived at different levels of abstraction. In the case of road and rail, observable physical links connect fixed points that have geographic reference, but in the case of social networks the links do not have – at least not permanently – an observable physical manifestation and the people linked do not generally have a fixed geographic reference. Consequently it is important to differentiate between different types of network, most importantly for archaeological purposes: pure networks, flow networks and transportation networks (Fischer 2004).

11.2.1 *Pure networks*

The 'purest' form of network, known to mathematicians as a *simple graph*, comprises a finite number of *nodes* connected by *edges*, such that each edge joins exactly

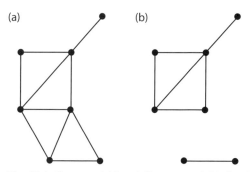

Fig. 11.1 Connected (a) and disconnected (b) simple graphs.

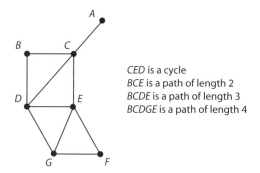

CED is a cycle
BCE is a path of length 2
BCDE is a path of length 3
BCDGE is a path of length 4

Fig. 11.2 Paths and cycles in a simple graph.

two nodes, there is no more than one edge per pair of nodes and edges do not have directionality (Wilson 1996). Social networks are readily represented using a simple graph since the nodes can be used to represent people and the edges the relationships between those people, in which case the rules about edges reflect the idea that human relationships are diadic, that any two people have only one relationship, that people do not have relationships with themselves and that relationships are mutual. A graph is said to be *connected* if every node can be reached from any other node by traversing one or more edges, otherwise it is said to be *disconnected* (Fig. 11.1). Thus in a connected social network it would be possible to deliver a letter to any other person by asking an acquaintance to pass it on to one of their acquaintances, and so on. If each person handled the letter only once then the sequence of edges by which it reached the final recipient would constitute a *path* (Fig. 11.2). If the sender and final recipient were the same person then the path would constitute a *cycle*. Note that the *length* of a path is simply the number of edges between the origin and destination nodes, something that is not so readily appreciated when the nodes happen to have a fixed geographic reference (i.e. geographical distance and path length are not necessarily correlated).

The information stored in a simple graph is purely topological, i.e. about the connectivity between the nodes only; in the above example it is about whether or not two people have a relationship. This is entirely appropriate for purposes such as

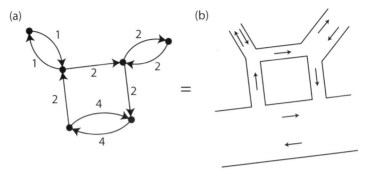

Fig. 11.3 A weighted digraph (a) of a road network (b). In this case the weights reflect the number of lanes.

Watts and Strogatz's (1998) investigation of what kind of social network underwrites the 'small-world' phenomenon – the observation that despite having a densely knit network of close friends we can also be connected to almost everyone else on the planet in just six steps. It may be less appropriate, however, for researching the influence of physical proximity on social network formation (see Gamble 1998 for an archaeological interest in this subject) since the placement of nodes in a simple graph provides no information about physical location.

In most GIS software, networks are represented as vector maps,[1] such that the nodes are represented as points and the edges as lines joining them. Two problems arise in attempting to represent a simple graph in this way. The first is the issue of planarity (see transportation networks below) and the second is that it will require the invention of arbitrary coordinates for the nodes. Consequently it is usually better to use specialist software, such as Pajek,[2] for the analysis of simple graphs. Such software also has the virtue of offering a wider range of graph theoretic measures than will normally be found in GIS packages. Of course, in the case of a network where the nodes do have fixed geographic reference then the appropriate coordinates can be assigned to the points representing the nodes. In this case, however, it is important to recognise that such locational information is not intrinsic to the graph and will therefore be ignored in the calculation of most graph theoretic measures (see Section 11.3.1).

11.2.2 *Flow networks*

Given an interest in the movement of goods from one location to another, then it is very likely that one would wish to model both the direction and quantity of the goods moved through a network. Networks in which direction is important can be represented using what mathematicians call a directed graph, or *digraph* (Fig. 11.3).

---

[1]It is theoretically possible to develop raster representations of networks using Tomlin's (1990) 'incremental-linkage' operator. This is seldom implemented in commercial software, but one exception is MFWorks (www.keigansystems.com/software/mfworks/index.html).

[2]http://vlado.fmf.uni-lj.si/pub/networks/pajek/default.htm.

In a digraph, edges have directionality, i.e. they point from one node to another. Consequently, it is permissible in a digraph to have more than one edge joining a pair of nodes so as to represent the bidirectional flow of goods, influence or whatever else is being modelled. It is usually also considered permissible to have edges that both start and end at the same node, perhaps in this case to represent the internal consumption of goods produced at a node. Note that some authors prefer the term *arc* for a directed link, reserving the label edge for an undirected link (e.g. Fischer 2004).

It is possible to model the quantities that flow through a network by attaching weights to the edges. In a *weighted digraph*, often referred to in the GIS literature as a valued graph (e.g. Chou 1997, p. 229), the weights (values) are usually chosen to represent either *impedance* or a *capacity constraint*. Impedance measures the relative or absolute ease with which material can flow between the nodes joined by an edge, while a capacity constraint represents the maximum amount of material that can flow between nodes. Such weights typically reflect real-world phenomena such as the width or surface quality of a road, the transport technology available on that route or even the distance between the relevant nodes.

It might not be immediately clear from a GIS perspective why the distance between nodes should be specified as a weight, when often it would appear to be an intrinsic property of the real-world distribution of the nodes. The pragmatic answer is that impedance and capacity constraints are rarely a function of the simple straight-line distance between nodes, but instead a function of the distance covered by (quite possibly winding) routes on the ground. Few GIS packages can automatically calculate such distances in the course of network analysis. The reason why distances are specified as weights is that the spatial element of a flow network is an abstraction of its topology rather than a representation of its exact physical layout. Consequently, given appropriate weights, it is perfectly possible to calculate flows without reference to the geographic coordinates of the nodes involved.

11.2.3 *Transportation networks*

The majority of GIS-based network analyses concern the location of facilities such as markets or the routing of deliveries on transportation networks, mostly road networks. Although much of this work can be carried out using abstracted flow networks, the demand from end-users for realism (for example, drivers want to be able to recognise an edge as a particular winding road on the ground) and the benefits that accrue from using existing GIS databases mean that it is desirable to perform network analyses on ordinary geographically referenced vector maps. The three requirements for transportation modelling can be met as follows.

1. It should be possible to attach weights to the lines representing edges. Since most vector maps already associate attribute values with each line this is normally only a matter of adding an additional field to the attribute table (see Chapter 2).

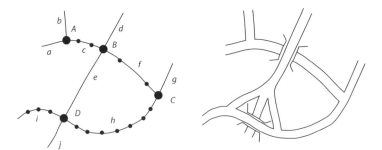

Fig. 11.4 A transport network. The nodes (large circles) carry topological information; the vertices (small circles) carry only topographical information.

2. It should not be necessary to eliminate information about the real-world course of a route in favour of a straight-line edge between the relevant nodes. All current GIS packages with network-analytic pretensions are capable of differentiating nodes that carry topological information, i.e. those representing junctions, from vertices that carry only topographical information, i.e. whose sole function is to mark a change in direction of the road, railway, etc. Provided this is the case, it is perfectly possible to perform network analysis on curved edges whose real-world course is approximated by many separate straight lines (Fig. 11.4).

3. Nodes should carry information about junctions. Figure 11.4 shows a common situation in which one road crosses another on a bridge, so that there is no junction at which a vehicle can leave one road and join the other. The easiest way of representing this situation in a network is to have the edges representing the two roads cross without a node. However, GIS software often enforces planarity in the process of creating a 'topologically correct' vector map, which effectively means that edges are not allowed to cross except at nodes. To understand the concept of planarity, imagine a network in which the nodes are represented by balls placed on a table and the edges by lengths of string tied between the relevant balls. A simple graph represented in this way would remain topologically constant even if one picked the balls up and moved them around, providing that the strings remained attached to the same balls. In the case of a *planar graph*, however, it is not permissible to pick up either the balls or strings, only to push them around on the table top. The theoretical significance of this restriction is that some arrangements of nodes that are considered topologically equivalent in a simple graph are not topologically equivalent in a planar graph (Fig. 11.5). The practical significance for transport analysis is that GIS software that enforces planarity requires a map to have nodes even where there is no possibility on the ground of moving from one edge to another. The most common solution to this problem uses a *turn table* (Fischer 2004). For example, ArcView's Network Analyst extension requires that for every node the user specify whether it is possible to move between each pair of edges joining that node. In the case of a bridge, the turn table might look like that depicted in Fig. 11.6. Compiling a turn table is tedious, but it has the virtue of flexibility in that it provides a means of representing a range of real-world complications, such as prohibited turns.

11.3 Analysing networks

The following sections provide detailed explanation of a wide and complex variety of measurement terms for networks. Although the terms themselves are mathematical and abstract, we do show how these can be applied to archaeological data.

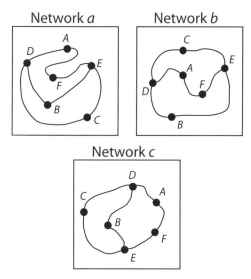

Fig. 11.5 Planar graphs. All three networks are topologically equivalent unless embedded in the plane, in which case $a = b \neq c$.

From	To	Permitted
e	h	1
e	i	1
e	j	1
h	e	1
h	i	1
h	j	0
i	e	1
i	h	1
i	j	0
j	e	1
j	h	0
j	i	0

Fig. 11.6 A turn table for node D in the transport network in Fig. 11.4.

The questions asked of networks fall into three main groups. First, there are questions about network structure or topology, i.e. how the nodes are connected. Second, there are questions about the location of particular facilities (usually sites) on the network. The third set of questions concerns the routing of information, goods or people through networks.

11.3.1 *Measures of network structure*
Measures of network structure, such as how well-connected nodes are to each other, potentially enable one to establish whether an ancient road network would survive

Table 11.1 *Basic measures of the networks in Fig. 11.1*

	N	E	G
Network *a*	7	10	1
Network *b*	7	7	2

Table 11.2 *Local measures for the nodes in Fig. 11.2*

	k_i	C_i	A_i	K_i
A	1	1.0	13	3
B	2	1.0	12	3
C	4	0.6	8	2
D	4	0.7	8	2
E	4	0.7	8	2
F	2	1.0	12	3
G	3	0.83	10	3

the severing of a few links, whether an ancient city may have gained importance by virtue of its accessibility, whether urban growth is scale free or whether some parts of a museum are more accessible to visitors than others by virtue of their intervisibility. We describe some of these examples in more detail below, but first we review some of the more widely used measures of network structure.

Since not all graph theoretic measures are independent of one another, there is some overlap in their interpretation. Consequently, the following scheme is not intended to be prescriptive, but simply to provide a starting point when choosing a measure for a particular problem.

Basic measures

Measures of network structure often require a few basic quantities, including:

> N The total number of nodes in a graph.
>
> E The total number of edges in a graph. Note that a simple graph may contain a maximum of $N(N-1)/2$ edges.
>
> G The number of components of a graph, i.e. the number of sections of the graph that are totally disconnected from one another.

The two networks shown in Fig. 11.1 have the basic measures shown in Table 11.1.

Local measures

A number of measures can be used to assess the location of an individual node in a network. The nodes in Fig. 11.2 have the local measures shown in Table 11.2.

Local connectivity

> The **nodal degree**, k_i, is simply the number of edges connected to a particular node. In a simple graph the maximum possible number of edges that can be connected to a node i is $N-1$. In the case of a directed graph it is possible to distinguish the in-degree from the out-degree.
>
> The **clustering coefficient** of node i, C_i, is calculated as
>
> $$C_i = \frac{2e}{n(n-1)} \qquad (11.1)$$
>
> where n is the number of nodes directly connected to i (including i itself) and e is the number of edges that connects those nodes to one another. In other words, C_i is the number of edges in the immediate neighbourhood of i expressed as a fraction of the maximum possible number of edges in that neighbourhood. This fraction ranges from 0, if i is completely disconnected, to 1, if all the nodes to which i is directly connected are also connected to one another. A social interpretation of C_i is that it measures the extent to which your friends are also your friends' friends.

Local accessibility While measures of local connectivity provide information about the immediate neighbourhood of a node, measures of accessibility provide information about how readily a node may be reached from further afield. Notice in Table 11.2 how the most accessible nodes (those with low A_i, i.e. C, D and E) also have the least clustered neighbourhoods (low C_i).

> The **accessibility index** of node i, A_i, is calculated as
>
> $$A_i = \sum_{j \neq i} l_{ij} \qquad (11.2)$$
>
> where l_{ij} is the shortest path length between nodes i and j. For those unfamiliar with this notation, the symbol $\sum j \neq i$ says to sum whatever follows, in this case the shortest path lengths, for all the nodes j to which i is connected, excluding i itself. Note that there is no instruction to sum the shortest path length to all nodes in the graph, i.e. from $j = 1$ to $j = N$, because it is possible that some nodes are not connected at all, in which case the path length between them is considered infinite.
>
> The **König index** is a measure of the centrality of a node. The König index of node i, κ_i, is simply the longest of the shortest path lengths to a node j to which i is connected. This can be stated formally as
>
> $$\kappa_i = \max l_{ij} \qquad (11.3)$$

Global measures

Sometimes the overall properties of a network are of more interest than those of specific nodes or, alternatively, one may wish to assess whether or not a node is typical by comparing its properties with those of an 'average' node. The networks in Fig. 11.7 have the global measures shown in Table 11.3.

Table 11.3 *Global measures for the networks in Fig. 11.7*

	K	β	γ	α	C	δ	D	L
Network a	1.71	0.86	0.29	0.0	0.79	5	50	2.38
Network b	4.57	2.29	0.76	1.11	0.89	2	26	1.24

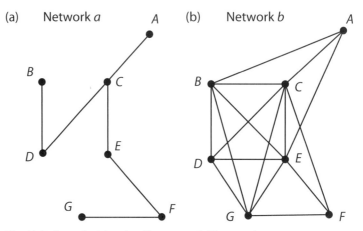

Fig. 11.7 Sparsely (a) and well-connected (b) networks.

Global connectivity

The **average degree**, K, of a network is calculated as

$$K = \frac{1}{N} \sum_{i=1}^{N} k_i \tag{11.4}$$

If the average degree of a simple graph is close to $N - 1$ then almost every node is directly connected to every other, whereas if it is considerably smaller then many nodes are not *directly* connected, although they may still be connected via intermediate nodes. Indirect connectivity can be quantified using accessibility measures.

The **beta index**, β, is simply the average number of edges available per node, calculated as

$$\beta = E/N \tag{11.5}$$

β ranges from 0 for a completely disconnected graph to $(N - 1)/2$ for a completely connected simple graph.

The **gamma index**, γ, is the ratio of number of edges actually present in a network to the maximum number possible. It is calculated for a simple network as

$$\gamma = E/E_{max} = E/[N(N - 1)/2] \tag{11.6}$$

The maximum possible number of edges in a planar network is always less than for a non-planar network with the same number of nodes, so in this case γ is calculated as

$$\gamma = E/E_{\max} = E/[3(N-2)] \tag{11.7}$$

γ measures essentially the same network properties as β, but makes it easier to compare different networks because it is constrained to range in value from 0 for a completely disconnected network to 1 for a completely connected network.

The **alpha index**, α, is the ratio of the actual number of cycles in a network to the maximum number possible. It is calculated as:

$$\alpha = (E - N + G)/(2N - 5) \tag{11.8}$$

α provides some indication of the amount of redundancy among the connections in a network, so that a network with high α might be thought more robust than one with a low α.

The **average clustering coefficient**, C, is calculated as:

$$C = \frac{1}{N} \sum_{i=1}^{N} C_i \tag{11.9}$$

A value of 1 would indicate that a network is made up of a number of globally disconnected neighbourhoods (components) that are each locally highly connected, whereas a value of 0 would indicate that no nodes share neighbours. In studies of social networks, C is used as a measure of 'cliqueiness'.

Global accessibility Measures provide some indication of how easy it is to travel between nodes that are connected, but not directly connected.

The **network diameter**, δ, is equal to the largest König index of any node in the network. It measures the maximum journey length that would be *required* to travel between two nodes. Of course, longer lengths might be possible by avoiding the shortest paths, but this is usually of less interest.

The **Shimbel index**, D, is defined as the total number of edges traversed by all the shortest paths between pairs of nodes in the network. It may be calculated as

$$D = \sum_{i} \sum_{j \neq i} l_{ij} \tag{11.10}$$

A network with a small Shimbel index is said to be compact, in the sense that most nodes are only a short path length away from others.

The **average path length**, L, is calculated as

$$L = \frac{2}{N(N-1)} \sum_{i} \sum_{j \neq i} l_{ij} \tag{11.11}$$

Note that $2/N(N-1)$ is the reciprocal of the number of pairs of nodes, which provides L with an advantage over the Shimbel index in that it scales the measure according to the network size.

Examples

The following examples have been chosen to illustrate the application of network analysis at both a regional scale and the scale of individual buildings. Gorenflo and

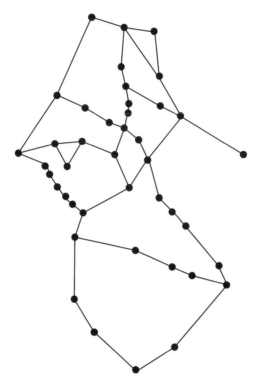

Fig. 11.8 A graph of Serbian trade routes in the thirteenth and fourteenth centuries (data from Carter 1969, Fig. 2.)

Bell (1991) describe several other examples concentrating on archaeological and historical transportation networks.

Settlement location Carter (1969) used measures of network structure to analyse the centrality of successive capitals of medieval Serbia in the thirteenth–fourteenth centuries AD. His aim was to identify the likely extent of the Serbian oecumene[3] and, in particular, to assess whether Stefan Dušan's choice of capital city ultimately contributed to the demise of the Serbian state. For this purpose he created an undirected planar graph of trade routes with 42 nodes representing medieval settlements (Fig. 11.8).

   Carter chose to analyse the trade network by representing it in matrix form, which is a common approach in network analysis. A C_1 matrix comprises a set of N rows and N columns, such that each entry is coded 1 if the row and column node are connected by an edge and 0 otherwise (Fig. 11.9). By raising the C_1 matrix to the power of the network diameter, in this case multiplying the C_1 matrix by itself

---

[3]The concept of an oecumene roughly equates to that 'portion of the state that supports the densest and most extended population and has the closest mesh of transportation lines' (Whittlesey 1944 cited in Carter 1969, p. 39).

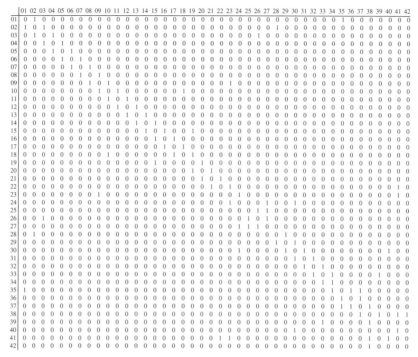

Fig. 11.9 The C_1 matrix for the Serbian trade network shown in Fig. 11.8.

11 times, he was able to obtain a result in which each entry gives the number of 11-step routes between the relevant pair of nodes. He then summed each row to obtain the 'gross vertex connectivity' of each node, i.e. the total number of 11-step routes to which it is connected. Carter found that the medieval capitals of Serbia were ranked 1, 5, 6, 7 and 17 in descending order of gross connectivity, with Dušan's chosen capital, Skoplje, ranked lowest.

A significant problem with gross vertex connectivity is that it includes redundant information: it seems unrealistic that a trader would prefer to do business with the settlement at the end of the largest number of 11-step routes as opposed to a settlement that is generally only a few steps away. Consequently, Carter constructed an $N \times N$ short-path matrix, in which each entry records the number of edges in the shortest path between the relevant pair of nodes. He again summed each row, this time obtaining the accessibility index A_i as defined above. The medieval capitals ranked 1, 2, 3, 6 and 8 in order of descending accessibility, that is increasing A_i, with Skoplje ranked lowest.

Carter concluded that Stefan Dušan's chosen capital was not best placed in terms of transportation links and that this may have been a contributory factor in the demise of the Serbian state. Perhaps more interestingly from a methodological point of view, he also created maps showing isolines[4] of accessibility (Fig. 11.10), which

---

[4] See Chapter 12 for an explanation of isolines.

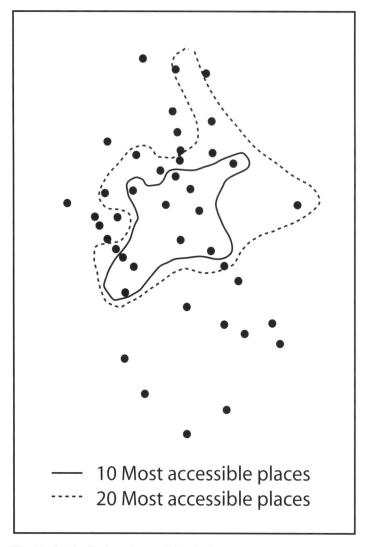

Fig. 11.10 Distribution of accessibility in the medieval Serbian oecumene (data from Carter 1969, Figs. 3 and 6).

he used to suggest that the extent of the medieval Serbian oecumene may have extended further west than hitherto realised. This suggestion also drew on more advanced work in which Carter calculated the eigenvectors of the connectivity matrix, a subject which falls beyond the scope of this book – interested readers should consult Gould's (1967) *On the Geographical Interpretation of Eigenvalues* and may also find a straightforward introduction to matrix algebra useful (e.g. Chapter 18 of Eason *et al.* 1980).

Building design There has been sporadic archaeological interest in space syntax, which comprises a theory of the human use of space and a collection of methods

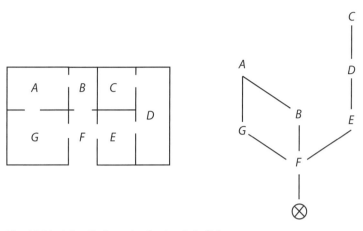

Fig. 11.11 A justified graph of a simple building.

for analysing the human use of space according to that theory. The main theoretical tenets of space syntax were laid out in Hillier and Hanson's (1984) *The Social Logic of Space* and its relationship with architectural practice further developed in Hillier's (1996) *Space is the Machine*. The space syntax method that has been most used by archaeologists is the construction of justified graphs. Such graphs are tree-like networks that show how discrete spaces in a building, or sometimes group of buildings, are accessible from one another (Fig. 11.11). They have been used to investigate issues such as social stratification and privacy in contexts including: Scottish Iron Age brochs (Foster 1989), English medieval nunneries and monasteries (Gilchrist 1997, pp. 160–169), North American pueblos (Bustard 1996) and Bulgarian tells (Chapman 1990).

Our concern here, however, is with recent work that uses measures of network structure to analyse the layout of buildings in terms of the intervisibility of spaces within them. Turner *et al.* (2001) calculate the intervisibility between all points on a 1-m grid within a building. They then construct a *visibility graph* (Floriani *et al.* 1994) in which the nodes represent the points on the grid and the edges indicate mutual visibility (Fig. 11.12). Note that in this case the nodes represent analytical units rather than real, clearly delineated, physical entities; this clearly demonstrates the flexibility of network analysis.

Turner *et al.* (2001) argue that network measures of visibility graphs can provide useful information about the way in which built spaces influence human behaviour. First, and most straightforwardly, the immediate neighbourhood of a node constitutes that node's isovist (see Chapter 10) and its nodal degree is linearly related to the isovist area. They argue that the local clustering coefficient, C_i, measures the 'proportion of intervisible space within the visibility neighbourhood of a point' (Turner *et al.* 2001, p. 110). By plotting a map of C_i for all nodes it is then possible to investigate how much the visual field changes as one moves around the building, since $C_i \rightarrow 0$ implies a large change in what is visible while $C_i \rightarrow 1$ implies little change. Finally, Turner *et al.* argue that the mean shortest path length *from each*

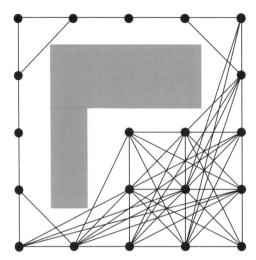

Fig. 11.12 A visibility graph for the exterior of an L-shaped building.

node provides a measure of visual accessibility which is sensitive to global, not just local, relationships. They have plotted this for a set of points in a major art gallery in London and found that is is correlated with the number of visits to rooms in the gallery. Importantly, the actual Euclidean distance between the points does not correlate with visits, leading Turner *et al.* to argue that mean shortest path length measures an aspect of intervisibility that influences the comprehensibility of space.

11.3.2 *Location on networks*

The problem of optimally locating facilities within a catchment is known as the *location–allocation* problem. In modern-day planning and commerce, *facilities* are typically things like schools and supermarkets (see Longley *et al.* 2001, pp. 313–316), but it is not difficult to think of other centralised resources more relevant to the past. Location–allocation problems can be solved for the placement of facilities in continuous space, or for their position on networks. Bell and Church (1985) provide archaeological examples of both, but it is the latter which interests us here (we have already discussed continuous space in Chapter 10).

Solving location–allocation problems on networks

As Gorenflo and Bell (1991) point out, networks can play two roles in location–allocation models: they can provide a locational constraint on the placement of facilities (i.e. the facilities must be on the network) or they can provide a means of modelling the interaction between candidate centres (e.g. edges that represent the flow and volume of goods). What constitutes the 'optimal' location of facilities in a network is determined by the *objective function*. The most commonly employed objective functions are designed to solve the following problems:

The ***p-median*** problem is to locate *p* centres offering facilities so as to minimise the total distance travelled from all demand locations to their nearest facility.

Coverage problems seek to locate centres offering facilities so as to ensure that all demand locations are within some specified distance of their nearest facility. Compared with the *p*-median solution, the average distance between a demand location and its nearest facility may be higher, but the maximum distance is likely to be lower. In contemporary planning, the coverage problem is often seen to provide the most appropriate solution for the location of emergency services, where it is the maximum response time that must be minimised.

Concerns have been raised that the use of optimality models merely serves to project modern capitalist values back into the past (e.g. Thomas 1991a, but see Mithen 1989 for a more sympathetic view). In the case of location–allocation modelling, two counter-arguments may be made. The first is that archaeologists are free to specify the objective function of their choosing, although admittedly this may require scripting or programming, since commercial GIS software is unlikely to offer built-in support for anything other than the standard *p*-median and coverage problems. The second argument concerns the inferential framework within which location–allocation modelling is to be applied. As archaeologists, we are not normally in the business of locating facilities, but instead seek to understand the location of those already established in the past. In this case, rather than simply asserting that the past was different, we may be able to establish how different by comparing locational solutions derived from modern objective functions against the archaeological evidence.

A more serious objection specific to location–allocation modelling is that the 'classical' (Bailey and Gatrell 1995, p. 369) approach, which includes the *p*-median and coverage problems as formulated above, assumes that people always use the closest facilities. This is not always the case today and may not have been in the past. *Spatial interaction* methods overcome this limitation by allowing the probabilistic allocation of demand to facilities. Bailey and Gatrell (1995, Chapter 9) provide an introduction to spatial interaction modelling, and Fotheringham and O'Kelly (1989) provide a more extended treatment.

An archaeological example
Mackie (2001) has used location–allocation modelling to study the relationships between shell midden sites on Vancouver Island, Canada. Taking the centroids of midden zones as nodes, he built a network based on shortest-path distances across water (Fig. 11.13). Then, treating all nodes as both demand locations and candidate centres (with equal capacity to function as such), he used ARC/INFO to solve the *p*-median problem for numbers of centres ranging from 1 to 25.

Mackie found that for $p = 1$ and $p = 5$ to $p = 9$, the middens chosen as centres had average areas larger than would be expected by chance alone, suggesting a link between centrality and intensity of use (Fig. 11.14). The importance of centrality *per se* was supported by the lack of any correlation between network accessibility

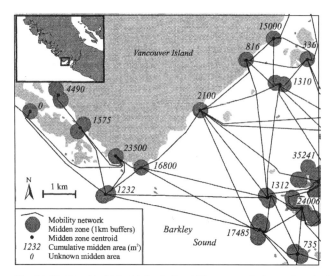

Fig. 11.13 Detail of Mackie's shell midden network (reproduced with permission from Mackie 2001, Fig. 6.3).

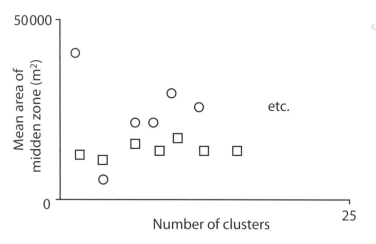

Fig. 11.14 The relationship between the number of centres, p, and the average area of the midden zones chosen as centres in Mackie's location–allocation analysis of shell midden sites (data from Mackie 2001, Fig. 7.3 and table 7.1). ○, actual solution sets; □, random solution sets.

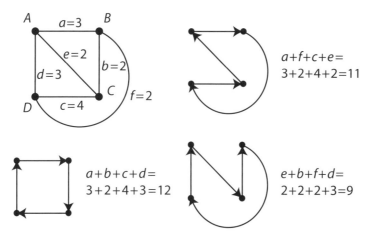

Fig. 11.15 The travelling salesman problem for 4 nodes. Route *ebfd* is shortest, assuming weights are totals rather than per-unit distance.

and the size of midden zones. Mackie (2001, p. 63) concluded from these results that he had discovered the scale at which 'habitual action makes both a significant and recognisable contribution to the archaeological signature'.

11.3.3 *Routing on networks*

Routing is an important element of many commercial applications of GIS (see Longley *et al.* 2001 for concrete examples). It is likely to become even more widespread with the proliferation of wireless devices that can be used to download and display data for real-time navigation. It has, however, found virtually no use in archaeological GIS. So far as logistics are concerned, archaeological fieldwork is rarely conceived on a scale that would justify the use of GIS for optimising the deployment of, say, field-walking teams. And in the case of research, it would appear that archaeologists have found few analogues for the problems that are routinely solved in commerce.

For these reasons we have restricted our discussion of routing to a brief account of the main applications – to serve as a stimulus for further thought if nothing else. Those who require a more detailed treatment should consult Fischer (2004) for further references.

The **travelling salesman problem** is to find 'the least cost tour through a set of nodes so that each node is visited exactly once' (Fischer 2004, p. 2). Note that as the number of nodes increases, so the number of possible tours increases very rapidly: there are 3 possible tours through 4 nodes (Fig. 11.15), 12 possible tours through 5 nodes, but 181 440 possible tours through 10 nodes (Longley *et al.* 2001, p. 317). As a result, it is usual for GIS software to provide an approximate rather than exact solution to the travelling salesman problem.

The **vehicle routing problem** is a generalisation of the travelling salesman problem to include situations where there is more than one salesperson and it is therefore necessary to decide which salesperson should visit which node. Additional complications can include multiple starting points, constraints on the number of visits that an individual salesperson can make (so-called *capacity constraints*) and also constraints on the visiting times for each node (Fischer 2004).

The **orienteering problem** is a variant of the travelling salesman problem in which it is not necessary to visit every node. Instead the aim is to maximise the gains from visiting nodes while simultaneously minimising the distance travelled (Longley *et al.* 2001).

11.4 Networks on continuous surfaces

11.4.1 *Least-cost paths*

Most users of GIS know the physical location of the network links that they wish to model – for example, roads, railways, waterways or power lines. Archaeologists, however, often do not know the exact route of transportation links because for much of history transport did not involve the construction of specialised infrastructure such as roads and artificial waterways. Even where it did, such infrastructure may not have been preserved. Under these circumstances GIS can be used to predict transport routes by deriving least-cost paths from an appropriate accumulated cost-surface (Chapter 10). Of course, prediction of 'lost' routes is not the only use for least-cost paths: they can be compared to known routes in order to help understand the location of those routes.

Calculating least-cost paths

As Husdal (2000) recounts, the idea of using cost-surfaces to derive least-cost paths dates back to the late 1970s and was effectively introduced into GIS by Tomlin (1990). Most, if not all, commercially available GIS software implements the calculation of a least-cost path as a two stage process. The first stage is to create a cost-surface that models the accumulated cost of travelling outward from the origin using the relevant transport technology. The second stage is to trace the route of steepest reduction in accumulated cost from the destination back to the origin. It follows that the validity of the final least-cost path is dependent upon the suitability of both the accumulated cost-surface and the path-finding algorithm. We have already discussed the first of these at length in Chapter 10, where the reader should pay particular attention to the problem of anisotropy. We discuss the second in more detail here.

Many least-cost paths generated using GIS are problematic, either because they fail to replicate known routes, or because they follow routes that seem intuitively unlikely. (There is, of course, a delicate balance to be struck in weighing counter-intuitive results from the application of a relatively crude GIS technique against the possible failings of common sense!) The most commonly encountered problems arise from the following (see also Harris 2000):

> **Shape of search neighbourhood** Least-cost paths often exhibit small-scale zig-zags, even when they purportedly represent the least costly route over a uniform landscape – which ought to be a straight line (Fig. 11.16). This frequently occurs when the

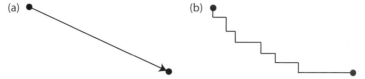

Fig. 11.16 Least-cost paths are seldom optimal, even on a uniform surface: (a) shows the optimal path between two nodes on a uniform surface, (b) shows how it is typically generated in a raster GIS.

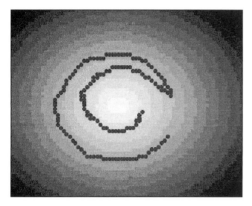

Fig. 11.17 Collischonn and Pilar's least-cost path on a mountain (reproduced from Collischonn and Pilar 2000, Fig. 8, with the permission of Taylor & Francis Ltd, www.tandf.co.uk/journals).

path-tracing algorithm and/or the cost-accumulation algorithm searches a neighbourhood with a radius of just one map cell. In the worst case, the von Neumann neighbourhood (Rook's move) only allows moves in the four cardinal directions, while the Moore neighbourhood (Queen's move) only permits moves in eight directions. There are two solutions to this problem, although both are likely to require some programming. The first, as explored by Xu and Lathrop (1995), is to increase the search radius, thereby increasing the number of directions in which it is possible to move. The second method, favoured by Douglas (1999), interpolates the exact course of the path through each map cell: this overcomes the need for paths to pass through the centres of map cells and as a result removes the limitation that a move can only be made in one of a finite number of directions.

Failure to model anisotropy Despite the occurrence of small-scale zig-zags, least-cost paths seldom exhibit the large-scale zig-zags that characterise mountain roads in many parts of the world. The absence of such paths when they might be expected is usually indicative of the failure to model the anisotropic cost of traversing sloping land adequately. As Collischonn and Pilar (2000) point out, the traditional procedures for finding a least-cost path cannot be applied to solve problems with direction-dependent costs because the direction of travel across each cell is not known at the time that the cost-of-passage surface is created. They have devised an algorithm that performs both steps together and which is capable of producing 'realistic' mountain roads (Fig. 11.17) provided that the costs attributed to different slopes are appropriate: as

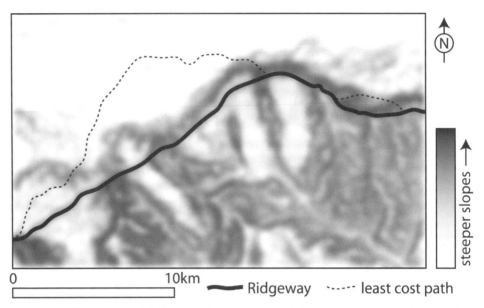

0   10km   ▬▬ Ridgeway   ·-·-· least cost path

Fig. 11.18 A globally suboptimal least-cost path (based on data from Bell and Lock 2000, Fig. 5). Elevation data © Crown Copyright. All rights reserved. Licence no. 100021184.

discussed in Chapter 10, in many cases steep downhill slopes should be considered more costly than gentle uphill slopes.

Assumption of steepest descent Another common objection to least-cost paths is that they often do not appear to follow the globally optimal route. For example, Bell and Lock (2000) generated a least-cost path between two locations on a prehistoric trackway in central England. Although the trackway follows a natural ridge, the GIS-generated least-cost path dropped off the ridge and then climbed back onto it (Fig. 11.18). Given that Bell and Lock assigned the lowest costs to flat land and gentle slopes, one might have expected the GIS path to follow the ridge, thereby avoiding the steep transverse slopes. In fact this result is characteristic of those obtained from path-tracing algorithms that seek the most rapid reduction in accumulated cost. Such algorithms essentially trace the path that water would take over the accumulated cost surface when flowing from the destination to the origin. Considered from the origin, such a path typically accumulates costs slowly at first and then at an ever greater rate as one approaches the destination. The problem with this is that people do not usually leave the hardest work until last, but instead seek a route along which costs accumulate relatively steadily.

Failure to model multiple destinations The least-cost path algorithms currently available in production GIS are designed to trace paths between exactly two locations. Thus in order to predict the most likely route to multiple locations one must make do with one of the following two methods. The first would be to treat that location as the origin and then trace paths separately to all other locations, which might be appropriate if there are reasonable grounds for treating one location as some kind of redistributive centre. The second method would be to treat each as the destination and then origin in turn, which might better suit, for example, a sequence of locations along a caravan route. Both methods suffer serious limitations: the first prevents the generation of substantially shared routes whose exact location is partly a function of the necessary compromises, while the second requires that one already knows the order in which locations were visited. At the time of writing specialised multiple destination least-cost path algorithms are the preserve of experimental GIS (see for example McIlhagga 1997 cited in Husdal 2000).

Failure to use ratio-scale costs It is common for least-cost paths generated for archaeological purposes to be derived from relative rather than absolute measures of cost, partly because of the difficulty of calibrating the costs of past transport technologies. Relative costs are usually measured on an ordinal or interval scale rather than a ratio scale. It is not widely appreciated that when costs are measured on an interval scale, adding or subtracting an arbitrary uniform amount from the costs will often alter the least-cost path because it alters the relationship between the costs incurred in traversing particular map cells (Longley *et al.* 2001, p. 319). Least-cost paths should, wherever possible, be generated using costs measured on a ratio scale.

Archaeological applications

Archaeological applications of least-cost path analysis may be divided into two groups: those that seek to replicate known routes and those that attempt to predict unknown routes.

Replication of routes The purpose of replicating routes is generally to aid in understanding the reasons for the location of routes. For example, Madry and Rakos (1996) sought to replicate known segments of the Celtic road network in the Arroux Valley, France, using several different determinants of 'cost'. They then used the best model – 'a combination of least change in elevation, low slope and preference to remain within line of sight of hillforts' (Madry and Rakos 1996, p. 115) – to predict the course of a missing segment of the road network. Similar studies include Bell and Lock's (2000) study of the Ridgeway prehistoric track, discussed above, and Kantner's (1996) attempt to replicate the location of known Anasazi road segments in Chaco Canyon, New Mexico.

Prediction of routes One of the more sophisticated attempts to predict the location of unknown routes was carried out by the Wroxeter Hinterland Project, which sought to reconstruct the Iron Age road network that existed prior to the development of the Roman city of Wroxeter, England. Van Leusen and his colleagues (see van Leusen 2002, Chapter 16) generated a road network by tracing least-cost paths from the locations of known settlement enclosures to Wroxeter (which was a centre of exchange in the Iron Age) and also the least-cost paths from the same known settlements to the larger multivallate enclosures. Broadly similar attempts to predict entire pathway or road networks have been made for the Bronze and Iron Age settlements of central Italy (Bell *et al.* 2002) and the Neolithic habitation of the Biferno Valley, also in Italy (Silva and Pizziolo 2001). A rather different example of route prediction is offered by Krist and Brown's (1994) study of possible Late Pleistocene/Early Holocene hunting sites in the Great Lakes region of North America. Here, least-cost paths were used to predict the likely migration routes

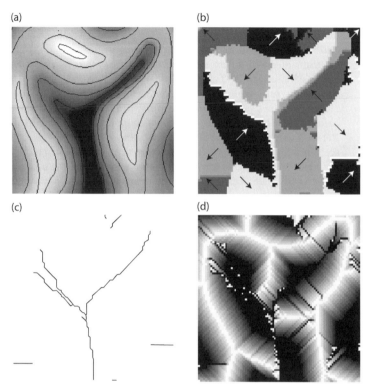

Fig. 11.19 A (a) DEM (white = high), (b) local drainage direction map, (c) stream channel (defined on flow accumulation $\geqslant 50$) and (d) flow accumulation map (white = low).

of caribou in order to ascertain whether they were in view of the possible hunting sites. Note that this study provides a well-documented example of the creation of a partially anisotropic accumulated cost-surface.

11.4.2 *Hydrology*

Archaeological GIS frequently include hydrological information in the form of vector maps of watercourses. Such maps are most commonly used for proximity analysis, for example, to identify sites that may be at risk from flooding, or as a possible predictor of site location. Vector maps of navigable watercourses can also be used for network analysis. For example, both Zubrow (1990) and Allen (1990) based their network models of the early European colonisation of North America on maps of the major river systems. In principle, most of the methods described above can be applied to hydrological networks.

Our concern here is with an alternative method of representing hydrology using *local drainage direction* (LDD) maps (Fig. 11.19b). LDD maps are a form of surface topology map. Such maps show how map cells are connected by some process, in this case the direction of water flow across each cell. Note that although topological relations such as previous cell (e.g. where the water came from) and next cell (e.g. where the water will flow) can be retrieved from a surface topology map (e.g. by following the direction of flow), they are not themselves stored in the map. In other words, whereas a vector map records topological relations explicitly, a surface topology map records them only implicitly.

There are two advantages in representing hydrology using an LDD map. The first is that it makes possible the automated derivation of watercourses where such data are either not available or data acquisition would be costly and/or time-consuming. The second advantage is that LDD maps can be used to derive additional information about a region's hydrology and landscape morphology which may in turn be useful for understanding archaeological site location.

Calculating LDD maps

Local drainage direction maps are usually implemented as raster maps, although they have also been created using TINs (see, for example, Jones *et al.* 1990). The computation of a raster LDD map involves two processes, which may be carried out iteratively until an acceptable result has been obtained.

Direction of flow Each cell in an LDD map is coded according to the direction in which water would flow out of it. The simplest method computes this as the direction of the steepest downhill slope within the Moore neighbourhood, i.e. within a window of radius one map cell. The use of such a small window only allows the direction to be determined to the nearest 45°, so that the cell at the centre of the window will typically be coded with an integer in the range 1–9 representing the bearing N, NE, E, SE, S, SW, W, NW or 'pit' (see below). Jensen and Domingue (1988) describe search strategies that can be employed when more than one map cell shares the steepest slope. Burrough and McDonnell (1998, p. 194) describe more sophisticated methods that also allow for the dispersion of water over several cells.

Pit removal Cells are coded 'pit' when all their neighbours have a higher elevation. Pits disrupt the surface topology because water that flows into them does not flow out again. They must therefore be removed, which can be achieved by increasing the elevation of the pit until at least one neighbour is lower or, alternatively, by decreasing the elevation of all the neighbours until at least one is lower. Both methods can be applied manually or automatically, but in either case the challenge is to remove only those pits that do not reflect reality. Methods have been devised (e.g. Deursen 1995) to ensure that pits are only removed if they fall below a certain size, specified in terms of area, depth or volume.

Derivatives of LDD maps

Once an LDD map has been computed it can be used to generate further information about the hydrology and topography of a region.

Hydrology Burrough and McDonnell (1998, pp. 195–198) provide a useful introduction to the many hydrological indices that can be derived from LDD maps,
focusing particularly on those that are used to model sediment transport. Here we
concentrate instead on the indices that are most likely to be of use for addressing
general locational questions.

> **Flow accumulation** This LDD derivative codes each map cell with the number of
> upstream cells that drain into it (Fig. 11.19d). Although the flow accumulation map
> provides a crude measure of the relative volume of water that would drain through
> each map cell, it is mostly used as an intermediate step in the computation of other
> indices.
>
> **Stream channel maps** These code each map cell according to whether they contain
> a watercourse (Fig. 11.19c). They can be generated from a flow accumulation map
> using simple map algebra to extract all cells with more than some minimum number
> of upstream cells. How many upstream cells are required to produce permanent
> running water is, of course, a function of land cover, soil type, underlying geology
> and precipitation. Nevertheless, in many cases stream channel maps provide a useful
> – and potentially more accurate – alternative to digitising watercourses from paper
> mapping.
>
> **Stream order** In natural language we often categorise watercourses using words such
> as 'stream', 'brook', 'river' and 'estuary'. These categories are typically defined on
> more than one property, so that, for example, 'streams' are narrow, fast flowing and
> have no tributaries, while 'brooks' are wider and have only streams as tributaries, and
> 'rivers' are wide, flow slowly and have many tributaries of all types. The categories
> used in GIS, so-called stream-order indices, are different in that they are typically
> based on only one property of a watercourse. Consequently, it is important to choose
> the most appropriate index for the problem at hand (see Haggett and Chorley 1969,
> pp. 8–16, for a useful survey of indices and Ward 1990 for a more recent treatment).
> For example, the *Strahler Index* provides a purely topological categorisation, such
> that watercourses at the tips of a network are coded 1, those formed by the confluence
> of two or more order-1 watercourses are coded 2, those formed by the confluence of
> two or more order-2 watercourses are coded 3 and so on (Fig. 11.20a). Note that the
> confluence of a lower-order watercourse with a higher-order watercourse does not
> alter the order of the latter. Consequently, the Strahler Index provides no information
> about the number of tributaries of a watercourse, rendering it unsuitable as even a
> loose proxy for the width or speed of flow of a watercourse. In contrast, the *Shreve
> Index* adds information about the number of tributaries by the device of assigning
> a new order at every confluence, where that order is the sum of the orders of the
> watercourses that join (Fig. 11.20b). As a result the Shreve Index provides a better
> indication of the likely relative sizes of watercourses.

Topography There are many ways in which one can attempt to characterise topography, including measures of surface roughness and the use of second-order derivatives (Chapter 9). Hydrological modelling adds the possibility of mapping watersheds (drainage basins) and ridges.

> **Watersheds** are usually defined for a specific point on a watercourse (the *pour point*)
> and constitute all the land that drains into that point (Fig. 11.21a, b). They are readily
> identified from an LDD map by stepping back up the drainage network from the
> pour point until there are no further cells that receive input from any other cell. The

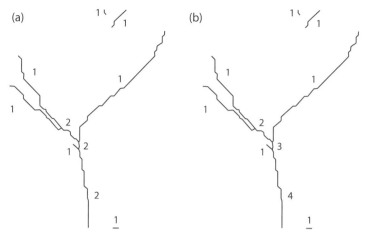

Fig. 11.20 Stream order coded using (a) the Strahler Index and (b) the Shreve Index.

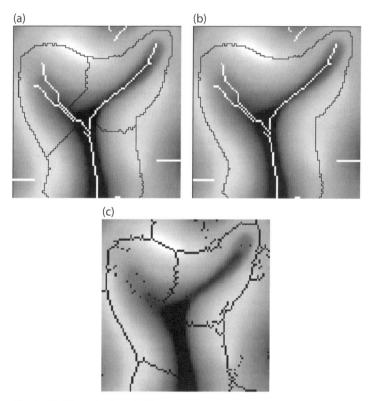

Fig. 11.21 Watersheds and ridges: (a) watersheds with pour point at accumulated flow of 1500; (b) watersheds with pour point at accumulated flow of 4500; (c) ridges.

complete set of cells traversed in this process constitutes the watershed for that pour point. Archaeologists usually conceive of watersheds at a landscape scale, relating them to economic and social concepts such as site catchments and territories. However, by appropriate choice of the pour point it is also possible to identify the local watersheds of individual sites, or even parts of sites, although the latter, in particular, will require a suitably high-resolution DEM. Such small-scale watersheds, or *upstream elements*, could potentially contribute to the understanding of site formation processes by mapping the likely sources of water-borne materials.

Ridges are the local elevation maxima that define the edges of watersheds. Either fact may be used to identify them from LDD maps, but which is most suitable depends on the question at hand. If one wishes to identify all ridges irrespective of whether they constitute slight rises between streams or the summits of mountains that separate entire river systems, then it is best simply to identify all local elevation maxima, which may be accomplished by extracting the set of cells that have no upstream elements (Fig. 11.21c). If the software in use does not permit topological queries on the LDD map, then the same effect can be achieved using map algebra to extract all cells with a value of 1 in the flow accumulation map.

Sometimes, however, the question demands that one identifies ridges of a particular scale: for example, the course of a long distance prehistoric trackway is more likely to have been influenced by the location of major ridges that extend for a considerable distance than it is by the location of relatively minor topographic features. In this case it may be most appropriate to identify ridges from the edges of watersheds, since the latter can be calculated at specific scales by careful choice of the pour points. For example, the ridges that bound the watersheds of pour points located on watercourses characterised by a high Strahler stream-order index will represent relatively large-scale topographic features, whereas those that bound the watersheds of pour points with a low stream-order index will represent small-scale topographic features. The main problem with this approach is that a set of watersheds associated with a given stream-order index will not include areas that drain directly into higher-order watercourses, thus leaving the ridges in those areas undefined.

Archaeological applications

Proximity to watercourses is routinely included in archaeological predictive models. Other aspects of hydrology that can be derived from LDD maps are included less often, probably owing as much as anything to a lack of familiarity with hydrological modelling. Indeed, one might, a priori, suppose that proximity to watercourses of a particular stream order (or that drain a certain size area) would be better predictors than proximity per se. In addition, there are other potential locational influences that can be derived from LDD maps, even though they are not normally available as part of the hydrological modelling functionality of mainstream GIS software. For example, it appears that many Palaeoindian/Early Archaic lithic scatters in SW Nebraska may be preferentially located at confluences of watercourses (Peterson 2004). Box 11.1 describes how a map of confluences can be created from a stream-order map.

Another use of hydrological modelling in archaeology is for palaeoenvironmental reconstruction, although there are few examples to date. One is Gillings' (1995, 1997) attempt to reconstruct the river network in the Tiza Valley, Hungary. The

Box 11.1 A method for locating confluences

This box describes a method for generating a map of confluences from a stream order map (Peterson 2004). The basic idea is very simple.

1. Use the hydrological modelling capabilities of software such as ArcGIS Spatial Analyst to create a map of the Strahler stream index.
2. If necessary, rasterise the stream-order map and reclassify it so that cells that do not contain a watercourse are coded NULL, while those that do are coded according to their order.
3. Pass a kernel of radius 1 over the rasterised stream-order map. If the central cell contains a stream then compare its value with the mean value of all other cells in the kernel that contain a stream. If the value of the central cell and the mean are different, then the central cell is located at a confluence; if they are equal then it is not located at a confluence.

This solution requires software that supports spatial offsets in map algebraic expressions, such as GRASS. The appropriate GRASS map algebra for step 3 above is:

```
confluences=eval(n=(if(isnull(stream_order[-1,-1]),0,1)+\
    if(isnull(stream_order[0,-1]),0,1)+\
    if(isnull(stream_order[1,-1]),0,1)+\
    if(isnull(stream_order[-1,0]),0,1)+\
    if(isnull(stream_order[0,0]),0,1)+\
    if(isnull(stream_order[1,0]),0,1)+\
    if(isnull(stream_order[-1,1]),0,1)+\
    if(isnull(stream_order[0,1]),0,1)+\
    if(isnull(stream_order[1,1]),0,1)),\
t=(if(isnull(stream_order[-1,-1]),0,stream_order[-1,-1])+\
    if(isnull(stream_order[0,-1]),0,stream_order[0,-1])+\
    if(isnull(stream_order[1,-1]),0,stream_order[1,-1])+\
    if(isnull(stream_order[-1,0]),0,stream_order[-1,0])+\
    if(isnull(stream_order[0,0]),0,stream_order[0,0])+\
    if(isnull(stream_order[1,0]),0,stream_order[1,0])+\
    if(isnull(stream_order[-1,1]),0,stream_order[-1,1])+\
    if(isnull(stream_order[0,1]),0,stream_order[0,1])+\
    if(isnull(stream_order[1,1]),0,stream_order[1,1])),\
m=if(n,t/n,0),\stream_order[0,0]!=m)
```

The above creates an output raster map called `confluences` from an input map called `stream_order`, both containing what their names suggest. Cells in the output map that do not contain watercourses are coded NULL, those that contain watercourses but are not at confluences are coded 0, and those that contain watercourses and are at confluences are coded 1. Note that the equation makes use of three intermediate variables before the final result is calculated on the last line: n is the number of cells in the kernel that contain a watercourse, t is the sum of the stream-order indices of those cells and m is the mean of the stream-order indices. It may help to know that isnull(A) is a logical function that returns TRUE if the map cell in A is NULL and FALSE otherwise. Similarly, the logical function if(A,B,C) takes the form: if the map cell in A is TRUE (i.e. non-zero) then return the result B but if A is not TRUE (i.e. zero) then return the result C.

problem faced by the Upper Tiza Project was that nineteenth century flood control had eliminated the annual flood regime, thus making it very difficult to understand past use of the landscape. The aim of the hydrological modelling was to 're-access those past environmental dynamics' (Gillings 1997). This research illustrates many of the processes described above. Briefly, in light of evidence that no large-scale river migration nor alluviation had taken place during the time period being studied, Gillings processed a modern DEM to identify and remove pits, distinguishing between those likely to represent artefacts of interpolation and those representing real features. He then created an LDD map and, specifying lowest points around the boundary of the study area as pour points, generated watersheds. This allowed him to create an accumulated flow map for the Tiza watershed, from which he generated watercourses by extracting all cells with an accumulated flow of 50 cells or more (representing a minimum catchment of 20 000 m^2). Gillings then vectorised the watercourses and merged them with the course of the Tiza, thus providing a reconstruction of the natural hydrology obliterated in the nineteenth century.

11.5 Conclusion

In this chapter we have explored applications of network analysis to archaeological problems. Techniques such as the generation of least-cost paths are well known, although by no means unproblematic. Others, such as the creation of visibility networks, hold considerable promise for the future. We have endeavoured to show how many different kinds of phenomena can be conceived as networks, while being careful to draw attention to the issues that must be considered when using GIS maps for network analysis.

12

Maps and digital cartography

12.1 Introduction

Cartographers have long recognised the influence that maps have on the shaping of spatial consciousness (Monmonier 1991; Wood 1992; Lewis and Wigen 1997). The purpose of this chapter is to explore the way maps, whether paper or digital, may be used to present spatial information and to highlight some design principles to maximise their effectiveness at this task. In doing so we describe a range of mapping techniques appropriate for the different sorts of data routinely handled by archaeologists. We also consider some major cartographic principles and design conventions that help make maps effective communication devices, and discuss the growing importance of the Internet and interactive mapping for the publication of spatial data.

12.2 Designing an effective map

As defined in Chapter 2, maps are traditionally divided into two categories: *topographic* and *thematic*. The former term describes maps that contain general information about features of the Earth's surface, whereas thematic maps are limited to single subjects, such as soils, geology, historic places, or some other single class of phenomena. Both types of map must contain some basic pieces of information so that the reader is able to comprehend and contextualise the data that is being presented. The most basic of these, without which a map is difficult if not impossible to understand, are: (i) a title; (ii) a scale; (iii) a legend and (iv) an orientation device, such as a north arrow (Table 12.1).

There are other items that may need to be included on a map in certain circumstances. The most important of these is reference information about the coordinate system used to create the map, and how the grid system relates to what is being depicted. Maps produced by national mapping agencies will always contain information about the coordinate system (as described in Chapter 2). This often takes the form of a few lines of text in the bottom left or right of the map describing the point of origin of the grid and the coordinate system (e.g. UK National Grid), and the ellipsoid that has been used (e.g. WGS84). This information is necessary for computing transformations between different mapping systems, and it can also be of use in archaeological contexts when attempting to relate data collected from a GPS receiver with existing topographic maps. Coordinate information, such as how the grid was established and the location of the 0, 0 datum, is also useful when

Table 12.1 *Essential map items*

Item	Description
Title	It cannot be assumed that common sense is a sufficient replacement for a title. For topographic maps, the title must provide the geographical context. For thematic maps, the title should identify the class of object or objects. Contour lines, for example, do not always represent elevation; they may represent temperature, rainfall or some other form of trend surface.
Scale	It is impossible to determine the scale of a map from visual assessment alone. Scales should either be given in easily multiplied linear units (1, 2, 5, 10, 100, etc.) or as an absolute scale (e.g. 1 : 25 000). In most cases, the latter style is more useful as it permits the reader to calculate approximate distances using a ruler. Many GIS and CAD systems have a facility for allowing absolute scales to be added to maps by automatically calculating the mathematical relationship between a map's geographical extent and the size of the printed version. As publishers may change the size of a map to fit the available space in a report or book, absolute scales will need to be recalculated. For this reason, despite being less useful, linear scales are often preferred.
Legend	This defines the thematic classification of the map. Legends, like the phenomena they represent, may either be continuous or discrete. In the case of the former, it is necessary to break the variables into categories or 'bins'. Some GIS programs create data bins that do not lend themselves to easy interpretation, and these therefore need to be changed manually. The number of legend categories used to define discrete data will ultimately be influenced by the number of objects there are in the class; however, it is worth keeping in mind that it is difficult to distinguish between large numbers of categories.
Orientation	A device to orientate the reader, usually in the form of a north arrow or grid overlay is essential. Although this in itself doesn't necessarily make the map more understandable, it does permit the reader to orientate the map and place it within a geospatial framework.

presenting large-scale data, such as plans of an archaeological excavation or field survey.

Information defining how the data were collected may also be of use and should be stored as associated *metadata*. Metadata transforms a map into a more complete record of the spatial information. For example, maps showing geophysical data, such as soil resistivity, should contain, in addition to the information described in the previous paragraph, short descriptions of the equipment used and the conditions under which the data were collected. Chapter 13 describes geospatial metadata standards in further detail, including tools for the recording of this information.

12.3 Map design

One of the disadvantages of the type of mapping facilities included in GIS software is that the resulting maps often do not adhere to basic cartographic design principles (Dent 1999, p. 6). Successful communication of spatial information requires at least some understanding of these principles. Although we are not advocating an approach that emphases style over content, it is necessary to be aware that design plays an important part in the effective presentation of spatial data. Cartographers have recognised this for some time, and have grouped issues of map design into three areas: (i) those related to object arrangement, (ii) those related to visual impact and (iii) those related to comprehension.

Object arrangement is an important component of map design and helps ensure proper balance and focus of attention. Automated map production is a common element in many GIS packages, and can significantly reduce the amount of time spent preparing maps. Unfortunately, automated mapping can never quite reach the skill of a good cartographer, and maps produced using the built-in functions of GIS packages often require substantial editing. General problems of these systems include poor arrangement and sizing of basic elements: titles are often inappropriately large or small, labels are incorrectly placed, scales are in unsuitable units, north arrows are too large and ornate. Fortunately, these can be manually edited, although specialised vector graphic packages offer more opportunities for cartographic manipulation.

Visual impact plays an equally important role in map communication. For example, the upper map in Fig. 12.1 shows a map of Thrace in which there are few visual aids to help distinguish between the mainland, islands and sea. The lower map in the same figure corrects this by using polygon shading, which immediately provides a mechanism for visually distinguishing between features. Colours may also help readers distinguish between map features, but the non-judicial use of colour can create maps that become unintelligible rainbows of information.

Humans have a limited ability to deal with complex classifications of data, so progressive shading or the use of different colours may help in highlighting differences between object classes. Alternatively, it is sometimes worth using higher-level categories to make complicated data more comprehensible. For example, an excavated archaeological site may have 20 different types of features and these could be grouped into fewer numbers of larger categories (e.g. hearth and ash deposits, pits and constructional features) each with their own distinctive colour ramp (e.g. reds, blues and greens). In cases where three or more categories of information need to be communicated, it may be preferable to use a separate map for each category.

12.4 Thematic mapping techniques

Thematic mapping often requires the use of specialised mapping techniques to convey information properly, of which there are five basic types: (i) the choropleth map, (ii) the continuous distribution map, (iii) the proportional symbol map, (iv) the dot density map and (v) the isarithmic map. Most GIS programs are capable of producing all of these map types.

12.4.1 *The choropleth map*

The choropleth map is the best way to depict the distribution of data classes in well-defined areas (called *enumeration units*). Choropleth maps do three things

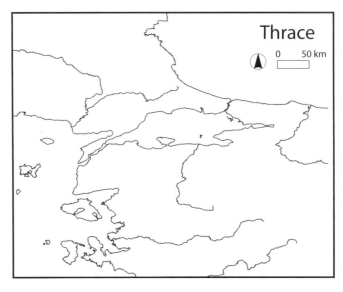

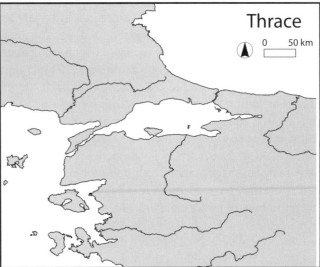

Fig. 12.1 The absence of polygon shading in the upper map makes it difficult to distinguish between the mainland, islands, rivers and sea. The addition of a polygon fill in the lower map allows these features to be more easily distinguished.

very effectively: (i) they show a quantitative or qualitative value associated with a geographical area, (ii) they give the reader a sense of the patterning of the mapped variables over a larger area and (iii) they provide a basis for comparing other values mapped using the same geographical boundaries (Dent 1999, p. 140). For example, the upper map in Fig. 12.2 shows the density of pottery sherds per survey unit (i.e. number of sherds/unit area). This form of mapping provides a means for determining the density of each unit in the survey map and, at the same

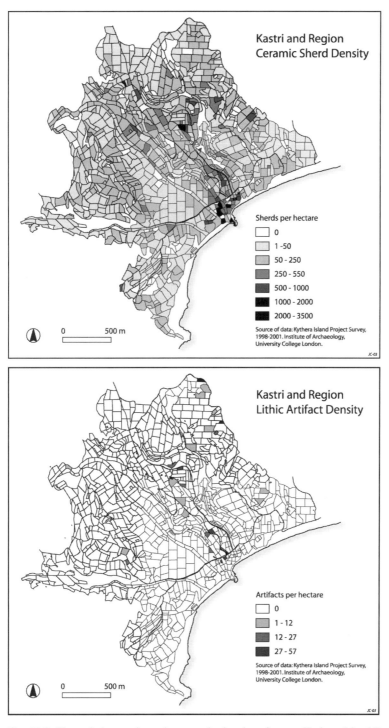

Fig. 12.2 Choropleth mapping using quantitative data. Source: Kythera Island Project. Used with permission.

time, provides information about the variability of the density in the study area. The lower map in the same figure shows the density of lithic artefacts (i.e. number of lithic artefacts/unit area). As both maps share the same enumeration units, it is easy to compare the distribution patterns of the two materials. Quantitative or qualitative data can be used for choropleth mapping. In the case of the former, the data must either be a total (such as the number of artefacts) or a ratio (such as the number of artefacts divided by the area of the enumeration unit). Unless the enumeration units are identical in area, ratio values are the more useful measure.

In both quantitative and qualitative forms of choropleth mapping, the underlying assumption is that the data are spread evenly throughout the enumeration unit. In some cases this assumption cannot easily be justified, yet this form of representation may still be the most appropriate mapping technique. In the previous map of pottery sherd distribution, for example, the artefacts cannot be assumed to be evenly distributed within each survey unit. This issue has been addressed by Lock *et al.* (1999) who suggest that choropleth maps bring major disadvantages to the representation of artefact distributions. Some concession to intra-enumeration-unit variability can be made by mapping a measure of the variability itself, using one of a variety of statistical measures that express the variability in a distribution of numbers. One simple measure is the *coefficient of variation*, which is the standard deviation divided by the mean. For example, Fig. 12.3 maps intra-unit variability for each enumeration unit for the ceramic sherd data in Fig. 12.2.

Standardising and normalising data

As noted, the choropleth technique works best with quantitative data when presented as a ratio and, most often, this will be a ratio of the data value to the area of the enumeration unit (i.e. a density). This standardises the data so that variability is not dependent on the size of the collection unit. Alternative ratio calculations can also be used to 'normalise' the data allowing disparate data to be compared on equal terms. For example, an observed value, such as a sherd count, could be used to normalise the distribution of another artefact category thus showing new values as a proportion to number of sherds recovered in that enumeration unit.

Determining class ranges

A major issue with choropleth mapping is categorising data values. Classes, or 'bins', are used to simplify patterns and make data easier to comprehend. Classification of data will invariably lead to generalisation and a loss of detail, but conventional cartographic theory, on the basis of experimentation, suggests that readers cannot distinguish between more than 11 grey-tone classes, and Dent (1999, p. 143) makes the recommendation that no more than 6 classes should be used. The classification method needs to be carefully controlled in order for it to be comprehensible. Some GIS programs use classification algorithms to determine the optimum number of classes, although user-intervention is often required. As described in Chapter 7, there are five basic approaches to numeric classifications for the

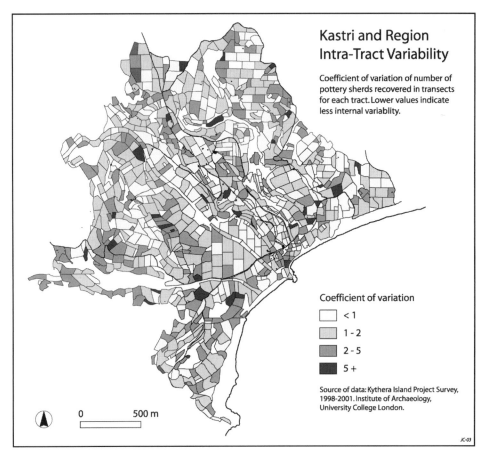

Fig. 12.3 Mapping enumeration-unit variability. Source: Kythera Island Project. Used with permission.

purposes of choropleth mapping: equal interval, natural break, standard deviation, quantile and equal area. As we previously explained, it is important to be aware of the structure of your data before choosing one of these methods (e.g. which of the four 'idealised' distributions it resembles in Fig. 7.15). This will help you choose the most appropriate classification method although you may need to edit the class ranges manually to present a more comprehensible picture of the data.

12.4.2 *Maps of continuous distribution*

Continuous distribution maps are used to display information about continuously varying quantitative data rather than discrete data. Maps of continuous distributions are similar in many ways to choropleth maps because they display values within an enumeration unit, within which the value is assumed to be representative. The major difference is that in maps of continuous distribution, the enumeration units are typically equal shapes and sizes (usually raster pixels, although other shapes such as hexagons can also be used) whereas choropleth maps may use different shaped

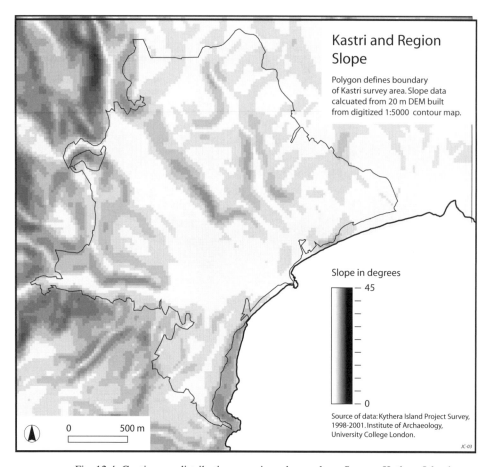

Fig. 12.4 Continuous distribution mapping: slope values. Source: Kythera Island Project. Used with permission.

polygons. The visualisation framework for maps of continuous distribution is also different, in that values are best represented using a ramped (or smooth) scale rather than discrete classes. The smooth gradation from the highest and lowest values also enhances the idea that the data being displayed are continuous in nature. Several colours can potentially be used in a colour 'ramp', for example a transition from green to yellow to red, to show changing elevation, temperature or rainfall values. Colour ramping can result in dramatic visual effects for continuously distributed data such as elevation. If done injudiciously, such as ramping between more than three or four colours, it can interfere with the interpretation of data patterning. Some data, such as slope values, are often better represented using a single ramped colour.

Figure 12.4 shows a map of slope values for the same study area used in the previous figures. In this case, the data categories are not individually identifiable; rather, an impression of a continuously varying surface is maintained by the use of

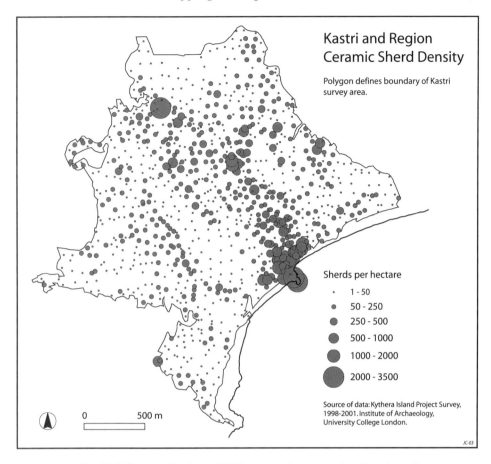

Fig. 12.5 Ceramic density variability mapped as proportional symbols. Source: Kythera Island Project. Used with permission.

ramped legend. It is important to emphasise that continuous distribution maps are not limited to environmental phenomena; they can be used effectively to show the distribution of a wide range of data. To cite one recent example, the mapping of fluted point distribution using continuous distribution techniques has been used to help understand the expansion of Palaeoindians (Steele *et al.* 1998; Anderson and Faught 2000).

12.4.3 *The proportional symbol map*
Proportional symbol maps are possibly the most popular form of thematic map devised. This is largely because of the fundamentally simple idea behind the technique of using the size of a symbol (typically circles, although squares, triangles or other shapes are also used) to represent the quantity of a phenomenon at a specific place on a map. Figure 12.5 shows a map of pottery sherd densities using proportional symbols.

Simple though this technique may be, there are some issues that need to be taken into account when creating proportional symbol maps, particularly with regards to the selection of the symbol and the manner in which the grading is calculated. Circles are traditionally the preferred shape because they can be easily scaled and related to a precise position on a map, but most programs offer a range of alternative symbols that may be more suited to the type of data that is being mapped. A major problem with complex shapes, however, is the difficulty they present for assessing scalar differences. Experiments have demonstrated that people both over- and underestimate the size of circles depending on the size of the neighbouring circles. The relative sizes of squares are most accurately estimated, although squares can create a rectangularity in maps that can distract from the data (Dent 1999, pp. 179–180).

Most GIS programs possess automatic scaling features for determining the size of the symbols in relation to their associated class ranges. Formulae for determining symbol size have been developed in cartography (e.g. Dent 1999, pp. 177–183), but it is unclear to what extent this has been adopted in GIS. Examination of the size grading in most systems suggests that it is based on linear calculations, so some user intervention may be needed for effective communication. Depending on whether circles, squares or some other shape is used, sizes may need to be adjusted to give a better impression of the differences between larger and smaller symbols.

12.4.4 *The dot-density map*

The rise of GIS-led cartographic production has seen a decline in the use of dot-density maps, which is unfortunate because they are an extremely useful and powerful way to present information about density values. Dot-density mapping is based on a simple premise: each dot represents a consistent unit of data, so that the total number of dots within an enumeration area equals the total data value. The map in Fig. 12.6 depicts ceramic distribution in the study area using this technique. As can be seen, this provides a very good impression of the underlying spatial structure of the distribution, although not the precise values for each enumeration unit, which is better represented by choropleth mapping. Additionally, as the dots are placed randomly within the enumeration unit, they do not show the specific location of the phenomena. This may appear rather limited compared to a map which shows the location of the units, but Fig. 12.6 arguably provides a better sense of the density variability than a simple choropleth map.

The effectiveness of this sort of mapping is based partly on the value of the dots, partly on the size of the dots and partly on how the dots are placed within the enumeration unit. If the dot value is too low or the dot size is too large, the map soon becomes crowded to such an extent that dots bleed into each other. Conversely, if the dot value is too high or the size too small, the map is too sparsely populated and any underlying spatial pattern is difficult or impossible to detect. To avoid creating a false sense of patterning, the dots also need to be randomly placed within their

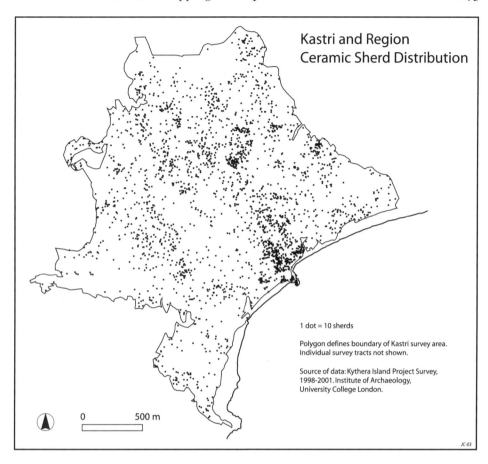

Fig. 12.6 Ceramic distribution as a dot-density map. Source: Kythera Island Project. Used with permission.

enumeration areas; any tendency to cluster within this space can undermine the very purpose of this type of mapping.

12.4.5 *The isarithmic map*

Isarithmic maps are used to portray three-dimensional surfaces (volumes) using line symbols referred to as *isolines*. This form of mapping is most recognisable when it is used to show variations in elevation using contour lines. The technique is, of course, not limited to showing elevation, and can be used to represent any expression of volume – or data that can be conceived as a volumetric – such as temperature or rainfall. The technique can be divided into two separate forms depending on the underlying data: *isometric mapping* and *isoplethic mapping*. The former term is used to describe data that are collected as points, whereas the latter term is used for data that occur over geographical areas (Dent 1999, p. 191). Examples of isometric maps used by archaeologists include elevation, rainfall and other environmental data

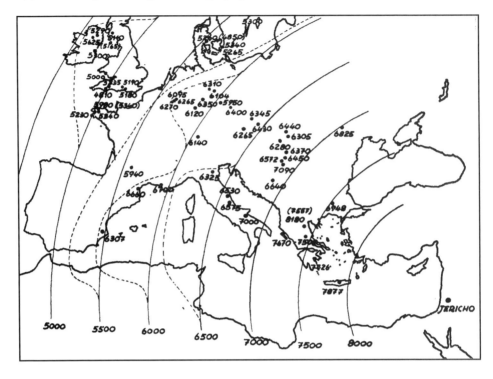

Fig. 12.7 Isochronic mapping of the spread of Neolithic farming, with dates in years BP (from Ammerman and Cavalli-Sforza 1971, p. 685). Dashed lines are expected regional variations. Reproduced with the permission of Blackwell Publishing. See Gkiasta *et al.* (2003) for more recent spatial modelling of the Neolithic radiocarbon record.

that have been collected by recording instruments or field observations. Isarithmic techniques have also been used to construct maps such as that in Fig. 12.7, which depicts the spread of Neolithic expansion in Europe using *isochrons*, where the locations and dates of Early Neolithic sites form the underlying point data (Ammerman and Cavalli-Sforza 1971).

In contrast, isoplethic techniques are used to depict spatial variability of data that have been collected in enumeration units, for example population density per square kilometre or the number of pottery sherds per hectare as shown in Fig. 12.8. Although the method of construction is similar to isometric maps, isoplethic mapping ultimately hides the scale of the collection unit. This is acceptable for truly continuous data (as this can often be found in the map documentation), but may cause confusion for quasi-continuous datasets as used in Fig. 12.8. For this reason, isoplethic maps are less suited for data collected in enumeration units, which are better mapped using choropleths.

Before methods for determining the placement of isolines were integrated into many common GIS packages, isarithmic mapping was a technically demanding

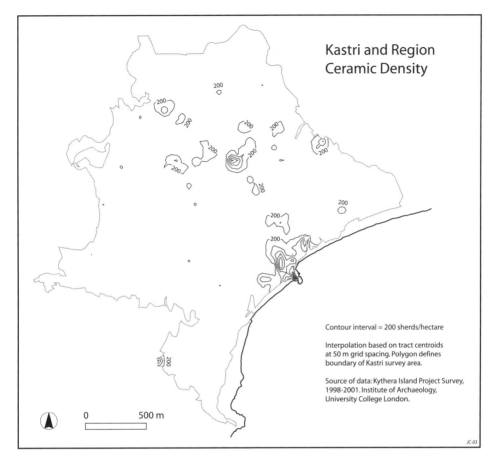

Fig. 12.8 Isoplethic mapping of pottery density. The base data are identical to that used to construct the maps in Figs. 12.2, 12.5 and 12.6. Source: Kythera Island Project. Used with permission.

exercise. Conceptually, the process can be equated to inserting a horizontal plane through a three-dimensional surface at a set value, and recording the line of intersection. In practice, this process could be approximated by 'threading' a line through an array of data values and then smoothing the line. This, of course, assumes that the data array contains values that match the intervals of the lines. If this is not the case, then data values will have to be estimated through the process of *interpolation* (as described in Chapter 6).

Isarithmic mapping is subject to the same sorts of errors that have been described previously; errors in data collection may produce faulty base data, improper interpolation algorithm might result in inaccuracies, edge effects can cause spurious results towards the borders of the distribution, the map may be improperly drawn and the finished map itself may be improperly interpreted by the reader. The use of

GIS for map generation does not necessarily mean that a map will be appropriately drawn, so some care also needs to be taken to make certain that the source information is both clearly and properly presented. There are some design strategies that can be used to assist this, such as making isolines appear dominant on a map by using heavier weighted lines than used for other map data, and making certain that the isoline labels are legible and orientated towards the user. Automated labelling of isolines, or other spatial objects, is not handled very well by GIS and the use of more sophisticated third-party automated labelling facilities or, alternatively, manually placing labels, will ensure greater legibility.

12.5 Internet mapping

As the use of the Internet and other forms of electronic dissemination of archaeological data increase, so does interest in presenting map data in such a way that it can take advantage of the interactive and hypertext facilities that multimedia authoring languages offer. Electronic publication has also changed the style of publication by providing the reader with more options to navigate text and data in non-linear ways, and to create their own interpretations of the evidence.

Hodder (1999, pp. 117–128) has discussed the impact of global information systems on archaeology and, in a lively debate, Hodder (1997) and Hassan (1997) also discuss the implications arising from Hodder's celebration of the erosion of the authority of authorship that has been seen as an implication of digital publication. Similar implications arising from digital publication of spatial information can be proposed: providing users with interactive access to complete spatial datasets – and thus the ability to create, interrogate and analyse subsets of this information – challenges the authority of the cartographer and presents opportunities for alternative interpretations. Standards for Internet GIS, or 'Web GIS' as it is also called, are still emerging (Smith *et al.* 2002; Peng and Tsou 2003); the development of technologies for interactive Internet mapping is consequently a relatively new enterprise in the rapid rise of GIS technologies, but is one that has the potential to bring GIS to a much wider non-specialist audience.

Archaeologists have been early users of this technology as it provides a logical extension of the traditional published site report to a more interactive and interpretable format. Facilities that permit hyperlinks between data tables, descriptions and related maps can increase the effectiveness of maps as communication media. A good example is the development of a 'Web-CD' for the West Heslerton Project (Powlesland 1998) described in Chapter 3. Another is the York Archaeological Trust's publication of 41–49 Walmgate (Macnab 2003), where within a web browser users are able to navigate at will between maps and data with ease: large-scale maps are hyperlinked to smaller-scale plans of individual burials and features, which are linked to data tables describing the contents and artefacts. These in turn are hyperlinked to Harris matrixes, the cells of which are linked back to other maps. This provides the reader with near-seamless movement between spatial data, description and synthesis, providing a more integrated site report than the traditional, paper-based, linear model.

While hypertext and hypermaps provide exciting avenues for the publication of archaeological information, they are dependent on predefined links between data that the user is then free to navigate. Fully 'interactive mapping', on the other hand, involves a different set of tools that mimic the functions of standalone GIS delivered via the Internet and accessed by a browser. This type of mapping involves an element of free navigation within and between maps and spatial datasets, including standard facilities like changing the scale and level of generalisation, panning and moving across maps, and enabling and disabling map themes (Cartwright *et al.* 2001). Many commercial GIS packages now offer the ability to distribute GIS data and GIS functionality over the Internet. When linked to a 'geolibrary' (Goodchild 1998) offering searchable access to spatial datasets, the potential for more exploratory analysis of spatial data relationships is increased. Some of the more common proprietary Web GIS platforms include ESRI's ArcIMS[1] and Internet Map Server (IMS),[2] and MapInfo's MapXtreme[3] software. Using these programs, it is possible to distribute GIS data from dynamic servers to users via web browsers, extending the user-base of spatial information to non-GIS specialists.

Web GIS has been extended by the definition of a markup language called Scalable Vector Graphics (SVG), which offers considerable improvement on HTML. Previously, maps accessed by web browsers had to be in raster formats and user interactivity was enabled by predefined hyperlinks, or by Java scripting which provided some degree of interactivity. SVG is a new non-proprietary grammar that extends the utility of XML and establishes a standard for describing two-dimensional vector graphics. Introductory guides to XML and SVG can be found in Ray and McIntosh (2002) and Eisenberg (2002). Although SVG only provides a mechanism for the creation of vector graphics (and their integration with raster images) it nevertheless offers a major enhancement to HTML by enabling the combination of raster and vector graphics in ways not previously possible. Adobe Illustrator[4] will export files as SVG, and extensions to several common GIS packages have been developed that enable the publication of map data using SVG, such as SVGMapper[5] for ESRI's ArcView, Map2SVG[6] for MapInfo Professional and GeoMedia WebMap[7] for Intergraph. A Web GIS application using SVG is shown in Fig. 12.9, which allows mouse-over querying of archaeological contexts from an excavation (Macnab 2003). Verhoeven (2003) has also described the application of SVG to interactive mapping of archaeological data from a Mesopotamian survey project.

---

[1]www.esri.com/software/arcims/.   [2]www.esri.com/software/internetmaps/.
[3]www.mapinfo.com/.   [4]www.adobe.com/svg/.   [5]www.svgmapper.com/.
[6]www.gis-news.de/svg/map2svg.htm.   [7]http://imgs.intergraph.com/gmwm/.

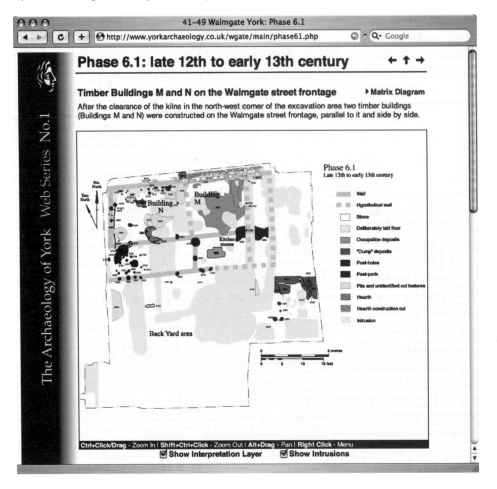

Fig. 12.9 An SVG map of late twelfth to early thirteenth century phases at Walmgate, York (Macnab 2003). Clicking on a given context pulls up a context description with links to photos and the stratigraphic matrix. The map can be zoomed and panned and thus provides many of the functions of GIS via a web browser. The system was built by Mike Rains using MySQL, PHP and Apache. Data and interface copyright ©York Archaeological Trust. Reproduced with permission.

12.6 Conclusion

Maps are wonderfully communicative documents that are able to hold and express a vast amount of spatial data that would otherwise be impossible to convey efficiently. A basic understanding of cartographic principles is extremely important for the effective use of maps, and the techniques described in this chapter will fulfil the mapping needs of most archaeological users of GIS. As is clear from the previous section, however, digital publication requires both a new set of skills and a rethinking of how data can be made available to the public. Although there will be a place for the traditional paper map in the future of GIS, and traditional map design is still a vital skill, Internet mapping will increasingly come to dominate GIS and will transform the mapping techniques that cartographers have come to rely on. The growing importance of the Internet as a primary vehicle for data dissemination, the sharing of map data between users in different countries and the provision of tools for the interrogation of map data within Internet browsers, are all part of this trend. In our opinion, this will continue to the stage when dynamic digital maps will become the primary vehicle with which users interact and explore archaeological datasets.

13

Maintaining spatial data

13.1 Introduction

The most valuable (non-human) resource that any organisation possesses is its data. Hardware and software are easily replaceable but the loss of data can be catastrophic for an organisation. Information loss, whether full or partial, is easily avoided through the routine taking of backups and the storage of data off-site. As there is plenty of readily available information on how best to implement a backup and data-recovery procedure, we do not consider it in any detail in this book. What is less obvious, particularly to those new to GIS and digital data, is the similarly important task of data maintenance. Consider, for example, the following three scenarios:

- An employee in a cultural resource management (CRM) unit is assigned the task of updating site locations from newly acquired GPS data. How should the fact that a few site locations have been updated be documented and where and how should the old data be stored?
- An aerial photograph of a portion of landscape has been rectified and georeferenced, and is ready to be used to delineate features of archaeological significance. How and where should information about the degree of error in the georeferencing be documented? Where and how should the errors for the newly digitised archaeological features be documented?
- A research student is collecting data on soil types for Eastern Europe from several different national agencies that each have different scales and recording systems. How is this student able to search and compare and ultimately integrate datasets in a manner that ensures the data will be appropriate for his/her needs?

Each of these three scenarios highlights the need for a way of recording and retrieving *metadata*, i.e., structured data about data. In a very real and practical sense, metadata provides users with a set of essential and standardised pieces of information about what the dataset is, when it was created, what its update cycle is, who created it, where the data refer to, and how to obtain more information about it. For any organisation that collects or updates data, the recording of metadata about each dataset is an essential step in data collection and maintenance. For individual researchers metadata is also very important, as it ensures that, for example, the sources of data are recorded so that they can be properly referenced in any ensuing publication.

Although the time investment associated with creating and maintaining metadata is not trivial, it is vital to ensure the long-term viability of data archives. The benefits of metadata are many and include greater longevity of information, improved understanding of a dataset, the facility to search for appropriate datasets based on several selection criteria (e.g. type of data, location and creation date), and expanded capabilities to share data between individuals and organisations. This chapter describes methods and international standards for the collection of metadata for geospatial datasets.

13.2 Metadata standards

What information about a dataset should be recorded? Standardisation of metadata categories is important, not least because of the increasingly common tendency of accessing information via the Internet from global gateways. There is a consequent need to be able to assess the relevant details about data from a standardised list of categories and descriptive terms. Additionally, as digital data become the de-facto form for many spatial disciplines like archaeology, standardised metadata are essential for providing users with the ability to assess both the quality and appropriateness of the broad range of commercial and free datasets that are encountered in a GIS environment. Metadata standards have been defined by a number of organisations, and one of the most common is the *Dublin Core Metadata Element Set*, also known as ISO Standard 15836-2003. This consists of 15 elements that describe a dataset: title, creator, subject, description, publisher, contributor, data, type, format, identifier, source, language, relation, coverage and rights (Dublin Core Metadata Initiative 2003).

The Dublin Core does not, however, contain elements that describe geospatial datasets, such as geographical location and scale. For that reason, several alternative standards have been defined to describe geospatial datasets. These include the Australia New Zealand Land Information Council (ANZLIC) *Working Group on Metadata: Core Metadata Elements Guidelines Draft 7*, the Canadian General Standards Board (CGSB) *Canadian Directory Information Describing Digital Georeferenced Data Sets*, European Committee for Standardisation (CEN) *Standard for Geographic Information*, the UK National Geospatial Data Framework (NGDF) metadata standard, and the US Federal Geographic Data Committee (FGDC) *Content Standard for Geospatial Metadata* (FGDC-STD-001-1998). Although each of these organisations have defined standards for their particular region, regional variations have recently been reduced by the creation of an international standard for geospatial metadata by the International Standards Organisation (ISO) Technical Committee (TC) 211 on Geographic Information and Geomatics, called *ISO 19115 (Geographic Information – Metadata)* (International Standards Organisation 2003). This standard is now closely followed by all the former regional organisations and establishes the current international standard for defining metadata elements appropriate for geospatial information.

ISO 19115 consists of over 400 hierarchically ordered metadata elements. Its structure is complicated, but also comprehensive and flexible. ISO 19115 also defines a 'core' set of 22 elements: 7 of which are mandatory, 4 that are conditionally mandatory (depending on the type of data) and 11 are optional (Table 13.1).

Table 13.1 *ISO 19115 core elements and entry examples*

Name	Type	ISO 19115 Element No.	Example entry
Dataset title	Mandatory	360	Kythera Digital Elevation Model 2 (KIPDEM2)
Dataset reference date	Mandatory	363	(creation) 2001-10-01
Dataset responsible party	Optional	367	James Conolly
Geographical location (four bounding coordinates)	Conditional	343–346	westBoundLongitude=22.89 eastBoundLongitude=23.11 northBoundLatitude=36.38 southBoundLatitude=36.13
Dataset language	Mandatory	39	en
Dataset character set	Conditional	40	utf-8
Dataset topic category	Mandatory	41	006 (elevation)
Spatial resolution	Optional	61	20m
Abstract describing dataset	Mandatory	25	The KIPDEM2 is a continuous raster map of elevation values from the Aegean island of Kythera. It has a 20-m cell size and was interpolated from a 5-m contour interval and spot heights base map (manually digitised from the Greek Military maps of Kythera). The DEM was created using Topogrid.
Distribution format	Optional	285	ArcGIS 8.3
Additional extent information (vertical/temporal)	Optional	355–358	Elevation range 0–250 m
Spatial representation type	Optional	37	raster
Spatial reference system	Optional	207	WGS84
Lineage statement	Optional	83	Derived from the 5-m contours and spot heights manually digitised from the 1 : 5000 Greek Military maps of Kythera.
Online resource	Optional	397	`www.ucl.ac.uk/kip`
Metadata file identifier	Optional	2	KIP.DEM2
Metadata standard name	Optional	10	ISO 19115 Geographic Information – Metadata
Metadata standard version	Optional	11	DIS-ESRI1.0
Metadata language	Conditional	3	en
Metadata character set	Conditional	4	utf-8
Metadata point of contact	Mandatory	377	James Conolly
Metadata date stamp	Mandatory	9	2003-07-21

Source: Open GIS Consortium (2001, Table 3). Note that this table is provided for information only and is not a guide to ISO 19115 metadata standards. For full details please refer to the standard's documentation (ISO, 2003).

Mandatory elements include such things as the title of the dataset, an abstract describing the data and the point of contact (i.e. a named individual) for the dataset. Conditional elements refer to those that must be completed if the data are of a particular type. Recording the geographic location of the dataset, for example, is necessary if the data are geospatial. Optional information includes items such as the type of spatial data, the spatial resolution of the dataset, the reference system and the distribution format. Although optional, these elements provide essential information and should be completed when possible. If strict adherence to the full ISO 19115 structure isn't necessary or appropriate, then this core set can be used for guidance for the minimum details that are needed to document a dataset.

Some national geospatial organisations continue to define their own set of core elements based on the international standard. For example, there are 32 proposed standard elements for the UK defined by UK Gemini (Walker 2003). As can be seen from Table 13.2, 17 of these are mandatory (M) and 15 are optional (O). It is designed to be compliant with ISO 19115 and will form the standard set of elements for UK geospatial metadata.

13.3 Creating metadata

It should be clear from this brief review of metadata standards that creating a full, ISO-19115-compliant, metadata database for each dataset in a project or organisation is a very time-consuming exercise. It can, however, be streamlined if some basic information about the data is assembled prior to creating the metadata record (cf. Land Information New Zealand 2003):

> **How many datasets are there?** During project development and analysis the number of spatial datasets may rapidly expand as new combinations of data are created. Keeping track of individual datasets and their relationships is an essential first step to proper data management and maintenance.
>
> **What is the purpose of the data?** Understanding what the data are used for and why they were created will also help in the assembly of metadata.
>
> **What do the data represent?** A clear definition of what is being represented by a set of geospatial data is needed for descriptive purposes.
>
> **How are the data represented?** The provision of this information is crucial as it simplifies the process of searching through catalogues of metadata to identify appropriate datasets. For example, elevation data may be stored as a set of points, contour lines or as a continuous grid, and although this is obvious when viewing a dataset, it must nevertheless be specified in metadata in order to facilitate search and retrieval.
>
> **Who created it?** Recording the identity of the individual(s) responsible for the creation of a dataset is important so that queries about its construction can be addressed to the right person.
>
> **What are the sources of information and resources (the 'lineage') that were used to create the data?** When creating data, whether by manually or automatically digitising paper maps, or by generating derived data such as a slope map, it is necessary to document the source of the base dataset, the methods of digitisation, the post-capture processing methods and the methods of transformation, as appropriate.

Table 13.2 *Standard metadata elements for the UK*

No.	Name	Type
1	Title	M
2	Alternative title	O
3	Dataset language	M
4	Abstract	M
5	Topic category	M
6	Subject	M
7	Date	M
8	Dataset reference date	M
9	Originator	O
10	Lineage	O
11	West bounding coordinate	M
12	East bounding coordinate	M
13	North bounding coordinate	M
14	South bounding coordinate	M
15	Extent	M
16	Vertical extent information	O
17	Spatial reference system	M
18	Spatial resolution	O
19	Spatial representation type	O
20	Presentation type	O
21	Data format	M
22	Supply media	O
23	Distributor	M
24	Frequency of update	M
25	Access constraint	O
26	Use constraint	O
27	Additional information source	O
28	Online resource	O
29	Browse graphic	O
30	Date of update metadata	M
31	Metadata standard name	O
32	Metadata standard version	O

What are the potential sources of error? Although this information does not form part of the ISO 19115 core element set, it is nevertheless an important piece of metadata for geospatial information. If, for example, data have been digitised from a paper map, then the relevant RMS errors must be recorded for reasons explained in Chapter 5.

When was it created and how long is it valid for? This information is particularly important for data that are subject to updates, such as a record of sites or find locations. Original datasets are often superseded when new information is made available and it is essential that the time of creation and the validity of the dataset is recorded so as to ensure that the most up-to-date information is being used at any given time.

13.3.1 *Recording methods*

The emerging standard for storing metadata is XML (eXtensible Markup Language), which itself is a standard for recording information about information.[1] As applied to metadata, it consists of a set of nested items with enclosed tags that describe the element followed by the record details, as in this segment from a longer XML record:

```
<idPurp>To provide a continuous map of elevation
             values for Kythera </idPurp>
    <idStatus>
     <!-- completed -->
        <ProgCd value="001"/>
    </idStatus>
    <idPoC>
        <rpOrgName>Kythera Island Project</rpOrgName>
        <rpCntInfo>
            <cntAddress>
                <delPoint>Institute of Archaeology</delPoint>
                <city>London</city>
                <adminArea>London</adminArea>
                <postCode>WC1H 0PY</postCode>
                <country>United Kingdom</country>
            </cntAddress>
            <cntOnlineRes>
            <linkage>http://www.ucl.ac.uk/kip</linkage>
            </cntOnlineRes>
        </rpCntInfo>
    </idPoC>
```

Although metadata can be entered manually in any text editor, the use of a dedicated XML editor with an ISO 19115 (or equivalent) template greatly facilitates the construction of structured records. A good cross-platform example of such an editor is the USGS-developed Java application *XMLInput*[2] (Fig. 13.1).

Many recent GIS programs also have facilities for recording information about metadata which adhere closely to the ISO 19115 standard. ESRI's ArcGIS, for example, comes with a program called ArcCatalogue, which has a 'wizard' for building ISO 19115 metadata that automatically stores the data in XML (Fig. 13.2).

Integrated tools also speed up the documentation process by automatically completing some fields (e.g. scale, geographical coordinates, time of creation, etc.) by querying the data itself. Integrated programs provide a reasonably straightforward

---

[1] Further information on XML can be found at www.w3.org/XML.
[2] Available from: ftp://ftpext.usgs.gov/pub/cr/mo/rolla/release/xmlinput/.

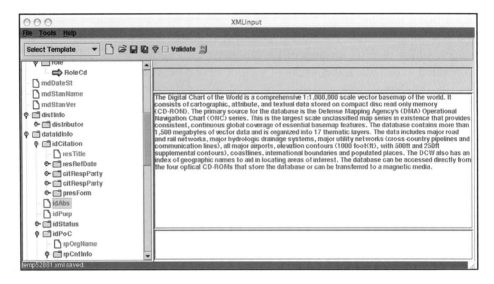

Fig. 13.1 The XMLInput editor with an ISO 19115 template file loaded for the Digital Chart of the World. Available from: `ftp://ftpext.usgs.gov/pub/cr/mo/rolla/release/xmlinput/`.

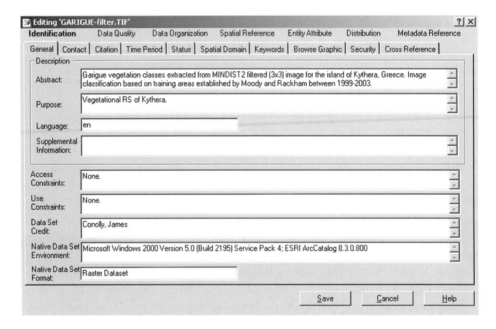

Fig. 13.2 The Metadata editor in ESRI's ArcCatalogue. Source: ESRI. ArcGIS software and graphical user interface are the intellectual property of ESRI and used herein with permission. Copyright © ESRI. All rights reserved.

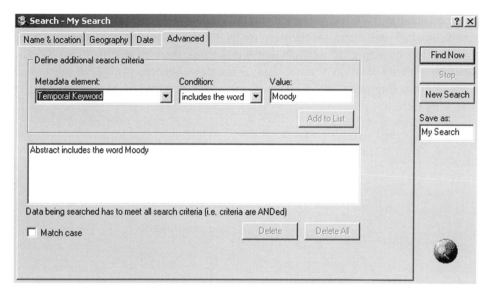

Fig. 13.3 The Metadata search tool in ESRI's ArcCatalogue. Source: ESRI. ArcGIS
software and graphical user interface are the intellectual property of ESRI and used
herein with permission. Copyright © ESRI. All rights reserved.

interface and centralised database for entering, storing and retrieving metadata. Furthermore, ArcCatalogue and similar programs also provide tools for implementing
metadata queries (Fig. 13.3).

Metadata queries can take the form of multiple search criteria (e.g. 'all raster
datasets describing elevation for location p, created in the last 12 months, with a
grid size of 500 m or better'). Additional software tools are available for geospatial
metadata creation: the USGS maintains a set of creation and validation software
tools, as well as guidance pages for creating FGDC compliant metadata (following
ISO 19115 standards).[3]

13.4 Conclusion

This brief review of the importance of properly maintaining spatial data using
geospatial metadata standards should be sufficient to convince most readers that
metadata are important and warrant the necessary investment to create compliant
records. In particular, the ability quickly to search and filter a database of geospatial
data and then quickly retrieve the most appropriate or up-to-date version of, for
example a distribution map, is of great utility to the user. Furthermore, proper
maintenance of data makes the sharing of information much easier, as it encourages

---

[3]http://geology.usgs.gov/tools/metadata/.

common standards for recording the source, quality and errors associated with any given dataset. Finally, and no less importantly, the provision of metadata contributes to the 'future-proofing' of the data that it describes, thereby helping to protect the investment in the creation of those data. Since these benefits justify the substantial costs of collecting metadata, their creation should be a routine part of any project involving GIS.

GLOSSARY

GIS terms

2.5D GIS These GIS typically represent the third-dimension by extruding vector objects by a z-attribute variable to create the impression of a three-dimensional surface or volume. They are not normally capable of answering fully three-dimensional queries. (Compare *3D GIS*.)

3D GIS A GIS that records the spatial location of *geographic features* in three dimensions such that it is capable of answering queries like 'find all the objects within a spherical radius of 1 m from this point'. (Compare *2.5D GIS* and *virtual reality*.)

Accessibility Graph theoretic measures of **local accessibility** provide information about how readily an individual *node* may be reached from other nodes outside its immediate *neighbourhood*. Measures of **global accessibility** provide similar information for the network as a whole. (Compare *connectivity*.)

Accumulated cost-surface A model of the cost of moving from a specified origin to one or more destinations. The cost recorded at the destination(s) is that incurred when following the least costly route from the origin, as computed by applying a *spreading function* to a *cost-of-passage map*.

Accuracy Consider taking the mean of several measurements to estimate some *attribute*, such as soil pH. The estimate would be accurate if the mean was close to the true value, even if the spread of measured values was wide. (Compare *precision*.)

Agent-based model A computer program in which a collection of – often interacting – autonomous software entities (agents) pursue their goals by carrying out one or more tasks in simulated environment. In archaeological examples, agents typically represent individual human beings or households.

AGNPS The AGricultural Non-Point Source Model is a process-orientated erosion model that attempts to predict soil loss by allowing sediment to 'flow' over a map.

Anisotropic Dependent on both the direction of travel and any directional attributes (e.g. aspect) of individual map cells. (Compare *isotropic*.)

ANSWERS The Areal Non-point Source Watershed Environmental Response Simulation model is a process-orientated erosion model similar to *AGNPS*.

Arc Another term for *polyline*.

Arc–node data structure A method that structures, stores and references *vector* data in a *relational DBMS* so that *vertices* (and *nodes*) construct *polylines* (arcs) and polylines construct *polygons*.

Area A two-dimensional geometrical primitive that may be represented by a *vector polygon*, or a contiguous set of *raster cells* that share the same *attribute* value.

Aspect The *azimuth* of the maximum rate of change of *elevation* (*slope*) in the downhill direction.

Attribute The term attribute usually refers to the non-locational properties of a *geographic feature* (e.g. the number of artefacts found at a site), but it is worth noting that the OpenGIS Reference Model (www.opengeospatial.org/specs/?page=orm) includes location among the attributes of a geographic feature.

Automated mapping The forerunner to GIS, this made possible the computerised storage and presentation of digital maps, but offered no analytical capabilities.

Azimuth A direction in the horizontal plane, often given as the number of degrees clockwise from north.

Binary viewshed map A *raster* or *vector* map that codes *cells* or *polygons* according to whether or not they fall inside a given *viewshed*.

Bit The smallest unit of digital information representing a binary state, such as 0 or 1, or true or false.

Boolean algebra Algebra that uses the logical (or set) operations AND (intersection), OR (union), XOR (exclusive disjunction) and NOT (complement).

Buffer An *area* containing all locations within a specified distance from a given *point, line* or areal feature.

Byte A unit of digital information made up of 8 *bits*. A kilobyte (kB) is either 1000 (10^3) or 1024 (2^{10}) bits, a megabyte (MB) 1 000 000 (10^6) or 1 048 576 (2^{20}) bits, etc., depending upon whether the writer is using SI or binary units (unfortunately it is not always easy to tell).

Cartesian coordinate The Cartesian coordinate system uses an x-axis and a y-axis placed so as to be orthogonal (i.e. at a right angle) to one another. The two axes intersect at an origin, which has the Cartesian coordinate $(0, 0)$. The Cartesian coordinate of other locations takes the form (x, y), where x is the distance from zero on the x-axis and y is the distance from zero on the y-axis. The system may be extended to three dimensions by the addition of a z-axis. (See also *easting, northing*; compare *polar coordinate*.)

Cartographic Relating to the production of maps (as distinct from the manipulation of spatial data).

CAD Computer Aided Design provides a means of storing, manipulating and displaying representations of two- or three-dimensional objects. Although it can be used to produce maps, CAD software does not geographically locate objects and is not capable of supporting most of the database and analytical functionality expected of a GIS.

Cell A single (usually square) area within the grid structure that forms a *raster* map.

Cellular automata A computer simulation in which identical cells arranged on a regular grid repeatedly update their state according to the state of their neighbours. The technique is particularly suitable for modelling spreading processes, such as the spread of wildfire.

Centroid The geometric centre of a *polygon*. Its location is often approximated by calculating the mean of the coordinates of all *vertices* that define the polygon.

Choropleth map A *thematic* map showing a quantitative or qualitative *attribute* value associated with each geographical *area* (e.g. the number of archaeological sites in each county).

Cleaning The process of cleaning a *vector* map entails removing redundant *vertices* and, more importantly, *digitising* errors that would otherwise disrupt the map's *topology*, such as *dangling lines, overhangs, overshoots* and *slivers*. (See also *snap*.)

Client A computer that makes use of a service, such as the authentication of legitimate users, which is provided by another computer to which it is networked. Alternatively, a computer software package that allows a user to retrieve and possibly manipulate data stored using other software, either on the same or a different computer. (Compare *server* and *front end*.)

Colour ramp A gradual change of colour used to represent ordinal *scale* (see statistical terms), interval scale or ratio scale *attribute* values. Normally the user specifies the exact colour to be associated with the minimum and maximum values and the software then interpolates the appropriate colour for intermediate values.

Command-line A facility for running computer programs, specifying operations and choosing options by typing text rather than using a *GUI*.

Connectivity *Graph* theoretic measures of **local connectivity** provide information about how well an individual *node* is connected to its neighbours. Measures of **global connectivity** provide similar information for the network as a whole. (Compare *accessibility*.)

Constrained interpolation The minimum and maximum values in a model generated by constrained *interpolation* must match the minimum and maximum values present in the original *sample*. (Compare *unconstrained interpolation*.)

Continuous field This model of space is appropriate when dealing with *attribute* values that vary continuously through space, such as *elevation*. It is usually represented using a *raster* map. (Compare *entity model*.)

Contour Another name for *isoline*, but usually used to refer specifically to an imaginary line joining locations at a specified *elevation*.

Corridor A *buffer* created around a *line*.

Cost-of-passage map A (normally *raster*) map that models the energetic, time or other cost of travelling across each map *cell*.

Cost-surface (See *accumulated cost-surface*.)

CRM Cultural Resource Management involves the identification, preservation, presentation and interpretation of archaeological and historical sites that are threatened by development, natural processes or damage inflicted by visitors.

Cross-tabulation The production of a table that records how the *attribute* values in one *raster* map are distributed with respect to the attribute values in another raster map.

Cumulative viewshed map A *raster* or *vector* map that codes *cells* or *polygons* according to how many *viewsheds* they fall inside (i.e. the arithmetic sum of two or more *binary viewshed maps*).

Cycle A *path* that begins and ends at the same *node* in a *graph*.

Dangling line A *digitising* error in which two adjacent line segments of what should be a single *polyline* fall short of one another, so terminating at two unwanted *nodes* rather than at a common *vertex*. (Compare *overshoot*.)

Database A collection of information organised according to a *data model*. The central component of any GIS is a database that stores information about *geographic features*, including both their *geographic location* and their *attributes*. Note, however, that many GIS practitioners use the term database to refer specifically to the *data structures* and/or software used to store non-locational attribute data.

Data model A conceptual scheme that defines what aspects of the real world are to be treated as features, what *attributes* they have and how they are related.

Data structure The way in which a *DBMS* actually organises data so that it can be stored in a computer.

DBMS A DataBase Management System is software that is used to store, manage and query data in a *database*.

Decimal degree When an angular measurement is given in decimal degrees then its fractional part is given in multiples of $1/10$, $1/100$, $1/1000$ and so on, rather than in minutes ($1/60$) and seconds ($1/3600$).

Delaunay triangulation A tessellation of triangular *polygons* constructed such that the closest *vertex* to any point within a given triangle is one of the vertices used to construct that triangle.

DEM A Digital Elevation Model is a digital map that provides a model of the elevation of (part of) the Earth's surface. (Compare *DTM*.)

Digitising Generally, the process of converting conventional paper maps and images into digital form. Among GIS practitioners the term is often used to refer specifically to those methods that produce *vector* rather than *raster* output, especially the use of a *digitising tablet* or *heads-up* digitising.

Digitising tablet A device for *digitising* paper maps by tracing over them with a *puck*. (Compare *scanner*.)

Dirichlet tessellation A tessellation made up of *Thiessen polygons* fitted to a set of *points*.

Dot-density map A map in which dots representing a consistent unit of data are placed randomly in each *enumeration area* such that the total number of dots within a given enumeration area represents the total data value within it.

DTM Digital Terrain Model is another term for *DEM*. Note, however, that some GIS practitioners restrict the term DTM to those maps (usually *TINs*) that explicitly model the location of landform features such as *ridges*. (Compare *DEM*.)

Dynamic modelling A form of modelling involving the computer simulation of change through time.

Easting The distance east of the origin (*x*-coordinate) in a *Cartesian coordinate* system. (See also *northing*.)

Edge A connection between two *nodes* in a *graph*, usually represented as a line joining them.

Edge effect The tendency for *spatial operations* to return incorrect values near the edge of a map, often because the *neighbourhood* used to calculate them has been artificially truncated.

Effective slope The *slope* that is actually experienced when traversing a map *cell* in a horizontal direction other than the *aspect*.

Elevation The height above some specified datum, often mean sea level.

Ellipsoid A relatively simple model of the shape of the Earth that approximates it as a sphere flattened at the poles. (Compare *geoid*.)

Entity model This model of space is appropriate when dealing with discrete *geographical features* such as find spots, roads or administrative districts. The location and *geometry* of each feature (entity) is usually recorded in a *vector* map and its attributes in an associated *database*. (Compare *continuous field*.)

Enumeration area An *area* treated as an indivisible whole for the purposes of plotting the distribution of *attribute* values across a map.

Environmental determinism A critical label applied to models that treat one or more – particularly locational – aspects of human behaviour as a purely functional response to environmental conditions such as the distribution of shelter and food resources.

Error propagation The increase in uncertainty that results from combining datasets and/or building models (e.g. by *interpolation*) from them. (See also *map generalisation*.)

ETRS 89 The European Terrestrial Reference System 1989 is the *geodetic datum* preferred for high-precision *GPS* survey in Europe. (Compare *NAD 27*, *NAD 83* and *WGS 84*.)

Euclidean Conforming to the axioms that define Euclidean *geometry*. This is the kind of geometry that underwrites what most of us are taught at school: for example, that the linear distance from A to B is the same as from B to A, and that the lengths of the sides of a right-angled triangle are related according to the formula $a^2 + b^2 = c^2$.

Exact interpolation A type of *interpolation* that leaves the *attribute* values at *sample* locations unchanged. (Compare *inexact interpolation*.)

Filter A *spatial operation* designed to remove variability from a map by computing the new *attribute* value of a given *cell* as a function of the values in that cell's *neighbourhood*.

Flat-file database A *database* comprising just one table that stores information about all the recorded *attributes* of each object. (Compare *relational database*.)

Flood-fill interpolation An *interpolation* algorithm designed specifically for the purpose of interpolating continuous surfaces from *isoline* (normally *contour*) data.

Flow accumulation map A map created by searching a *local drainage direction* map to compute the number of upstream *cells* that drain into each cell. Usually, but not necessarily, used for *hydrological* modelling.

Flow network A *network* that represents the movement of, for example goods, between *nodes*. This requires that it includes information about the direction and possibly the magnitude of flow. (Compare *network* and *transportation network*.)

Friction map Another term for *cost-of-passage map*.

Front end A user interface to a GIS or other computer system, especially one that has been customised for a particular subset of users and/or which is a *client* of a *server*.

Fuzzy A state of uncertainty, usually either in the *geographic location* of some phenomenon, such as a boundary, or in the membership of a set, such as the set of *cells* visible from a site.

Geodesy The science of measuring the shape of the Earth and the location of points on its surface.

Geodetic datum A coordinate system designed to provide the best possible fit with all or part of the *geoid*.

Geographic coordinate Geographic coordinates use *latitude* and *longitude* to specify a location on the surface of the Earth.

Geographic feature A feature associated with a *geographic location*.

Geographic location A location relative to the Earth's surface.

Geoid A model of the shape of the Earth that takes into account deviations from the *ellipsoid* such that its surface largely coincides with mean sea level.

Geolibrary A collection of searchable spatial datasets, typically made available to users via *Web GIS*.

Geometry The branch of mathematics concerned with spatial relationships. GIS practitioners often use the term 'geometric' to refer to spatial aspects of a *geographic feature* (e.g. its shape) other than its *geographic location*. Note also that 'a geometry' is a formal spatial language, e.g. *Euclidean* geometry.

Georectification The combined process of correcting distortion in an image (such as an aerial photograph) and *georeferencing* it.

Georeferencing The process of placing spatial data (such as remote-sensing imagery or *digitised* paper maps) in its correct *geographic location* by transforming it to fit an appropriate coordinate system.

Geospatial A term used to describe data (or methods applied to it) about *geographic features*, in other words, data in which the spatial component includes location relative to the Earth.

Global operation A *spatial operation* that computes the new *attribute* value at a given location from the attribute values at all locations for which data are available. (Compare *local operation*.)

GPS The Global Positioning System allows users with suitable electronic receivers to determine their *geographic location* by comparing the time taken to receive signals broadcast from three or more (usually at least four) satellites. Handheld **navigation-grade GPS** receivers are suitable for mapping features on the landscape to within 10–20 m of their true location. In North America, the Wide Area Augmentation System (**WAAS**) and, in Europe, the European Geostationary Navigation Overlay Service (**EGNOS**) transmit information on accuracy of GPS positioning signals, which can enhance the accuracy of suitably equipped navigation-grade GPS receivers to ±3 m. **Differential GPS** (DGPS) are accurate to between 0.5 and 5 m and therefore suitable for archaeological site survey and larger-scale mapping.

Graph A very abstract kind of *network* simply comprising a collection of *nodes* linked by *edges*.

Graticule The 'grid' formed by displaying the lines of *latitude* and *longitude* on a map. The exact appearance of the graticule depends on the choice of *projection*.

Gravity model A locational model which assumes that the intensity of interaction between locations is directly proportional to some quantity at those locations and inversely proportional to the intervening distance.

Ground control point A location that can be identified on a map and whose real *geographic location* is known. Ground control points play an important role in *georeferencing*.

GUI A Graphical User Interface is a facility for running computer programs, specifying operations and choosing options by using a pointing device (mouse) to select from choices presented as, for example, 'drop-down menus' and 'radio' buttons. (Compare *command-line*.)

Header The header of a *raster map* usually records the number of rows and columns in the map, the *geographic location* of its corners and the size (on the ground) of each *cell*.

Heads-up digitising The process of *digitising* a map by using a mouse or other pointing device to trace over a *scanned* copy that is displayed on a computer screen. Also called **on-screen** digitising. (Compare *digitising tablet*.)

High-pass filter A *filter* designed to remove long-range variability from a map and which is therefore often used to accentuate local features such as the edges of fields.

Histogram equalisation A technique for *classifying* a continuous variable (e.g. *elevation*) so that each *class* contains the same number of observations.

Hydrological modelling The process of modelling the movement of water over the Earth's surface. (See also *local drainage direction map*.)

Hypermap A digital map, designed to be viewed in a web browser, that contains fixed hyperlinks (URLs) to more detailed maps and/or *attribute* data. (Compare *interactive map*.)

Inexact interpolation A type of *interpolation* that does not necessarily preserve the *attribute* values at *sample* locations. (Compare *exact interpolation*.)

Interactive map Like *hypermaps*, interactive maps are designed to be viewed in a web browser, but rather than relying on fixed hyperlinks they allow free navigation within and between maps by providing standard GIS facilities such as the ability to pan across maps, to change the scale and level of generalisation, and to enable and disable map themes. (See also *Web GIS*.)

Interpolation A mathematical technique for estimating *attribute* values (e.g. *elevation*, soil type) at unsampled locations from those measured at sampled locations, where the unsampled locations fall within the spatial distribution of sampled locations.

Intervisibility Locations A and B are computed to be intervisible when a straight 'line-of-sight' projected from A to B does not intersect an *elevation* surface representing potential obstructions such as rising ground or buildings. (See also *reciprocity*.)

Inverse distance weighting (IDW) A form of *interpolation* in which the influence of a sampled location is inversely proportional to its distance from the unsampled location whose *attribute* value is being estimated.

Irradiance The amount of solar energy received per unit area, also referred to as **solar gain**.

Isarithmic Isarithmic maps are used to portray three-dimensional surfaces (volumes) using *isolines*.

Isoline An imaginary line passing through a set of locations that share the same value of a particular attribute. (Compare *contour*.)

Isometric map An *isarithmic* map that depicts the distribution of *point attributes*. (Compare *isoplethic*.)

Isometric view A visual representation of a three-dimensional object (or a surface such as elevation) in which the angles between the x-, y- and z-axes are equal, as are the scales along them. Note that neither condition is true of a perspective drawing.

Isoplethic map An *isarithmic* map that depicts the distribution of *areal attributes*. (Compare *isometric*.)

Isotropic Independent of the direction of travel. (Compare *anisotropic*.)

Justified graph *Space syntax analysis* uses *graphs* to depict which spaces in a building or urban area are directly accessible from which others (e.g. via a doorway). A justified graph shows these relationships relative to a specified starting space, often the outside of a building.

Isovist The set of all locations *intervisible* with a given viewpoint.

Kernel The *neighbourhood* used in a *spatial operation* such as *filtering*.

Key A unique identifier that can be used to distinguish between individual records in a *database* table. A **primary key** uses just one field in the table, whereas a **composite key** uses a combination of fields. A **foreign key** is used to build relationships between tables in a *relational database*.

Laplacian filter A particular kind of *high-pass filter* that is often used for edge detection in images. Its *kernel* weights are chosen to approximate the second derivatives in the definition of the Laplace operator.

Latitude An angular measurement giving the location of a point on the Earth's surface north or south from the equator. Both latitude and *longitude* are required for a complete *geographic coordinate*.

Least-cost path A route that minimises the total cost of moving between two locations on an *accumulated cost-surface*.

Line A one-dimensional geometrical primitive. Also a basic *vector* object comprising a straight-line segment defined by two terminating *nodes*. A linear *geographic feature* can be represented in a vector map using the basic line object if it is straight, or a *polyline* (*arc*) if it is curved. Linear geographic features can also be represented in a *raster* map as a sequence of raster *cells* that share the same *attribute* value.

Local drainage direction map A *hydrological* model, usually presented as a *raster* map, in which the *attribute* value in each *cell* represents the direction in which water would flow out of that cell.

Local operation A *spatial operation* that computes the new *attribute* value at a given location from the attribute values at locations within a *neighbourhood* that comprises a (usually small) subset of the locations for which data are available. (Compare *global operation*.)

Location–allocation modelling Location–allocation models provide solutions to the problem of optimally locating facilities (such as a trading post) within a catchment. Note that the solutions assume that people always use the nearest facility. (Compare *spatial interaction modelling*.)

Longitude An angular measurement giving the location of point on the Earth's surface east or west from the Greenwich Meridian. Both *latitude* and longitude are required for a complete *geographic coordinate*.

Low-pass filter A *filter* designed to remove short-range variability from a map and which is therefore often used to smooth a surface.

Map algebra The application of arithmetic and/or logical operators to one or more *raster* maps so as to compute new *attribute* values on a *cell*-by-cell basis.

Map generalisation The process of adjusting the amount of detail in a map when it is reproduced at a different *scale* or *resolution* so as to avoid the errors that would otherwise arise from ignoring the limitations in accuracy set by the original scale.

Mass points The *points* used to build a *TIN*.

Metadata Information about a dataset, usually provided in a standardised format, and typically recording what the dataset contains, its spatial location, when it was created, who created it, how it was created, etc.

MIDAS The Monument Inventory Data Standard, which provides a standardised terminology for the inventory of archaeological and historical features in the UK.

Multiple viewshed map A *raster* or *vector* map that codes *cells* or *polygons* according to whether or not they fall inside one or more given *viewsheds* (i.e. the logical union of two or more *binary viewshed maps*).

NAD 27 The North American Datum 27 is the *geodetic datum* that was used for much of the twentieth century mapping of North America. It is now being replaced by *NAD 83*.

NAD 83 A recent North American *geodetic datum* that better captures the deviations between the true shape of the Earth and the Clarke *ellipsoid* on which the earlier *NAD 27* was based. (Compare also *ETRS 89* and *WGS 84*.)

Neighbourhood The set of locations used by a *spatial operation* to compute a new *attribute* value at a given location. Note that the locations in a neighbourhood may or may not be spatially contiguous. An example of a contiguous neighbourhood commonly used when *filtering* a *raster* map is the target *cell* plus the eight immediately adjacent cells. The term has a different meaning in *network* analysis where it refers to the set of *nodes* to which a given node is connected by some specified number of *edges*.

Network A representation of the connections between some phenomena (such as cities), especially one in which the basic *graph* is augmented with additional information such as the *flow* of goods or a *turn table*.

Node In a vector map a node is a *vertex* that represents the end of a discrete line (which may be a *polyline*), or the intersection of one or more discrete lines. Alternatively, in a *graph* or *network*, a node is an object that is connected by zero, one or more *edges*.

Normalisation The process of splitting tables in a *relational database* so that it conforms to a set of 'normal forms' designed to prevent duplication and ensure data integrity.

Northing The distance north of the origin (*y*-coordinate) in a *Cartesian coordinate* system. (See also *easting*.)

Object-orientated A *data model* and/or associated computer programming paradigm that packages *attribute* data (both locational and non-locational) and functionality (i.e. behaviour) together into modular units called objects.

Observer offset When computing *intervisibility* most software allows this extra height to be added to the viewpoint *elevation* in order to ensure that the line-of-sight is projected from eye level rather than ground level. (Compare *target offset*.)

ODBC Open DataBase Connectivity is an application programming interface for connecting to database management systems (*DBMS*). *Client* software that implements ODBC (e.g. the mail-merge facility in a word processor) can access data in a DBMS that also implements ODBC, even if the client software was written in a different programming language and runs on a different operating system.

Open source software The label 'open source' is often used to refer collectively to software released under various licences that permit or even require the distribution of source code, generally at little or no cost to the user. More specifically, open source software is that distributed according to the terms of the Open Source Definition (see www.opensource.org/docs/definition.php).

Orthorectification The process of removing *elevation*-induced distortion from *remote-sensing* images. (Compare *georectification*.)

Overhang A *digitising* error in which one *polygon* overlaps another. (Compare *sliver*.)

Overshoot A *digitising* error in which two adjacent line segments of what should be a single *polyline* are not joined at a common *vertex*, but instead cross before each terminating at an unwanted *node*. (Compare *dangling line*.)

Palmtop Small handheld computing devices mostly used as personal organisers, but increasingly able to run a wider range of software including GIS.

Path A sequence of *edges* connecting two *nodes* in a *graph* such that no edge occurs more than once.

Photogrammetry The process of determining three-dimensional coordinates from two or more photographs of the same subject taken from different positions. Photogrammetry is sometimes used to derive *elevation* data from stereoscopic aerial photographs.

Pit A map *cell* whose neighbours all have a higher elevation. Pits may or may not accurately represent real terrain features, but either way they are often removed prior to *hydrological modelling* because they disrupt the calculation of *local drainage direction*.

Pixel Another term for *cell*. Some GIS practitioners prefer the use of pixel for raw raster images and cell for fully *georectified* raster maps.

Plan convexity A second-order derivative of a surface that measures the amount of curvature in the horizontal plane. If the surface is an *elevation* model, then positive plan convexity indicates a location that is on a convex surface (perhaps a hill), while negative plan convexity indicates a location that is on a concave surface (perhaps a natural basin). (Compare *profile convexity*.)

Plotter A device for printing maps, particularly one designed to print on very large sheets of paper (larger than A3) by literally drawing with a 'pen'.

Polar coordinate Polar coordinates use a distance from a fixed point and one or more angles (depending how many dimensions are relevant) to define a location. In contrast, *Cartesian coordinates* use only distances along one or more orthogonal axes. *Geographic coordinates* are essentially an abbreviated form of polar coordinate in which only the angles (*latitude* and *longitude*) are given because it is assumed that all locations of interest lie (approximately) on the *ellipsoid*, from which it follows that the distance from the centre of the Earth is redundant information.

Precision Consider taking the mean of several measurements to estimate some *attribute*, for example, soil pH. The estimate would be precise if the spread of measured values was narrow, even if the mean was not close to the true value. (Compare *accuracy*.)

Point A zero-dimensional geometric primitive that is represented by a single *vertex* in a *vector* map or (rather imperfectly) a single *cell* in a *raster* map. In reality, many point *geographic features* are not zero dimensional, but they are represented as such because their exact spatial extent is not relevant and/or is too small to be recorded given the *resolution* of the digital data.

Point digitising A means of using a *digitising tablet* or of *heads-up digitising* in which the *puck* or mouse is used to place *vertices* manually on the map object. (Compare *stream digitising*.)

Point operation A point operation computes the new *attribute* value at a given location without reference to the attribute value at any other location. It may, however, involve the use of attribute values at the same location in other maps. (Compare *spatial operation*.)

Polygon A *vector* object used to represent an *areal geographic feature*.

Polygon overlay A type of *spatial query* that is used to determine the *area* that is defined by the intersection of two or more *polygons*.

Polyline A *vector* object comprising two or more connected straight *lines* which together represent a curving linear *geographic feature*. The *vertices* at which a polyline terminates are often referred to as *nodes*.

Pour point Computation of a *watershed* proceeds by following a *local drainage direction* map upstream from a specified pour point on a watercourse.

Predictive model Usually a mathematically defined *function*, such as a logistic *regression* equation, that relates the probability (or odds) of site presence to one or more spatially varying *attributes* such as elevation, proximity to water, etc. Predictive models are often presented to the end-user in the form of a *raster* map in which the attribute value of each *cell* represents the probability that archaeological evidence will be found in that location.

Primary data Data collected by actual measurement of the phenomenon in question, for example a plan of field boundaries created by field survey. (Compare *secondary data*.)

Profile convexity A second-order derivative of a surface that measures the amount of curvature in the vertical plane. If the surface is an *elevation* model, then positive profile convexity indicates a location that is on a convex surface (perhaps the side of a hill), while negative profile convexity indicates a location that is on a concave surface (perhaps the side of a valley). (Compare *plan convexity*.)

Projection The transformation required to represent the curved surface of the Earth on a flat plane, such as a map. Projections are grouped into families according to whether they first project the surface of the Earth onto the surface of a cylinder (**cylindrical projection**), cone (**conic projection**) or flat plane (**azimuthal projection**). They also fall into groups according to how they manage the distortion caused by the transformation from a curved surface to a flat plane: i.e. whether they preserve the orthogonal layout of the lines of latitude and longitude (**conformal projection**), the area of a *geographic feature* (**equal-area projection**), the distance between two *points* (**equidistant projection**) or the direction of a line drawn between two points (**true-direction projection**).

Proportional symbol map A map that uses the size of a symbol to represent the *attribute* value at a specific location.

Proximal tolerance When creating a *TIN*, the minimum horizontal distance between *vertices* used to create the tessellation. (Compare *weed tolerance*.)

Puck An electronic pointing device used to record the location of points of interest on a map placed on a *digitising tablet*.

Quadrat A rectangular area used as a sampling unit during fieldwork. (Compare *tract*.)

Quadtree A method used to reduce the storage requirements of a raster map by means of a hierarchical tessellation.

Query The selection of *geographic features* according to their *attribute* values and/or spatial properties. (Compare *spatial query*.)

Raster map A raster map represents spatial data using a grid of equally sized *cells* or *pixels*. Each cell contains a value recording some *attribute* at that location. The geographic location of each cell is usually calculated from information provided in the map *header*.

Reciprocity *Intervisibility* is said to be reciprocal if location A is computed to be visible from location B, and B is also computed to be visible from A. Note that intervisibility is not necessarily reciprocal if the *observer offset* is different from the *target offset*.

Reclassification The process of simplifying a dataset by altering the *classes* or categories used to record *attribute* values.

Relational database A *database* made up of separate tables such that all records in a given table have all the *attributes* that appear as fields (normally columns) in that table. (Compare *flat-file*.)

Resolution GIS have display tools that allow digital data to be viewed and printed at a variety of *scales*. Consequently, the traditional concept of scale does not measure an intrinsic property of a digital dataset. Instead it is often helpful to think in terms of the resolution of the dataset, that is the smallest *geographical features* that it distinguishes.

Ridge Local elevation maxima that define the upstream edges of *watersheds*.

RMSE The Root Mean Square Error of a transformation (e.g. during *georectification*) is a quantitative measure of the goodness-of-fit between the desired and actual locations.

Run length compression A method used to reduce the storage requirements of a raster map by eliminating contiguous duplicate numbers from a sequence.

Scale The ratio between a distance on a map and the distance that it represents on the Earth's surface. Large-scale maps have a small ratio and usually cover small areas in detail, whereas small-scale maps have a large ratio and usually cover large areas in less detail. (Compare *resolution*; not to be confused with the statistical usage of *scale*.)

Scanner A device used to capture a *raster* image of something (e.g. a paper map) by moving a sensor over it.

Secondary data Data acquired from an existing record, for example a plan of field boundaries created by *digitising* a paper map. (Compare *primary data*.)

Sensitivity analysis The process of repeating an analysis with different parameter values or different *samples* in order to gauge how much confidence can be placed in the results.

Server A computer that provides a service, such as the authentication of legitimate users, to another computer to which it is networked. Alternatively, a computer software package, such as a *DBMS*, that stores data that is accessed and possibly manipulated using other software running on the same or a different computer. (Compare *client*.)

Shaded relief map A map (usually of *elevation*) shaded so as to give it a three-dimensional appearance, as if illuminated by low sunlight.

Site catchment The geographical region exploited and/or controlled by the inhabitants of a site.

Sliver A *digitising* error in which there is a small gap between two *polygons* that should share a common boundary. (Compare *overhang*.)

Slope The maximum rate of change of the *elevation* at a given location.

Smoothing The application of a *low-pass filter*.

Snap Many *digitising* programs have a snap feature that automatically finds and connects *vertices* within a user-defined radius in order to help prevent *dangling lines* and *overshoots*.

Space syntax A theory and collection of methods for studying the human use of space in the built environment that together place great emphasis on the importance of the 'configuration' of (i.e. connections between) spaces.

Spatial interaction modelling Unlike *location–allocation* models, spatial interaction models allow the probabilistic allocation of demand when attempting to locate facilities optimally.

Spatial operation A spatial operation computes the new *attribute* value at a given location from the attribute values at one or more other locations in the same map. (Compare *point operation*; see also *neighbourhood*.)

Spatial query The selection of *geographic features* according to their spatial properties as well as, or instead of, their *attribute* values. (See also *buffer*, *polygon overlay* and *query*.)

Spline An *interpolation* method that joins together a number of polynomial functions to describe a smooth surface that passes through all the *attribute* values at the sampled locations.

Spot height An elevation value associated with a single *point* rather than a *contour*, often but not necessarily recording a local minimum or maximum.

Spreading function The function used to generate an *accumulated cost-surface* from a *cost-of-passage map*.

SQL Structured Query Language provides the industry-standard mechanism for users to create, modify and select entries in a *relational database*.

Stream channel map A map depicting the location of watercourses. Many stream channel maps are created by *hydrological modelling* rather than survey.

Stream order A *classification* of a watercourse according to some attribute such as how many tributaries it has or its location within the drainage network.

Stream digitising A means of using a *digitising tablet* or of *heads-up digitising* in which *vertices* are placed automatically while the *puck* or mouse is traced over the map object. (Compare *point digitising*.)

SVG Scalable Vector Graphics is an extension of *XML* that provides a non-proprietary standard for describing two-dimensional vector graphics in a manner that allows them to be rendered by suitably enabled web browsers and other applications.

Target offset When computing *intervisibility* some software allows extra height to be added to each cell that is being viewed in order to ensure that the line-of-sight is projected towards the relevant object (such as the top of a signal station) rather than ground level. (Compare *observer offset*.)

Tension A parameter that can be used to increase the roughness of a surface *interpolated* using *splines* so that it better fits the *attribute* values at the sampled locations.

Thiessen polygon A polygon that contains exactly one of a set of points and that also contains all the space that is closer to that point than any other in the set.

Thematic map A map whose content is limited to a single subject, such as soil, geology or historic places. (Compare *topographic map*.)

TIN A Triangulated Irregular Network is a *vector DEM* that represents the land surface as a tessellation of triangular *polygons* (actually a *Delaunay triangulation*).

Topographic map A map that provides general information about features of the Earth's surface. Unlike *thematic maps*, topographic maps include information about several subjects, usually including elevation, watercourses, landcover, buildings, roads, etc.

TOPOGRID A proprietary method of *interpolation* developed by ESRI to produce *hydrologically correct DEMs* from *contour* data, *spot heights* and, preferably, additional hydrological data.

Topology is the branch of *geometry* concerned with those spatial properties of an object that remain unchanged when the object is subject to continuous distortion (i.e. stretching or knotting). Consequently, the topological aspects of a *geographic feature* include whether it directly abuts, contains or is contained by another feature, but not its shape, size or *geographic location*.

Total station An electronic survey instrument that is able to record horizontal and vertical angles and linear distances from itself to a target and then automatically convert this data into *eastings*, *northings* and *elevation* values.

Tract An area used as a sampling unit during fieldwork. Whereas *quadrats* are defined by a grid, tracts are often irregular in shape and at least partially defined by features such as field boundaries.

Transportation network A *network* that represents the infrastructure of a transport system such as a road or rail network. It will typically record the actual *geographic location* of *edges* (e.g. the bends in roads), the nature of the connections between edges at *nodes* (e.g. prohibited turns) and possibly also the properties of edges (e.g. road width). (See also *turn table*.)

Travelling-salesman problem The problem of finding the least-cost *path* through a set of *nodes* in a *network* so that each node is visited exactly once.

Trend surface analysis The process of fitting a mathematically defined two-dimensional surface to a set of *points*. Trend surface analysis is occasionally used as a method of global *interpolation*, but more often to model a spatial process.

Turn table A table used to specify whether it is actually possible on the ground to move between each pair of *edges* joining at a *node* in a *transportation network*.

Unconstrained interpolation The minimum and maximum values in a model generated by unconstrained *interpolation* may be less than or greater than the minimum and maximum values present in the original *sample*. (Compare *constrained interpolation*.)

USLE The Universal Soil Loss Equation links observed rates of soil loss at a location with the erosivity of the rainfall and various other topographic *attributes* such as slope and landcover. Unlike *AGNPS* it does not actually model the process of erosion.

UTM The Universal Transverse Mercator *projection* is a cylindrical projection that divides the world into 60 vertical zones, each 6° of *longitude* wide. A grid is superimposed on each zone, making it possible to specify a *geographic location* using UTM coordinates, which comprise the zone, an *easting* and a *northing*.

Vector map A vector map represents spatial data using *points*, *lines* and *polygons*, which are in turn stored as lists of coordinates and possibly also *topological* information and/or a link to a *database* containing *attribute* values.

Vertex An element in a *vector* map that represents an isolated *point*, the beginning or end of a *line* (including lines that are part of a *polyline*), or the corner of a *polygon*. (Compare *node*.)

Viewshed The set of locations that are *intervisible* with a given viewpoint.

Visibility graph A *graph* in which *nodes* representing *geographic locations* are linked by edges if they are *reciprocally intervisible*.

Voronoi diagram Another name for *Dirichlet tessellation*.

VR Virtual reality is the computer simulation of an environment. Whereas *3D GIS* provides for the storage, manipulation and display of data recorded in three dimensions, virtual reality provides ways of actually interacting with three-dimensional objects.

Watershed The area from which water drains to a specified point (the *pour point*) on a watercourse.

Web-CD Electronic publication of data on a CD-ROM in which hyperlinks provide immediate cross-referencing between maps, plans, illustrations, tables, descriptive text, etc.

Web GIS Use of the Internet to publish digital spatial data in a way that affords users at least some of the functionality of conventional GIS. (See *interactive map*.)

Weed tolerance When building a *TIN*, the minimum distance along a *contour* before a *vertex* is used to create the tessellation. (Compare *proximal tolerance*.)

WGS 84 The World Geodetic System 1984 is a *geodetic datum* that can be used for *GPS* surveying anywhere in the world. (Compare *NAD 27*, *NAD 83* and *ETRS 89*.)

XML eXtensible Markup Language is a general-purpose self-documenting markup language capable of describing many different kinds of data. It is particularly useful for storing metadata and for sharing data between systems connected via the Internet.

Statistical terms

Autocorrelation In statistics, autocorrelation means that observations are not independent, such that each observation tends to be similar to its neighbours. **Spatial autocorrelation** thus refers to a situation where the difference in *attribute* value between any two *points* is correlated with the distance between those points. The correlation may be positive (i.e. attribute values are more similar the closer two points are together) or negative (i.e. values are more similar the further away two points are from each other).

Binary connectivity A measure of the *topological* relationship between a set of *n* objects. Typically calculated in a $n \times n$ matrix, such that each pair of objects is recorded as either being connected (1) or not (0).

Case-control Refers to a form of *predictive modelling* in which the location of sites is known, but the location of non-sites is unknown. The result is consequently an odds, rather than an absolute probability measure for site presence.

Chi-squared test A commonly used *non-parametric* statistical test for independence. Often used to test for independence in data arranged in a *contingency table*.

Class A subset of observations or objects produced by the process of *classification*.

Classification The process of dividing a set of observations or objects into two or more subsets (i.e. *classes*) based on their qualitative or quantitative (numerical) properties, e.g. through the application of *cluster analysis*. Commonly used numerical classification methods for *choropleth* mapping include **standard deviation** (elements are grouped according to their distribution around the mean); **quantile** (classes contain equal numbers of elements, as in quartiles where each class possesses 25 per cent of the elements); **natural break** (where class boundaries are defined at 'natural' intervals based on the distribution pattern of the data, as found by routines such as *Jenk's optimisation*); **equal interval** (classes defined at equal ranges of values); and **geometric interval** (class boundaries change systematically to increase class width in skewed distributions).

Cluster analysis A type of *classification* that involves creating groups (through a variety of *cluster definition* methods) of elements based on the elements' spatial location or some other *attribute(s)*, such as size or morphology.

Cluster definition A cluster analysis may take many forms, although the more common are **hierarchical** methods in which small clusters with few elements may form a smaller number of larger groups; **density** methods in which clusters are defined around high-density *areas* (e.g. of *points*, or of *attribute* values in a continuous distribution); and **partitioning** methods in which elements are sequentially placed into one of two or more groups by iteratively ascertaining the group to which each object is most similar.

Coefficient of determination A statistic, r^2, that expresses the amount of dependence between two variables, usually labelled x and y. It can range from 0 (i.e. no dependency) to $+1$ or -1 (i.e., respectively, a completely positive or completely negative dependency).

Coefficient of variation A statistic that expresses the variability in a distribution. It is usually expressed as a percentage and calculated as: $CV = (\text{standard deviation/mean}) \times 100$.

Co-kriging A type of *kriging* that uses two or more variables (and thus two or more *semi-variograms*) for establishing the parameters for an *interpolation*.

Confounding Two variables are said to be confounded when they are not independent, and it is thus difficult to ascertain which variable is responsible for the observed effect. For example, in *predictive modelling*, high *elevation* and large *viewshed* area might influence site presence, but these two variables are confounded because they are not independent of each other (i.e. higher elevations tend to have larger viewshed areas), and thus it is difficult to determine which variable is actually influencing site presence.

Contingency table A table of counts constructed by *classifying* objects by two or more nominal-scale or ordinal-scale variables. For example, a distribution of sites may be classified into *slope class* (e.g. low, medium or high) and date (e.g. Palaeoindian, Archaic, Woodland). Measures of association in contingency tables may be determined by the *Chi-squared test*.

Correlation Two variables are said to be correlated if the values of one variable predictably change with the value of the other variable. If both increase together, then they are positively correlated; if one decreases as the other increases, then they are negatively correlated. The strength of the relationship can be measured by a *correlation coefficient*.

Correlation coefficient A statistic that measures the degree of relationship between two variables, usually labelled x and y. The *Pearson Product–Moment Correlation Coefficient* is the most commonly used, and is denoted by r.

Density analysis (intensity analysis) A set of methods for measuring the changing density of an *attribute* value (such as the number of points, or a *population*) over a given *area*.

Dependent variable A variable that is influenced by, or is thought to be influenced by, an *independent variable*. For example, the dependent variable 'site location' may be influenced by the independent variable 'soil type'.

Design variable In the context of *predictive modelling*, a design variable is a numeric variable that is derived from a nominal-*scale* variable.

Distribution A measure of the relative frequency of occurrence (i.e. probability of occurrence) of values from a number of observations of a single variable. If values are distributed equally around the mean (i.e. mean $\approx$ mode $\approx$ median) then the distribution is said to be **normal** (i.e. a 'bell curve', or Gaussian distribution). A **skewed** distribution occurs when values are not equally distributed around the mean. More specifically, if the mode $>$ mean (i.e. small numbers of low values) then the distribution is said to be negatively skewed; if mode $<$ mean (i.e. small numbers of high values) then the distribution is said to be positively skewed.

Diversity The number of different values in a *cell's neighbourhood*.

Function A relation (e.g. equation) in which each element of a set is associated with another element of the same or another set. For example, $x = 3y$ is a function.

Getis's G_i^* statistic A statistical test for determining whether a location and its surrounding regions form a cluster of higher (or lower) than average *attribute* values.

Geostatistics Statistical methods that deal with the spatial relationships between objects.

Heteroscedastic Describes a situation where errors in an *independent variable* are drawn from different *distributions* (i.e. two or more separate processes are being expressed). This may be identified by the presence of clustering in an x, y-plot. (Compare *homoscedastic*.)

Homoscedastic A situation when errors are drawn from the same distribution for all independent variables. (Compare *heteroscedastic*.)

Independent variable The variable (normally denoted by x) that influences the *dependent* variable (normally denoted by y).

Interaction The description, analysis or prediction of *flow* (i.e. interaction) between defined regions or centres (e.g. between one population centre and another).

Intercept The point on the y-axis at which it intersects a *line of regression*.

Interdependence Describes a relationship between two variables in which it is difficult or impossible to identify which is *dependent* and which is *independent*. (Compare *confounding*.)

Jenk's optimisation A statistical method for devising 'natural-break' *class* boundaries (see *classification*) by minimising the sum of the squared deviations from class means.

k-Means analysis A commonly used method of *cluster* analysis that uses a partitioning method for *cluster definition*.

Kolmogorov–Smirnov A commonly used *non-parametric* statistical test used to determine whether two frequency (probability) *distributions* differ from each other.

Kriging A form of *interpolation* that relies on *geostatistics* to calculate the distance weighting of surrounding values.

Lag The distance between pairs of *points* in a spatial distribution (usually grouped into lag intervals for the purposes of constructing a *variogram*).

Line of regression A straight line through a distribution of x, y-variables that is positioned to minimise the sum of the squared vertical distances. The line has two *regression constants*: a *y-intercept* and a *slope*, which are used to derive the linear equation.

Mann–Whitney U test A commonly used *non-parametric* statistical test used to determine whether ordinal- or higher-*scale* data are drawn from a single *population*.

Monte-Carlo simulation A statistical technique used to reduce the uncertainty inherent in random *samples* by taking repeated random samples (typically 1000 or more). The distribution of values of some statistic (such as the sample mean) can then be examined in order to obtain a better estimate of the *population* mean.

Multivariate More than one variable, as in multivariate statistics.

Nearest neighbour analysis A simple method for determining whether a set of *points* in space tends towards a regular, random or clustered spatial pattern.

Non-parametric test A type of statistical test (such as the *Chi-squared test*) that does not require the *distribution* of values to conform to a specific shape. (Compare *parametric*.)

Null hypothesis An explanation that is being statistically tested, usually expressed as either 'no difference' (e.g. between *samples*) or 'random', and denoted by H_0. If H_0 is rejected, then the **alternate hypothesis** (H_1) is favoured (usually expressed as a 'significant difference' between samples, or 'non-randomness').

One-sample test A statistical test in which an observed pattern is compared to a (random) *sample* of independent observations.

Outlier An unusually high or low value relative to other values in a set of data. Outliers may occur because of human error (e.g. in observation or in data entry), because the measurement comes from a different *population*, or because the value is recording a rare event in a single population.

Parametric test A type of statistical test (such as *Student's t*) that requires a certain shape of *distribution* (typically a normal distribution). (Compare *non-parametric*.)

Partitioning Around Medoids (PAM) A method of *cluster analysis* that is similar, but more robust, than *k-means*.

Point distribution A set of *points* in space. The arrangement of points may be described as tending towards randomness (i.e. each point is independent of every other point), clustered or regular in distribution. See also *nearest neighbour* and *Ripley's K*.

Population The set of entities about which statistical inferences are to be made, typically by drawing a *sample* from the population.

Predictive gain A measure of the utility of a *predictive model* which, when calculated for a specified probability of site occurrence, ranges from 1 (high predictive utility) through 0 (no predictive utility) to -1 (the model predicts the reverse of what it is supposed to).

Range The difference between the highest and lowest values in a *sample* of data (such as a *neighbourhood* of *cells*).

Regression analysis A statistical technique that, in the simplest sense, finds the line or curve that best fits a set of x, y-data points. More specifically, regression analysis determines the values of parameters (e.g. the *regression constants*) of the *function* that describes the best-fit line or curve. In **linear regression** this function describes a straight line; **non-linear regression** analysis defines the shape of a curved line. **Logistic regression** analysis attempts to fit an S-shaped (sigmoidal) curve to a range between 0 and 1 to minimise the frequency of intermediate values; it is thus ideal for *predictive modelling* where 0 represents the absence of a site, and 1 the presence of a site.

Regression constants The *y-intercept* and *slope* of a line in a linear equation, or the potentially several parameters in a non-linear equation.

Residual The observable difference between an actual value and its predicted value in a *sample*. For example, in linear *regression analysis* the residual is the difference between the actual *dependent* (y) value, and the value predicted by the *line of regression*.

Ripley's *K*-function A *function* used to compare an observed point pattern against a theoretical random distribution at a range of spatial scales in order to ascertain whether the observed pattern is significantly more clustered or more regularly distributed than expected.

Sample A set of entities drawn from a *population* from which inferences about the population are to be made.

Scale In statistical terms, scale refers to the type of data. **Nominal**-scale data are classificatory values that have no inherent order or distance between them (e.g. 'beaker', 'bowl', 'plate'); **ordinal**-scale data are categories that can be ordered, but distances between them are not measurable (e.g. 'small', 'medium', 'big'); **interval** data have the properties of an ordinal scale, but also the property of known distances between the categories (e.g. 1000 BCE, 500 BCE, 60 BCE); **ratio**-scale data have the properties of interval data, but have a fixed zero point (e.g. 1000 m, 500 m, 60 m).

Semi-variance Semi-variance is a spatial statistic that estimates the degree of *correlation* between the *attribute* values of *points* and the distance between them (i.e. spatial *autocorrelation*).

Significance level The probability level at which a *null hypothesis* is rejected in favour of the *alternate hypothesis* in a statistical test, and denoted either by α or p. Significance levels are usually set at no more than 10 per cent ($\alpha < 0.1$), most often 5 per cent ($\alpha < 0.05$), but at times 1 per cent ($\alpha < 0.01$) or less. As the significance level moves from large to small, the probability of making a *type 1 error* decreases and the probability of making a *type 2 error* increases.

Slope In statistical terms, slope refers to the gradient of a line in a *regression analysis* and is one of the *regression constants*.

Spatial analysis The set of statistical and related methods (e.g. visualisation techniques) used for the analysis of spatial data.

Spatial modelling The set of statistical and related methods (e.g. *viewshed* analysis) used to understand the spatial relationships between different phenomena (e.g. between archaeological sites and their environmental correlates).

Spatial regression A geostatistical method of *regression analysis* that incorporates spatial data as a variable to reduce the errors that arise when performing standard regression on data that are known or suspected of being spatially *autocorrelated*.

Spatial statistics The set of statistics that are concerned with the description and/or analysis of spatial phenomena.

Student's *t* A statistical distribution defined by W. S. Gosset in 1908 that is used in Student's *t*-test to ascertain whether the means of two normally *distributed samples* are drawn from the same *population*.

Testing sample A *sample* of sites (typically 50 per cent) withheld from the sample of all known sites that is used to test the accuracy of a *predictive model*.

Training sample A *sample* of sites (typically 50 per cent) selected from the sample of all known sites that is used to develop a *predictive model*.

Two-sample test A statistical test between two *samples* drawn from the same (or suspected same) *population*.

Type 1 error Incorrectly rejecting a *null hypothesis*.

Type 2 error Incorrectly accepting a *null hypothesis*.

Validation The testing of a model to determine its accuracy.

Variance A measure of the *distribution* around the mean of a *sample* of numbers.

Variogram A plot of *semi-variance* against distance between points (i.e. the *lag*, denoted by h) is called a *variogram* and is used to estimate the parameters necessary for *interpolation* by *kriging*. An **experimental variogram** is a known function that defines the best-fit line between points on the variogram, and is usually based on a linear, spherical or Gaussian model.

Remote-sensing terms

Active sensor A *remote-sensing* system that transmits energy and reads how it is reflected back from phenomena. (Compare *passive sensor*.)

Colour composite An image that resembles a colour image, but has been created by combining information from individually captured *spectral bands* from a *multispectral* sensor. Also called a **false colour composite** when the colours do not resemble what would be seen to the naked eye (e.g. when spectral bands that are strongly sensitive to the presence of vegetation are not coloured green).

Contrast stretch A mathematical technique used to expand a narrow range of *pixel* values in a digital image by 'stretching' the values to the upper and lower limits permitted (typically between 0 and 255).

GPR Ground Penetrating Radar is an *active sensor remote-sensing* tool, usually handheld or on a small wheeled trolley, that transmits electromagnetic radiation (typically somewhere between 1.5 GHz to 100 MHz) beneath the ground and reads the reflected signal to detect subsurface features (such as burials or building foundations).

Ground truthing An essential stage in *image classification* in which areas defined by *supervised classification* or *unsupervised classification* are physically checked for accuracy by visiting the area in question.

Hyperspectral See *multispectral*.

IFSAR Interferometric Synthetic Aperture Radar: an *active sensor* mounted on space craft (such as the *Space Shuttle*) or aircraft to collect *elevation* data.

Image classification The process of converting the continuous data recorded in one or more *spectral bands* into discrete *classes* (or probability values for classes) that represent different types of features or vegetation. This is usually done via an *unsupervised classification* or *supervised classification* procedure.

Infrared Radiation between the visible and microwave portions of the electromagnetic spectrum. Near-infrared (NIR) begins at wavelengths of about 0.7 μm (i.e. 0.0007 mm) and stretches to wavelengths of about 1000 μm in the far-infrared (FIR) range.

LiDAR Light Detection And Ranging: an *active sensor* mounted on aircraft to measure *elevation*.

Multispectral More than one *spectral band*. If there are very many narrow bands recorded (e.g. in excess of 20), then the data may be referred to as *hyperspectral*. (Compare *panchromatic*.)

Panchromatic A single spectral band that records visible light in a format equivalent to a 'black and white' (i.e. greyscale) image. (Compare *multispectral*.)

Passive sensor A *remote-sensing* system that records energy that is either generated by the targeted phenomenon or is being reflected from some other source (e.g. the Sun). (Compare *active sensor*.)

Remote sensing The art and science of recording and interpreting the nature of phenomena without coming into physical contact with them. Usually associated with some form of device that records energy waves (such as visible light, infrared light or radar).

Spectral band The range of electromagnetic wavelengths recorded by a single sensor on a *remote-sensing* device. Typically, spectral bands correspond to a named frequency range such as near-*infrared*, visible green, visible red, etc.

Spectral clustering See *unsupervised classification*.

SRP The Spectral Response Pattern is a distinctive pattern of energy values recorded in one or more *spectral bands* for a specific feature or phenomenon (e.g. buildings or a plant species) or group of phenomena (e.g. a plant community).

SRTM The Shuttle Radar Topography Mission, which uses an *IFSAR* device to collect world-wide *elevation* data.

Supervised classification A process of image interpretation that begins by delineating a *sample* of *training areas* in a digital image in order to identify and define a *spectral response pattern* for the phenomenon in question.

Training area A defined area on the ground that contains a specific feature or phenomenon (e.g. an archaeological site, or a type of vegetation or plant community) that can also be delineated on the digital image and thus used in a *supervised classification*.

Unsupervised classification A process of image interpretation that begins by statistical pattern recognition, typically using some form of *multivariate* statistics to identify clusters across two or more *spectral bands*. These *spectral clusters* are assumed to represent distinctive features or phenomena and can thus form the basis for an *image classification*.

Vegetative index A mathematical combination of different *spectral bands* through *map algebra* to create a new image that represents spatial variation in some aspect of vegetation (e.g. the Normalised Difference Vegetation Index, or NDVI, combines the red and near-*infrared* bands to produce a new map with *cell* values typically between 0.1 to 0.6, with higher values representing 'healthier' green vegetation).

REFERENCES

Abe, Y., Marean, C. W., Nilssen, P. J., Assefa, Z. and Stone, E. (2002). The analysis of cutmarks on archaeofauna: a review and critique of quantification procedures, and a new image-analysis GIS approach. *American Antiquity*, 67: 643–663.

Alcock, S. and Cherry, J., eds. (2004). *Side-by-Side Survey: Comparative Regional Studies in the Mediterranean World*. Oxford, Oxbow Books.

Aldenderfer, M. (1996). Introduction. In Aldenderfer, M. and Maschner, H. D. G., eds., *Anthropology, Space and Geographical Information Systems*, pp. 3–18. New York, Oxford University Press.

(1998). Quantitative methods in archaeology: a review of recent trends and developments. *Journal of Archaeological Research*, 6: 91–1220.

ALGAO (2001). *Local Records – National Resource: An ALGAO Strategy for Sites and Monuments Records in England*. London, Association of Local Government Archaeology Officers (ALGAO).

(2002). *Historic Environment Records: Benchmarks for Good Practice*. London, English Heritage/ Association of Local Government Archaeology Officers (ALGAO).

Allen, J. R. L. and Fulford, M. G. (1996). The distribution of south-east Dorset Black Burnished Category 1 pottery in south-west Britain. *Britannia*, 27: 223–281.

Allen, K. M. S. (1990). Modelling early historic trade in the eastern Great Lakes using geographic information systems. In Allen, K. M. S., Green, S. W. and Zubrow, E. B. W., eds., *Interpreting Space: GIS and Archaeology*, pp. 319–329. London, Taylor & Francis.

Ammerman, A. J. and Cavalli-Sforza, L. L. (1971). Measuring the rate of spread of early farming in Europe. *Man*, N.S. 6: 674–688.

Anderson, D. G. and Faught, M. K. (2000). Palaeoindian artefact distributions: evidence and implications. *Antiquity*, 74: 507–513.

Anderson, R. C. (1982). Photogrammetry: the pros and cons for archaeology. *World Archaeology*, 14: 200–205.

APPAG (2003). *The Current State of Archaeology in the United Kingdom: First Report of the All-Party Parliamentary Archaeology Group*. London, The All-Party Parliamentary Archaeology Group.

Atkinson, P. (2002). Surface modelling: what's the point? *Transactions in GIS*, 6: 1–4.

Aurenhammer, F. and Edelsbrunner, H. (1984). An optimal algorithm for constructing the weighted Voronoi diagram in the plane. *Pattern Recognition*, 17: 251–257.

Bailey, T. C. and Gatrell, A. C. (1995). *Interactive Spatial Data Analysis*. Harlow, Longman.

Baker, W. A. (1992). Air archaeology in the valley of the River Severn. Unpublished Ph.D. thesis, University of Southampton.

Ball, G. and Hall, D. (1970). A clustering technique for summarising multivariate data. *Behavioral Science*, 12: 153–155.

Barker, P. (1998). *Techniques of Archaeological Excavation*, 3rd edition. London and New York, Routledge.

Barrett, J. C. (1999). The mythical landscapes of the British Iron Age. In Ashmore, A. and Knapp, A. B., eds., *Archaeologies of Landscape*, pp. 253–265. Oxford, Blackwell.

Barton, M. B., Bernabeu, J., Aura, E. and Garcia, O. (1999). Land-use dynamics and socioeconomic change: an example from the Polop Alto Valley. *American Antiquity*, 64: 609–634.

Barton, M. B., Bernabeu, J., Aura, E., Garcia, O. and Roca, N. L. (2002). Dynamic landscapes, artifact taphonomy and land-use modeling in the western Mediterranean. *Geoarchaeology*, 17: 155–190.

Batchelor, D. (1999). The use of GIS for archaeological sensitivity and visibility analysis at Stonehenge, Avebury and associated sites, World Heritage site, United Kingdom. In Box, P., ed., *GIS and Cultural Resource Management: A Manual for Heritage Managers*, pp. 118–128. Bangkok, UNESCO.

Batty, M. (2001). Exploring isovist fields: space and shape in architectural and urban morphology. *Environment and Planning B: Planning and Design*, 28: 123–150.

Baxter, M. (1994). *Exploratory Multivariate Analysis in Archaeology*. Edinburgh, Edinburgh University Press.

Beardah, C. (1999). Uses of multivariate kernel density estimates. In Dingwall, L., Exon, S., Gaffney, V. Laflin, S. and van Leusen, M., eds., *Archaeology in the Age of the Internet: Computer Applications and Quantitative Methods in Archaeology 1997*. BAR International Series S750. Oxford, Archaeopress.

Beardah, C. and Baxter, M. (1996). The archaeological use of kernel density estimates. *Internet Archaeology*, 1. `http://intarch.ac.uk/journal/issue1/beardah_index.html` (accessed 05/11/2004).

Beasley, D. and Huggins, L. (1991). *ANSWERS User's Manual*. W. Lafayette, IN, Agricultural Engineering, Purdue University.

Beck, A. and Beck, M. (2000). Computing, theory and practice: establishing the agenda in contract archaeology. In Roskams, S., ed., *Interpreting Stratigraphy: Papers Presented to the Interpreting Stratigraphy Conferences 1993–1997*, pp. 173–181. Oxford, Archaeopress.

Bell, T. and Lock, G. (2000). Topographic and cultural influences on walking the Ridgeway in later prehistoric times. In Lock, G., ed., *Beyond the Map: Archaeology and Spatial Technologies*, pp. 85–100. Amsterdam, IOS Press.

Bell, T., Wilson, A. and Wickham, A. (2002). Tracking the Samnites: landscape and communication routes in the Sangro Valley, Italy. *American Journal of Archaeology*, 106: 169–186.

Bell, T. L. and Church, R. (1985). Location–allocation modelling in archaeological settlement pattern research: some preliminary applications. *World Archaeology*, 16: 354–371.

Ben-Dor, E., Portugali, J., Kochavi, M., Shimoni, M. and Vinitzky, L. (1999). Airborne thermal video radiometry and excavation planning at Tel Leviah, Golan Heights, Israel. *Journal of Field Archaeology*, 26: 117–127.

Benedikt, M. L. (1979). To take hold of space: isovists and isovist fields. *Environment and Planning B: Planning and Design*, 6: 47–65.

Bevan, A. (2003). The rural landscape of Neopalatial Kythera: a GIS perspective. *Journal of Mediterranean Archaeology*, 15: 217–256.

Bevan, A. and Bell, T. (2004). *A Survey of Standards for the English Archaeological Record Community: A Report on Behalf of English Heritage*. London, English Heritage.

Bevan, A. and Conolly, J. (2004). GIS, archaeological survey and landscape archaeology on the Island of Kythera, Greece. *Journal of Field Archaeology*, 29: 123–138.

(in press). Multi-scalar approaches to settlement distributions. In Lock, G. and Molyneaux, B., eds., *Confronting Scale in Archaeology: Issues of Theory and Practice*. London, Kluwer Press. `http://www.tuare.trentu.ca/njconolly/papers/bevan-conolly-2005.pdf` (accessed 22/08/05).

Bewley, R., Braasch, O. and Palmer, R. (1996). An aerial archaeology training week, 15–22 June 1996, held near Siofok, Lake Balaton, Hungary. *Antiquity*, 70: 745–750.

Bewley, R., Donoghue, D., Gaffney, V., van Leusen, M. and Wise, A. (1998). *Archiving Aerial Photography and Remote Sensing Data: A Guide to Good Practice*. Arts and Humanities Data Service Guides to Good Practice. Arts and Humanities Data Service. `http://ads.ahds.ac.uk/project/goodguides/apandrs` (accessed 05/11/2004).

Bewley, R. and Raczkowski, W., eds. (2002). *Aerial Archaeology: Developing Future Practice*. Oxford, IOS Press.

Beynon-Davies, P. (1992). *Relational Database Design*. Oxford, Blackwell Scientific.

Bibby, J. S., Douglas, H. A., Thomasson, A. J. and Robertson, J. S. (1991). *Land Capability Classification for Agriculture*. Aberdeen, Macaulay Land Use Research Institute.

Binford, L. R. (1989). The 'New Archaeology' then and now. In Lamberg-Karlovsky, C. C., ed., *Archaeological Thought in America*, pp. 50–62. Cambridge, Cambridge University Press.

Binford, L. R. and Binford, S. R., eds. (1968). *New Perspectives in Archaeology*. Chicago, IL, Aldine.

Bintliff, J., Kuna, M. and Venclova, N., eds. (2001). *The Future of Surface Artefact Survey in Europe*. Sheffield, Sheffield Academic Press.

Bishop, I. D. (2002). Determination of thresholds of visual impact: the case of wind turbines. *Environment and Planning B: Planning and Design*, 29: 707–718.

Bouchet, J.-M. and Burnez, C. (1990). Le camp Néolithique de Réjolles à Biron Charente-Maritime. *Bulletin de la Société Préhistorique Française*, 87: 10–12.

Bourn, R. (1999). Events and monuments: a discussion paper. *SMR News*, 8: 3–7.

Bove, F. J. (1981). Trend surface analysis and the Lowland Classic Maya collapse. *American Antiquity*, 46: 93–112.

Bradley, R. (1998). Ruined buildings, ruined stones, enclosures, tombs and natural places in the Neolithic of south-west England. *World Archaeology*, 30: 13–22.

(2000). *An Archaeology of Natural Places*. London, Routledge.

Bradley, R., Harding, J., Rippon, S. and Mathews, M. (1993). A field method for investigating the distribution of rock art. *Oxford Journal of Archaeology*, 12: 129–145.

Brock, J. C., Wright, C. W., Sallenger, A. H., Krabill, W. B. and Swift, R. N. (2002). Basis and methods of NASA Airborne Topographic Mapper LiDAR surveys for coastal studies. *Journal of Coastal Research*, 18: 1–13.

Broodbank, C. (1999). Kythera survey: preliminary report on the 1998 season. *Annual of the British School at Athens*, 94: 191–214.

Buck, C., Cavanagh, W. and Litton, C. (1988). The spatial analysis of site phosphate data. In Rahtz, S., ed., *Computer and Quantitative Methods in Archaeology 1988*, BAR International Series 446, pp. 151–160. Oxford, BAR.

Bunge, W. W. (1966). *Theoretical Geography*. Lund Studies in Geography 6, Series C, General and Mathematical Geography. Lund, Gleerup.

Burrough, P. A. and McDonnell, R. (1998). *Principles of Geographical Information Systems*. Oxford, Oxford University Press.

Bustard, W. (1996). Space as Place: Small and Great House Spatial Organisation in Chaco Canyon, New Mexico, 1000–1150 AD. Unpublished Ph.D. thesis, University of New Mexico.

Campbell, J. B. (1996). *Introduction to Remote Sensing*, 2nd edition. New York, The Guilford Press.

(2002). *Introduction to Remote Sensing*, 3rd edition. New York, Guilford Publications.

Campbell, M. (2000). Sites and site types on Rarotonga, Cook Islands. *New Zealand Journal of Archaeology*, 22: 45–74.

Cañamero, D. and de Velde, W. V. (2000). Emotionally grounded social interaction. In Dautenhahn, K., ed., *Human Cognition and Social Agent Technology*, pp. 137–162. Amsterdam, John Benjamins.

Capper, J. (1907). Photographs of Stonehenge, as seen from a war balloon. *Archaeologia*, 60: 571.

Carrara, A., Bitelli, G. and Carla, R. (1997). Comparison of techniques for generating digital terrain models from contour lines. *International Journal of Geographical Information Science*, 11: 451–474.

Carter, F. W. (1969). An analysis of the Medieval Serbian Oecumene: a theoretical approach. *Geografiska Annaler*, 51: 39–52.

Cartwright, W., Crampton, J., Gartner, G., *et al.* (2001). Geospatial information visualisation user interface issues. *Cartography and Geographic Information Science*, 28: 45–60.

Cassels, R. (1972). Locational analysis of prehistoric settlement in New Zealand. *Mankind*, 8: 212–222.

Chapman, H. and Gearey, B. (2000). Palaeoecology and the perception of prehistoric landscapes: some comments on visual approaches to phenomenology. *Antiquity*, 74: 316–319.

Chapman, J. (1990). Social inequality on Bulgarian tells and the Varna problem. In Samson, R., ed., *The Social Archaeology of Houses*, pp. 49–92. Edinburgh, Edinburgh University Press.

Chen, P. P. S. (1976). The entity-relationship model: toward a unified view of data. *ACM Transactions on Database Systems*, 1: 9–36.

Chorley, R. J. and Haggett, P., eds. (1967). *Models in Geography*. London, Methuen.

Chou, Y.-H. (1997). *Exploring Spatial Analysis in Geographic Information Systems*. Albany, NY, OnWord Press.

Clark, A. J. (1996). *Seeing Beneath the Soil: Prospecting Methods in Archaeology*. London, B. T. Batsford.

Clark, P. and Evans, F. (1954). Distance to nearest neighbour as a measure of spatial relationships in populations. *Ecology*, 35: 445–453.

Clarke, D. L. (1968). *Analytical Archaeology*. London, Methuen.

ed. (1972). *Models in Archaeology*. London, Methuen.

ed. (1977). *Spatial Archaeology*. London, Academic Press.

Cliff, A. D. and Ord, J. K. (1981). *Spatial Processes, Models and Applications*. London, Pion.

Clifford, P. and Richardson, S. (1985). Testing the association between two spatial processes. *Decisions and Statistics, Supplement Issue No. 2*, pp. 155–160.

Clowes, A. and Comfort, P. (1982). *Process and Landform*. Edinburgh, Oliver & Boyd.

Codd, E. F. (1970). A relational model of data for large shared data banks. *Communications of the ACM*, 13(6): 377–387.

Collischonn, W. and Pilar, V. (2000). A direction-dependent least cost path algorithm for roads and canals. *International Journal of Geographical Information Science*, 14: 397–406.

Couclelis, H. (1992). People manipulate objects (but cultivate fields): beyond the raster–vector debate in GIS. In Frank, A. U., Campari, I. and Formentini, U., eds., *Theories and Methods of Spatio-Temporal Reasoning in Geographic Space*, pp. 65–77. Berlin, Springer-Verlag.

(1999). Space, time, geography. In Longley, P. A., Goodchild, M. F., Maguire, D. J. and Rhind, D. W., eds., *Geographical Information Systems*, Vol. I, *Principles and Technical Issues*, pp. 29–38. New York, John Wiley & Sons.

Cox, C. (1992). Satellite imagery, aerial photography and wetland archaeology. *World Archaeology*, 24: 249–267.

Cunliffe, B. W. (1971). Some aspects of hill-forts and their cultural environments. In Jesson, M. and Hill, D., eds., *The Iron Age and its Hill-Forts*, University of Southampton Monograph Series 1, pp. 53–70. Southampton, University of Southampton.

Curry, M. R. (1998). *Digital Places: Living with Geographic Information Technologies*. London, Routledge.

Dacey, M. F. (1960). The spacing of river towns. *Annals of the Association of American Geographers*, 50: 59–61.

D'Andrea, A., Gallotti, R. and Piperno, M. (2002). Taphonomic interpretation of the Developed Oldowan site of Garba IV (Melka Kunture, Ethiopia) through a GIS application. *Antiquity*, 76: 991–1002.

Daniel, I. R. (2001). Stone raw material availability and Early Archaic settlement in the southeastern United States. *American Antiquity*, 66: 237–265.

DeLoach, S. R. and Leonard, J. (2000). Making photogrammetric history. *Professional Surveyor*, 20: 6–10.

DeMers, M. N. (1997). *Fundamentals of Geographic Information Systems*. New York, John Wiley & Sons.

Dennell, R. W. and Webley, D. (1975). Prehistoric settlement and land use in southern Bulgaria. In Higgs, E. S., ed., *Palaeoeconomy, Being the Second Volume of Papers in Economic Prehistory by Members and Associates of the British Academy Major Research Project in the Early History of Agriculture*, pp. 97–109. Cambridge, Cambridge University Press.

Dent, B. D. (1999). *Cartography: Thematic Map Design*, 5th edition. London, WCB/McGraw Hill.

Deursen, W. P. A. V. (1995). Geographical Information Systems and Dynamic Models. Unpublished Ph.D. thesis, Utrecht University. Available as Nederlandse Geografische Studies 190. `http://pcraster.geog.uu.nl/publications.html` (accessed 16/08/04).

Dibble, H. L., Chase, P. G., McPherron, S. P. and Tuffreau, A. (1997). Testing the reality of a 'living floor' with archaeological data. *American Antiquity*, 62: 629–651.

Douglas, D. H. (1999). Least cost path in GIS using an accumulated cost surface and slope lines. `http://www.hig.se/~dds/research/leastcos/cumcost4.htm` (accessed 10/02/2002).

Dreyfus, H. (1972). *What Computers Can't Do: A Critique of Artificial Reason*. New York, Harper & Row.

Dublin Core Metadata Initiative (2003). Dublin Core Metadata Element Set, Version 1.1: Reference Description. `http://dublincore.org/documents/dces/` (accessed 08/09/2004).

Duncan, R. B. and Beckman, A. (2000). Site location in Pennsylvania and West Virginia. In Westcott, K. L. and Brandon, R. J., eds., *Practical Applications of GIS for Archaeologists: A Predictive Modeling Kit*, pp. 33–58. London, Taylor & Francis.

Dunning, A. (2001). Managing change with digital data: the case of the Essex Sites and Monuments Record. *Internet Archaeology*, 15. `http://ahds.ac.uk/creating/case-studies/essex/` (accessed 12/11/2004).

Earl, G. and Wheatley, D. (2002). Virtual reconstruction and the interpretive process: a case-study from Avebury. In Wheatley, D., Earl, G. and Poppy, S., eds., *Contemporary Themes in Archaeological Computing*, University of Southampton Department of Archaeology Monograph 3, pp. 5–15. Oxford, Oxbow Books.

Eason, G., Coles, C. W. and Gettinby, G. (1980). *Mathematics and Statistics for the Bio-Sciences*. Chichester, Ellis Horwood.

Eastman, J. R. (1989). Pushbroom algorithms for calculating distances in raster grids. In Auto–Carto, eds., *Auto–Carto 9: Ninth International Symposium on Computer–Assisted Cartography*, Baltimore, MD, 2–7 April. Falls Church, VA, American Society for Photogrammetry and Remote Sensing, American Congress on Surveying and Mapping, pp. 288–297.

(1997). *Idrisi Version 2: Guide to GIS and Image Processing*, Vol. 1. Worcester, MA, Clark Labs.

(2001). *Idrisi32 Release 2: Guide to GIS and Image Processing*, Vol. 1. Worcester, MA, Clark Labs.

Ebert, D. (2002). The potential of geostatistics in the analysis of fieldwalking data. In Wheatley, D., Earl, G. and Poppy, S., eds., *Contemporary Themes in Archaeological Computing*, University of Southampton Department of Archaeology Monograph 3, pp. 82–89. Oxford, Oxbow Books.

Egenhofer, M. J. (1991). Extending SQL for cartographic displays. *Cartography and Geographic Information Systems*, 18: 230–245.

(1994). Spatial SQL: a query and presentation language. *IEEE Transactions on Knowledge and Data Engineering*, 6: 86–95.

Eisenberg, J. D. (2002). *SVG Essentials*. Cambridge, MA, O'Reilly.

Eiteljorg, H. (2000). The compelling computer image: a double-edged sword. *Internet Archaeology*, 8. `http://intarch.ac.uk/journal/issue8/eiteljorg_index.html` (accessed 12/01/2004).

ESRI (1999). Splines. ArcInfo Version 7.2.1 Documentation. Redlands, CA, Environmental Systems Research Institute.

(2002). TIN in ArcInfo 8.0.1. ArcInfo Version 8.0.1 Documentation. Redlands, CA, Environmental Systems Research Institute.

Eve, S. (2004). Chersonesos Multi Agent Modelling System (CMAMS v1.2). Unpublished M.Sc. thesis, Institute of Archaeology, University College London.

Exon, S., Gaffney, V., Woodward, A. and Yorston, R. (2000). *Stonehenge Landscapes: Journeys Through Real-and-Imagined Worlds*. Oxford, Archaeopress.

Fanning, P. C. and Holdaway, S. J. (2001). Stone artifact scatters in western NSW, Australia: geomorphic controls on artifact size and distribution. *Geoarchaeology*, 16: 667–686.

FAO (1974). *Approaches to Land Classification, Soils Bulletin* 22. Rome, Food and Agriculture Organisation.

FAO (1976). *A Framework for Land Evaluation, Soils Bulletin* 32. Rome, Food and Agriculture Organisation. `http://www.fao.org/docrep/X5310E/X5310E00.htm` (accessed 03/09/2004).

Felleman, J. P. (1986). Landscape visibility. In Smardon, R. C., Palmer, J. F. and Felleman, J. P., eds., *Foundations for Visual Project Analysis*. New York, pp. 47–62. John Wiley & Sons.

Fernie, K. and Gilman, P. (2000). *Informing the Future of the Past: Guidelines for SMRs*. Swindon, English Heritage.

Finzi, C. V. and Higgs, E. S. (1972). Prehistoric economy in the Mount Carmel area of Palestine: site catchment analysis. *Proceedings of the Prehistoric Society*, 36: 1–37.

Fischer, M. M. (2004). GIS and network analysis. In Hensher, D., Button, K., Haynes, K. and Stopher, P., eds., *Handbook of Transport Geography and Spatial Systems*. Amsterdam, Elsevier Science. `http://www.ersa.org/ersaconfs/ersa03/cdrom/papers/433.pdf` (accessed 25/08/2004).

Fisher, P. and Unwin, D., eds. (2002). *Virtual Reality in Geography*. London and New York, Taylor & Francis.

Fisher, P. F. (1991). First experiments in viewshed uncertainty: the accuracy of the viewshed area. *Photogrammetric Engineering and Remote Sensing*, 57: 1321–1327.

(1993). Algorithm and implementation uncertainty in viewshed analysis. *International Journal of Geographical Information Systems*, 7: 331–347.

Fisher, P. F., Farrelly, C., Maddocks, A. and Ruggles, C. L. N. (1997). Spatial analysis of visible areas from the Bronze Age cairns of Mull. *Journal of Archaeological Science*, 24: 581–592.

Floriani, L. D., Marzano, P. and Puppo, E. (1994). Line-of-sight communication on terrain models. *International Journal of Geographical Information Systems*, 8: 329–342.

Foley, J. D., van Dam, A., Feiner, S. K. and Hughes, J. F. (1990). *Computer Graphics: Principles and Practice*. Reading, MA, Addison-Wesley.

Foley, R. A. (1977). Space and energy: a method for analysing habitat value and utilisation in relation to archaeological sites. In Clarke, D. L., ed., *Spatial Archaeology*, pp. 163–187. London, Academic Press.

Forer, P. and Unwin, D. (1999). Enabling progress in GIS and education. In Longley, P. A., Goodchild, M. F., Maguire, D. J. and Rhind, D. W., eds., *Geographical Information Systems*. Vol. 2, *Management Issues and Applications*, pp. 747–756. New York, John Wiley & Sons.

Foresman, T. W. (1998). GIS early years and the thread of evolution. In Foresman, T. W., ed., *The History of GIS*, pp. 3–17. London, Prentice Hall.

Foster, S. M. (1989). Analysis of spatial patterns in buildings (access analysis) as an insight into social structure: examples from the Scottish Iron Age. *Antiquity*, 63: 40–50.

Fotheringham, A. S., Brunsdon, C. and Charlton, M. (2000a). *Geographically Weighted Regression: The Analysis of Spatially Varying Relationships*. London, John Wiley & Sons.

(2000b). *Quantitative Geography*. London, Sage.

Fotheringham, A. S., Charlton, M. E. and Brunsdon, C. (1998). Geographically weighted regression: a natural evolution of the expansion method for spatial data analysis. *Environment and Planning A*, 30: 1905–1927.

Fotheringham, A. S. and O'Kelly, M. E. (1989). *Spatial Interaction Models: Formulations and Applications*. Dordrecht, Kluwer.

Fowler, M. (1996). High-resolution satellite imagery in archaeological application: a Russian satellite photograph of the Stonehenge region. *Antiquity*, 70: 667–671.

Franke, R. (1982). Smooth interpolation of scattered data by local thin plate splines. *Computers and Mathematics with Application*, 8: 237–281.

Franklin, W. R. (2000). Applications of analytical cartography. *Cartography and Geographic Information Science*, 27: 225–237.

Fritz, J. M. and Plog, F. T. (1970). The nature of archaeological explanation. *American Antiquity*, 35: 405–412.

Gaffney, V. and Stančič, Z. (1991). *GIS Approaches to Regional Analysis: a Case Study of the Island of Hvar*. Ljubljana, Znanstveni inštitut Filozofske fakultete.

(1992). Diodorus Siculus and the island of Hvar, Dalmatia: testing the text with GIS. In Lock, G. and Moffett, J., eds., *Computer Applications and Quantitative Methods in Archaeology 1991*, British Archaeological Reports International Series 557, pp. 113–126. Oxford, Tempus Reparatum.

Gaffney, V., Stančič, Z. and Watson, H. (1996). Moving from catchments to cognition: tentative steps toward a larger archaeological context for GIS. In Aldenderfer, M. and Maschner, H. D. G., eds., *Anthropology, Space and Geographic Information Systems*, pp. 132–154. Oxford, Oxford University Press.

Gaffney, V. and van Leusen, P. M. (1995). Postscript: GIS, environmental determinism and archaeology. A parallel text. In Lock, G. R. and Stančič, Z., eds., *Archaeology and Geographical Information Systems: A European Perspective*, pp. 367–382. London, Taylor & Francis.

Gamble, C. S. (1998). Palaeolithic society and the release from proximity: a network approach to intimate relations. *World Archaeology*, 29: 426–449.

Garcia-Sanjuan, L. and Wheatley, D. (1999). The state of the Arc: differential rates of adoption of GIS for European heritage management. *European Journal of Archaeology*, 2: 201–228.

Gavrilova, M. (n.d.). Weighted Voronoi diagrams in biology. http://pages/cpsc.ucalgary. ca/~marina/vpplants/ (accessed 05/11/2004).

Gibson, J. J. (1986). *The Ecological Approach to Perception*. Hillsdale, Lawrence Erlbaum Associates.

Gilbert, N. and Troitzsch, K. G. (1999). *Simulation for the Social Scientist*. Buckingham, Open University Press.

Gilchrist, R. (1997). *Gender and Material Culture: The Archaeology of Religious Woman*. London, Routledge.

Gillings, M. (1995). Flood dynamics and settlement in the Tisza valley of north-east Hungary: GIS and the Upper Tisza Project. In Lock, G. R. and Stančič, Z., eds., *Archaeology and Geographic Information Systems: A European Perspective*, pp. 67–84. London, Taylor & Francis.

(1997). Not drowning but waving? The Tisza flood-plain revisited. In Johnson, I. and North, M., eds., *Archaeological Applications of GIS: Proceedings of Colloquium II, UISPP XIIIth Congress*, Forli, Italy, September 1996. Sydney University Archaeological Methods Series 5. Sydney, Archaeological Computing Laboratory. CD-ROM.

(2005). The real, the virtually real, and the hyperreal: the role of VR in archaeology. In Smiles, S. and Moser, S., eds., *Envisioning the Past: Archaeology and the Image*, pp. 223–239. Oxford, Blackwell Publishing.

Gillings, M. and Goodrick, G. T. (1996). Sensuous and reflexive GIS: exploring visualisation and VRML. *Internet Archaeology*, 1. http://intarch.ac.uk/journal/issue1/ gillings_index.html (accessed 30/08/2004).

Gillings, M., Mattingly, D. and van Dalen, J., eds. (1999). *Geographical Information Systems and Landscape Archaeology*. The Archaeology of Mediterranean Landscapes 3. Oxford, Oxbow Books.

Gillings, M. and Sbonias, K. (1999). Regional survey and GIS: the Boeotia Project. In Gillings, M., Mattingly, D. and van Dalen, J., eds., *Geographical Information Systems and Landscape Archaeology*, The Archaeology of Mediterranean Landscapes 3. Oxford, Oxbow Books.

Gilman, P. (2004). Sites and Monuments Records and Historic Environment Records in England: is Cinderella finally going to the ball? *Internet Archaeology*, 15. http://intarch.ac.uk/journal/issue15/gilman_toc.html (accessed 11/06/2004).

Gimblett, H. R., ed. (2002). *Integrating Geographic Information Systems and Agent-Based Modeling Techniques for Simulating Social and Ecological Processes*. Oxford, Oxford University Press.

Gkiasta, M., Russell, T., Shennan, S. and Steele, J. (2003). Neolithic transition in Europe: the radio-carbon record revisited. *Antiquity*, 77: 45–63.

Goodchild, M. F. (1998). The geolibrary. In Carver, S., ed., *Innovations in GIS 5: Selected Papers from the Fifth National Conference on GIS Research UK (GISRUK)*, pp. 59–68. London, Taylor & Francis.

Gorenflo, L. J. and Bell, T. L. (1991). Network analysis and the study of past regional organisation. In Trombold, C. D., ed., *Road Networks and Settlement Hierarchies in the New World*, pp. 80–98. Cambridge, Cambridge University Press.

Gorenflo, L. J. and Gale, N. (1990). Mapping regional settlement in information space. *Journal of Anthropological Archaeology*, 9: 240–274.

Goudie, A. S. (1987). Geography and archaeology: the growth of a relationship. In Wagstaff, J. M., ed., *Landscape and Culture: Geographical and Archaeological Perspectives*, pp. 11–25. Oxford, Basil Blackwell.

Gould, P. R. (1967). On the geographical interpretation of eigenvalues. *Transactions of the Institute of British Geographers*, 42: 53–86.

Grove, A. T. and Rackham, O. (2003). *The Nature of Mediterranean Europe: An Ecological History*. New Haven, CT, Yale University Press.

Hageman, J. B. and Bennett, D. A. (2000). Construction of digital elevation models for archaeolog-ical applications. In Westcott, K. L. and Brandon, R. J., eds., *Practical Applications of GIS for Archaeologists: A Predictive Modeling Kit*, pp. 113–127. London, Taylor & Francis.

Haggett, P. (1965). *Locational Analysis in Human Geography*. New York, John Wiley & Sons.

Haggett, P. and Chorley, R. J. (1969). *Network Analysis in Geography*. London, Edward Arnold.

Haines, E. (1994). Point in polygon strategies. In Heckbert, P., ed., *Graphics Gems IV*, pp. 24–46. London, Academic Press.

Haining, R. (1990). The use of added variable plots in regression modelling with spatial data. *The Professional Geographer*, 42: 336–345.

(2003). *Spatial Data Analysis: Theory and Practice*. Cambridge, Cambridge University Press.

Haraway, D. (1991). *Simians, Cyborgs, and Woman: The Reinvention of Nature*. London, Free Asso-ciation Books.

Harris, E. C. (1979). *Principles of Archaeological Stratigraphy*. London, Academic Press.

Harris, T. (2000). Moving GIS: exploring movement within prehistoric cultural landscapes using GIS. In Lock, G., ed., *Beyond the Map: Archaeology and Spatial Technologies*, pp. 116–123. Amsterdam, IOS Press.

Harvey, D. (1969). *Explanation in Geography*. London, Edward Arnold.

Hassan, F. (1997). Beyond the surface: comments on Hodder's 'reflexive excavation methodology'. *Antiquity*, 71: 1020–1025.

Haughton, C. and Powlesland, D. (1999). *West Heslerton: the Anglian Cemetery*, Archaeological Monograph 1. Yedingham, Landscape Research Centre.

Hernandez, M. J. (2003). *Database Design for Mere Mortals: A Hands-On Guide to Relational Database Design*, 2nd edition. Boston, MA, Addison-Wesley Professional.

Higgs, E. S. and Finzi, C. V. (1972). Prehistoric economies: a territorial approach. In Higgs, E. S., ed., *Papers in Economic Prehistory: Studies by Members and Associates of the British Academy*

Major Research Project in the Early History of Agriculture, pp. 27–36. Cambridge, Cambridge University Press.

Higgs, E. S., Vita-Finzi, C., Harris, D. R. and Fagg, A. E. (1967). The climate, environment and industries of Stone Age Greece: part II. *Proceedings of the Prehistoric Society*, 33: 1–29.

Higuchi, T. (1983). *The Visual and Spatial Structure of Landscapes*. Cambridge, MA, MIT Press. (Trans. Charles S. Terry.)

Hill, J. B. (1998). Ecological variability and agricultural specialisation among the protohistoric pueblos of central New Mexico. *Journal of Field Archaeology*, 25: 275–294.

Hillier, B. (1996). *Space is the Machine*. Cambridge, Cambridge University Press.

Hillier, B. and Hanson, J. (1984). *The Social Logic of Space*. Cambridge, Cambridge University Press.

Hodder, I. (1972). Locational models and the study of Romano-British settlement. In Clarke, D. L., ed., *Models in Archaeology*, pp. 887–909. London, Methuen.

(1982). *Symbolic and Structural Archaeology*. Cambridge, Cambridge University Press.

(1986). *Reading the Past*. Cambridge, Cambridge University Press.

(1990). *The Domestication of Europe*. Oxford, Basil Blackwell.

(1997). Always momentary, fluid and flexible: towards a reflexive excavation methodology. *Antiquity*, 71: 691–700.

(1999). *The Archaeological Process*. Oxford, Blackwell.

Hodder, I. and Hassell, M. (1971). The non-random spacing of Romano-British walled towns. *Man*, N.S. 6: 391–407.

Hodder, I. and Orton, C. (1976). *Spatial Analysis in Archaeology*. Cambridge, Cambridge University Press.

Holt-Jensen, A. (1988). *Geography: History and Concepts, a Student's Guide*. London, Paul Chapman Publishing. (Trans. B. Fullerton.)

Hoobler, B. M., Vance, G. F., Hamerlinck, J. D., Munn, L. C. and Hayward, J. A. (2003). Applications of land evaluation and site assessment. *Journal of Soil and Water Conservation*, 58: 105–113.

Horn, B. K. P. (1981). Hill shading and the reflectance map. *Proceedings of the IEEE*, 69: 14–47.

Hosmer, D. W. and Lemeshow, S. (1989). *Applied Logistic Regression*. New York, John Wiley & Sons.

Hudson-Smith, A. and Evans, S. (2003). Virtual cities: from CAD to 3-D GIS. In Longley, P. A. and Batty, M., eds., *Advanced Spatial Analysis: The CASA Book of GIS*, pp. 41–60. Redlands, CA, ESRI Press.

Hunt, E. D. (1992). Upgrading site-catchment analysis with the use of GIS: investigating the settlement patterns of horticulturalists. *World Archaeology*, 24: 283–309.

Husdal, J. (2000). How to make a straight line square: network analysis in raster GIS. Unpublished M. Sc. thesis, University of Leicester. http://husdal.com/mscgis/thesis/ (accessed 05/07/2004).

Hutchinson, M. F. (1989). A new method for gridding elevation and stream line data with automatic removal of pits. *Journal of Hydrology*, 106: 211–232.

Hutchinson, M. F. and Dowling, T. I. (1991). A continental hydrological assessment of a new grid-based digital elevation model of Australia. *Hydrological Processes*, 5: 45–58.

Iliffe, J. C. (2000). *Datums and Map Projections, for Remote Sensing, GIS, and Surveying*. London, Whittles Publishing.

Ingold, T. (1993). The temporality of the landscape. *World Archaeology*, 25: 152–174.

Izraelevitz, P. (2003). A fast algorithm for approximate viewshed computation. *Photogrammetric Engineering and Remote Sensing*, 69: 767–774.

International Standards Organisation (2003). ISO 19115: 2003 Geographic information: Metadata. http://dublincore.org/documents/dces/ (accessed 08/09/2004).

Jenks, G. F. and Caspall, F. C. (1971). Error in choropleth maps: definition, measurement, reduction. *Annals of the Association of American Geographers*, 61: 217–244.

Jensen, J. R. (2002). *Remote Sensing of the Environment*. New Jersey, Prentice Hall.

Jensen, S. K. and Domingue, J. O. (1988). Extracting topographic structure from digital elevation data for geographic information system analysis. *Photogrammetric Engineering and Remote Sensing*, 54: 1593–1600.

João, E. M. (1998). *Causes and Consequences of Map Generalisation*. London, Taylor & Francis.

Jochim, M. A. (1976). *Hunter-Gatherer Subsistence and Settlement: A Predictive Model*. New York, Academic Press.

Johnston, R. J. (1999). Geography and GIS. In Longley, P. A., Goodchild, M. F., Maguire, D. J. and Rhind, D. W., eds., *Geographical Information Systems*. Vol. I, *Principles and Technical Issues*, pp. 39–47. New York, John Wiley & Sons.

Jones, C. (1997). *Geographical Information Systems and Computer Cartography*. Harlow, Longman.

Jones, N. L., Wright, S. G. and Maidment, D. R. (1990). Watershed delineation with triangle-based terrain models. *Journal of Hydraulic Engineering*, 116: 1232–1251.

Judge, W. J. and Sebastian, L., eds. (1988). *Quantifying the Present and Predicting the Past: Theory, Method and Application of Archaeological Predictive Modeling*. Washington, DC, US Bureau of Land Management, Department of Interior, US Government Printing Office.

Kantner, J. (1996). An evaluation of Chaco Anasazi roadways. `http://sipapu.ucsb.edu/roads/SAA96.pdf` (accessed 20/08/2004). Paper presented at the 61st SAA Annual Meeting, New Orleans, LA.

Kaufman, L. and Rousseeuw, P. J. (1990). *Finding Groups in Data: An Introduction to Cluster Analysis*. New York, John Wiley & Sons.

Ketz, D. D. (2001). Managing archaeological surveys through geospatial information. *Pipeline and Gas Journal*, 228: 37–40.

King, G. (1996). *Mapping Reality: An Exploration of Cultural Cartographies*. London, Macmillan.

Klein, F. (1939). *Elementary Mathematics from an Advanced Standpoint, Vol. 2, Geometry*. London, Macmillan. (Trans. E. R. Hedrick and C. A. Noble from the third German edition).

Kohler, T. A. and Gumerman, G. J., eds. (2000). *Dynamics in Human and Primate Societies: Agent Based Modeling of Social and Spatial Processes*. Oxford, Oxford University Press.

Kohler, T. A. and Parker, S. C. (1986). Predictive modelling for archaeological resource location. In Schiffer, M. B., ed., *Advances in Archaeological Method and Theory*, Vol. 9, pp. 397–452. New York, Academic Press.

Krist, F. J. and Brown, D. G. (1994). GIS modelling of Palaeo-Indian period caribou migrations and viewsheds in northeastern Lower Michigan. *Photogrammetric Engineering and Remote Sensing*, 60: 1129–1137.

Kvamme, K. L. (1983). Computer processing techniques for regional modeling of archaeological site locations. *Advances in Computer Archaeology*, 1: 26–52.

(1985). Determining relationships between the natural environment and prehistoric site locations: a hunter-gatherer example. In Carr, C., ed., *For Concordance in Archaeological Analysis: Bridging Data Structure, Quantitative Technique and Theory*, pp. 208–238. Kansas City, KS, Westport.

(1988). Development and testing of quantitative models. In Judge, W. J. and Sebastian, L., eds., *Quantifying the Present and Predicting the Past: Theory, Method and Application of Archaeological Predictive Modeling*, pp. 325–427. Washington, DC, US Bureau of Land Management, Department of Interior, US Government Printing Office.

(1990a). The fundamental principles and practice of predictive archaeological modeling. In Voorrips, A., ed., *Mathematics and Information Science in Archaeology: A Flexible Framework*, Studies in Modern Archaeology 3, pp. 257–295. Bonn, Holos-Verlag.

(1990b). GIS algorithms and their effects on regional archaeological analyses. In Allen, K. M. S., Green, S. W. and Zubrow, E. B. W., eds., *Interpreting Space: GIS and Archaeology*, pp. 112–125. London, Taylor & Francis.

(1990c). One-sample tests in regional archaeological analysis: new possibilities through computer technology. *American Antiquity*, 55: 367–381.

(1990d). Spatial autocorrelation and the Classic Maya collapse revisited: refined techniques and new conclusions. *Journal of Archaeological Science*, 17: 197–207.

(1992a). A predictive site location model on the High Plains: an example with an independent test. *Plains Anthropologist*, 37: 19–40.

(1992b). Terrain form analysis of archaeological location through geographic information systems. In Lock, G. and Moffett, J., eds., *Computer Applications and Quantitative Methods in Archaeology 1991*, British Archaeological Reports International Series 577, pp. 127–136. Oxford, Tempus Reparatum.

(1993). Spatial statistics and GIS: an integrated approach. In Andresen, J., Madsen, T. and Scollar, I., eds., *Computing the Past: Computer Applications and Quantitative Methods in Archaeology 1992*, pp. 91–103. Aarhus, Aarhus University Press.

Kwan, M. P. (2002). Is GIS for woman? Reflections on the critical discourse in the 1990s. *Gender, Place and Culture*, 9: 271–279.

Ladefoged, T. N. and Pearson, R. (2000). Fortified castles on Okinawa Island during the Gusuku Period, AD 1200–1600. *Antiquity*, 74: 404–412.

Lake, M. W. (2000a). MAGICAL computer simulation of Mesolithic foraging. In Kohler, T. A. and Gumerman, G. J., eds., *Dynamics in Human and Primate Societies: Agent-Based Modelling of Social and Spatial Processes*, pp. 107–143. New York, Oxford University Press.

(2000b). MAGICAL computer simulation of Mesolithic foraging on Islay. In Mithen, S. J., ed., *Hunter-Gatherer Landscape Archaeology: The Southern Hebrides Mesolithic Project 1988–98*, Vol. 2, *Archaeological Fieldwork on Colonsay, Computer Modelling, Experimental Archaeology, and Final Interpretations*, pp. 465–495. Cambridge, The McDonald Institute for Archaeological Research.

(2004). Being in a simulacrum: electronic agency. In Gardner, A., ed., *Agency Uncovered: Archaeological Perspectives on Social Agency, Power and Being Human*, pp. 191–209. London, UCL Press.

Lake, M. W. and Woodman, P. E. (2000). Viewshed analysis of site location on Islay. In Mithen, S. J., ed., *Hunter-Gatherer Landscape Archaeology: The Southern Hebrides Mesolithic Project 1988–98*, Vol. 2, *Archaeological Fieldwork on Colonsay, Computer Modelling, Experimental Archaeology, and Final Interpretations*, pp. 497–503. Cambridge, The McDonald Institute for Archaeological Research.

(2003). Visibility studies in archaeology: a review and case study. *Environment and Planning B: Planning and Design*, 30: 689–707.

Lake, M. W., Woodman, P. E. and Mithen, S. J. (1998). Tailoring GIS software for archaeological applications: an example concerning viewshed analysis. *Journal of Archaeological Science*, 25: 27–38.

Land Information New Zealand (2003). New Zealand Government Geospatial Metadata Standard v. 1.2 Draft: Part 1 – Profile Definition. www.linz.govt.nz/rcs/linz/pub/web/root/core/Topography/ProjectsA%ndProgrammes/geospatialmetadata/index.jsp (accessed 08/09/2004).

Langmuir, E. (1997). *Mountaincraft and Leadership*. Glasgow, The Scottish Sport Council/The Mountain Leader Training Board.

Levine, N. (2002). *CrimeStat: A Spatial Statistics Program for the Analysis of Crime Incident Locations (v 2.0)*. Houston, TX, Ned Levine & Associates/Washington, DC, National Institute of Justice.

Lewis, M. and Wigen, K. (1997). *The Myth of Continents: A Critique of Metageography*. Berkeley, CA, University of California Press.

Lillesand, T. M., Chipman, J. W. and Kiefer, R. W. (2003). *Remote Sensing and Image Interpretation*, 5th edition. New York, John Wiley & Sons.

Lillesand, T. M. and Kiefer, R. W. (2000). *Remote Sensing and Image Interpretation*, 4th edition. New York, John Wiley & Sons.

Lindley, D. V. and Scott, W. F. (1984). *Cambridge Elementary Statistical Tables*. Cambridge, Cambridge University Press.

Llobera, M. (1996). Exploring the topography of mind: GIS, social space and archaeology. *Antiquity*, 70: 612–622.

(2000). Understanding movement: a pilot model towards the sociology of movement. In Lock, G., ed., *Beyond the Map: Archaeology and Spatial Technologies*, pp. 65–84. Amsterdam, IOS Press.

(2001). Building past landscape perception with GIS: understanding topographic prominence. *Journal of Archaeological Science*, 28: 1005–1014.

(2003). Extending GIS-based visual analysis: the concept of 'visualscapes'. *International Journal of Geographical Information Science*, 17: 25–48.

Lloyd, C. D. and Atkinson, P. M. (2004). Archaeology and geostatistics. *Journal of Archaeological Science*, 31: 151–164.

Lock, G. (2003). *Using Computers in Archaeology*. London, Routledge.

Lock, G., Bell, T. and Lloyd, J. (1999). Towards a methodology for modelling surface survey data: the Sangro Valley Project. In Gillings, M., Mattingly, D. and van Dalen, J., eds., *Geographical Information Systems and Landscape Archaeology*, The Archaeology of Mediterranean Landscapes 3, pp. 55–63. Oxford, Oxbow Books.

Lock, G. R. and Harris, T. M. (1996). Danebury revisited: an English Iron Age hillfort in a digital landscape. In Aldenderfer, M. and Maschner, H. D. G., eds., *Anthropology, Space and Geographic Information Systems*, pp. 214–240. Oxford, Oxford University Press.

Longley, P. A., Goodchild, M. F., Maguire, D. J. and Rhind, D. W. (1999). Introduction. In Longley, P. A., Goodchild, M. F., Maguire, D. J. and Rhind, D. W., eds., *Geographical Information Systems*, Vol. I, *Principles and Technical Issues*, pp. 1–20. New York, John Wiley & Sons.

(2005). Geographic Information Systems and Science, 2nd edition. Chichester, John Wiley & Sons.

Loots, L. (1997). The use of projective and reflective viewsheds in the analysis of the Hellenistic city defence system at Sagalassos, Turkey. *Archaeological Computing Newsletter*, 49: 12–16.

Lowry, R. (2003). Concepts and applications of inferential statistics. http://faculty.vassar.edu/lowry/webtext.html (accessed 08/07/03).

Mackie, Q. (2001). *Settlement Archaeology in a Fjordland Archipelago: Network Analysis, Social Practice and the Built Environment of Western Vancouver Island, British Columbia, Canada since 2000 BP*, British Archaeological Reports International Series 926. Oxford, Archaeopress.

Macnab, N. (2003). Anglo-Scandinavian, Medieval and Post-Medieval Urban Occupation at 41–49 Walmgate, York, UK. www.yorkarchaeology.co.uk/wgate/ (accessed 07/09/2004).

Madry, S. and Rakos, L. (1996). Line-of-sight and cost surface techniques for regional archaeological research in the Arroux river valley. In Maschner, H. D. G., ed., *New Methods, Old Problems: Geographic Information Systems in Modern Archaeological Research*, pp. 104–126. Carbondale, IL, Southern Illinois University Center for Archaeological Investigations.

Manber, U. (1989). *Introduction to Algorithms: A Creative Approach*. Reading, MA, Addison-Wesley.

Manly, B. F. J. (1991). *Randomization and Monte Carlo Methods in Biology*. London, Chapman & Hall.

Marble, D. F. (1990). The potential methodological impact of geographic information systems on the social sciences. In Allen, K. M. S., Green, S. W. and Zubrow, E. B. W., eds., *Interpreting Space: GIS and Archaeology*, pp. 9–21. London, Taylor & Francis.

Marean, C. W., Abe, Y., Nilssen, P. J. and Stone, E. C. (2001). Estimating the minimum number of skeletal elements (MNE) in Zooarchaeology: a review and a new image-analysis GIS approach. *American Antiquity*, 66: 333–348.

Maris, M. and te Boekhorst, R. (1996). Exploiting physical constraints: heap formation through behavioural error in a group of robots. In IEEE/RSJ, ed., *Intelligent Robots and Systems, Proceedings of the 1996 IEEE/RSJ International Conference on Intelligent Robots and Systems (IROS96) Part III*, pp. 1655–1661. New Jersey, IEEE.

Maschner, H. D. G. and Stein, J. W. (1995). Multivariate approaches to site location on the northwest coast of North America. *Antiquity*, 69: 61–73.

Matheron, G. (1971). *The Theory of Regionalized Variables and its Applications*. Les Cahiers du Centre de Morphologie Mathématique, Fasc. 5. Fontainebleau, Centre de Géostatistique.

McIlhagga, D. (1997). Optimal path delineation to multiple targets incorporating fixed cost distance. Unpublished Honours B.A. thesis, Carleton University.

McKee, B., Sever, T. and Sheets, P. (1994). Prehistoric footpaths in Costa Rica: remote sensing and field verification. In Sheets, P. and McGee, B., eds., *Archaeology, Volcanism, and Remote Sensing in the Arenal Region, Costa Rica*, pp. 142–157. Austin, TX, University of Texas Press.

Menard, S. (2001). *Applied Logistic Regression Analysis*. Thousand Oaks, CA, Sage Publications.

Merwin, D. A., Cromley, R. G. and Civco, D. L. (2002). Artificial neural networks as a method of spatial interpolation for digital elevation models. *Cartography and Geographic Information Science*, 29: 99–110.

Milner, G. R. (1996). Native American interactions: multiscalar analyses and interpretations in the Eastern Woodlands. Book reviews. *Antiquity*, 70: 992–995.

Minetti, A. E., Ardigò, L. P. and Saibene, F. (1993). Mechanical determinants of gradient walking. *Journal of Physiology*, 471: 725–735.

Mitas, L., Mitasova, H., Brown, W. M. and Astley, M. (1996). Interacting fields approach for evolving spatial phenomena: application to erosion simulation for optimized land use. In *Proceedings, Third International Conference/Workshop on Integrating GIS and Environmental Modeling*, Santa Fe, NM, January 21–26, 1996. Santa Barbara, CA, National Center for Geographic Information and Analysis. www.ncgia.ucsb.edu/conf/SANTA_FE_CD-ROM/main.html (accessed 29/09/04).

Mitasova, H., Mitas, L., Brown, W. M., *et al.* (1995). Modelling temporally and spatially distributed phenomena: new methods and tools for GRASS GIS. *International Journal of Geographic Information Systems*, 9: 433–446.

Mithen, S. J. (1989). Evolutionary theory and post-processual archaeology. *Antiquity*, 63: 483–494.

ed. (2000). *Hunter-Gatherer Landscape Archaeology: The Southern Hebrides Mesolithic Project 1988–98*, Vol. 2, *Archaeological Fieldwork on Colonsay, Computer Modelling, Experimental Archaeology, and Final Interpretations*. Cambridge, McDonald Institute for Archaeological Research.

Mlekuz, D. (2004). Listening to the landscapes: modelling soundscapes in GIS. *Internet Archaeology*, 16. http://intarch.ac.uk/journal/issue16/mlekuz_toc.html (accessed 23/05/05).

Monk, D. (2001). Spatial Statistics v. 1.0 for ArcView. http://arcscripts.esri.com/details.asp?dbid=11828 (accessed 03/09/2004).

Monmonier, M. (1991). *How to Lie with Maps*. Chicago, IL, University of Chicago Press.

Moran, P. A. P. (1950). Notes on continuous stochastic phenomena. *Biometrika*, 37: 17–23.

Müller, J. (1988). *The Chambered Cairns of the Northern and Western Isles*, Occasional Paper 16. Edinburgh, Department of Archaeology, University of Edinburgh.

Nearing, M. A., Lane, L. J. and Lopes, V. L. (1994). Modeling soil erosion. In Lal, R., ed., *Soil Erosion Research Methods*, 2nd edition, pp. 127–156. Delray Beach, FL, Soil and Water Conservation Society/St. Lucie Press.

Neiman, F. D. (1997). Conspicuous consumption as wasteful advertising: a Darwinian perspective on spatial patterns in Classic Maya terminal monument dates. In Barton, M. C. and Clark, G. A., eds., *Rediscovering Darwin: Evolutionary Theory and Archaeological Explanation*, Archaeological Papers of the American Anthropological Association 7, pp. 267–290. Washington, DC, American Anthropological Association.

Neteler, M. and Mitasova, H. (2002). *Open Source GIS: A GRASS GIS Approach*. Boston, MA, Kluwer Academic Press.

Newman, M. (2002). *SMR Content and Computing Survey 2002*. London, Data Services Unit, English Heritage.

Nigro, J. D., Ungar, P. S., de Ruiterand, D. J. and Berger, L. R. (2003). Developing a Geographic Information System (GIS) for mapping and analysing fossil deposits at Swartkrans, Gauteng Province, South Africa. *Journal of Archaeological Science*, 30: 317–324.

Open GIS Consortium (1999). Document 99-049: OpenGIS simple features specification for SQL, revision 1.1. `http://www.opengis.org/techno/specs/99-049.pdf` (accessed 21/5/03).

(2001). The OpenGIS Abstract Specification. Topic 11: OpenGIS Metadata (ISO/TC 211 DIS 19115). `http://portal.opengeospatial.org/files/?artifact_id=1094` (accessed 22/08/05).

Ord, J. K. and Getis, A. (1995). Local spatial autocorrelation statistics: distributional issues and an application. *Geographical Analysis*, 27: 286–306.

Pannatier, Y. (1996). *VARIOWIN: Software for Spatial Data Analysis in 2D*. New York, Springer-Verlag.

Passmore, R. and Durnin, J. V. G. A. (1955). Human energy expenditure. *Physiological Review*, 35: 801.

Pélissier, R. and Goreaud, F. (2001). A practical approach to the study of spatial structure in simple cases of heterogeneous vegetation. *Journal of Vegetation Science*, 12: 99–108.

Peng, Z.-R. and Tsou, M.-H. (2003). *Internet GIS: Distributed Geographic Information Services for the Internet and Wireless Network*. New York, John Wiley & Sons.

Peregrine, P. (1995). Networks of power: the Mississippian world system. In Nassaney, M. S. and Sassaman, K. E., eds., *Native American Interactions: Multiscalar Analyses and Interpretations in the Eastern Woodlands*, pp. 247–265. Knoxville, TN, University of Tennessee Press.

Perlès, C. (1999). The distribution of *magoules* in Eastern Thessaly. In Halstead, P., ed., *Neolithic Society in Greece*, Sheffield Studies in Aegean Archaeology, pp. 42–56. Sheffield, Sheffield Academic Press.

(2001). *The Early Neolithic in Greece*. Cambridge, Cambridge University Press.

Peterson, M. (2004). Developing predictive models for prehistoric settlement patterns on the High Plains of Western Nebraska. Unpublished M.Sc. thesis, Institute of Archaeology, University College London.

Philip, G., Donoghue, D., Beck, A. and Galiatsatos, N. (2002). CORONA satellite photography: an archaeological application from the Middle East. *Antiquity*, 76: 109–118.

Pickles, J. (1999). Arguments, debates, and dialogues: the GIS-social theory debate and the concern for alternatives. In Longley, P. A., Goodchild, M. F., Maguire, D. J. and Rhind, D. W., eds., *Geographical Information Systems*, Vol. I, *Principles and Technical Issues*, pp. 49–60. New York, John Wiley & Sons.

Pollard, J. and Gillings, M. (1998). Romancing the stones: towards an elemental and virtual Avebury. *Archaeological Dialogues*, 5: 140–164.

Popper, K. (1963). *Conjectures and Refutations: The Growth of Scientific Knowledge*. London, Routledge & Kegan Paul.

Portugali, J. and Sonis, M. (1991). Palestinian national identity and the Israeli labour market: Q-analysis. *The Professional Geographer*, 46: 256–279.

Poulter, A. and Kerslake, I. (1997). Vertical photographic site recording: the "Holmes Boom". *Journal of Field Archaeology*, 24: 221–232.

Powlesland, D. (1997). Publishing in the round: a role for CD-ROM in the publication of archaeological fieldwork results. *Antiquity*, 71: 1062–1066.

(1998). The West Heslerton assessment. *Internet Archaeology*, 5. `http://intarch.ac.uk/journal/issue5/westhes_toc.html` (accessed 30/08/2004).

Powlesland, D., Clemence, H. and Lyall, J. (1998). West Heslerton: WEB-CD: the application of HTML and WEB tools for creating a distributed excavation archive in the form of a WEB-CD. *Internet Archaeology*, 5. http://intarch.ac.uk/journal/issue5/westhescd_toc.html (accessed 31/08/2004).

Powlesland, D., Lyall, J. and Donoghue, D. (1997). Enhancing the record through remote sensing. The application and integration of multi-sensor, non-invasive remote sensing techniques for the enhancement of the Sites and Monuments Record. Heslerton Parish Project, N. Yorkshire, England. *Internet Archaeology*, 2. http://intarch.ac.uk/journal/issue2/pld_index.html (accessed 05/11/2004).

Premo, L. (2004). Local spatial autocorrelation statistics quantify multi-scale patterns in distributional data: an example from the Maya Lowlands. *Journal of Archaeological Science*, 31: 855–866.

Ray, E. T. and McIntosh, J. (2002). *Perl & XML*. Cambridge, MA, O'Reilly.

Relph, E. (1976). *Place and Placelessness*. London, Pion.

Renfrew, C. (1976). *Before Civilisation: The Radiocarbon Revolution and Prehistoric Europe*. Harmondsworth, Pelican.

Renfrew, C. and Dixon, J. (1976). Obsidian in Western Asia: a review. In Sieveking, G. d. G., Longworth, I. H. and Wilson, K. E., eds., *Problems in Economic and Social Archaeology*, pp. 137–150. London, Duckworth & Co.

Renfrew, C., Dixon, J. E. and Cann, J. R. (1968). Further analysis of Near East obsidian. *Proceedings of the Prehistoric Society*, 34: 319–331.

Renfrew, C. and Level, E. (1979). Exploring dominance: predicting polities from centers. In Renfrew, C. and Cooke, K. L., eds., *Transformations: Mathematical Approaches to Culture Change*, pp. 145–168. New York, Academic Press.

Ripley, B. D. (1976). The second order analysis of stationary point process. *Journal of Applied Probability*, 13: 255–266.

  (1981). *Spatial Statistics*. New York, John Wiley & Sons.

Robert, C. P. and Casella, G. (2004). *Monte Carlo Statistical Methods*, 2nd edition. New York, Springer-Verlag.

Roberts, B. K. (1996). *Landscapes of Settlement: Prehistory to the Present*. London, Routledge.

Roberts, M. B. and Parfitt, S. A. (1999). *Boxgrove. A Middle Pleistocene Hominid Site at Eartham Quarry, Boxgrove, West Sussex*. English Heritage Archaeological Report 17. London, English Heritage.

Robinson, A. H., Jorrison, J. L., Muehrcke, P. C., Kimerling, A. J. and Guptill, S. C. (1995). *Elements of Cartography*, 6th edition. New York, John Wiley & Sons.

Robinson, J. M. and Zubrow, E. (1999). Between spaces: interpolation in archaeology. In Gillings, M., Mattingly, D. and van Dalen, J., eds., *Geographical Information Systems and Landscape Archaeology*, The Archaeology of Mediterranean Landscapes 3, pp. 64–83. Oxford, Oxbow Books.

Rogerson, P. A. (2001). *Statistical Methods for Geography*. London, Sage.

Roper, D. C. (1979). The method and theory of site catchment analysis: a review. *Advances in Archaeological Method and Theory*, 2: 119–140.

Rose, J., Ralston, H. J. and Gamble, J. G. (1994). Energetics of walking. In Rose, J. and Gamble, J. G., eds., *Human Walking*, pp. 45–72. Baltimore, MD, Williams & Wilkins.

Roskams, S. (2001). *Excavation*. Cambridge Manuals in Archaeology. Cambridge, Cambridge University Press.

Rossiter, D. (1996). A theoretical framework for land evaluation. *Geoderma*, 72: 165–190.

Ruggles, C. L. N. and Medyckyj-Scott, D. J. (1996). Site location, landscape visibility, and symbolic astronomy: a Scottish case study. In Maschner, H. D. G., ed., *New Methods, Old Problems: Geographic Information Systems in Modern Archaeological Research*, Occasional Paper 23, pp. 127–146. Carbondale, IL, Southern Illinois University Center for Archaeological Investigations.

Saile, T. (1997). Landscape archaeology in central Germany: site catchment analysis using GIS. In Johnson, I. and North, M., eds., *Archaeological Applications of GIS: Proceedings of Colloquium*

II, UISPP XIIIth Congress, Forli, Italy, September 1996, Sydney University Archaeological Methods Series 5. Sydney, Archaeological Computing Laboratory. CD-ROM.

Searle, J. (1992). *The Rediscovery of the Mind*. Cambridge, MA, MIT Press.

Sever, T. L. and Wagner, D. (1991). Analysis of prehistoric roadways in Chaco Canyon using remotely sensed digital data. In Trombold, C. D., ed., *Ancient Road Networks and Settlement Hierarchies in the New World*, New Directions in Archaeology, pp. 42–52. Cambridge, Cambridge University Press.

Shanks, M. and Tilley, C. (1987a). *Re-Constructing Archaeology*. Cambridge, Cambridge University Press.

(1987b). *Social Theory and Archaeology*. Cambridge, Polity Press.

Sheets, P. and Sever, T. L. (1991). Prehistoric footpaths in Costa Rica: transportation and communication in a tropical rainforest. In Trombold, C., ed., *Ancient Road Networks and Settlement Hierarchies in the New World*, New Directions in Archaeology, pp. 53–65. Cambridge, Cambridge University Press.

Shennan, S. (1988). *Quantifying Archaeology*. Edinburgh, Edinburgh University Press.

Silva, M. D. and Pizziolo, G. (2001). Setting up a 'human calibrated' anisotropic cost surface for archaeological landscape investigation. In Stancic, Z. and Veljanovski, T., eds., *Computing Archaeology for Understanding the Past. Proceedings of the CAA2000 Conference*, British Archaeological Reports International Series 931, pp. 279–286. Oxford, Archaeopress.

Silverman, B. W. (1986). *Density Estimation for Statistics and Data Analysis*. London, Chapman & Hall.

Slocum, T. (1998). *Thematic Cartography and Visualisation*. New Jersey, Prentice Hall.

Smith, C., Aberline, P. and Bellman, C. (2002). Investigation and prototyping of emerging web standards for web GIS. *Cartography*, 31: 63–76.

Smith, D. P. and Atkinson, S. F. (2001). Accuracy of rectification using topographic map versus GPS ground control points. *Photogrammetric Engineering and Remote Sensing*, 65: 565–570.

Sneath, P. and Sokal, R. (1973). *Numerical Taxonomy: The Principles and Practice of Numerical Classification*. San Franciso, CA, W. H. Freeman & Co.

Snyder, J. P. and Voxland, P. M. (1989). *An Album of Map Projections*, US Geological Survey Professional Paper 1453. Washington, DC, US Geological Survey.

Sokal, R. R., Harding, R. M. and Oden, N. L. (1989). Spatial patterns of human gene frequencies in Europe. *American Journal of Physical Anthropology*, 80: 267–294.

Sokal, R. R. and Sneath, P. H. A. (1963). *Principles of Numerical Taxonomy*. San Franciso, CA, W. H. Freeman & Co.

Soule, R. G. and Goldman, R. F. (1969). Energy costs of load carried on the head, hands, or feet. *Journal of Applied Physiology*, 27: 687–690.

Spikins, P., Conneller, C., Ayertaran, H. and Scaife, B. (2002). GIS based interpolation applied to distinguishing occupation phases of early prehistoric sites. *Journal of Archaeological Science*, 29: 1235–1245.

Stancic, Z., Gaffney, V., Ostir-Sedej, K. and Podobnikar, T. (1997). GIS analysis of land-use, settlement patterns and territories on the island of Brac. In Johnson, I. and North, M., eds., *Archaeological Applications of GIS: Proceedings of Colloquium II, UISPP XIIIth Congress*, Forli, Italy, September 1996, Sydney University Archaeological Methods Series 5. Sydney, Archaeological Computing Laboratory. CD-ROM.

Steele, J., Adams, J. and Sluckin, T. (1998). Modelling Paleoindian dispersals. *World Archaeology*, 30: 286–305.

Steinberg, J. M. (1996). Ploughzone sampling in Denmark: isolating and interpreting site signatures from disturbed contexts. *Antiquity*, 70: 368–393.

Sterud, E. and Pratt, P. (1975). Archaeological intra-site recording with photography. *Journal of Field Archaeology*, 2: 151–167.

Stopher, P. R. and Meyburg, A. H. (1979). *Survey Sampling and Multivariate Analysis for Social Scientists and Engineers*. Lexington, Lexington Books.

Strahler, A. N. (1952). Dynamic basis of geomorphology. *Bulletin of the Geological Society of America*, 63: 923–938.

Sui, D. Z. (1994). GIS and urban studies: Positivism, post-positivism and beyond. *Urban Geography*, 15: 258–278.

Sydoriak, K. (1985). Pattern recognition at the intra-site level using trend surface analysis. *American Archaeology*, 5: 59–63.

Thioulouse, J., Chessel, D., Dolédec, S. and Olivier, J.-M. (1997). ADE-4: a multivariate analysis and graphical display software. *Statistics and Computing*, 74: 75–83.

Thomas, J. (1991a). The hollow men? A reply to Steven Mithen. *Proceedings of the Prehistoric Society*, 57: 15–20.

(1991b). *Rethinking the Neolithic*. Cambridge, Cambridge University Press.

(1993). The politics of vision and the archaeologies of landscape. In Bender, B., ed., *Landscape: Politics and Perspectives*, pp. 19–48. Oxford, Berg.

(1996). *Time, Culture and Identity: An Interpretative Archaeology*. London, Routledge.

(2004). *Archaeology and Modernity*. London, Routledge.

Thurston, J., Poiker, T. K. and Moore, J. P. (2003). *Integrated Geospatial Technologies: A Guide to GPS, GIS, and Data Logging*. Hoboken, NJ, John Wiley & Sons.

Tiefelsdorf, M. and Boots, B. (n.d.). GAMBINI (multiplicative weighted Voronoi diagram). http://info.wlu.ca/~wwwgeog/special/download/gambini.htm (accessed 05/11/2004).

Tilley, C. (1994). *A Phenomenology of Landscape*: *Paths, Places and Monuments*. Oxford, Berg.

(1996). The powers of rocks: topography and monument construction on Bodmin Moor. *World Archaeology*, 28: 161–176.

Tilley, C. and Bennet, W. (2001). An archaeology of super-natural places. *Journal of the Royal Anthropological Institute*, 7: 335–362.

Tobler, W. R. (1959). Automation and cartography. *Geographical Review*, 49: 526–534.

Tomlin, C. D. (1990). *Geographic Information Systems and Cartographic Modelling*. Englewood Cliffs, NJ, Prentice-Hall.

Tomlinson, R. (1998). The Canada geographic information system. In Foresman, T. W., ed., *The History of GIS*, pp. 21–32. London, Prentice Hall.

Tschan, A. P. (1999). An introduction to object-oriented GIS in archaeology. In Barceló, J. A., Briz, I. and Vila, A., eds., *New Techniques for Old Times, CAA98, Computer Applications and Quantitative Methods in Archaeology: Proceedings of the 26th Conference*, Barcelona 1998, British Archaeological Reports International Series 757, pp. 303–316. Oxford, Archaeopress.

Tschan, A. P., Raczkowski, W. and Latalowa, M. (2000). Perception and viewsheds: are they mutually inclusive? In Lock, G., ed., *Beyond the Map: Archaeology and Spatial Technologies*, pp. 28–48. Amsterdam, IOS Press.

Tuan, Y. F. (1974). Space and place: humanistic perspective. In Board, C., Chorley, R. J., Haggett, P. and Stoddart, D. R., eds., *Progress in Geography 6*, pp. 211–252. London, Edward Arnold.

(1978). Literature and geography: implications for geographical research. In Ley, D. and Samuels, M. S., eds., *Humanistic Geography: Prospects and Problems*, pp. 194–206. Chicago, IL, Maaroufa.

Turner, A., Doxa, M., O'Sullivan, D. and Penn, A. (2001). From isovists to visibility graphs: a methodology for the analysis of architectural space. *Environment and Planning B: Planning & Design*, 28: 103–122.

Ur, J. (2003). CORONA satellite photography and ancient road networks: a northern Mesopotamian case study. *Antiquity*, 77: 102–116.

van de Laan, M. J., Pollard, K. S. and Bryan, J. (2002). A new partitioning around medoids algorithm. www.bepress.com/ucbbiostat/paper105 (accessed 07/09/ 2004).

van Leusen, P. M. (1993). Cartographic modelling in a cell-based GIS. In Andresen, J., Madsen, T. and Scollar, I., eds., *Computing the Past: Computer Applications and Quantitative Methods in Archaeology 1992*, pp. 105–123. Aarhus, Aarhus University Press.

(1999). Viewshed and cost surface analysis using GIS (cartographic modelling in a cell-based GIS II). In Barceló, J. A., Briz, I. and Vila, A., eds., *New Techniques for Old Times–CAA98–Computer Applications and Quantitative Methods in Archaeology: Proceedings of the 26th Conference*, Barcelona 1998, British Archaeological Reports International Series 757, pp. 215–223. Oxford, Archaeopress.

(2002). Pattern to Process: Methodological Investigations into the Formation and Interpretation of Spatial Patterns in Archaeological Landscapes. Unpublished. Ph.D. thesis, University of Groningen. http://www.ub.rugul.eldoc/dis/arts/p.m.van.leusen/ (accessed 02/08/2004).

Venables, W. N. and Smith, D. M. (2003). An introduction to R: a programming environment for data analysis and graphics. http://cran.r-project.org (accessed 03/09/2004).

Verhagen, P., Gili, S., Micó, R. and Risch, R. (1999). Modelling prehistoric land use distribution in the Rio Aguas Valley (SE Spain). In Dingwall, L., Exon, S., Gaffney, V., Laflin, S. and van Leusen, M., eds., *Archaeology in the Age of the Internet. CAA 97, Computer Applications and Quantitative Methods in Archaeology: Proceedings of the 25th Anniversary Conference*, University of Birmingham, April 1997, British Archaeological Reports International Series 750. Oxford, Archaeopress. CD-ROM.

Verhoeven, K. (2003). From satellite and survey to web mapping: the Mesopotamian alluvial plain (MAP) as SVG on the web. Poster presented at *Enter the Past: Computer Applications in Archaeology 2003*, Vienna, 8–12 April 2003.

Vita-Finzi, C. (1978). *Archaeological Sites in their Setting*. London, Thames & Hudson.

Wagstaff, J. M. (1987). The new archaeology and geography. In Wagstaff, J. M., ed., *Landscape and Culture: Geographical and Archaeological Perspectives*, pp. 26–36. Oxford, Basil Blackwell.

Walker, R. (2003). *UK GEMINI: A Geo-spatial Metadata Interoperability Initiative. Proposed Metadata Standard*. London, Association for Geographic Information. www.gigateway.org.uk/metadata/metadataspecs.html (accessed 08/09/2004).

Wand, M. P. and Jones, M. C. (1995). *Kernel Smoothing*. London, Chapman & Hall.

Ward, R. C. (1990). *Principles of Hydrology*. New York, McGraw Hill.

Warren, R. E. and Asch, D. L. (2000). Site location in the Eastern Prairie Peninsula. In Westcott, K. L. and Brandon, R. J., eds., *Practical Applications of GIS for Archaeologists: A Predictive Modeling Kit*, pp. 5–32. London, Taylor & Francis.

Washburn, J. (1974). Nearest neighbour analysis of Pueblo I–III settlement patterns along the Rio Puerco of the East, New Mexico. *American Antiquity*, 39: 315–335.

Watson, J. W. (1955). Geography: a discipline in distance. *Scottish Geographical Magazine*, 71: 1–13.

Watts, D. J. and Strogatz, S. H. (1998). Collective dynamics of 'small-world' networks. *Nature*, 393: 440–442.

Westcott, K. L. and Brandon, R. J., eds. (2000). *Practical Applications of GIS for Archaeologists: A Predictive Modeling Kit*. London, Taylor & Francis.

Whallon, R. (1974). Spatial analysis of occupation floors, II. The application of nearest neighbour analysis. *American Antiquity*, 39: 16–34.

Wheatley, D. (1993). Going over old ground: GIS, archaeological theory and the act of perception. In Andresen, J., Madsen, T. and Scollar, I., eds., *Computing the Past: Computer Applications and Quantitative Methods in Archaeology 1992*, pp. 133–138. Aarhus, Aarhus University Press.

(1995). Cumulative viewshed analysis: a GIS-based method for investigating intervisibility, and its archaeological application. In Lock, G. and Stančič, Z., eds., *Archaeology and Geographical Information Systems*, pp. 171–186. London, Taylor & Francis.

(1996). The use of GIS to understand regional variation in earlier Neolithic Wessex. In Maschner, H. D. G., ed., *New Methods, Old Problems: Geographic Information Systems in Modern Archaeological Research*, Occasional Paper 23, pp. 75–103. Carbondale, IL, Southern Illinois University Center for Archaeological Investigations.

(2004). Making space for an archaeology of place. *Internet Archaeology*, 15. http://intarch. ac.uk/journal/issue15/10/toc.html (accessed 11/06/2004).

Wheatley, D. and Gillings, M. (2000). Vision, perception and GIS: developing enriched approaches to the study of archaeological visibility. In Lock, G., ed., *Beyond the Map: Archaeology and Spatial Technologies*, pp. 1–27. Amsterdam, IOS Press.

(2002). *Spatial Technology and Archaeology: The Archaeological Applications of GIS*. London, Taylor & Francis.

Whittlesey, D. (1944). *The Earth and the State: A Study of Political Geography*, 2nd edition. New York, Holt.

Wilkinson, T. (1993). Linear hollows in the Jazira, upper Mesopotamia. *Antiquity*, 67: 548–562.

Williams, J. T. (1993). Spatial autocorrelation and the Classic Maya collapse: one technique, one conclusion. *Journal of Archaeological Science*, 20: 705–709.

Wilson, J. (1999). Local, national, and global applications of GIS in agriculture. In Longley, P. A., Goodchild, M. F., Maguire, D. J. and Rhind, D. W., eds., *Geographical Information Systems*, Vol. 2, *Management Issues and Applications*, pp. 981–993. New York, John Wiley & Sons.

Wilson, R. J. (1996). *Introduction to Graph Theory*, 4th edition. Harlow, Longman.

Wischmeier, W. H. and Smith, D. D. (1978). *Predicting Rainfall Erosion Losses: A Guide to Conservation Planning*. US Department of Agriculture (USDA) Handbook 537. Washington, DC, US Government Printing Office.

Witcher, R. (1999). GIS and landscapes of perception. In Gillings, M., Mattingly, D. and van Dalen, J., eds., *Geographical Information Systems and Landscape Archaeology*. The Archaeology of Mediterranean Landscapes 3, pp. 13–22. Oxford, Oxbow Books.

Wood, D. (1992). *The Power of Maps*. London and New York, The Guilford Press.

Wood, J. (1996). The geomorphological characterisation of digital elevation models. Unpublished Ph.D. thesis, University of Leicester. www.geog.le.ac.uk/jwo/research/dem_char/thesis/ (accessed 20/12/03).

Woodman, P. E. (2000a). Beyond significant patterning, towards past intentions: the location of Orcadian chambered tombs. In Buck, C., Cummings, V., Henley, C., Mills, S. and Trick, S., eds., *Proceedings of the UK Chapter of Computer Applications and Quantitative Methods in Archaeology 1999*. British Archaeological Reports International Series 844, pp. 91–105. Oxford, Archaeopress.

(2000b). A predictive model for Mesolithic site location on Islay using logistic regression and GIS. In Mithen, S., ed., *Hunter-Gatherer Landscape Archaeology: The Southern Hebrides Mesolithic Project 1988–98*, Vol. 2, *Archaeological Fieldwork on Colonsay, Computer Modelling, Experimental Archaeology, and Final Interpretations*, pp. 445–464. Cambridge, McDonald Institute for Archaeological Research.

Worboys, M. F. (1995). *GIS: A Computing Perspective*. London, Taylor & Francis.

Wright, D. J., Goodchild, M. F. and Proctor, J. D. (1997). Demystifying the persistent ambiguity of GIS as 'tool' versus 'science'. *The Annals of the Association of American Geographers*, 87: 346–362. http://dusk.geo.orst.edu/annals.html (accessed 11/10/2004).

Xu, J. and Lathrop, R. G. (1995). Improving simulation accuracy of spread phenomena in a raster-based geographic information system. *International Journal of Geographical Information Systems*, 9: 153–168.

Yang, X. and Holder, T. (2000). Visual and statistical comparisons of surface modeling techniques for point-based environmental data. *Cartography and Geographic Information Science*, 27: 165–175.

Young, R. A., Onstad, C. A., Bosch, D. D. and Anderson, W. P. (1989). AGNPS: a nonpoint-source pollution model for evaluating agricultural watersheds. *Journal of Soil and Water Conservation*, 44: 168–173.

Zarky, A. (1976). Statistical analysis of site catchments at Ocós, Guatemala. In Flannery, K. V., ed., *The Early Mesoamerican Village*, pp. 117–130. New York, Academic Press.

Ziebart, M., Holder, N. and Dare, P. (1998). Field digital data acquisition (FDA) using total station and pencomputer: a working methodology. In Wheatley, D., Earl, G. and Poppy, S., eds., *Contemporary Themes in Archaeological Computing*. University of Southampton Department of Archaeology Monograph 3, pp. 58–64. Oxford, Oxbow Books.

Zubrow, E. B. W. (1990). Modelling and prediction with geographic information systems: a demographic example from prehistoric and historic New York. In Allen, K. M. S., Green, S. W. and Zubrow, E. B. W., eds., *Interpreting Space: GIS and Archaeology*, pp. 307–318. London, Taylor & Francis.

(1994). Knowledge representation and archaeology: a cognitive example using GIS. In Renfrew, C. and Zubrow, E. B. W., eds., *The Ancient Mind: Elements of a Cognitive Archaeology*, pp. 107–118. Cambridge, Cambridge University Press.

Index